CRITICAL
INSIGHTS

The
Harry Potter Series

CRITICAL INSIGHTS

The
Harry Potter Series

Editors
Lana A. Whited
M. Katherine Grimes

SALEM PRESS
A Division of EBSCO Information Services, Inc.
Ipswich, Massachusetts

GREY HOUSE PUBLISHING

Publisher's Cataloging-In-Publication Data
(Prepared by The Donohue Group, Inc.)

The Harry Potter series / editors, M. Katherine Grimes, Lana A. Whited.
-- [First edition].

   pages ; cm. -- (Critical insights)

   Edition statement supplied by publisher.
   Includes bibliographical references and index.
   ISBN: 978-1-61925-519-7 (hardcover)

   1. Rowling, J. K. Harry Potter series. 2. Rowling, J. K.--Criticism and interpretation. 3. Children's stories, English--20th century--History and criticism. 4. Children's stories, English--21st century--History and criticism. 5. Fantasy fiction, English--20th century--History and criticism. 6. Fantasy fiction, English--21st century--History and criticism. I. Grimes, M. Katherine. II. Whited, Lana A., 1958- III. Series: Critical insights.

PR6068.O93 Z94 2015
823/.914

LCCN: 2015942119

First Printing

PRINTED IN THE UNITED STATES OF AMERICA

Contents

The Book and The Author

Critical Contexts

Critical Readings

Resources _____

About This Volume

M. Katherine Grimes & Lana A. Whited

As Colette Drouillard's essay in this book reminds us, an entire generation of readers has grown up reading J. K. Rowling's seven-volume series about Harry Potter. Now that these young readers have matured, the books they loved to read as children and teenagers can become the works they enjoy studying as adults. We hope this volume, as well as the phenomenal number of other sources available about the series, will help them do just that.

Critical Insights: The Harry Potter Series is a collection of essays by scholars, some of whom are established international specialists in such fields as children's literature, fantasy, and even Harry Potter studies. Some are creative writers themselves. Others are more recent college graduates, some still in master's and doctoral programs, who read J. K. Rowling's famous series in their youth and are now taking their places among the dozens of other academics who have examined the Harry Potter series from hundreds of angles.

The writers with essays in this book have approached the seven-volume series about the wizard in various ways:

First, several essayists have provided background on the author and the works. Laurie Adams has written about author Joanne Rowling's life and surveyed both Rowling's works and books and articles written about Harry Potter series. In his essay "J. K. Rowling: Author(ing) Celebrity," Saradindu Bhattacharya discusses the way Rowling's fame contributes to Harry Potter's and vice versa. In addition, Lana A. Whited has examined in depth the popular and critical reception of the series in her essay "A Survey of the Critical Reception of the Harry Potter Series," and M. Katherine Grimes, in the introduction, suggests educational and scholarly ways to view the books.

Other essayists have studied J. K. Rowling's work in a historical context. Grimes' essay "'Contemporary' Is Not 'Modern': The Harry Potter Series as a Sampler of Western Literature" provides an overview of historical literary periods and discusses into what eras the books might fit. In "The Once and Future Wizard: Arthurian (and Anti-Arthurian) Themes in the Harry Potter Series," Danny Adams examines Rowling's works in the context of legends surrounding King Arthur and his knights, while Christina Vourcos' essay, "Mentoring in the Wizarding World: Dumbledore and His Literary Ancestors," relates Albus Dumbledore to Arthur's mentor, Merlin, as well as to Gandalf in J. R. R. Tolkien's Lord of the Rings trilogy.

Additional mentors, as well as characters' roles and role models, are the subjects of Jeanne Hoeker LaHaie's essay about women in the series, "Mums Are Good: Harry Potter and the Traditional Depictions of Women," and Danielle Bienvenue Bray's piece about male characters, "Rock Cakes and Reciprocity: Food and the Male Performance of Nurturing in Harry Potter." Leigh A. Neithardt examines characters as well, focusing on those perceived as having disabilities, in her essay entitled "'Splinched': The Problem of Disability in the Harry Potter Series."

Like Vourcos and Danny Adams, Crystal Wilkins, in her essay "Moral Ambiguity in Authority Figures in The Hunger Games, Divergent, and the Harry Potter Series," relates the later Harry Potter books to other literary works, this time to more recent ones, specifically Suzanne Collins' The Hunger Games trilogy and Veronica Roth's Divergent series, focusing on dystopian elements in all three sets of novels.

Todd Ide and Jenn Coletta examine the Harry Potter series in a wider context, with Ide looking at politics in both the wizarding world and our own in "The Dark Lord and the Prince: Machiavellian Elements in Harry Potter" and Coletta viewing the series in a Christian context in her essay "Morals vs. Christianity: How Harry Potter Goes Beyond Goodness to Godliness." Whited's essay on the quest for immortality in the series, "From Sorcerer's Stone to Deathly Hallows: The Failed Quest for Immortality in the Harry Potter Series," is also a thematic exploration, one that argues against J. K. Rowling's own interpretation of a major theme in the books.

In her essay "Growing Up with Harry Potter: What Motivated Youth to Read the Harry Potter Series?," Colette Drouillard discusses studies of young readers themselves to ascertain why they began reading the series and why they remained loyal to the books throughout their childhoods and teen years. Margaret Zeegers also addresses the way the worlds of Harry Potter, other literature, and readers intersect to give young people a genuine and valuable reading experience in her piece "Harry Potter and the Chronotope: Suggestive Possibilities for Theoretical Engagement."

Critical Insights: The Harry Potter Series, then, examines J. K. Rowling's series thematically as well as in larger literary and historic contexts. The essayists and editors hope that, in the future, Harry Potter readers will introduce the books they love to their children and students, first as readers, then as thinkers, and finally as scholars themselves.

THE BOOK
AND THE
AUTHOR

On J. K. Rowling's Harry Potter Series_____

M. Katherine Grimes

When I was a child, I read as a child. Sometimes I still do. I read for entertainment, for excitement, and for escape, identifying with a character who has adventures that provide me with vicarious enjoyment devoid of real danger, but leaving me with a sense of accomplishment and triumph nonetheless.

Now, however, I also read as an adult, analyzing characters, examining themes, evaluating style, investigating allusions, and considering pedagogy because this adult is not only a reader, but also a teacher. My primary teaching job is helping my four sons become good readers—not just competent decipherers of words on a page, but explorers of ideas. My other teaching task is helping my college students learn to read and think about literature so that they can use it to understand themselves and their world.

The child in me has loved reading the Harry Potter books and now listening to Jim Dale and Stephen Frye read them to me as I drive. The English major in me loves to think about themes, character development, political ideas, and social commentary. The parent in me rejoices that three of my sons have already finished the series (one has only a book to go), and three have attended a Hogwarts course in Ferrum College's Summer Enrichment Camp. The professor in me thinks about ways to use Harry Potter in literature classes. And as coordinator of the English program at Ferrum, I am proud that we have recently instated a course in our curriculum called Harry Potter and the Hero Myth. Not surprisingly, it is taught by Dr. Lana Whited, editor of the first collection of scholarly essays concerning J. K. Rowling's series about the Boy Who Lived. Furthermore, as a member of the academic world, I am pleased that scholars have realized that the Harry Potter series deserves serious academic discussion, despite at times having been dismissed as a collection of books for children and scorned for its popularity.

On J. K. Rowling's Harry Potter Series   3

Regardless of Rowling's claims to the contrary, the first book in the Harry Potter series is definitely a children's story. But somewhere along the way, those of us who bought Harry Potter books for our nieces and nephews and children and grandchildren began to love them, too. There's a danger in forgetting that what we think of as children's tales can hold the truth. When the first collection of scholarly essays about J. K. Rowling's Harry Potter novels, *The Ivory Tower and Harry Potter,* was published in 2002, when Rowling was just over halfway finished with her series, author and journalist William Safire had already declared the books mere children's fare, inappropriate for adults. Based on his reading of only *Harry Potter and the Sorcerer's Stone*, which is certainly the most elementary book in the series, Safire, in *The New York Times*, compared Rowling's achievements to Porky Pig cartoons. He even warned that "[s]cholarly tomes will be written about the underlying motifs of the Potter series, justifying its adult readership." And sure enough, within a year of the publication of *The Ivory Tower*, Elizabeth Schafer and Giselle Anatol published collections of scholarly essays on Rowling's novels, and it was obvious that the Harry Potter series was not just a fad, but literature that the academic community was taking seriously, probably much to Safire's annoyance and satisfaction, for after all, he had predicted just that consequence. Literary critic Harold Bloom had much the same reaction, again after reading the first book in the series. In *The Wall Street Journal*, he wrote that J. K. Rowling was contributing to the dumbing down of American readers, especially American children.

It is true that children's books are usually more straightforward, with fewer moral dilemmas than those found in critically acclaimed novels for adults. We almost always know what the characters in children's books should do and then watch the young people figure that out and do it. Then, things usually turn out for the good. For example, in Bill and Vera Cleaver's *Where the Lilies Bloom*, young Mary Call Luther eventually realizes, as does the reader, that the promise her father had her make before his death will doom the family, and she must go against him in order to save her siblings and her father's land. Mary Call has a dilemma, but the reader really does not. In Richard Wright's *Native Son*, on the other hand, most readers are torn between feeling sympathy for Bigger Thomas because he is a victim of a greedy, racist society, which is trying him for a crime that did not occur—the rape and murder of Mary Dalton—and feeling anger at him for the murder of his girlfriend Bessie Mears.

Flannery O'Connor dismissed Harper Lee's *To Kill a Mockingbird*, calling it "a child's book," writing, "When I was fifteen I would have loved it," but admitting that "for a child's book it does all right" (411). While Lee's book certainly lacks the intellectual sophistication of O'Connor's *Wise Blood*, it contains truths about the racism and hypocrisy of the South, about good and evil, and even about truth itself, which many of us adults need reminding of from time to time. Rowling herself cautions us not to forget the importance of children's books. After Hermione Granger receives Albus Dumbledore's bequeathal of *The Tales of Beedle the Bard*, Ron Weasley dismisses it as just stories for children—of "The Tale of the Three Brothers," he says, "That's just one of those things you tell kids to teach them lessons, isn't it?" (Rowling, *Deathly Hallows* 414). Yet this volume proves to be the key to Harry, Ron, and Hermione's figuring out about the Deathly Hallows. It is also a key to our understanding a bit about death: it might be tricked, but it cannot be defeated, so the happiest are those who—like the brother in possession of an invisibility cloak—know to avoid death until it can no longer be avoided and then accept it when it comes. Perhaps that seems an obvious lesson, but John Donne, Edward Taylor, Dylan Thomas, and even Shakespeare's Hamlet struggle with the concept of death.

It is true that the Harry Potter series rarely presents the reader with moral dilemmas. We know that Harry should obey Albus Dumbledore, fight Voldemort, remain true to his friends, even disobey school rules when other goals are more important. However, the books do raise questions that adults face: How do we know whom to trust? What do we do when we think our friends have betrayed us? What do we do when figures in authority treat us badly, even cruelly? How do we try to find fairness in an unfair world? The importance of the maturation novel is twofold: First, what we experience as children makes us into who we become as adults. Second, children are people; they are not creatures whose lives and thoughts belong to a world in which adults do not live.

One fact about children's stories that is rarely true of adult ones is that, in childhood, we usually read stories or have them read to us over and over. As adults, we read them to our children until both we and they memorize lengthy passages, if not entire books. Just think for a minute about how many Dr. Seuss lines you can recite without trying hard. In our adult years, especially once we hit middle age, we realize that just to read once all the books on our bucket list would take many lifetimes, so unless we're teaching a book or reading it to our children, we think that we haven't the luxury of third and fourth readings. But we miss much by thinking that one reading is enough. We should never forget how to read as children do.

Understanding why it is easy to dismiss popular books and films is not difficult. After all, Stephenie Meyer's Twilight series and accompanying movie saga are popular successes, while the works of Seamus Heaney and Toni Morrison are literary and critical triumphs. But we should remember that the works of Mark Twain and Charles Dickens are both. A book that is a popular success is fun to read. One that is a literary success is fun to think about, to read again, to analyze, and to discuss. Often literary scholars seem to think that treating popular books as worthy of their attention will cause their colleagues to see them as less than serious, as insufficiently academic; therefore, they leave best sellers to the popular culture scholars and turn their literary analytical attention to the established canon, or at least to contemporary writers who have been honored with Man Booker or Pulitzer Prizes.

Now that the excitement accompanying the release of each new Harry Potter book and film has died down, when children who read the novels for the first time can finish the entire series at their own pace and see all the movies without waiting, one wonders whether series such as Suzanne Collins' Hunger Games and Veronica Roth's Divergent will knock J. K. Rowling's books off the literary shelf and, eventually, out of the canon. Those of us who waited outside bookstores and theatres are saddened at that possibility. Those of us who see the books as more than just ways for J. K. Rowling, Time Warner, and Universal to make money hope that the universality and timelessness of the themes in the novels, as well as the unique elements of the characters and plots, will keep the books rolling from the shelves into the hands of readers, both young and old, longer than Sir Nicholas de Mimsy Porpington.

It is obvious that the Harry Potter phenomenon has not lost its allure and that the marketers have managed to maneuver the books into money-making magic, to manipulate a literary wildfire into merchandise in order to make themselves gallons of galleons. Universal Studios has already opened two Harry Potter theme parks, Daigon Alley and Hogsmeade, in The Wizarding World of Harry Potter in Orlando, Florida, with the Hogwart's Express connecting the two parks. Universal also has a Wizarding World of Harry Potter theme park at Universal Studios in Osaka, Japan, and plans to open another in Hollywood, California, in 2016.

The US Quidditch Association lists almost 170 Quidditch teams from Rhode Island to Hawaii, most at universities, but some in adult communities and high schools. The teams carry names such as the Rutgers Nearly Headless Knights, the New York Badassilisks, and the Harvard Horcruxes. Yes, there is an International Quidditch Association, too, with its own World Cup. It now boasts over three hundred teams in twenty countries.

One could have concern that the popular success of the Harry Potter commercial phenomenon could lead to pooh-poohing by scholars. After all, if something such as Fox News appeals to the masses, it is often suspect. But in the case of Harry Potter, scholars seem to be able to see past the commerce to the value of the literary series.

Whole camps or parts of camps from Maryland to Utah are related to Harry Potter. Intergenerational events such as the Edinboro (Pennsylvania) Potterfest, which includes the Ravenclaw Academic Conference, and Harry Potter fan conventions such as LeakyCon[1] and conferences such as the one held annually at Chestnut Hill College in Philadelphia bring together fans and scholars to enjoy and discuss the series. More importantly, numerous colleges and universities, including Cal Tech, Swarthmore, Yale, and University of Birmingham in England, are offering courses related to Harry Potter, as Harold Bloom predicted: "The cultural critics," he wrote disdainfully in 2000, "will soon introduce Harry Potter into their college curriculum . . . ."

Those of us old enough to remember television before cable understand how that medium and movies at the theatre united people in a culture. In the 1940s, almost everyone in the United States knew Lucille Ball and Humphrey Bogart; in the 1950s, Ed Sullivan and James Stewart; in the 1960s, Andy Griffith and Julie Andrews; in the 1970s, Alan Alda and Jane Fonda; in the 1980s, Bill Cosby and Meryl Streep. But now, with hundreds of television channels and movies available by subscription to such services as Netflix, six people in the same household can simultaneously watch six different shows and know so little in common that they have nothing to discuss at the dinner table. John Granger, author of several books about Rowling's series, wrote in a *Washington Post* article, "Harry's seven adventures are the first twenty-first-century shared text—a ubiquitous narrative that everyone has read or heard of." While I wouldn't say "everyone," I have found that my college students are more likely to know Harry Potter than perhaps any other protagonist I name except Jesus. If Harry Potter is our common ground, if most high school and college students have seen the films even if they haven't read all the books, we can use that shared experience to begin a conversation.

How can students use their interest in Harry Potter in the classroom? My experience as a professor is that those students who have read the Harry Potter series are almost always among the brightest in my classes and also often creative as well as perceptive. Because many educators allow students to choose their own project and research topics, students can propose essay ideas and science project designs related to J. K. Rowling's work. Roger Highfield's *The Science of Harry Potter: How Magic Really Works* should lead to ideas in chemistry and physics. *Harry Potter and History* by Nancy R. Reagin can help students of history, especially that of England and other parts of Europe. Students in philosophy classes can turn to William Irwin's *The Ultimate Harry Potter and Philosophy: Hogwarts for Muggles* and David Baggett's *Harry Potter and Philosophy: If Aristotle Ran Hogwarts.* Students in psychology class can use Neil Mulholland's *The Psychology of Harry Potter: An Unauthorized Examination of the Boy Who Lived.*[2] Jenn Sims has edited a collection aimed at those studying sociology: *The Sociology of Harry Potter: 22 Enchanting Essays on the Wizarding World.* And business students can use Susan Gunelius' *Harry Potter: The Story of a Global Business Phenomenon* as they discuss the success of Fred and George Weasley's joke shop as well as J. K. Rowling's phenomenal rise to tremendous wealth. Language students can compare the books in the languages they speak with those in the languages they are studying as well as examining Rowling's invention of words. (Pokémon fans might be interested in comparing the names of the Pokémons with names of characters in the Harry Potter books.) And students of literature can find numerous works to help them analyze the Harry Potter series, including the first two essay collections, *The Ivory Tower and Harry Potter*, edited by Lana A. Whited, and *Reading Harry Potter: Critical Essays*, edited by Giselle Liza Anatol, who has also compiled a more recent collection, *Reading Harry Potter Again: New Critical Essays.* Of course hundreds of essays—including those in this collection—can supplement the dozens of books now available about Harry Potter and almost every subject taught in high schools and colleges.

How should teachers and professors use the interest of our students in the Harry Potter series? Many colleges and universities (Arcadia, Appalachian State, Harvard, and more) have at least one freshman seminar section related to Rowling's works. Freshman courses are great places to start. The first three or four films can begin the class for students not familiar with the series, and the last books can become the texts. Professors are tailoring courses to their own disciplines and other interests. Examples include "Harry Potter's Bookshelf" (Kansas State University), "Finding Your Patronus" (Oregon State), "Muggles, Magic, and Mayhem: The Science and Psychology of Harry Potter" (Alfred University), and

"Battling Against Voldemort" (Swarthmore).[3] Harry Potter study abroad courses are also on the rise; the University of California at San Marcos plans a three-week course in the United Kingdom in June 2015.

Professors of introductory classes can also use the series to help students delve into numerous subjects. Business and marketing classes can investigate the phenomenal success of the book series, as well as the economics and marketing of films, merchandise, theme parks, and more. Those classes can also study the portrayal of various shops and industries, such as banking, in Rowling's novels. Classes in law and legal issues can review copyrights, patents, and J. K. Rowling's agents' threats to authors and editors of books on the series. Economics professors can discuss the way various socioeconomic classes are depicted in the wizarding world and the stasis of those classes. Sociologists might also discuss socioeconomic class divisions, as well as stereotyping, vilification of the Other, gender identity and relations, the role of the family, and the dynamics of servitude (the House-Elves). Psychology courses can use the Harry Potter series to study concrete vs. formal reasoning; intellectual, social, psychological, and moral development; and the nature vs. nurture argument; in fact, a developmental psychology class at Vanderbilt University travelled to England during its study of Harry Potter.

Classes in religion can examine the battle of good vs. evil, humanism, forgiveness, and the idea of free will; a quick check of college classes that relate to Harry Potter finds theology courses at the University of Missouri, Florida State University, Yale, and many others. Courses in political science, such as one that uses the Harry Potter series as text at the University of the Americas, might tackle the portrayal of the Ministry of Magic, the courting of factions by those who would rule, the terrorizing of the opposition in order to expand power, political schemes for world takeover, the Machiavellian aspects of Voldemort, and the use of the media to manipulate the masses. Historians might point out to their students the parallels between Voldemort and Adolph Hitler, the treatment of minorities in world history and in the Harry Potter series, allegiances, and infighting and civil war, especially in relation to the self-destruction of the giants.

A professor at Frostburg State uses Harry Potter to discuss physics, and the website TeachEngineering provides instructions for using Harry Potter activities to teach high school students life science, physical science, and chemistry. Perhaps horticulture professors could relate their lessons to some of those at Hogwarts, as well. Courses in technology can examine the ways people in the real world accomplish without magic what the witches and wizards do in the Harry Potter books, such as how Skype resembles the way wizards' heads appear in fireplaces in head-only transport through the Floo network, or recent advances in cloaking technology with military applications.

Health and human performance programs can use Quidditch in their coaching classes, especially at colleges and universities with Quidditch teams; the discussions of the game should not be separated from the books, however, as discussions of Minerva McGonnagall's willingness to break rules for an athlete can lead to useful discussions of the problems with athletics in academia. The willingness of adults to risk children's lives for the Triwizard Tournament is even more troubling than the obsession with Quidditch. Discussions of the Quidditch World Cup scenes in *Harry Potter and the Goblet of Fire* can lead to investigations of the Olympics and soccer World Cup tournaments in relation to sports and international relations, including a look at hooliganism at soccer events.

Professors of film, especially those who teach classes in literature and film, can certainly use the Harry Potter movies to discuss adaptations of novels for the screen. Popular culture classes can study the phenomenal rise of the book series and the films, as well as the influence of the books and the films on popular culture. Linguists can use the adaptations of the British Harry Potter books into American English as a means to discuss dialect as well as tracing the etymologies of words Rowling created. Language professors can use translations of the Harry Potter books to help students learn languages, and the importance of speaking to others in their own language is evident when Albus Dumbledore speaks to the merpeople in Mermish in *Harry Potter and the Goblet of Fire.*

Education professors can use the Hogwarts frame to discuss effective versus ineffective teaching techniques and styles, the boarding school system, favoritism, experiential learning, problems with bullying, the role of sports in education, and even cheating (how much of Ron's and Harry's homework does Hermione actually do for them?). Even though the students sometimes do not respect their professors, especially Severus Snape and Sybill Trelawney, often for valid reasons, it becomes increasingly obvious throughout the books that the education they are receiving is valuable, as it saves their lives time after time. The books teach that even those with gifts must do their work and pay attention in class, as Hermione does, in order to learn how to use those gifts.

Classes involving current events can use the series to try to understand a very confusing world. For example, after a massacre in Nigeria in early January 2015, one survivor described the fighting that preceded the slaughter. Reporters for ABC News cite an Associated Press report in which Ibrahim Gambo "said that he was part of a civilian militia that, bolstered by a belief that its fighters were protected from bullets by a magical charm, initially had success in resisting Boko Haram insurgents," but that the militia pulled back when the army told it to do so in order for a plane to attack, and the slaughter occurred when the plane didn't come. Gambo is quoted as saying, "It is sad that our fortification charm became ineffective once we showed fear" (Umar and Torchia). Of course, Neville Longbottom and Dumbledore's Army are like the civilian militia, fighting for the right. The Death Eaters are like Boko Haram, although the real-life group is much more horrid. And the protego charm is like the magical charm of which Gambo speaks. Magical charms might not be real, but the belief in them might be, as might the courage of those who stand and fight for their families and their communities.

Above all, though, J. K. Rowling's Harry Potter series is literature, and it is in such classes where it is most valuable. Classes in folklore can discuss folkloric elements of Harry Potter—magic, mentors, good characters versus evil ones, journeys, quests, and more—as well as J. K. Rowling's use of folklore in *The Tales of Beedle the Bard*, especially "The Tale of the Three Brothers." Professors of literature can use the books to discuss allusions, especially mythological allusions, but also religious ones, such as the serpent image. The novels can also be used to teach point of view, for whereas most of the books in the series are limited to Harry's point of view, we are also privy to scenes in the British prime minister's office, Malfoy Manor, the locations of Tom Riddle's childhood, and other places where Harry is not present. Professors of literature as well as creative writing can use the books to teach story construction, as most of them follow Freitag's pyramid individually, and the entire series also has its own plot diagram. Character development is a major part of the series, as we see individuals who remain static, such as Bellatrix Lestrange, and others who grow tremendously, such as Neville Longbottom.

While a curriculum entirely based on the Harry Potter series might be extreme, both high school teachers and college faculty with an interest in J. K. Rowling's works can find ways to use that literature to connect students with other academic materials.

Where will scholars go with the Harry Potter (HP) series in the future? One decision to be made will be the definition of the HP canon. Will the seven-book series be the canon, with the film adaptations and peripheral materials—such as the Christmas 2014 short stories, *The Tales of Beedle the Bard*, *Fantastic Beasts and Where to Find Them,* and *Quidditch through the Ages*—consulted occasionally, but rarely considered in published works on the series? Or will the entire output of Rowling's continued creation and expansion of the wizarding world be considered one *ouvre*?[4] It is possible that Rowling will revise the original books themselves, as they have been criticized for minor discrepancies and awkward styling (backfill is particularly amateurish).[5] In fact, one such discrepancy has already been corrected. In *Harry Potter and the Goblet of Fire,* Rowling explains that with the spell *priori incantatum*, Voldmort's wand will spit out images of his victims in reverse chronological order, but then she has Harry's father appear before Harry's mother, even though James was killed before Lily (667). Later editions correct the mistake. So which version of the book belongs in the canon, the original or the revised? If Rowling revises further, scholars will be faced with decisions like those facing Walt Whitman editors: are the original editions definitive, or should we replace them with revised, and presumably better, ones? In addition, although Rowling and almost all of her characters are British, much of the Harry Potter scholarship has been done on the other side of the Atlantic, using the American versions of the novels. Will future scholars continue to use the books adapted for readers who aren't familiar with the dialects and spelling of the United Kingdom, or will they agree with scholars such as Philip Nel that the works should be studied as they were written?[6] After all, if we attempt Shakespeare in the original, how could Rowling be too difficult?

To some these questions might seem pedantic and esoteric. However, the fact that we are asking them is indicative of the seriousness with which the study of the Harry Potter series is being taken.

Wallace Stevens wrote a poem called "Anecdote of the Jar," a poem about a jar on a hill and the idea of order. The poem is useful in teaching symbolism, but it isn't particularly interesting. Samuel Beckett wrote a play called *Waiting for Godot*, a play about men waiting for another man to show up. Spoiler alert: He never shows up. Again, the play is useful in discussing the modern condition and the possibility that God does not exist, or at least that no deity will come at our bidding. But the drama isn't particularly interesting. Italo Calvino wrote a book called *If on a Winter's Night a Traveler*, a novel in which characters keep finding beginnings of books, but can't find the rest of the novels. It is an interesting work for discussing postmodernism and meta-fiction, but it is highly unsatisfying as a novel. Literature can be accessible, interesting, and satisfying and still be useful and instructive. The Harry Potter novels, like the works of George Eliot, Alice Walker, Charles Dickens, Thomas Hardy, Carson McCullers, Mary Shelley, Mariama Ba, Mark Twain, and hundreds of other writers, demonstrate that fact.

Notes

1. Recently renamed "GeekyCon."

2. Mulholland's title shows the decision to accept J. K. Rowling's agents' request to use the term "unauthorized," a decision that most scholars have since eschewed.

3. College and university campuses also include many Harry Potter-themed student organizations, such as the large Wizards and Muggles Club at the College of William and Mary and the Order of the Nose-Biting Teacups at College of New Jersey.

4. A good discussion of the canon issue may be found in Lesson 10 of the podcast *Mugglenet Academia*, available from mugglenet.com.

5. A reader having Harry's story explained for the fourth or fifth time, presumably to make each book capable of standing alone, might be reminded of the preschool children's television show *Blues Clues*, which aired each episode five times. During the first viewing, children were intrigued. As their familiarity with the material increased during subsequent viewings, they felt proud of themselves for having learned the answers to all the questions. This sort of unusual dramatic irony might be the way that young readers of the Harry Potter series feel when they see explanations of events with which they are already familiar—a sort of self-congratulation that they are already in on this knowledge, but some people must not be, as it is being explained again. Older readers, on the other hand, certainly find that intrusive narration a bit condescending. As news stories continue sometimes for weeks, good journalists learn how to provide backfill that informs readers who have somehow missed earlier reports without insulting those who have kept up all along. J. K. Rowling might benefit from observing how reporters and news editors accomplish this task skillfully, as opposed to writing such lines as ". . . Harry Potter wasn't a normal boy. As a matter of fact, he was as not normal as it is possible to be. Harry Potter was a wizard . . ." (*Chamber of Secrets* 3).

6. Nel's essay on this subject, "'You Say Jelly, I Say Jell-O,'" appears in Whited, *The Ivory Tower and Harry Potter*.

Works Cited

Bloom, Harold. "Can 35 Million Book Buyers Be Wrong? Yes." *Wall Street Journal Western Edition* 11 July 2000: A2. *General OneFile*. Web. 30 Dec. 2014.

Granger, John. "Imagining a World without Harry Potter." *Washington Post* 14 Jul. 2011. *WashingtonPost.com*. Web. 28 Dec. 2014.

O'Connor, Flannery. *The Habit of Being: Letters of Flannery O'Connor*. New York: Farrar, Straus & Giroux, 1979.

Rowling, J. K. *Harry Potter and the Chamber of Secrets*. New York: Arthur A. Levine/Scholastic, 1999.

_____. *Harry Potter and the Deathly Hallows*. New York: Arthur A. Levine/Scholastic, 2007.

Safire, William. "Besotted with Potter." *New York Times* 27 Jan. 2000. *NYTimes.com*. Web. 27 Dec. 2014.

"Top Colleges for Harry Potter Fans." *About Education*, n.d. Web. 2 January 2015.

Umar, Haruna, & Christopher Torchia. "Survivors of Nigeria Attack Describe Killings." *ABCNEWS.go.com*. ABC News, 12 Jan. 2015. Web. 15 Jan. 2015.

"What Is Harry Potter Canon?" *Mugglenet Academia*. Hosts Keith Hawk & John Granger. Lesson 10. 23 Sept. 2012. *Mugglenet.com*. Web. 2 Jan. 2015.

Whited, Lana A., ed. *The Ivory Tower and Harry Potter*: *Perspectives on a Literary Phenomenon*. Columbia, U of Missouri P, 2002.

The Sustaining Power of Imagination: Biography of J. K. Rowling_____

Laurie Adams

Talent and intelligence never yet inoculated anyone against the caprice of the Fates. (J. K. Rowling, YouTube, 2011)

Who better to write the chronicles of "the boy who lived" than an author whose personal history is fraught with moments of hardship and loss? J. K. Rowling's work was informed by her experiences of adaptation and despair and an early-budding, steadily honed power of creative expression, which helped her to endure episodes of intense personal struggle. Examined through this lens, Rowling's life and the triad of guiding interior influences of imagination, expression, and agency made her perfectly suited to be the teller of the tale.

Born to parents Peter and Anne (née Volant) on July 31, 1965, Joanne (J. K.) Rowling took her first wavering steps into writing at the age of six, unaware that her creative gifts would help to carry her on the bumpy road to her eventual career as a successful novelist. In fact, before literary glory came, her knack for making up characters and envisioning their exploits would provide a constant in her life that stood her in good stead through various moments of change and grief.

Rowling describes her early childhood as happy and comfortable, if working-class and filled with the solemnity of many funerals. In an interview for the BBC, she noted "my sister [Diana] and I were born into an old family. Not in the sense of noble, but in the sense of aged" (Harrypottertheend1). Besides the loss of elderly family members, there was the upheaval of moving. The Rowlings left the author's earliest childhood home in Gloucestershire, England, when she was five, settling into a neighborhood in Winterbourne (Nel 8). There, she made the acquaintance of a family of high-spirited youngsters named "Potter," whose name she would later immortalize

(Nel 8). A less happy move occurred some four years later when the Rowlings relocated to Tutshill. This removed young Joanne from her friends and placed her in a primary school she did not like and in the classroom of a teacher, Mrs. Morgan, whose tactics would be recalled in the character of Severus Snape (Nel 9). But Mrs. Morgan and the Potter children were not the only real-life images that Rowling would extract from these early years. The surrounding countryside, including the Forest of Dean, and another friend she chanced upon in her teens—Séan Harris, whose personality was translated onto the page in the form of Ron Weasley—were other examples of Rowling's keen eye lighting upon steady anchors in reality for her fiction (Nel, 11, 16).

This mental retention of places, impressions, personalities, and odd mythology not only fed Rowling's imagination, but its synthesis into her written work gives a small inkling of the interior dynamics of imagination, expression, and agency. Imagination piqued would be given expression in a very determined, productive way. Even her earliest tale, "Rabbit," scribbled down when she was six years old, was written with the expectation that it would be published. Rowling noted in a 2001 interview for the BBC that "as soon as I knew that *people* wrote books, that they didn't just arrive . . . I knew [writing] was what I wanted to do . . . I can't remember not wanting to be a writer" (Vashetti). Though Rowling was secretly convinced she would one day make a writing career for herself, and her family was aware of her penchant for story-telling, she did not assert that conviction openly in order to avoid discouragement (Harvard).

There was discouragement enough in other forms. Though she was a strong enough student to be promoted to Head Girl by the final year of secondary school, Rowling was often bored living in the country and was occasionally bullied in school (Nel 12, 16). Additionally, Rowling's mother, Anne, was diagnosed with an aggressive form of multiple sclerosis when Rowling was fifteen, creating a home environment that Rowling often fled with the assistance of her friend Séan Harris (Nel 15, 16). Though the diagnosis cast a pall over her middle and late teens, it would be some years before its full impact crashed down upon Rowling's life.

In the interim, there was still school and, with it, deeply personal decisions to be made. Upon graduating from secondary school, Rowling set off for the University of Exeter, and despite having apparently given in to her parents' preference of a course that would fit her to be a bilingual secretary, she veered instead into a course that would feed her ever-hungry creative side (Nel 16). Pursuing Greek and Roman studies and French instead of the more pragmatic path was the first of several gambles Rowling would take toward fulfilling her literary ambition.

Following her graduation from Exeter, Rowling was hired by Amnesty International as a researcher in its African Research Department in London (Harvard). It would be here that the interaction among imagination, expression, and agency intensified. While Rowling's gift for expression was already well-established in its connection with agency—transferring story idea into completed work—Rowling's experiences with Amnesty International tightened the connection between imagination and agency. During these years, assisting in the documentation of abuses against political prisoners and refugees, Rowling's conceptualization of imagination evolved from an element of creativity into a more expansive view. She began to view imagination as a positive sustaining force—igniting empathy to inspire the demand for political change and further the cause of social justice (Harvard). Imagination, then, became for Rowling not a passive form of sustaining oneself through trying circumstances by daydreaming, but a catalyst, inspiring others to intervene on behalf of the at-risk, so that they might be rescued (Harvard).

In a very short time, however, Rowling herself would be in need of both forms of assistance. From 1990 to 1994, Rowling endured a series of personally devastating events, beginning with the death of her mother and quickly followed by a short-lived marriage that produced a daughter, but was otherwise regarded by Rowling as "catastrophic" (Archives). The rapid dissolution of the marriage and profound sadness over her mother's loss precipitated an unexpected descent into dire financial straits and depression (Nel 20). A single mother in a time when British politicians were setting up single mothers as scapegoats for crime and other social problems, Rowling could not find full-time employment and was forced to apply for public assistance benefits (Nel 20; Bryfonski 16). Despite this small income, her own earnings from part-time work, and the friends and family members who helped Rowling in other small ways throughout this time, she admits she was "as poor as it's possible to be in modern Britain without being homeless" (Rowling Archives).

Throughout this time, Rowling was sustaining herself emotionally with her imagination and agency in her more typical way—by doggedly working on the manuscript that would become *Harry Potter and the Philosopher's Stone*. Rowling said that the idea for Harry Potter first occurred to Rowling on a train in 1990, only months before her mother's death. Within six months of that event, she was hard at work on the first drafts of the story (Nel 18). With the help and encouragement of friends, she continued, writing "at least fifteen drafts" of the first chapter of the book (Vashetti). Completing the novel in 1995, Rowling then poured her effort into finding an agent and was ultimately signed by Christopher Little of the Christopher Little Literary Agency.

The story of Little's attempts to sell the book to a publisher has now passed into legend, with twelve rejections (Oprah Interviews), complaints about length (Nel 22), and the kindly-meant, but thoroughly discouraging assertion "You'll never make money out of children's books, Jo" (Bryfonski 44; Vashetti). One year after *Harry Potter and The Philosopher's Stone*—bought by Bloomsbury for around £2000—had been winning awards and gained a solid British fan-base, that same doubted, disparaged little book would earn its author one of the highest advances ever paid by a US publisher—$105,000 (Nel 22, 23; Vashetti).

For the next eleven years, up to the publication of *Harry Potter and the Deathly Hallows* in 2007, Rowling's life would be utterly transformed by the juggernaut that the series became. The seven books spawned movies with a seemingly endless array of licensed merchandise, as well as the Wizarding World theme park at Universal Studios and the Pottermore interactive website. Over 400 million books sold and continue to sell. Rowling's work has made her a billionaire.

Though her increased fame and fortune saddled Rowling with unforeseen new challenges in the form of a sometimes antagonistic relationship with the press, the comforting constant that writing had been for her since age six kept propelling her forward. Still harboring the imagination-fuelled empathy awakened by her years at Amnesty International, Rowling found that her new-found status afforded a platform and clout for causes that captured her imagination and spurred her to act. Two spin-off books based on the world of Harry Potter raised millions for children's charities (Bryfonski 17). Rowling also contributed her resources and voice to other efforts, writing impassioned opinion articles decrying the vilification of single parents (Spartz) and exposing the suffering of "caged children" in European orphanages and institutions ("My Fight"). Rowling noted that she found the needs of children in crisis to be singularly compelling, as a mother to three children herself, including her daughter from her first marriage and a son and daughter with her second husband, whom she married in 2001 (Jkrowling. com; Bryfonski 17, 18).

Rowling's deep desire to inspire her type of empathy-to-action response in her readers and cause them to ask difficult questions about the trials of others they might ordinarily avoid would also underpin her first post-Harry Potter novel, *The Casual Vacancy*. Rowling describes the purposely unsettling tale as being about "exclusion and prejudice and outsider status and division" (Harrypottertheend1). Rowling told BBC interviewer James Runcie, "I do get angry when I hear people talk and I think, 'can you not engage your imagination to the *tiniest* degree so that you understand what it might be like not to be you?'" (Harrypottertheend1).

The Casual Vacancy, published in 2012, examines the tensions within a small British town and the friction between middle-class residents leery of the residents of subsidized housing nearby (Harrypottertheend1). It would be followed in 2013 with Rowling's venture into gritty detective stories, *The Cuckoo's Calling*, which she published under the pen name Robert Galbraith (Jkrowling. com).

In the interim between the publication of the first Galbraith novel and its follow-up, *The Silkworm*, in June of 2014, Rowling became active in the mounting discussion leading up to the referendum vote to decide Scottish independence. Rowling's pleading appeal to retain unity with Britain, published in *The Telegraph*, outlined her concerns and instantly stirred controversy. Rowling's misgivings included her fears that medical research—to which she had contributed in memory of her mother—would be derailed and that politicians clamoring for a "yes" vote were underestimating the difficulties of secession and the risks involved therein. Rowling thrust herself into the midst of the increasingly heated debate not only with her words, but with a million-dollar contribution to the Better Together unity campaign, earning her the enmity of Scottish nationalists (Rowling, "Anti-Scottish Independence").

Critics of Rowling pointed to her ties with British politicians as the impetus for her leanings ("Scottish Independence"). However, given her consistent habit of following the dictates of imagination to act and express herself in service of sustaining that which is in jeopardy, it makes sense that she would favor unity, if sufficiently concerned about an independent Scotland's sustainability. Only time will tell if that interior impulse, which guided her so unerringly in the past, will place her on the right side of history on this question.

J. K. Rowling has not abandoned Harry Potter and his companions; in late 2014 she released twelve new pieces on her website *Pottermore*. Such inclusions are likely to continue.

Works Cited

Bryfonski, Dedria, ed. *Political Issues in J.K. Rowling's Harry Potter Series*. New York: Greenhaven, 2009.

Harrypottertheend1. "J. K. Rowling – Writing for Grownups 2012." *YouTube*. YouTube, 30 Sept. 2012. Web. 9 Sept. 2014.

Harvard Magazine. "J. K. Rowling Speaks at Harvard Commencement." *YouTube*. YouTube, 15 Sept. 2011. Web. 9 Sept. 2014.

Mills, Alice. "Harry Potter: Agency or Addiction?" *Children's Literature in Education* 41.4 (2010): 291–301. *Academic Search Complete.* Web. 15 Sept. 2014.

Nel, Philip. *J. K. Rowling's Harry Potter Novels*. New York: Continuum International, 2001.

Rowling, J. K. *Harry Potter and the Deathly Hallows*. New York: Scholastic, 2007.

_____. *Harry Potter and the Order of the Phoenix*. New York: Scholastic, 2003.

_____. "My Fight." *jkrowling.com*. 2 May 2006. Web. 21 Apr. 2015.

_____. *jkrowling.com*. n.d. Web. 9 Sept. 2014.

_____. "J. K. Rowling's Anti-Scottish Independence Statement in Full." *Telegraph.co.uk*. Telegraph Media Group, Limited, 11 Jun. 2014. Web. 9 Sept. 2014.

_____. *Pottermore.com*. Pottermore Limited, n.d. Web. 9 Sept. 2014.

Rowling Archives. "Oprah Interviews J. K. Rowling, Full Video." *YouTube*. YouTube, 24 July 2013. Web. 9 Sept. 2014.

"Scottish Independence: J.K. Rowling Donates £1m to Pro-UK group." *BBC.com*. BBC, 11 Jun. 2014. Web. 9 Sept. 2014.

Spartz, Emerson. "Rowling: 'I am Prouder of My Years as a Single Mother than Any Other Part of My Life.'" *MuggleNet.com*. 18 Sept. 2013. Web. 9 Sept. 2014.

Vashetti. "J. K. Rowling – Harry Potter and Me (BBC, 2001)" *YouTube*. YouTube, 21 May 2014. Web. 9 Sept. 2014.

CRITICAL
CONTEXTS

"Contemporary" Does Not Mean "Modern": The Harry Potter Series as a Sampler of Western Literary Traditions_____

M. Katherine Grimes

When I try to get my undergraduate students to discuss literary periods, they sometimes act as though I am Professor Binns droning through History of Magic classes—until they actually see how *Oedipus Rex* tells the story of a Classical tragic hero and how Beowulf differs from Oedipus because Grendel's killer is a Medieval hero. Then we get to the Modern period, and the students who understand, who are really thinking, make such statements as "I thought everything being written right now would be Modern"; then I explain the difference between the Modern literary period and contemporary literature.

J. K. Rowling's series of books about the boy wizard are contemporary novels; they were all written and published within the past twenty years. But they are not Modern novels. In fact, even though they were written in what some scholars call the Post-postmodern period, they do not have all the characteristics of any specific literary period, but serve as a sort of sampler of Western literature—works written in Europe, Northern Africa, and the Americas—through the centuries.

For hundreds of years, authors had no idea that they belonged to specific literary and artistic periods. Later scholars saw patterns in the visual art, architecture, music, drama, dance, and literature of historical periods, as well as connections between those patterns and the philosophy, religion, economics, social systems, and historical events of those eras. Once the scholars observed these patterns, they gave names to the artistic periods. It is important to remember that, while most of the important authors who write during specific periods exhibit characteristics of the art of their periods, the fact that a writer is *in* a literary period does not mean that he or she is *of* that period. That fact is certainly true of Harry Potter's creator, J. K. Rowling.

Harry Potter and Ancient Literature

The Mesopotamian epic *Gilgamesh* illustrates well the Ancient period, a time when most people in the Western world were illiterate, and myths, legends, and folktales were passed down orally. The long poem, which Lana Whited discusses in her essay on immortality in this book, is believed to be the earliest epic, with parts of it written around 2000 BCE. It focuses on a hero who is changed for the better because of friendship and undertakes a quest related to immortality. Harry Potter is certainly transformed from his lonely existence with his aunt, uncle, and cousin, the Dursleys, to a much richer life with his friends, Ron Weasley, and Hermione Granger. He, too, undertakes a quest related to the idea of immortality, not to gain his own immortality, but to prevent that of the evil Voldemort. Both works portray the quest for immortality as unwise.

The ancient world, in addition, gave us the Hebrew scriptures, especially the Torah or the Pentateuch, which became the first five books in the Christian Bible. These writings, which most scholars date to the fifth or sixth century BCE, also contain elements that appear in the Harry Potter series, such as the quest for forbidden knowledge. This motif is illustrated in the story of Adam and Eve in Genesis, in the search of Albus Dumbledore and Gellert Grindelwald for the Deathly Hallows, which would make them nearly invincible, and in the creation by Voldemort of Horcruxes, which would do the same for him. The story of Moses as a reluctant hero, who leads his people away from a cruel leader, serves as a prototype for Harry Potter, who leads Dumbledore's Army to fight the evil Voldemort. Like many heroes, both Harry and Moses begin their tales as swaddled infants left to be discovered and reared by people other than their parents.[1]

Thus from the ancient world, we get some of the most universal of themes, themes echoed through the ages and found now in the Harry Potter series: the hero archetype, the desire for knowledge, the power of temptation, the importance of friendship, the quest motif, and the search for immortality.

Harry Potter and Classical Literature

In the ninth century BCE, the Greek and Roman Empires became the models for Western culture. Architectural marvels such as the Parthenon in Greece and the Roman Coliseum as well as amazing statuary rivaled the great literature of the time. Epics including Homer's *Iliad* and *Odyssey* and Virgil's *Aeneid* continued the earlier tradition of combining heroic action with references to the gods, a sort of meshing of legend and mythology. J. K. Rowling does not refer to God or gods, but her novels are rife with legends: the legend of the three brothers, the legend of the sorcerer's stone, the legends of the nearly interminable quidditch matches, the legend of the baby Harry's defeat of the vile Lord Voldemort.

Greek and Roman drama was clearly divided into tragedy and comedy. Tragedy in Classical drama explored the fall of the hero (or occasionally the heroine) due to his own flaw, or mistake, or *hamartia*, which was often hubris, or excessive pride. An example of such a tragedy is Sophocles' *Oedipus Tyrannus*, or *Oedipus Rex*, both titles meaning "Oedipus the King." In this play, the king and queen of Thebes, Laios and Iocaste, have been told of a prophecy that their son will kill Laios, so when Oedipus is born, they send him to a mountain to die of exposure. The messenger cannot bring himself to leave the boy to perish, so he gives him to a shepherd, who in turn gives him to another king and queen. When Oedipus reaches adulthood, he goes to the oracle at Delphi to learn his fate, hears that he is prophesied to kill his father and marry his mother, and so leaves his home. His travels take him near Thebes, where, in a fit of road rage, he kills a man and most of the man's entourage. Oedipus proceeds to Thebes, where he solves the riddle of the Sphinx, a creature who has been tormenting the city. His reward for ridding Thebes of the Sphinx is to marry the widowed queen and rule jointly with her and her brother, Creon. Of course, the reader learns that the man killed on the road was Oedipus' father, and Iocaste is his mother. In a wonderful example of dramatic irony, the reader figures out the mystery long before the hero does because Oedipus is too arrogant to see himself for what he is. When Iocaste learns that she has married her son, she kills herself, whereupon Oedipus puts out his eyes and goes into exile.

The hubris that causes Oedipus to kill Laios and to be blind to his own identity as the murderer is not a trait we see in the hero of J. K. Rowling's novels. Harry Potter is generally humble and controlled, especially for a child. Voldemort has a tragic flaw, but he isn't the hero. However, like Sophocles' play, the Harry Potter novels are filled with the dilemma of prophecy: the conflict between fate and free will. Just as we ask whether Oedipus' fate was foreseen or predetermined by the oracle at Delphi, Harry Potter asks whether the prophecy that either he or Voldemort will die at the hands of the other determines what Harry must do or merely describes it.

Classical comedies are related to fertility rituals and are often extremely broad—unsophisticated, physical comedy—and bawdy. For example, *Lysistrata* by Aristophanes tells the story of Greek women banding together to stop the Peloponnesian War by denying their menfolk sex until peace is achieved. The Harry Potter novels certainly do not fit the definition of broad or bawdy comedy; however, they do feature a theme common in classical comic drama: mistaken identity, the discovery of which often leads to the rise of the hero. We see this in the Roman Plautus' *Menaechmi*, a farce in which twins separated in childhood are mistaken for one another and, after a series of silly misadventures, reunited, resulting in one of the men leaving his jealous wife to go live with his brother. In a nod to *Menaechmi*, twins George and Fred Weasley are often mistaken for one another, and Polyjuice potion fools many characters into believing that someone is someone else; in short, appearances deceive. Harry is revealed to be not the orphaned son of a couple killed in a car accident, as he had been told, but a wizard who has survived what should have been a fatal attack. He becomes the hero of the wizarding world. And of course comedy, even dark comedy, restores the status quo at the end, usually concluding with marriage, as befits its role as part of a fertility ritual. The Harry Potter series ends with the evil Voldemort destroyed, Harry and Ginny Weasley married, Hermione Granger and Ron Weasley married, and the next generation of wizarding children boarding the train to Hogwarts; the status quo is restored.

Satire, or making fun in order to correct, is a major part of Classical comedy, as well. That satire comes in two primary forms, both influenced by Roman authors: Horatian, named after Horace, a gentle sort of poking fun, and Juvenalian, from Juvenal, a sharper attack; both forms aim to improve society. Aristophanes' *The Wasps* satirizes the courts of Athens, while his play *The Clouds* makes fun of esoteric education and portrays Socrates as a useless sophist, someone who is interested in learning merely for the sake of learning and not for any practical purpose. In J. K. Rowling's works, the attacks on both the Ministry of Magic and the press, thinly disguised representatives of the British government and the paparazzi of British tabloids, are harshly satirized, as Minister of Magic Cornelius Fudge foolishly tries to hide the return of Voldemort, while reporter Rita Skeeter in the form of an insect, a beetle—a true bug—spies on more sympathetic characters and fabricates lies about them. Horatian satire is represented by the portrayals of author Gilderoy Lockhart, who uses other people's stories and then loses his own memory during an act of selfish cowardice, and of Xenophilius Lovegood, who prints articles about the Crumple-Horned Snorkack. Where does the portrayal of Percy Weasley fall? When he is cocky about his appointment to head boy and his Ministry of Magic job trying to standardize cauldron thickness, his siblings' amusement is Horatian; but when he becomes the sycophantic toady to Bartemius Crouch, Sr. and isolates himself from his family, he is portrayed as part of a dangerously disillusioned and deceitful government. Thus his character becomes less amusing and more frightening.

The epic found in the Ancient period continues to flourish during the Classical period. *The Odyssey* by Homer tells the tale of Odysseus (called Ulysses by the Romans), who has fought in the Trojan War and spends ten years trying to return to his wife, Penelope, and son, Telemachus. His well-known adventures include blinding and outwitting the one-eyed giant, or Cyclops, Polyphemus; fending off the call of the Sirens; and defeating the suitors of Penelope. He does this with the help of the goddess Athena, who takes the form of the old man Mentor, from whose name comes the term we now use for an older and wiser person who helps a younger one. Harry Potter's tale, too, is a long one in which he must defeat the evil Voldemort, fend off the temptation to forego his quest, and defeat the Death Eaters in a battle like the one Oedipus fought against the Trojans. Like Odysseus, he has a mentor, Dumbledore.[2] And like Odysseus, Harry ends up with his true love in the end, despite Ginny's suitors who have provoked the monster of jealousy in him.

J. K. Rowling herself studied the classics, including Roman and Greek history and literature. We see the influence of these studies not just in the classical themes in the Harry Potter series, but in names and spells derived especially from Latin and Greek. A few character names with classical origins are Minerva, the Roman goddess of wisdom, whose Greek counterpart is Athena; Remus, who, with his brother Romulus, was suckled as an infant by a wolf and who was killed by Romulus, the founder of Rome; Draco, a word whose etymology can be traced to both Greek and Latin words meaning a huge reptile or serpent; Severus, from the Latin for stern; and Albus, which probably comes from a Roman family name and means "white," just as albumen is the white of an egg. Spells with Latin origins include "wingardium leviosa," as "levis" is Latin for "light in weight"; "avada kedavra," with the reference to a cadaver, from Latin words for both a dead body and the verb meaning "to fall"; "impedimentum," a Latin word itself, meaning "obstacle"; "expelliarmus," from the Latin "expellere," meaning "to drive out"; and, of course, "stupefy," from the Latin "stupere," meaning "stunned."

Harry Potter and Medieval Literature

The Classical period ended about the time of the fall of the Roman Empire, around 476 CE, and was followed by the Medieval period, or the Middle Ages, during which Christianity spread throughout Europe and provided a sort of unity hitherto based primarily on military conquest. So while the Roman and Ottoman Empires, for example, had forcibly united many peoples under one political regime, Christianity united many peoples under one belief system and one religious leader, the pope. Norse, Roman, and Greek gods were replaced with one deity. Latin, the official language of the Roman Catholic Church, became the *lingua franca*, the language that most educated people knew. Paradoxically, both religion and superstition abounded. Emphasis lay on the soul and its salvation, but people also believed in witches and witchcraft. An example of the two sets of beliefs—in God and witchcraft—is found in stories about the plague of the fourteenth century, when estimates are that over half of all Europeans died. Historians say that many Christians thought that the plague was caused by God's anger at the people and tried to appease God by killing people accused of witchcraft, who were thought to associate with the devil, and even by killing cats, which were associated with witches. Some theories about the rapid spread of the disease hold that killing cats allowed the rapid growth of the flea-carrying rat population, causing the plague to spread throughout Europe as rapidly as the fire spread through London in 1666. Ironically, in the Harry Potter novels, the non-magical people are often the ones persecuted by the Death Eaters.

Heroic literature also still abounded during the Middle Ages: Perhaps the best known English epic, *Beowulf*, written around one thousand years ago, give or take a century, is a work in which the Norse hero Beowulf defeats a giant, the giant's mother, and a dragon. The man who became the legendary King Arthur, if he actually existed, probably lived sometime in the first two medieval centuries, and King Arthur and his knights became the subjects of numerous histories and poems over the next several hundred years. In his twelfth-century *History of the Kings of Britain*, Welsh scholar Geoffrey of Monmouth writes at length of King Arthur. Sir Gawain of Green Knight fame is portrayed as a knight of Arthur's Round Table, as is Galahad, who went on a quest for the Holy Grail, a dish or chalice associated with Jesus' last celebration of the Passover. The young knight in the "Wife of Bath's Tale" from Geoffrey Chaucer's *Canterbury Tales* is also a member of King Arthur's court.[3]

Certainly, the Harry Potter novels remind us of the Middle Ages. Hogwarts is a castle where suits of armor populate the halls; classes are held in the dungeon and in turrets; dragons must be fought; and, of course, people are witches and wizards. Albus Dumbledore is Order of Merlin, which obviously recalls us to the story of King Arthur. The Sword of Gryffindor certainly alludes to Arthur's sword, Excalibur, and the quest for the Horcruxes reminds us of quests such as the one for the Holy Grail.

Christian allegory abounds in medieval literature. The morality play *Everyman* is a good example. From the late 1400s, it tells the story of a man whose life is a pilgrimage and who, upon death, must account for his life. The conflict is between good and evil, and Everyman himself represents all people.

The Harry Potter novels serve as a sort of allegory, as well, with Voldemort and his Death Eaters representing evil and Dumbledore and the Order of the Phoenix representing good. Harry's choice in the Sorting Hat scene in *Harry Potter and the Philosopher's/Sorcerer's Stone* shows him as Everyman, choosing the good—Gryffindor—as opposed to what he sees as the bad—Slytherin. Voldemort's serpent-like appearance and his association with snakes certainly lead one to see a connection with the serpent in the book of Genesis, and Dumbledore's association with the phoenix, Fawkes, connects him with the idea of rebirth, of everlasting life, a Christian concept, as well as a promise of many other religions.

Harry Potter and Renaissance Literature

Chaucer's tales come near the end of the Middle Ages, in the late 1300s; the medieval period ends around the time of Chaucer's death in 1400, replaced in Europe by the Renaissance, which began in Italy and moved northward. The Renaissance was marked by emphasis on the physical world. While the spiritual domain remained a dominant theme, portrayal of that realm was much more worldly. The art of the Renaissance demonstrates this connection. Think of the Sistine Chapel in Rome, whose ceiling Renaissance artist Michelangelo painted five hundred years ago: while the scenes are religious, such as the creation of the world as described in the Hebrew and Christian scriptures, the paintings of the people are quite realistic. Writers who are best known during this period include Miguel de Cervantes

Saavedra, author of *Don Quixote de la Mancha*, and Cervantes' contemporary, William Shakespeare.

The writing of the Renaissance reflect a humanistic attitude, an emphasis on human beings as worthy of note and capable of improvement and understanding. Whereas in Europe in the Middle Ages Christians were taught that they were sinful and in need of intervention from the Catholic Church, the Renaissance brought about the Reformation and the idea that individuals were not answerable to an earthly authority such as a pope. One of the emphases of Renaissance philosophers was education, not just for the purpose of enhancing knowledge, but also for the advancement of the individual. The idea is not extremely different from the study today of the humanities—language, philosophy, history, art, music, and literature. The Harry Potter books certainly emphasize education, albeit not so much for the purpose of human perfectibility as for the skill of wizardry.

The focus on the human being and the value of the individual is certainly present in the series. As J. K. Rowling writes when Harry Potter realizes that his task includes succumbing to death, "he felt more alive and more aware of his own living body than ever before" (*Deathly Hallows* 692).

Harry Potter's parallels with Renaissance literature seem obvious as we look at two of the most famous works of the period: William Shakespeare's *Hamlet* and Miguel Cervantes' *Don Quixote*. In the play as in the Harry Potter novels, a father has been killed, and his son believes that he must avenge the death. Someone close to the father has betrayed him—Hamlet's uncle Claudius and James Potter's friend Peter Pettigrew. The main character hesitates—Hamlet to kill his uncle and Harry to kill Pettigrew. But in the end, the murderers and traitors are destroyed. The importance of honor and human emotion, topics common in Renaissance literature, are extolled. In the Spanish novel, too, honor is central. Although Don Quixote is mad during much of the novel, it is not his madness but his courage that we must admire. Probably the most iconic scene is Quixote's tilting at windmills, thinking them to be giants. Thus we speak of quixotic actions, bravery in the face of overwhelming odds.

Harry Potter, too, faces nearly impossible odds, yet carries on what he sees as his duty, even when he believes that he cannot possibly survive the attempt let alone triumph—like walking into the forest without his wand to meet Voldemort. In all three works, *Hamlet*, *Don Quixote*, and the Harry Potter series, appearances are deceiving, and the main characters often do not know who is trustworthy. But in all cases, the individual overcomes the deception and learns that he must trust himself.

Distrust of earthly power also raises its head in literature of the Renaissance. Just as the Reformation revealed a lack of trust in the vastly powerful Roman Catholic Church, Thomas More refused to accept Henry VIII's declaration of the king's supremacy as the head of the Church of England. More's book *Utopia* is also of interest, as it created, five hundred years ago, a fictional nation that, it argued, was superior to the Europe of the time. Albus Dumbledore's disrespect for the Ministers of Magic seems to reflect this view of earthly authority as questionable, and the headmaster's attempts to make Hogwarts a haven that protects children from such authority and from the evil Voldemort, lead Harry to see the school as a sort of utopia, an isolated place that is greatly superior to the world in which Harry spent most of his childhood.

Harry Potter and Neoclassical Literature

Around the middle of the seventeenth century, art and literature moved from the Renaissance to the Neoclassical period, also called the Enlightenment. An examination of the architecture in a place such as Williamsburg in Virginia shows that the Neoclassical period—so called because it revived the ideas of the Greek and Roman Classical age—emphasized order, balance, and perfectibility. Like many other writers, British poet Alexander Pope saw a hierarchy from God to the lowest creatures on earth as the order of the universe, and he asserted in the poem "Essay on Man" that "Whatever is, is right." It seems ironic, then, that the Enlightenment was also the time of both the American and the French Revolutions, for the notion of perfectibility carried over into government and politics. Far from seeing that "Whatever is, is right," the revolutionaries emphasized the concept of working to improve this world. Thomas Jefferson drafted the Declaration of Independence, asserting that "all men are created equal" and that governments should exist only by consent of the governed. Also called the Age of Reason, the Enlightenment emphasized the intellect and thinking for oneself. In fact, Thomas Paine wrote an essay called "The Age of Reason" in which he argued, as he and other Deists thought, that we should believe only what religious ideas can be substantiated by our observation. Thus, we should believe in a creator because there is a creation, but we need not believe parts of the Bible that we did not witness ourselves, such as people's reports of the appearance of angels.

The Harry Potter novels show the influence of the Neoclassical age in at least two ways. First is the emphasis on reason and logic. Hermione's use of reason gets the children through any number of adventures and out of any number of scrapes. For example, it is Hermione who figures out which bottles will move the children forward and backward, using Severus Snape's potions and clues, in *Harry Potter and the Sorcerer's Stone*. Increasingly, all three of the young people use logic to save themselves, Hogwarts, and the wizarding world. In *Harry Potter and the Deathly Hallows*, they use the clues that Albus Dumbledore has given them to find and destroy the Horcruxes that would have kept Voldemort's soul alive and to figure out the identities and locations of the Hallows themselves. Reason is so important to the wizarding world that an entire house at Hogwarts, Ravenclaw, is dedicated to the idea that "Wit beyond measure is man's greatest treasure" (Rowling, *Deathly Hallows* 588).

The idea of revolution is a second Neoclassical concept in the Harry Potter series. It manifests itself in two basic ways. First, the oppression by wizards of non-wizards leads us back to the oppression of American people in the English colonies by the British king, as well as the oppression of the French common people by the French royalty and aristocracy. Of course, other types of mistreatment of those not in power abound in the history of the world, but during the Neoclassical period, the American colonists and French common folk were the ones who overthrew their oppressors. The house-elves and goblins do not achieve the same success. However, the wizards who are victims of Voldemort and his hench-people at the Ministry of Magic do revolt and overthrow those who are abusing their power, and in *Deathly Hallows*, the house-elves join the battle that defeats Voldemort and the Death Eaters. The connection to the time of revolution becomes clearer if we see Cornelius Fudge and others in similar positions as the Tories, who want to deny that a problem exists, and see Albus Dumbledore and the members of the Order of the Phoenix and Dumbledore's Army as the revolutionaries. The goals of the revolutions during the eighteenth century and in the Harry Potter series were to improve the world, even if perfectibility might be too lofty an aim.

Harry Potter and the Romantic Period

At the end of the eighteenth century, the pendulum swung from Neoclassicism to Romanticism. Although the idea of revolution remained, most other ideas from the Enlightenment were replaced by new concepts. Two British poets, William Wordsworth and Samuel Taylor Coleridge, consciously outlined ways that their writing would be different from the writing of the generation preceding them. In *Lyrical Ballads*, first published in 1798 and presented in a second edition two years later, they explained and then demonstrated the concepts they saw as important to the poetic aesthetic of the nineteenth century. Those explanations and descriptions of Romantic literature show us that writing of this period focuses on nature, common people and their language, the supernatural, and emotion.

We see the emphasis on nature in Wordsworth's poem "I Wandered Lonely as a Cloud," in which the poet describes the joy that seeing a field of daffodils brings him at the time and in later contemplation. The focus on common people and their language is evident in American romantic poet Walt Whitman's "Song of Myself," which includes lists of people from all areas of North America and from all walks of life and declares them equal. The supernatural we see in Samuel Taylor Coleridge's "The Rime of the Ancient Mariner," when the dead sailors are animated and rise up to sail the ship. And we see emotion in Edgar Allan Poe's "The

Raven," when the narrator asks whether he will ever overcome the pain of losing his lost Lenore, knowing all the while that the bird will respond, "Nevermore."

We see the influence of every aspect of Romanticism on the Harry Potter series. In *Harry Potter and the Deathly Hallows*, Harry, Ron, and Hermione take refuge in nature while they are on the run from Voldemort and on their quest to destroy the Horcruxes. And when Harry thinks that he is about to die, it is the natural world, besides of course his loved ones, that he bemoans losing: "Every second he breathed, the smell of the grass, the cool air on his face, was so precious . . ." (697). Also, while Harry Potter is a wizard and an extraordinary one at that, he goes out of his way to celebrate the ordinary, the people whom pureblood wizards condemn. Harry's best friends are Ron Weasley, a boy from a relatively poor family, and Hermione Granger, who is Muggle-born. When the free house-elf Dobby is killed, Harry digs the grave himself, by hand, without magic. The Romantic idea of the language of the common people is celebrated in the Harry Potter books in their accessibility to children. The supernatural is evidenced in magic and ghosts and people's spirits returning from the dead to help Harry. For example, Rowena Ravenclaw's daughter, Helena, the Grey Lady, helps Harry find her mother's diadem, which Voldemort had used as a Horcrux, in a way similar to the dead sailors who rose in Coleridge's poem to help the mariner. And, of course, emotion is at the forefront, for the books deal with adolescents, people fairly squirming with emotion. Characters experience fear, anger, love, jealousy, sorrow, grief, and joy. Harry himself fears Voldemort, feels fury at Severus Snape and Dolores Umbridge, falls in love with Ginny Weasley, feels jealous of Ginny's early boyfriends, experiences sorrow upon the death of his owl Hedwig, grieves the loss of his parents and his friends during the battle at Hogwarts, and knows joy when he and Ginny are reunited. Children's and comparative literature scholar Maria Nikolajeva convincingly argues that much of Harry Potter's appeal is that he is a Romantic hero; in fact, her essay in Elizabeth Heilman's collection is entitled "*Harry Potter*; a Return to the Romantic Hero."

Harry Potter and Realism

In the mid-nineteenth century, the pendulum swung again, this time away from Romanticism and toward Realism. The focus moved from the ideal to the portrayal of the world as it is. Realistic writers, such as Mark Twain, had often been reporters, and the style of the Realists was often journalistic. In addition, Realism often focused on the growing middle class, as we see in such works as William Dean Howells' *The Rise of Silas Lapham*. A major branch of Realism is Psychological Realism, as we see in the works of Henry James. In his novella *The Turn of the Screw*, for example, we read about a governess who might or might not see ghosts and who becomes obsessed with protecting her charges from those ghosts, real or imagined. The important question is not really whether the ghosts actually exist, but the effect the perception of them has on the governess' psyche and her behavior toward the children.

Three aspects of the Harry Potter series are connected to the Realistic period. First is the reminder that Harry Potter is a Realistic character, despite his being a wizard.[4] He has friends, gets embarrassed, falls in love, gets in trouble for talking in class, struggles with homework, rebels against authority, and just generally acts like an adolescent, when he isn't doing magic or fighting the Dark Lord. Second is the presentation of the Dursleys, who are decidedly middle class, with their emphasis on being normal and their dedication to Vernon Dursley's career in the drill-making industry. The third is the Psychological Realism we get, especially in *Harry Potter and the Deathly Hallows*, when Harry experiences self-doubt and fear that he will die. In many ways, what goes on inside Harry's head is more interesting than the physical action in the novels, especially the final one.

Harry Potter and Naturalism

Around the turn of the nineteenth century, Realism moved into Naturalism, retaining its journalistic nature, but in some ways combining it with Romantic elements. Again, the focus was on the common people, as it was during the Romantic period. But this time, the literary aspects were combined with philosophical ones, and the result led to a sort of sociological treatise. Naturalism was based on the idea of philosophical determinism, the notion that free will is an illusion because our choices are limited by biology, environment, and economics. Stephen Crane's *Maggie: A Girl of the Streets* epitomizes Naturalism, as does Thomas Hardy's *Tess of the D'Urbervilles*. In Crane's novella, Maggie is the victim of drunk parents, poverty, and her gender. Her boyfriend ruins her reputation, then leaves her. Her choices then are limited to prostitution and death. Hardy's novel presents similar situations for Tess; her parents are poverty-stricken drinkers; the son of her employer rapes her and leaves her pregnant; her baby dies; she marries, but her husband leaves her when he finds out about her past; her work on farms is insufficient to help her family; and her choices are basically limited to becoming the mistress of her rapist and death. Naturalistic novels often have as one of their goals exposing society's deficiencies and pointing out ways we allow others to suffer.

The Harry Potter novels are certainly not realistic in the way that Naturalistic literature is. However, they do have an element of determinism. House-elves are born to be slaves; wizards and witches are born to be magical, even if their parents weren't; young Harry Potter is at the mercy of the insufferably mundane Dursleys; and Harry Potter is fated to destroy Voldemort or be destroyed by him. While that fact isn't really Naturalistic, it does show that we are not always in control of our fate. It is also important to note the Voldemort is in many ways a Naturalistic character. Born to a Muggle father, Tom Riddle, Sr., who never recognized the child as his son, and a witch mother, Merope Gaunt, who died soon after Tom Riddle, Jr., was born, he was reared in a Muggle orphanage. A half-blood wizard in a Muggle world, young Tom never felt as though he belonged. Like many Naturalistic works about criminals, such as Truman Capote's *In Cold Blood*, the difficult childhood helps explain the deviant behavior, even though it does not excuse the criminality.

Harry Potter and Modernism

Most literary scholars see Naturalism as short-lived, lasting only until about the time of World War I. However, Lana A. Whited, in her dissertation entitled "Naturalism, the New Journalism, and the Tradition of the American Fact-Based Homicide Novel," argues that the period lasted at least until the 1960s, when Truman Capote wrote *In Cold Blood.* It is certainly possible for two or more literary periods to coexist. While Naturalism might have continued for six decades or more, the disaster that was the First World War ushered in a period of literary pessimism and even despair. Modern poet T. S. Eliot wrote a long work called *The Wasteland,* which is filled with classical allusions but basically points out the fact that the world has deteriorated into meaninglessness. Modernist literature is often cynical. Characters and authors themselves seem alienated and filled with despair, as well as unable to communicate. While *The Wasteland* is the epitome of Modernism, Eliot's "The Love Song of J. Alfred Prufrock" shows even more directly the feelings of insignificance associated with the period, as well as the failure of language. Prufrock says more than once, "That is not what I meant at all." At its extreme, Modernism is nihilistic, seeing little or no meaning in the universe. In Franz Kafka's Modern novella *The Metamorphosis*, a man turns into an insect. His family becomes more and more alienated from him until he dies. The tone of the work is one of despair and misery. Perhaps the best way to understand the Modern attitude is to read about how the Dementors make people feel. In *Harry Potter and the Prisoner of Azkaban*, a Dementor is described as having a "dead, slimy hand" and "rattling breath like an evil wind." "Where there should have been eyes," Rowling writes, "there was only thin, gray scabbed skin, stretched blankly over empty sockets. But there was a mouth . . . a gaping, shapeless hole, sucking the air with the sound of a death rattle." The Dementor has "putrid breath" and "strong, clammy hands." Harry's reaction is "paralyzing terror" (384). Ron Weasley says after a Dementor enters the Hogwarts Express car where he, Harry, and others are riding, "I felt weird, . . . [l]ike I'd never be cheerful again . . ." (85). George Weasley says of the creatures, "They suck the happiness out of a place, Dementors. Most of the prisoners [in Azkaban, where the Dementors are guards] go mad in there" (Rowling, *Prisoner of Azkaban* 97). After all, the name itself implies that the creatures will make people lose their sanity, become demented. For the Dementor's kiss sucks out one's soul. Yet as Harry realizes that he must fight the Dementors, Modernists continue to search for meaning in a universe where they find none.

But despite the Dementors, the Harry Potter novels are not Modern in the sense of belonging to the Modern literary period. The universe does have meaning, and characters do not remain alienated. After all, even Percy Weasley is reunited with his family in the end; Voldemort is defeated; and the wizarding world is saved. However, the despair and disillusionment of the literature of the Modern period are evident, especially in the last book. Harry has certainly felt alienated before his teenage years; after all, he was ignored or tormented from his second year through his tenth. For all intents and purposes, he has no family from the time of his parents' death until he marries Ginny Weasley. In *Harry Potter and the Deathly Hallows*, he is literally separated from his school, which has become his home, and from all his friends except Hermione Granger. His parents, godfather, and headmaster/mentor are dead. In almost every way, he is having the experience the Modernists describe. However, he still has purpose, and that is why he is not a Modern character. And the novels have a happy ending, so they are not Modern works.

Harry Potter and Postmodernism

As the horrors of World War One led to Modernism, those of the Second World War led to Postmodernism. As in Modernism, the later period was basically nihilistic, agreeing that the universe is basically meaningless and the search for meaning is futile, even absurd. However, the Postmodernists saw that lack of meaning as freeing. Instead of thinking that they must search for a meaning that doesn't exist, they often felt freed to enjoy life and revel in its absurdity. Skepticism about absolute meaning caused Postmodernists to question science, language, and other means of interpreting reality. Focus was on the author, and interpretation of reality was subjective. One group of Postmodernists, the Beats, or Beat Generation, saw themselves as outsiders to the society of the 1950s, a society of conformity and capitalism, especially in the United States. Allen Ginsberg's poem "Howl" calls these outsiders—poets, drug addicts, homosexuals, the mentally ill—"the best minds of my generation." In the Postmodern period, heroes are replaced by anti-heroes, characters who seem, in many ways, the opposite of the heroes of myth and romance. While anti-heroes are certainly not new to Postmodernism, the alienation they represent is definitely appropriate to the age. Therefore, we see such protagonists as Holden Caulfield in *The Catcher in the Rye* by J. D. Salinger and Billy Pilgrim in Kurt Vonnegut's *Slaughterhouse Five.*

Harry Potter often feels like an outsider, sometimes completely alone and other times one of a small group of outsiders. The Harry Potter books show a generation that questions the reality presented by an earlier generation. The Ministry of Magic becomes an absolutely absurd place when Voldemort and his Death Eaters take over, using the ministry to persecute those wizards who were Muggle-born or half-bloods. Changes in identities with the use of Polyjuice potion make reality questionable. However, the Harry Potter books are not Postmodern because they do not assert that the world is meaningless and because, as Maria Nikolajeva points out, Harry is a traditional hero, not an anti-hero. Although the wizarding world has been turned topsy-turvy, it can be righted again, and it is, in the end, with Harry's heroism as the prime correction to the evil that has threatened the norm, such as it is.

Harry Potter and Post-Postmodernism, or Pseudomodernism, or Digimodernism

Postmodernism lasted until near the end of the twentieth century. Various names have been given to the period that began with the new millennium. But whether the period is Post-postmodern, Pseudomodern, Digimodern, or something else, general agreement is that the reader is more involved in the work than ever before. Instead of merely reading a book or watching a movie, consumers can participate in shaping narratives. For example, reality television shows let viewers vote. Radio shows let listeners call in.

The Harry Potter series itself is not Post-postmodern or Digimodern, but the experience of its readership often is. The Internet lets readers post and read one another's fan fiction and comments about the Harry Potter series. Even author J. K. Rowling participates, posting new Harry Potter content on her website *Pottermore*. Readers and authors are less isolated from one another, as are readers from other readers. This kind of shared experience in a virtual world takes us back to questions asked in the introduction to this volume of essays: What is the Harry Potter canon? Is it just the seven books in the series? Or does it include other works by J. K. Rowling, even her Internet posts?[5]

Harry Potter as Contemporary Literature

Whatever literary period we are in currently is contemporary—now. People rarely are conscious of the period they are creating or living in; usually periods are named later. And not everyone in a period is influenced by it. In fact, during the beginning of any period, most writers are still writing as though they are in the previous period, just as Beethoven composed like a Neoclassical musician at first, then like a Romantic one.

J. K. Rowling's Harry Potter series is eclectic; it represents numerous literary periods, not just one. The castle gives the books a Medieval setting, although Diagon Alley is more Victorian, like England during the nineteenth century when Victoria was on the throne, the time of Charles Dickens.[6] The tone is Romantic. The heroism is Classical. The way people move around in photographs and portraits is like a magical version of the Digimodern age. But the theme itself, the idea that one must fight evil and come to terms with one's own demons, is Ancient, going back all the way to Gilgamesh.

Notes

1. See Otto Rank's *The Myth of the Birth of the Hero* for additional characteristics of traditional heroes and "Harry Potter: Fairy Tale Prince, Real Boy, and Archetypal Hero" by M. Katherine Grimes

in *The Ivory Tower and Harry Potter*, ed. Lana A. Whited, for application of Rank's theories to Rowling's novels.

2. See Christina Vourcos' essay on mentors in this volume.

3. See Danny Adams' essay in this volume for a full discussion of the connection between the legends of King Arthur and the Harry Potter series.

4. See Grimes, "Harry Potter: Fairy Tale Prince, Archetypal Hero, and Real Boy" for further discussion of Harry as a realistic character.

5. An extensive discussion of the Harry Potter canon can be found in Lesson 10 of the *MuggleNet Academia* podcast, available from MuggleNet.com.

6. As many Harry Potter readers know, Daniel Radcliffe played the title role in a BBC adaptation of Dickens' *David Copperfield*.

Works Cited

Aristophanes. *Lysistrata*. 411 BCE. Trans. Charles T. Murphy. *Norton Anthology of World Masterpieces*. 5th Continental ed. Ed. Maynard Mack, et al. New York, Norton, 1987. 395–431.

La Chanson de Roland (The Song of Roland). c. 1090 CE. Student Edition. Ed. Gerard J. Brault. University Park, PA: Pennsylvania State UP, 1984.

Chaucer, Geoffrey. *The Canterbury Tales*. c. 1400 CE. Trans. David Wright & Christopher Cannon. New York: Oxford UP, 2011.

Crane, Stephen. *Maggie: A Girl of the Streets*. 1893. Ed. Thomas A. Gullason. New York: Norton, 1979.

Eliot, T. S. "The Love Song of J. Alfred Prufrock." *Poetry*. 1915. *The Complete Poems and Plays 1909–1935*. New York: Harcourt, Brace, 1958. 3–7.

_____. *The Wasteland*. 1922. *The Complete Poems and Plays 1909–1935*. New York: Harcourt, Brace, 1958. 37–55.

The Epic of Gilgamesh. c. 7th cent. BCE. Trans. N. K. Sandars. New York: Penguin Putnam, 1972.

Geoffrey of Monmouth. *History of the Kings of Britain*. c. 1136 CE. Trans. Lewis Thorpe. New York: Penguin, 1977.

Ginsburg, Allen. "Howl." 1955. *Howl and Other Poems*. 1956. *Poetry Foundation*. Poetryfoundation.org, n.d. Web. 1 Jan. 2015.

Homer. *The Odyssey*. 8th cent. BCE. Ed. Bernard Knox. New York: Penguin, 2006.

James, Henry. *The Turn of the Screw*. 1907–09. *The Aspern Papers and The Turn of the Screw*. By Henry James. Ed. Anthony Curtis. London: Penguin, 1984. 143–262.

Kafka, Franz. *The Metamorphosis*. 1915. Trans. Stanley Corngold. *The Norton Anthology of World Masterpieces*. 5th Continental Ed. Ed. Maynard Mack, et al. New York: Norton, 1987. 2301–41.

Nikolajeva, Maria. "Harry Potter: A Return to the Romantic Hero." *Harry Potter's World: Multidisciplinary Critical Perspectives*. Ed. Elizabeth E. Heilman. New York: Routledge Falmer, 2003. 125–40.

Plautus. *Manaechmi; Or, The Twin Brothers*. c. 200 BCE. Trans. Henry Thomas Riley. Digireads.com, 2007.

Poe, Edgar Allan. "The Raven." 1845. *Poetry Foundation*. Poetryfoundation.org, n.d. Web. 1 Jan. 2015.

The Quest of the Holy Grail. 13th cent. CE. Trans. Pauline M. Matarasso. New York: Penguin, 1969.

Rank, Otto. *The Myth of the Birth of the Hero*. 1909. Trans. F. Robbins & Smith Ely Jelliffe. *In Quest of the Hero*. Ed. Robert Segal. Princeton, NJ: Princeton UP, 1990. 1–86.

Rowling, J. K. *Harry Potter and the Chamber of Secrets*. Illustrations by Mary Grandpré. New York: Arthur A. Levine/Scholastic, 1999.

_____. *Harry Potter and the Deathly Hallows*. Illustrations by Mary Grandpré. New York: Arthur A. Levine/Scholastic, 2007.

_____. *Harry Potter and the Goblet of Fire*. Illustrations by Mary Grandpré. New York: Arthur A. Levine/Scholastic, 2000.

_____. *Harry Potter and the Half-Blood Prince*. Illustrations by Mary Grandpré. New York: Arthur A. Levine/Scholastic, 2005.

_____. *Harry Potter and the Order of the Phoenix*. Illustrations by Mary Grandpré. New York: Arthur A. Levine/Scholastic, 2003.

_____. *Harry Potter and the Prisoner of Azkaban*. Illustrations by Mary Grandpré. New York: Arthur A. Levine/Scholastic, 1999.

_____. *Harry Potter and the Sorcerer's Stone*. Illustrations by Mary Grandpré. New York: Arthur A. Levine/Scholastic, 1998.

Shakespeare, William. *The Complete Pelican Shakespeare*. Eds. Stephen Orgel & A. R. Braunmuller. New York: Penguin Random House, 2002.

Sir Gawain and the Green Knight. 14th cent. CE. Trans. Simon Armitage. New York: Norton, 2008.

Sophocles. *Oedipus the King*. c. 430 BCE. Trans. Robert Fagles. *Norton Anthology of World Masterpieces*. 5th Continental Ed. Ed. Maynard Mack, et al. New York, Norton, 1987. 310–58.

Whited, Lana A., ed. *The Ivory Tower and Harry Potter: Perspectives on a Literary Phenomenon*. Columbia: U of Missouri P, 2002.

Whitman, Walt. "Song of Myself." 1855. *Whitman: Poetry and Prose*. Ed. Justin Kaplan. New York: Library of America, 1982. 27–88.

Wordsworth, William. *Lyrical Ballads, with Other Poems*. 1800. Gutenberg EBook, 2005. Web. 31 Dec. 2014.

_____ & Samuel Taylor Coleridge. *Lyrical Ballads*. 1798. London: Penguin, 2007.

A Survey of the Critical Reception of the Harry Potter Series_____

Lana A. Whited

A person who types "Harry Potter" into the search box on Amazon. com will get approximately 216,500 items: books, movies, clothing (including costumes), jewelry, fine art collectibles, cell phone accessories, wands, room décor, Lego building sets, jigsaw puzzles, music and musical instruments, video games—from twenty-eight Amazon departments, ranging from "Books" to "Pet Supplies" (the "Expecto Patronum" dog feeding mat, for example) and "Tools and Home Improvement" (the "Lumos Nox" switch plate cover). Eliminating all the selections except "Books" narrows the list to about 16,000 items. Turning to more traditional research methods only adds to the abundance: searching "Harry Potter" in Gale Research's *One Search* database at the end of 2014 returns over 100,000 hits, including over 65,000 news items, more than 20,000 magazine articles, 2,114 articles in scholarly journals, and 197 books. Obviously, a reader hoping to learn something about the critical reception of the books needs assistance sorting through the bounty of words about Harry Potter by authors other than J. K. Rowling.

Critical Reputation: A Primer

As this is a volume intended primarily for undergraduate and advanced high school students, it may be useful to discuss how critical reputation is assessed. Who are the players in the overall act of assessing a book, and what are their roles? What is the difference between a book critic and a literary scholar?

Even before a book is released, the publisher (Bloomsbury or Scholastic, in the case of Harry Potter) develops a marketing plan that includes sending out advance copies to people in a position to recommend books to others, especially if they will recommend them to large audiences in a publication such as a newspaper, magazine, or journal. Publishers provide free copies to these publications.

Reviewers generally fall into two categories. Some are staff members at newspapers or magazines (print, online, or both) and usually have at least an undergraduate degree in a field involving writing, such as journalism or English; they may also have expertise in a certain area and write reviews about that area, such as food or film. If they are specifically assigned to write reviews, they may write many each month. A well-known and well-respected writer at a major publication can really boost a book's sales with a positive review. In July 2014, former *Roanoke Times* reporter Beth Macy published her first book, *Factory Man*. The book got much attention early on, and Macy got a number of national interviews because of high praise from *New York Times* reviewer Janet Maslin, who wrote in her summer books survey, "Early warning: 'Factory Man' (coming July 15) is an illuminating, deeply patriotic David vs. Goliath book. They give out awards for this kind of thing" ("When the Water's Too Cold").

Although scholars also write reviews sometimes, their work has less impact on a book's success because scholarly reviews are seldom published close to the time of the book's publication; scholars usually write for professional journals published one, two, or four times a year. Scholars have graduate degrees (a master's and perhaps also a doctorate) and are generally asked to review new books only in their specific areas of expertise. Of greater significance than their reviews is the original writing scholars produce, based on their own research questions; just as a medical researcher might examine tissue samples to look for the presence of a particular disease, a literary researcher might examine a book to look for the presence of certain ideas or patterns. Writing based on this research is called literary scholarship or literary criticism, although "criticism" in this context can be misleading. To say that a scholar writes literary criticism does not mean that he or she only makes negative comments about a book; rather, it suggests that the scholar makes a thorough examination of a text with a goal in mind, such as discussing what attitudes toward slavery Mark Twain includes in *Adventures of Huckleberry Finn*.

Combining the work of many literary scholars writing about the same book (or series) can help to determine its overall value.

Artistic works, including books, are judged according to two criteria: literary quality and popularity. Quality evaluations involve scholarly criteria and are generally made by experts, and assessments of popularity involve everyone who buys, reads, or recommends a book. In addition to reviews, criteria used to determine quality include awards and prizes given by boards and organizations, most private, and based on a pre-established set of criteria (such as the aspects of literature taught to students in a literature course). In the United States, the major literary awards are the Pulitzer prizes, which are awarded in a variety of categories (some non-literary) and the National Book Awards. In the United Kingdom, major literary awards include the Man-Booker Prize, the British Book Awards (or "Nibbies"), and the Costa (formerly Whitbread) Award. For the most part, these awards and prizes are qualitative measures of a book's success, but some, such as the Costa Award, also take into account a book's popularity.

Lists of notable books are usually measures of popularity when they are based exclusively on sales or polls of readers. (They may also be compiled by reviewers; Janet Maslin compiles a "Best Books of" list at the end of every year.) Lists are usually published by organizations and publications, and the most prestigious such list in North American publishing is the *New York Times* Bestseller lists, for which books are chosen in several categories. On special occasions, an organization or publication may compile a special list, such as the Modern Library list of Top 100 Books of the Twentieth Century, released at the turn of the twenty-first century.[1] ("100 Best Novels"). In a contrast of qualitative and populist assessments, Modern Library compiled both a list voted on by its editorial board and a list selected by readers. The board selected Irish writer James Joyce's *Ulysses* as its top selection, while readers chose Ayn Rand's *Atlas Shrugged*. Rand had three novels in the top ten of the reader's list; *Ulysses* was number eleven. No Ayn Rand novel appeared on the editorial board's top one hundred ("100 Best Books").

Another group of people who influence a book's reputation are those who put books in readers' hands or recommend them, including librarians, teachers, and bookstore employees. In the reader study discussed by Colette Drouillard elsewhere in this volume, all three of these groups had played roles in introducing Harry Potter to young readers, although not to the same degree as family and friends. This category reflects measures of both quality and popularity, as teachers, librarians, and book store employees have opinions about books shaped by both sets of criteria and may also have varying levels of expertise. They may read reviews or the recommendations of professional organizations such as the American Library Association, but they also pay attention to book lists and to what young readers are buying or borrowing.

Thus, a critical reputation is a stew containing ingredients from many sources, some experts and some not. What, then, are the elements of the Harry Potter series' critical reputation?

The Role of Children

In June 1997, Bloomsbury released the first press run of *Harry Potter and the Philosopher's Stone*: 500 books, 300 of which went to libraries. In July 2000, *Goblet of Fire* was launched with a press run of 1.5 million in hardback in the United Kingdom and 3.9 million in the United States (Brown). What is interesting about this difference is that the groundswell of popularity the series experienced in those three years did not come initially from the press or from book communities (that is, reviewers, librarians, teachers). It came, instead, from child- and young adult readers who noticed that there was something special about Harry. One reader of particular note was Alice Newton, whose father was chairman of Bloomsbury Publishing when Rowling's agent, Christopher Little, dropped off a sample of Harry Potter in June 1996. Little had taken on Rowling as a client after his young assistant, Bryony Evans, had read the three-chapter sample, laughing regularly (McGinty). By the time it came to Bloomsbury, the sample had been rejected by eight to twelve other publishers.[2] Eight-year-old Alice went to her room and came back a short while later "glowing." She said, "Dad, this is so much better than anything else," and she continued to nag him about reading more of Harry Potter's story ("Revealed"). Aware that his Bloomsbury colleague Roger Cunningham[3] was compiling a portfolio of fantasy books by new authors, Nigel Newton made his best business investment ever: he wrote a check to Joanne Rowling for two-thousand-five-hundred pounds—at the time, about $4000 ("Revealed") .

Alice Newton was not alone in her enthusiasm for Harry Potter. In 1997, *Harry Potter and the Philosopher's Stone* was selected for the gold medal in the nine- to eleven-year-olds category of the Nestlé Smarties Prize—an award based on children's votes. In 1998, it won every major British award selected by children (Eccleshare). Significantly, Drouillard, explains, identification with the protagonist was an enormous factor in the appeal of the Harry Potter series: "This group of young readers had the singular opportunity to grow up at approximately the same pace and in the same time period as Harry Potter and his friends" (Drouillard). The study reflects that well over 80 percent of young readers said they both were influenced to read the books by friends and family and, in turn, recommended the books to other friends and family members. In some cases, readers picked up a book after observing another young person absorbed in reading it. So strong was the peer influence as Harry Potter fanhood swelled that British booksellers timed the 1999 release of *Prisoner of Azkaban* for 3:45 p.m. to prevent eager young readers from skipping school to get it (Cowell). (With the publication of *Goblet of Fire*, the release moved permanently to weekends.)

Of course, the endorsement of adults—especially those in positions of authority where literature is concerned—helped to fan the flames already ignited by young enthusiastic readers.

Reviews of the Harry Potter Novels
In what is perhaps the first published review of a Harry Potter novel, Lindsey Fraser wrote in *The Scotsman* (Edinburgh) two days after the publication of *Harry Potter and the Philosopher's Stone* that Rowling "uses classic narrative devices with flair and originality and delivers a complex and demanding plot in the form of a first-rate

thriller. She is a first-rate writer for children" (qtd. in Nel 53). *The Herald* (Glasgow) wrote, "I have yet to find a child who can put it down." Reviews in the London papers *The Guardian*, *The Sunday Times*, *The Mail on Sunday*, and *The Financial Times* were also very positive, and *The Sunday Telegraph* called it "a terrific book" (Eccleshare). *The Times* (also London) reviewer described Rowling as "a sparkling new author brimming with delicious ideas, glorious characters and witty dialogue" (Johnson). It was clear from these early reviews that Rowling was off to a fine start at home.

By the time Harry Potter "crossed the pond," the first volume of his adventures was already a celebrated book, thanks largely to its having garnered major British prizes and turned up on impressive lists. The groundswell of support that had begun with child readers only grew as American reviewers got their hands on *Harry Potter and the Sorcerer's Stone*, the name having been changed (with Rowling's endorsement) because her American editor, Arthur A. Levine, felt that the word "philosopher" would be ineffective with young American readers.[4] In an often-quoted review in the *New York Times*, Michael Winerip lauds the book and its author. Winerip calls Harry "a terrific person we'd love to have for a best friend" and says that Rowling "has a gift for keeping the emotions, fears and triumphs of her characters on a human scale, even while the supernatural is popping out all over." Winerip recognizes similarities between Harry's creator and Roald Dahl, the best-loved British children's author immediately before Rowling; Dahl had died in 1990. Like many reviewers, Winerip finds Rowling's use of humor particularly Dahlian: "Professor McGonagall watched them turn a mouse into a snuffbox—points were given for how pretty the snuffbox was, but taken away if it had whiskers" (Rowling, qtd. in Winerip). The review also reflects an important reason for the book's initial success when Winerip compares Harry's anxiety as a Hogwarts novice to his own first day at Harvard thirty years earlier, amid classmates fresh from elite boarding schools. As M. Katherine Grimes has noted, it is the "Real Boy" with whom readers connect.

An interesting aspect of the American critical reception is the time gap between the publication of *Sorcerer's Stone* and the appearance of reviews in the places where good reviews are most coveted. In the first six months or so, reviews appeared primarily in publications devoted to children's literature or libraries. These were positive, but appeared in sources with narrow circulation, such as *School Library Journal* and *Cooperative Children's Book Center Choices*. In his assessment of the book's reception in the *20th Century American Bestsellers* database, Jordan Brown writes,

> [T]he book in these early reactions was judged as spectacular within the framework of children's fantasy literature, and the initial reviews, while overwhelmingly positive, seem to have a slight condescension about them typical of children's literature reviews, not praising or critiquing those elements of plot and characterization so vital to adult fiction.

The late response of mainstream book critics may reflect hesitation about embracing a book wildly successful with child readers; although Rowling has claimed that she began writing without a target audience, Bloomsbury certainly accepted it with an audience of child fantasy readers in mind, and Arthur A. Levine (who bought the US rights) works for Scholastic, one of the primary American publishers of children's books. Perhaps it simply took a while for grown-up book critics to get on board the Hogwarts train. Not before late 1998 did reviews began appearing in places such as the *New York Times* and *The Boston Globe*. By early 1999, the floodgates had opened, and praise for Harry Potter appeared almost everywhere.

Around the time of *Chamber of Secrets'* US publication on June 20, 1999, the Harry Potter phenomenon took a much more commercial turn when Warner Brothers bought the film rights to the series. The second book debuted in the top spot on the *New York Times* bestseller list, and when *Prisoner of Azkaban* debuted in the United States three months later, the books held the top three spots (Sept. 8). By spring 2000, the books had been on the *NYT* fiction bestsellers list for twenty weeks and were still in the top five positions. Frustration mounted among major publishers whose titles were pushed down (or off), and *Goblet of Fire* was due out in July, so the newspaper finally created a "Children's Bestsellers" list. As popularity grew, the critical reception became slightly more varied. As Philip Nel has observed, "Either the growing popular appeal of the series was beginning to make some critics more skeptical, or the hype beginning to surround the books was raising expectations" (*J. K. Rowling's* 55). Rowling herself was so concerned about living up to the hype that she submitted the *Chamber of Secrets* manuscript on time, then took it back for six weeks of revision (Sexton 77–78).

Although many reviewers considered *Chamber of Secrets* as strong as its predecessor, notices for the novel were more likely to contain a "but" accompanying the near-universal praise. The book was "slightly less magical" wrote Michael Dirda in the *Washington Post* (maybe because the concept was no longer new). *But* the plot was very similar to the first book, based on a secret hidden under the Hogwarts School. This was a complaint of Graeme Davis, who also felt that the climactic scene where Fawkes rescues and heals Harry is a *deux ex machine*[5] or contrived resolution; how, for example, would Fawkes know where to find Harry? (Davis wrote nine years later that he considered *Chamber* the weakest book in the series.) And some reviewers continued to find the books derivative of earlier British adolescent fiction, such as the work of Enid Blyton. Others raised content-based concerns: Mary Stuart said that some episodes were too frightening for younger readers, while Tammy Nezol found elements of the book disturbing, including Harry's withholding information from Dumbledore and the human-like behavior of the mandrakes, which herbology students were perceived as slaughtering. One begins to suspect that reviews had been so positive that some reviewers were digging for minor quibbles, perhaps to demonstrate their own powers of discernment.

No other content-based objections to the Harry Potter series rose to the level of the response from some conservative Christians, mostly in the United States. These objections focus, of course, on the practice of wizardry and witchcraft, with detractors citing passages in Leviticus that they claim expressly condemn sorcery. The groundswell of this objection came just before the July 2000 publication of *Goblet of Fire*; *Newsweek* published the first chapter as part of a cover story called "Here's Harry!" and reported that the books had been challenged in at least twenty-five school districts in seventeen states (Jones). But it was not an exclusively American campaign. Three months before the publication of *Goblet of* Fire, a Church of England primary school banned the first three books outright, the head teacher maintaining that "devils, demons, and witches are real and pose the same threat as, say, a child molestor" (Knight). And in September 2000, a Canadian school superintendent sent all 100 elementary schools in his system guidelines concerning the use of Harry Potter novels in the classroom (Jones). The most objective account of this crusade is "Hunting Down Harry Potter" by Kimbra Wilder Gish, a fifth-generation conservative Christian who describes, but does not endorse, the arguments. Undeniably, the publicity surrounding this controversy had a "forbidden fruit" effect with some readers, including young readers who reported to some school librarians that they had to read Harry Potter novels at school because they were not allowed to read them at home.

If some critics found fault with *Chamber of Secrets*, a controversy concerning *Prisoner of Azkaban* really drew out the Harry Potter detractors. The novel was a contender for the prestigious Whitbread, along with Irish poet (and Nobel laureate) Seamus Heaney's translation of *Beowulf*. Just before the award, *Independent* (London) critic Philip Hensher expressed dismay that a children's book—as he saw it—would even be considered for a serious literary prize. Acknowledging the series' benefits in encouraging reading, Hensher nevertheless announced that the Harry Potter phenomenon "is all getting seriously out of hand." Considering *Prisoner of Azkaban* for a major literary prize, to Hensher, represents "the infantilisation of adult culture, the loss of a sense of what a classic really is." Those who would put Rowling's novel in the same class as Heaney's *Beowulf* should "grow up," he asserted (Hensher). Citing Hensher's remarks, William Safire of the *New York Times* called the Whitbread Award to Heaney "a relief," arguing that the Harry Potter series lacks levels of deeper meaning that draw adults to fiction intended for younger readers, such as *Adventures of Huckleberry Finn*. Of Harry Potter generally, Safire declares, "prizeworthy culture it ain't; more than a little is a waste of adult time."

Nevertheless, many prominent critics weighed in with praise for *Prisoner*. The Cooperative Children's Book Center reviewer said that Rowling was getting better with every volume, and both the *School Library Journal* and *USA Today* reviewers concurred that Rowling was "three for three." In each volume, Rowling introduced inventive new devices that drew reviewers' praise; in *Prisoner of Azkaban* it was the Time-Turner and the Weasley Whereabouts clock, and many reviewers noted the overall complexity of the plot and the interesting use of time travel. A *New York Times* reviewer called it "maybe the best Harry Potter book yet." And writing in *The New York Review of Books,* fiction writer Alison Lurie declares Harry's story "a metaphor for the power of childhood: of imagination, of creativity, and of humor."

At the time of Philip Hensher's and William Safire's articles, *Goblet of Fire* was at the top of Amazon.com's sales list—although it would not be published for nearly seven more months. It was released on July 8, 2000, ushering in the era of simultaneous UK/US release and the midnight bookstore experience. Soon thereafter, two heavyweight US literary scholars weighed in—one to express reservations about the Harry Potter craze and the other to express outright scorn. The former is (now retired) German professor Jack Zipes, also a prominent expert on fairy tales, and the latter is the dean of contemporary American literary criticism, Harold Bloom.

In April 2000, during an interview about other subjects, Jack Zipes made "a passing remark" to a Minnesota newspaper reporter that he found the Harry Potter books "formulaic and sexist." During a public radio talk show soon thereafter, he was "aggressively attacked by 90 percent of the callers (all adults) for demeaning J. K. Rowling's works" (Zipes, Lecture). In *Sticks and Stones: The Troublesome Success of Children's Literature from Slovenly Peter to Harry Potter*, Zipes writes that although most readers appeared "mesmerized" by the series, he is "aware of a minority of professional critics who have misgivings about the quality of the Harry Potter books" (171). Zipes' perception of the books' "formulaic" nature is illustrated in his comment that "one dimensional characters are planted in each one of the novels to circle around Harry with his phallic wand and to function in a way that will highlight his extraordinary role as Boy Scout/detective" (Zipes, *Sticks* 180). Ultimately, he finds that Rowling "remains within the happy-ending school of fairy-tale writers" (182). Despite these examples of what he perceives to be the series' conventionality, Zipes spends most of his time exploring the difficulty of assessing literary merit in the case of a commercial phenomenon as huge as Harry Potter. Zipes perceives the series as more a commodity than a literary achievement, although he does issue a call for literary experts to "pierce the phenomenon" and figure out "why such a conventional work of fantasy has been fetishized, so that all sorts of magical powers are attributed to the very act of reading these works" (172). Although Zipes does not explore in detail his comments about the conventional or formulaic aspects of Rowling's work, his stature as a scholarly luminary undoubtedly influenced other children's literature experts.

Fourteen years later, in an address before students and faculty in the graduate programs in children's literature at Hollins University in Virginia, Zipes expressed surprise that the books continue to be popular and reiterated his contention that Rowling "has had to comply with the conventions of the culture industry." He said he continued to feel that the books "do not have inherent meaning," but instead have had meaning bestowed upon them. However, he did appear to soften his position slightly; the series had only appeared through *Goblet of Fire* at the time *Sticks and Stones* was published, and Zipes conceded that he had not noticed then how the Harry Potter stories "hark back to stories about sorcerers and magicians noted and written down" all the way back to the Greco-Roman period. These stories touch on "core human dispositions" and conventional ideas, such as that good and dark magic "are two sides of the same coin." The success of such a hero, Zipes said, depends entirely on whether he willingly shares his magic to help the world or whether he reserves it for his own gain. By that measure, he acknowledged, Harry would be considered a successful—if still conventional— hero.

Responding, in July 2000, to the publication of *Goblet of Fire* as well as the *New York Times'* establishment of a Children's

Bestsellers list, Harold Bloom delivered a scorching put-down of *Sorcerer's Stone*, the only Harry Potter novel he claims to have read. In a now famous *Wall Street Journal* article, Bloom, surely one of the longest-serving literature professors in the United States,[6] deprecates not only Rowling's novel, but most of children's literature: "I read new children's literature when I can find some of any value." Bloom terms the book "not well written" and "lacking an authentic imaginative vision." Like Zipes, he concludes that the book's "remarkable success" must be accounted for by some factor other than literary merit. Posing the question "Why read [Harry Potter]?" he responds, "Presumably, if you cannot be persuaded to read anything better . . . . Why read, if what you will read will not enrich minds or spirit or personality?" He does consider whether his response to Rowling is "merely a highbrow snobbery," and many readers suspect that to be his most accurate comment.

With the appearance of *Goblet of Fire*, a new era of Harry Potter commodity was ushered in: the UK and U.S. versions were released simultaneously for the first time (and thereafter); the bookstore-at-midnight release party was launched, and release moved permanently to weekends. Called *Harry Potter and the Doomspell Tournament* until the official title announcement just two weeks before publication, *Goblet of Fire* was released with an unprecedented combined first printing of over five million copies ("Potter Timeline"). An environmental impact analysis by faculty at the State University of New York at Albany revealed that Federal Express required about 100 planes and 9,000 trucks to deliver the 250,000 advance copies sold by Amazon.com alone (Yagelski). In the United Kingdom, Bloomsbury consigned a specially outfitted train designated "the Hogwarts Express" to carry J.K. Rowling from King's Cross Station to Perth selling and signing copies (Pigott). The celebrity critique of Harry Potter continued with horror writer Stephen King's *Goblet of Fire* review in the *New York Times*. King declared the book "every bit as good as Potters 1 through 3" and said the series became "a kind of lifeline" for him while he was recovering from a broken leg after being hit by a car. King says the book represents the sort of "simple, uncomplicated fun" ideal for summer reading and praises Rowling's "punning, one-eyebrow-cocked sense of humor" (a source of reader's praise throughout the series) manifest in new devices such as Rita Skeeter's "Quick-Quotes Quill." He was also one of the first reviewers to note Rowling's indebtedness to the mystery genre, declaring that the books "are, at heart, satisfyingly shrewd mystery tales" (King, "Wild"). And he noted that the notion of champions and tasks associated with the Triwizard Tournament should appeal to fans of Greek and Roman myths. King also credits realistic aspects of the books (such as the importance of being invited to the Yule Ball) for their appeal to adolescent readers. Ultimately, his endorsement of Rowling rings clear: "The fantasy writer's job is to conduct the willing reader from mundanity to magic. This is a feat of which only a superior imagination is capable, and Rowling possesses such equipment" (King, "Wild").

The presence of other celebrity writers and reviewers besides Stephen King in the ranks of *Goblet* reviewers testifies to the series' prominence by this time: Joan Acocella (*The New Yorker*), George Will (*The Washington Post*), Janet Maslin (*New York Times*), former Booker Prize winner Penelope Lively (*The Independent*), E. Nesbit biographer Julia Briggs (*Times Literary Supplement*), and children's author Tim Wynne-Jones (*Ottawa Citizen*). Maslin speaks for a multitude of critics in her *New York Times* appraisal: "Ms. Rowling offers her clearest proof yet of what should have been wonderfully obvious: what makes the Potter books so popular is the radically simple fact that they're so good." *Goblet of Fire* is the only Harry Potter book to win a Hugo Award (for science fiction or fantasy) in the Best Novel category.

Nevertheless, sprinkled throughout the *Goblet* reviews were discussions of flaws, most notably focused on Rowling's prose style and her depiction of foreigners. *USA Today* reviewer Dierdre Donahue called it "hurried . . . highlight[ing] Rowling's ability to crank out pages but show[ing] less of her creativity." Perhaps a good example of Rowling's "crank[ing] out" unimaginative prose is the long section after the last Triwizard task, when Voldemort goes on at length in a summary of his overall plan. Jen Larsen calls this passage "when the Bad Guy pauses in his Evil Preparations to take a moment and explain his Nefarious Plot, step by step" and laments that Rowling did not heed that old writer's standby advice: "Show, don't tell." For *Horn Book*, Martha V. Parravano wrote, "Some [readers] will find [it] wide-ranging, compellingly written, and absorbing; others, long, rambling, and tortuously fraught with adverbs." Perhaps appropriately (considering the plot), David Kipen of the *San Francisco Chronicle* called it "a perfect teenager of a book . . . spotty . . . opinionated . . . . often strangely endearing . . . . Most of all, as widely reported, it's ungainly."

Comments about the sociopolitical worldview of the series also began to surface with *Goblet*. This is perhaps not surprising, considering that the skepticism Rowling displays about the effectiveness of government is introduced in *Prisoner of Azkaban* (in the subplot about the condemnation of Buckbeak) and developed in *Goblet of Fire* through the characterizations of Bartemius Crouch and Cornelius Fudge. Writing in *Socialist Review* after the publication of *Goblet*, Carmen Brown calls the series "depressingly derivative, conservative and dispiritingly nostalgic for a bygone notion of a middle class Britain of public school and jolly hockey sticks (Quidditch at Hogwarts) that I thought had gone out of fashion when I grew out of Enid Blyton." Brown did note, however, that *Goblet* contained "unexpected and amusing moments of class politics," noting students' familiarity with the goblin wars and Hermione's campaign on behalf of the house-elves.

Rowling's depictions of students from other wizarding academies, a French school for beautiful and sophisticated girls and a Northern European school featuring military-style training for macho boys, drew some comments about stereotyping. Jen Larsen describes this tendency:

Awkwardly, Rowling slaps vaguely French and Russian accents and stereotypes all over her international students—most notably, the French-ish students and headmistress say things like "zees ees an outrage!" while the Russian-esque students wrap themselves in large bear furs and take dawn swims in icy lakes.

Reviews of the film adaptation of *Goblet* also noted this problem, pointing out "prevalent stereotypes of foreign nations," with the Beauxbatons and Durmstrang students "portrayed as beautiful, well buil[t], or attractive," but also "arrogant," while . . . most of the British characters are portrayed as relatable and genuine" (asydlow). Fortunately, non-British students who endure in later books, most notably Fleur Delacour, subsequently achieve more dimension.

For readers, the most agonizing time during the books' publication was the three-year gap before *Order of the Phoenix* appeared. Over two hundred million books had been sold in about the same number of countries and in fifty-five languages by the time the fifth book appeared June 20, 2003. Readers had passed the time focused on the rumor about which character close to Harry would die in the fifth installment. Again, reviews were primarily positive. Whereas some critics had found *Goblet of Fire* a slower narrative, *New York Times* critic John Leonard praised the new book's pace, which "starts slow, gathers speed and then skateboards, with somersaults, to its furious conclusion." Leonard also admires the increased intricacy of Rowling's storyline: "All of a sudden, like puberty, everything is more complicated and ambiguous." Increasingly, Harry is learning the truth of Sirius Black's advice: "The world isn't split into good people and Death Eaters" (Rowling, *Deathly Hallows* 263). (Along the lines of oversimplifying, Leonard does find both Draco Malfoy and Voldemort one-dimensional.) John Leonard articulates strengths many reviewers found in *Phoenix*, including the pace and overall complexity, as well as Harry's believable adolescent emotional turmoil. His review is representative, but also superior, due largely to his very witty prose style and his vast knowledge of the works of myth and fantasy to which Rowling is indebted. And any Harry Potter fan will be satisfied with his eloquent swipe at naysayers of Rowling specifically and children's literature in general. It is clear from the *Phoenix* reviews that both the hero and his saga are maturing. In Leonard's words, "J. K. Rowling is the real magician. . . . As Harry gets older, Rowling gets better."

On her official website, J. K. Rowling has declared *Harry Potter and the Half-Blood Prince* one of her favorites of the series and indicated that it was one of the most difficult to plan. After having to rewrite large portions of *Order of the Phoenix* in order to comply with her overall strategy, the author says she spent two months reviewing the *Half-Blood Prince* blueprint before beginning to write (Rowling, "Title"). Some reviewers have maintained from the beginning that Rowling owes a debt, in her plotting techniques, to classic English mystery novelists such as Agatha Christie and Dorothy L. Sayers. The painstaking plan for the *Half-Blood Prince* narrative substantially increased the frequency of this comparison (Rowling, "Title"). For example, it is a misdirection worthy of Agatha Christie herself that Snape's mother proves to be the "half-blood Prince" of Rowling's title.

With the fifth and sixth volumes of the series, critics also began expressing more lavish praise for the expansiveness of Rowling's fictional universe. It evokes comparisons to Tolkien's Middle Earth and is described by reviewers as a "consummately well imagined alternate reality" (Schillinger) and "a richly imagined and utterly singular world" (Kakutani, "Harry"). The *Wall Street Journal* reviewer tied the richness of the fantasy world to the praise about the unity of Rowling's overall vision, writing, "It is only as we proceed—and ideas seemingly thrown casually into the mix ripen into great significance—that it becomes clear that it's a world she has seen in its fantastic complexity all along" (qtd. "Harry Potter," *Arthur A. Levine*).

In general, with the series drawing toward its close, reviewers seemed inclined to deliver grand pronouncements on Rowling's accomplishment. *The Boston Globe* reviewer, Liz Rozenburg, said, "The book bears the mark of genius on every page." And Christopher Paolini, author of the Inheritance Cycle tretralogy (who began reading Harry Potter with *Goblet of Fire* when he was only sixteen years old), declared that Rowling's "epic stands as one of the great achievements in fantasy literature."

Critics also had nothing but praise for Rowling's deft handling of the death of Albus Dumbledore, but also became more sensitive to the appropriateness of violent scenes for all readers. The *New York Times'* Michiko Kakutani suggested that the scene "may well be too alarming for the youngest readers" ("Harry"). Of the headmaster's intensely emotional death and burial, the *Los Angeles Times* critic wrote, "I haven't cried so hard since Charlotte the Spider died" (Green). Reviewers also recognizes the sense of peril increasing in the final pages, in what Kakutani called "a thoroughly harrowing denouement [as the tone] grows progressively more somber, eventually becoming positively Miltonian in its darkness" ("Harry"). Schillinger describes the ending as "a finish so scorchingly distressing that the reader closes the book quaking," wondering "how on earth Harry will cope." Noting that the first four volumes in the series were written before the Sept. 11 attacks, Schillinger argues that the first half of the "gave children a thrilling escape into fantasy," whereas *Order of the Phoenix* and *Half-Blood Prince*, both post-Sept. 11 novels, "provide the opposite release: an escape from a reality that can now seem scarier than the prison of Azkaban." It is difficult not to agree with Emily Green that "This is a book for children of mettle." Critics also continued to note that the darkness of the narrative was relieved by Rowling's trademark humor, including "well-observed personality quirks and some first-class toilet humor" (Green)—the toilet humor, of course, being associated with Fred and George Weasley's joke shop.

As for flaws, the tendency of Rowling's characters to over-explain their plans or motivations continued to be noted. Kakutani calls it "an excess of exposition" observing that "[s]ome of Dumbledore's speeches to Harry have a forced, summing-up quality" ("Harry"). She also contends that Rowling is perhaps too obvious about pointing out connections with *Half-Blood Prince*'s parallel book, *Chamber of Secrets* (Rowling nearly used the book six title for book two). Kakutani writes, "the reader can occasionally feel Ms. Rowling methodically setting the stage for developments to come or fleshing out scenarios put in play by earlier volumes" (most notably, "Harry Potter and the Chamber of Secrets," with its revelations about the young Voldemort, "Harry"). But what Kakutani describes as too apparent, other critics (most notably John Granger) describe as illustrations of the ingenious scaffolding of the overall saga.

If it seemed staggering that *Goblet of Fire* debuted with a first printing of just over five million copies, who could ever have predicted that a publisher would print twelve million copies before even one was placed into the hands of a customer? Yet twelve million was *Deathly Hallows'* US press run alone ("Record") and within the first year, *Deathly Hallows* had sold forty-four million copies worldwide ("#9 J. K. Rowling"). About two weeks after the final installment was released, Stephen King described the difficulty faced by reviewers of Harry Potter books since the middle of the series: "Due to the Kremlin-like secrecy surrounding the books, all reviews since 2000 or so have been strictly shoot-from-the-lip." Even the most famous or esteemed of the Rowling reviewers worked with a big book and a short time frame and, consequently, according to King, "very few of the Potter reviewers have said anything worth remembering" (King, "J. K. Rowling's"). While the last statement is certainly debatable, it is true that Harry Potter's reviewers have worked under very unusual writing conditions, considering the length of the books. King's opinion notwithstanding, many of them have done an admirable job.

It is difficult to say whether the reviewers' task is easier or harder when confronted with the last book in a seven-volume series. Certainly the hype had never been bigger, except perhaps with the debut of *Chamber of Secrets*, when reviewers and readers alike were wondering if Rowling could strike gold in the same place twice. Many of the *Deathly Hallows* reviews focused on the stamina Rowling has demonstrated in sustaining Harry Potter's story over seventeen years (from initial conception to final publication). Claiming, "there's no one else like Rowling," the *Publishers Weekly* reviewer asks (rhetorically), "Who else has sustained such an intricate, endlessly inventive plot over seven thick volumes and so constantly surprised her readers with twists, well-laid traps and Purloined Letter–style tricks?" (qtd. in "Harry Potter," *Arthur A. Levine)*.

Another general theme in the *Deathly Hallows* reviews is the skill with which Rowling brings together elements introduced throughout the series, both the critical (small details reflecting Snape's allegiance to Lily Potter) and the apparently mundane (appearances of minor characters on trading cards). As Michiko Kakutani puts it, "With this volume, the reader realizes that small incidents and asides in earlier installments (hidden among a huge number of red herrings) create a breadcrumb trail of clues to the plot, that Ms. Rowling has fitted together the jigsaw-puzzle pieces of this long undertaking with Dickensian ingenuity and ardor" ("Epic"). Kakutani praises Rowling in particular for the author's deftness in combining in the narrative seemingly disparate elements—"the magic and the mundane," for example—while maintaining the original identity of each. Early on, she notes Rowling's "astonishingly limber voice," which "moves effortlessly between Ron's adolescent sarcasm and Harry's growing solemnity."

Guardian reviewer Catherine Bennett also praises Rowling's artistry in [weaving] together clues, hints and characters from previous books into a prodigiously rewarding, suspenseful conclusion in which all the important questions . . . are punctiliously resolved." Bennett's review is in many ways emblematic of *Deathly Hallows*' critical reception, as Bennett combines soaring praise, a nod to Rowling's ongoing stylistic deficits, and the conclusion that the strengths ultimately lead one not to care so very much about the weaknesses. Of the flaws, Bennett observes the number of clichés Harold Bloom spotted on one page of *Sorcerer's Stone*, noting that Rowling's detractors find her style "mediocre," "unsophisticated," and "contaminated by her participation in a crass celebrity culture." In short, critics seems generally to agree that style isn't Rowling's forte.

But despite this flaw and the occasional tendency toward heavy-handed exposition (a problem also noted by Kakutani in her review of the seventh volume), Bennett thoroughly admires the "colossal energy and wit" that have gone into most elements of Rowling's work on the series. Ultimately, her praise for the Harry Potter series is high; she calls it "altogether a towering fictional edifice whose vividness and sheer scale are enough to compensate, for many of us, for any deficiencies in design" (Bennett).

Two episodes in *Deathly Hallows* come up frequently in casual discussions between or among readers: the long sequence when

Harry, Ron, and Hermione are camping in the forest and the epilogue in which Harry's generation of students are all parents sending their own children off to Hogwarts. Some readers feel the forest sequence is long and tedious, with not much happening (although, to be fair, a lot happens inside the characters' heads). As for the epilogue, readers seem to either love or hate it, although there is a small community (to which I belong) of readers who understand the rationale for the epilogue (order has been restored; Voldemort is truly gone), but do not particularly like it. It is interesting to note that discussion of these two scenes is almost entirely absent from published reviews of the novel.

Research and Scholarship on Harry Potter

In addition to those reviewers writing about new Harry Potter releases mostly on short deadlines, as Stephen King has noted, there have also been notable contributions to the Harry Potter conversation by literary scholars who, to extend King's culinary metaphor, have had the opportunity of "savor[ing] every mouthful" before producing longer, more contemplative works. This category encompasses a surprising number of volumes, considering the relatively short lifespan of the primary sources and also a variety of approaches: anthologies, books focusing on particular topics, and even podcasts devoted to continuing academic discussion of the books.

For any student of the Harry Potter series interested in the critical response, anthologies are the logical starting point due to the rigorous editorial process an anthology undergoes in production, as well as the variety of critical perspectives afforded the reader. An anthology or collection of essays will contain the work of twelve to fifteen individuals. Around the midpoint of the Harry Potter series, the first anthologies of literary criticism began to appear.

The Ivory Tower and Harry Potter (edited by me) appeared in late 2002 and contains essays describing subgenres of literature that appear to influence Rowling, including fantasy, epic, myth, folktales, and the boarding school story; discussions of authority (including government) and values systems illustrated in the books; issues having to do with gender and language, and topics related to contemporary culture (including British politics) and technology. *Ivory Tower* was republished in a paperback edition in 2004, incorporating discussion of *Goblet of Fire* and an afterword focused on the theme of race-based persecution in the series.

Giselle Liza Anatol's *Reading Harry Potter*, published in 2003, has three main sections: "Reading Harry Potter Through Theories of Child Development," which includes discussion of psychosocial development (especially of preadolescents), cognition, archetypes, and authority; "Literary Issues and Historical Contexts," covering the boarding school novel, fairy tale influences, textual ancestors of Hermione's house-elf anti-slavery campaign, and technologies in the books; and "Morality and Social Values: Issues of Power," in which contributors discuss the moral complexity of Rowling's heroes, law, and legal concepts in the wizarding world, ethnic Otherness, class and socioeconomic identity, and gender. Anatol produced a second volume, *Reading Harry Potter Again*, in 2009, with essays encompassing the entire Harry Potter series. Additions to the subject matter include religion and morality, as well as eight new essays concerning politics (race, gender, class) and sociocultural impact of the novels.

Elizabeth Heilman's *Critical Perspectives on Harry Potter* (2008) is divided into four sections. The first section concerns identity and morality, including essays on conservative Christian objections to the series and on the character of Severus Snape (who, as previously noted, gets little space in Harry Potter scholarship). The second is "Critical and Sociological Perspectives," and novel topics here include an essay on the series as comedy and one on teachers. The third section concerns literary elements and genre considerations and includes an exploration of connections with the *Orestia* of classical Greek tragedy, source of one of Rowling's epigrams for *Deathly Hallows*. The final section focuses on culture and the mass media and includes essays on the film adaptations of the Harry Potter books and on fan fiction.

Cynthia Hallett edited two collections of Harry Potter critical essays, *Scholarly Studies in Harry Potter* (2005) and *J. K. Rowling: Harry Potter* (2012), with Peggy Huey). Topics of special interest in Hallett's collections include time travel and rule-breaking, maps and mapping, the Harlequin influence in the Weasley twins, magical creatures (including an essay entirely devoted to the Phoenix), food, the influence of the *Bildungsroman*,[7] free will and determinism, the occult, identity (essays about biracial identity and masculinity), medicine, maternal figures, and two interesting essays about Albus Dumbledore, "Dumbledore and the Closet" and "Dumbledore's Ethos of Love."

Two collections edited by Travis Prinzi, *Hog's Head Conversations* (2009) and *Harry Potter for Nerds* (2011), round out the category. In terms of content not addressed in other anthologies or contributors-you-really-don't-want-to-miss, this collection includes essays on the imagination by Prinzi and myth/fantasy scholar Amy Sturgis; an analysis of Ginny Weasley's role intriguingly titled, "Ginny Weasley: Girl Next-Doormat?"; an essay by John Granger (dubbed "The Dean of Harry Potter Scholars" by *Time* magazine) on the *Deathly Hallows* epigraphs; a discussion of *Tom Riddle's Diary*; and an exploration of the significance (or insignificance) of authorial intention entitled "If Rowling Says Dumbledore is Gay, Is He Gay?" The second collection, *Harry Potter for Nerds*, contains two important analyses of the overall architecture of the saga, J. Steve Lee's essay on the influence of the chiasmus[8] and John Granger's essay on the "turtleback" structure of the books. Also included are essays on wizarding expressions and insults ("Merlin's pants!"), alchemy, and the influences of the poetry of Dante, Edmund Spenser, and George MacDonald.

Of final note, with regard to collections, are two volumes devoted entirely or partially to teaching Harry Potter. The first (chronologically) is Elizabeth D. Schafer's *Exploring Harry Potter* (2000), not a true anthology, but a volume in the Beacham's Sourcebooks series, intended to be of practical use to parents, teachers, librarians, students, and researchers. *Exploring Harry Potter* is organized as a topic-by-topic guide to the books; it should be noted that due to its publication date, it does not cover the entire series and its list of resources is limited now. The second is popular culture scholar Valerie Estelle Frankel's *Teaching with Harry Potter*,[9] a collection of essays based on experiences in teaching Harry Potter, from elementary school through the college and university level. All of these collections have achieved good reviews, and a Harry Potter reader or fan who reads all of them would have a very extensive knowledge base in relevant issues of interpretation and analysis. Unfortunately, anthologies tend to be pricier than books by single authors and are, therefore, found mostly in library collections (but may usually be borrowed through interlibrary loan).

In addition to the anthologies, there are dozens of topic-oriented Harry Potter books by individual scholars encompassing perspectives from the humanities (especially literature, language, and philosophy); the natural sciences (particularly the intersection of science and technology with magic); and the social sciences. Titles customarily clarify the focus: *The Wisdom of Harry Potter* (Edmund Kern, 2003); *The Science of Harry Potter* (Roger Highfield, 2002); *The Psychology of Harry Potter* (Neil Mulholland, 2007); and *Harry Potter and History* (Nancy Reagin, 2011).

A book of critical significance not currently in print is John Granger's *Harry Potter as Ring Composition and Ring Cycle* (2010). Granger, a classics scholar who was already publishing analyses of the Harry Potter phenomenon when many of the early critical volumes were still in concept or manuscript, is author of *The Hidden Key to Harry Potter* (2002), *The Deathly Hallows Lectures* (2008), and half a dozen other Harry Potter-related books. Granger's ring composition theory was developed from a lecture he delivered in 2010 before a New York-based Harry Potter society and which has become better known in Harry Potter fandom due to his roles as a Potter pundit on the *Leaky Cauldron* website's *Pottercast* and as co-host of the podcast *MuggleNet Academia*. Granger's is the most thoroughgoing analyst of the series' overall structure, which he terms "the neglected artistry of Harry Potter" (4). The theory was formulated as Granger, preparing for a lecture on C. S. Lewis' *Space Trilogy*, encountered Sanford Schwartz's observation about the ring structure of each of the *Ransom* novels (in the trilogy), with the effect that "'later sections of the work circle back to the beginning,' as deliberate echoes or answers to the chapters reflected at the opposite side of the ring." (qtd. in Granger 5). Realizing that "writing in circles" was common in great literature, Granger "re-read each of the Harry Potter novels wearing [his] circular glasses, just like Harry" (5). The result is one of the most interesting and important works of Harry Potter critical analysis and one that obviously could not have been fully realized prior to the completion of the series (although Granger also argues that each Harry Potter volume has its own ring structure). One hopes that *Harry Potter as Ring Composition and Ring Cycle* will soon be widely available again. In the meantime, Granger is a widely-traveler speaker, and students of Harry Potter should take advantage of any attempt to hear him.

Lately, the focus of Harry Potter-related studies has shifted to primary research in the social sciences, including an American political science professor studying political attitudes and voting behaviors and a team of Italian researchers investigating young people and prejudice. This encouraging new research focuses on how reading the Harry Potter series has impacted the social and political beliefs of young people who came of age reading Harry Potter novels.

University of Vermont political science professor Anthony ("Jack") Gierzynski published *Harry Potter and the Millennials* in May 2013. Gierzynski and his team undertook the first comprehensive research on how growing up with Harry Potter has shaped the political attitudes of millennials, many of whom are now old enough to vote. As part of a general study about connections between popular culture and political opinion, Gierzynski surveyed eleven hundred college students nationwide and reached the following conclusions:

> Harry Potter fans are more open to diversity and are more politically tolerant than nonfans; fans are also less authoritarian, less likely to support the use of deadly force or torture, more politically active, and more likely to have had a negative view of the [George W.] Bush administration. Furthermore, these differences do not disappear when controlling for other important predictors of these perspectives, lending support to the argument that the series indeed had an independent effect on its audience. (*"Harry Potter and the Millennials"*)

Gierzynski believes that the Harry Potter series played a role in shaping the political climate that resulted in President Barack Obama's election ("Professor").

The findings of a team of Italian social scientists, published in the *Journal of Applied Social Psychology* in summer 2014, are consistent with Gierzynski's results. Professor Loris Vezzali and his colleagues explored the effects of what psychologists call *extended contact* on children's and adolescents' attitudes toward marginalized groups, such as immigrants and homosexuals. Based on the notion that prejudice and stigma often dissolve with personal interaction, the researchers investigated the effect when the interaction is in the form of reading and the characters are fictional. In other words, would extended contact have the same effect of dissolving prejudice when the marginalized populations or "out groups" are Mudbloods, house-elves, half-giants, and werewolves, not real-world groups? Vezzali and his colleagues conducted three investigations with different age groups of young people in Italy and England and found the answer to be a resounding "yes."

Recent work in international relations also suggests that reading the Harry Potter series has helped millennials to make sense of the problem of global terrorism by providing young readers with a vocabulary for discussing it. Daniel Nexon, author of *Harry Potter and International Relations*, who teaches in the distinguished School of Foreign Service at Georgetown University, tells this story: one of his colleagues asked a student if she'd been part of a group the previous evening celebrating the death of Osama bin Laden outside the White House. "Of course!" she responded. "I mean, they got Voldemort!" (Nexon, "Terror"). For many young people who came of age along with Harry Potter, the battle against Voldemort and the Death Eaters is synonymous with the problem of global terrorism, which explains why Harry Potter texts are sometimes required in political science and international studies courses. Part of this effect is an accident of timing: the attacks on the World Trade Center and the Pentagon occurred a little over a year after Harry Potter fans got *Harry Potter and the Goblet of Fire*, the novel that provided the first look at the Death Eaters in action, carrying out a terrorist-style attack at the Wizarding World's primary sporting event, the Quidditch World Cup. Daniel Nexon has noted, "Such tropes surely already resonated in the United Kingdom—the 'Good Friday' accords[10] were, after all, signed in 1998—but they took on new dimensions with the attacks of September 11, 2001, and the Bush Administration's policy responses" ("Terror"). The notion of government-sanctioned torture is reinforced when Dolores Umbridge shows up at Hogwarts, and the response includes both a counter-terrorism group, Dumbledore's Army, and a Dumbledore-led "clandestine paramilitary organization," the Order of the Phoenix (Nexon, "Terror").

Impact of the Harry Potter Series

The strength of the Harry Potter critical reception, especially the range and depth of scholarly interest in the books, testifies to the remarkable nature of J. K. Rowling's achievement. In September 2014, Facebook tallied up results from user posts of "10 Books that Moved Me," and the Harry Potter books were at the top of the list in all six countries posting 20,000 results or more. The series bested the perennial favorites *To Kill a Mockingbird, The Lord of the Rings,* and *Pride and Prejudice*, and all of these works were mentioned more often than the Bible. Of course, we take social media surveys with a grain of salt, especially as Facebook users were not directed to rank books in order of importance, but merely to list ten books that had been influential in their lives. Of perhaps sturdier import is a BBC canvas for the British reading public's "best loved novel" of all time ("Big Read"). After a year-long process and polling that included over a quarter million votes, *Harry Potter and the Goblet of Fire* was selected as number five, and Rowling was the only author to have four titles listed in the top 100, with the three other Harry Potter titles at 22, 23, and 24, in order of publication ("Big Read").[11]

These facts speak for themselves: as of July 2013, the Harry Potter books had sold over 450 million copies. The last four books set records as the fastest-selling books in history, and eleven million copies of *Deathly Hallows* were sold in the first twenty-four hours of release alone. The series has also been translated into seventy-three languages, making Harry Potter not only one of the best-selling book series of all time, but one of the most successful on a global scale. And for devoted readers of the series, the most common criticism of J. K. Rowling has always been this one, articulated by "Paul" on an online discussion board: "I have only one problem with J. K. Rowling's books. I read quicker than she writes."

Notes

1. Modern Library is an "imprint," or brand, of Random House publishing company.

2. Nigel Newton said eight; Stephen McGinty wrote twelve in *The Scotsman* on June 16, 2003.

3. Cunningham is said to have recommended that Rowling get a day job, advising her that writing for children is not lucrative (Beals).

4. In the time since the publication of *Sorcerer's Stone*, Rowling has said that she regrets having agreed to change the title, but felt she lacked the clout to protest at the time.

5. Literally, "god from the machine," this expression refers to the practice, in Greek drama, of having the gods lowered onto the stage to sort out matters in the plays' resolution. It has come to be used to describe endings that seem forced and improbable.

6. Bloom has been a member of Yale's literature faculty since 1955 and has also taught at New York University since 1988.

7. A German word for the "novel of formation" or coming-of-age novel.

8. *Chiasmus* is a Latin term derived from the Greek word for the letter "X" and means "shaped like the letter X." It is sometimes used to refer to plot patterns in literature.

9. Disclaimer: Frankel's collection opens with my essay "From Hogwarts Academy to the Hero's Journey."

10. A peace deal signed by British Prime Minister Tony Blair and Irish Taoiseach (head of government) Bertie Ahern establishing independent government in Northern Ireland and intended to bring an end to politically-motivated violence there.

11. It should be noted that after the first round of voting, largely because all four Harry Potter novels in publication were in the top 25, the

second-round voting was limited to 21 authors, each represented by one book. In Rowling's case, this was *Goblet of Fire*, and for Tolkien, it was *The Lord of the Rings*, which, like the Harry Potter series, might be regarded as a long novel in installments. A more level contest might have represented both authors with a single novel or both with an entire series. Nevertheless, Rowling's results were remarkable, outpacing such legendary authors as Jane Austen and Charles Dickens.

Works Cited

"#9 J. K. Rowling." *The Celebrity 100*. *Forbes*. 11 Jun. 2008. Web. 8 Jan. 2015.

Acocella, Joan. "Under the Spell: Harry Potter Explained." *The New Yorker*. 31 Jul. 2000: 74–78.

Anatol, Giselle Liza. *Reading Harry Potter: Critical Essays*. New York: Praeger, 2003. Contributions to the Study of Popular Culture ser.

_____. *Reading Harry Potter Again: New Critical Essays*. New York: Praeger, 2009.

asydlow. "*Harry Potter and the Goblet of Fire*: A Very Enjoyable Film, but Recognize Cultural Bias." *Internet Movie Database*. 12 Oct. 2010. Web. 8 Jan. 2015.

Bennett, Catherine. "A Send-Off Fit for a Wizard." Review of *Harry Potter and the Deathly Hallows*. *The Guardian* (London). 28 Jul. 2007. Web. 14 Jan. 2015.

"The Big Read." *BBC Home*, n.d. Web. 4 Jan. 2015.

Blais, Jacqueline. "Harry Potter Has Been Very Good to J. K. Rowling. *USA Today* 9 Jul. 2005. Web. 31 Dec. 2014.

Bloom, Harold. "Can 35 Million Book Buyers Be Wrong? Yes." *Wall Street Journal*. 11 Jul. 2000. Web. 6 Jan. 2015.

"British Publishers Delayed the Release of the Third Harry Potter Book so Kids Wouldn't Skip School." *OMG Facts*. March 6 (no year given). Web. 3 Jan. 2015.

Brown, Carmen. "Harry Potter: Cashing in on Pester Power." *Socialist Review* 244 (2000). Web. 2 Jan. 2015.

Brown, Jordan. "Rowling, J.K., *Harry Potter and the Sorcerer's Stone*." *20th Century American Bestsellers*. Ed. John Unsworth. *Brandeis University*. Web. 6 Jan. 2015.

Cowell, Alan. "Investors and Children Alike Give Rave Reviews to Harry Potter Books." *New York Times* 18 Oct. 1999. Web. 4 Jan. 2015.

Davis, Graeme. "Re-reading Harry Potter and the Chamber of Secrets." *Re-Read Harry Potter and the Chamber of Secrets Today! An Unauthorized Guide*. Ann Arbor: Nimble Books, 2008.

Dirda, Michael. "*Harry Potter and the Chamber of Secrets*." Review. *Washingtonpost.com*. The Washington Post, 4 Jul. 1999. Web. 31 Dec. 2014.

Donahue, Dierdre. "'Goblet of Fire' Burns Out." *USA Today*. 10 Jul. 2000: 1D. Web. 4 Jan. 2015.

Eccleshare, Julia. "The Publishing of a Phenomenon." *A Guide to the Harry Potter Novels*. London: Bloomsbury-Continuum, 2002. 7–14. Print.

Garcia, Elena. "Harry Potter Author Reveals Books' Christian Allegory, Her Struggling Faith." *Christian Post*. 18 Oct. 2007. Web. 6 Jan. 2015.

Gierzynski, Anthony. *Harry Potter and the Millennials: Research Methods and the Politics of the Muggle Generation*. Baltimore: Johns Hopkins U P, 2013. Print.

Gish, Kimbra Wilder. "Hunting Down Harry Potter: An Exploration of Religious Concerns about Children's Literature." *Horn Book* May/June 2000: 262-71.

Granger, John. "The Hogwarts Saga as Ring Composition and Ring Cycle." October/November 2010. PDF emailed to the author. 17 Dec. 2014.

Green, Emily. "Harry's Back, and Children Must Be Brave." Review of *Harry Potter and the Half-Blood Prince* by J. K. Rowling. *Los Angeles Times*. 16 Jul. 2005. Web. 4 Jan. 2015.

Grimes, M. Katherine. "Harry Potter as Fairy-Tale Prince, Real Boy, and Archetypal Hero." *The Ivory Tower and Harry Potter: Perspectives on a Literary Phenomenon*. Ed. Lana A. Whited. Columbia: U of Missouri P, 2002. 89–122.

"*Harry Potter and the Half-Blood Prince*." *Arthur A. Levine Books*. Arthur A. Levine Books, 2001–2005. Web. 6 Jan. 2015.

"*Harry Potter and the Sorcerer's Stone*." *Arthur A. Levine Books*. Arthur A. Levine Books, 2001–2005. Web. 6 Jan. 2015.

"Harry Potter Reviews, Awards, and Distinctions." *Cooperative Children's Book Center*. School of Education. University of Wisconsin-Madison, n.d. Web. 8 Jan. 2015.

Heilman, Elizabeth. *Critical Perspectives on Harry Potter*. New York: Routledge, 2008. Print.

Hensher, Philip. "Harry Potter, Give Me a Break." *The Independent* (London). 25 Jan. 2000: 1.

Highfield, Roger. *The Science of Harry Potter: How Magic Really Works*. New York: Penguin, 2003.

Johnson, Sarah. "First Review: New Harry Potter's 'a Cracker.'" *The Times* (London). 8 Jul. 2000: 1–2. Web. 28 Dec. 2014.

_____. "Go for Good Writing." *The Times* (London). 23 Aug. 1997. Web. 28 Dec. 2014.

Jones, Malcolm. "Why Harry's Hot." *Newsweek*. 16 Jul. 2000. Web. 12 Jan. 2015.

Kakutani, Michiko. "An Epic Showdown as Harry Potter is Initiated into Adulthood." *New York Times*. 19 Jul. 2007. Web. 14 Jan. 2015.

_____. "Harry Potter Works His Magic Again in a Far Darker Tale: Review of *Harry Potter and the Half-Blood Prince* by J. K. Rowling." *New York Times*. New York Times Company, 16 Jul. 2005. Web. 14 Jan. 2015.

King, Stephen. "J. K. Rowling's Ministry of Magic." *Entertainment Weekly*. 10 Aug. 2007. Web. 10 Jan. 2015.

_____. "Wild About Harry." *New York Times*. 23 July 2000. Web. 10 Jan. 2015.

Kipen, David. "Trouble with Harry: J. K. Rowling's Fantasy Series Hits an Awkward Teenage Phase with 'Goblet.'" *San Francisco Chronicle*. 10 July 2000. Web. 8 Jan. 2015.

Knight, India. "The Trouble with Harry." *Sunday Times* (London). 2 April 2000. *Dow-Jones Interactive*. Stanley Library of Ferrum College. 10 June 2001.

Larsen, Jen. "A Series Grows Up: J. K. Rowling's *Harry Potter and the Goblet of Fire*." *Strange Horizons*. 1 Sept. 2000. Web. 14 Jan. 2015.

Lawless, John. "Nigel Newton." *Bloomberg Businessweek Magazine* 29 May 2005. Web. 3 Jan. 2015.

Lively, Penelope. "Harry's in Robust Form, Although I'm Left Bug-eyed." Review of *Harry Potter and the Goblet of Fire*. *The Independent* (London). 13 July 2000: 5. Print.

Leonard, John. "Nobody Expects the Inquisition: *Harry Potter and the Order of the Phoenix*." Review. *New York Times*. 13 July 2003. Web. 4 Jan. 2015.

Lurie, Alison. "Not for Muggles." Review of *Harry Potter and the Goblet of Fire*. *New York Review of Books*. 16 Dec. 1999. Web. 10 Jan. 2015.

"100 Best Novels." *Modern Library*. *Random House*. Web. 4 Jan. 2015.

Maslin, Janet. "At Last, the Wizard Gets Back to School." *New York Times*. 10 July 2000: E1. Web. 8 Jan. 2015.

_____. "When the Water's Too Cold, Something Else to Dive Into: A Critic's Survey of Summer Books." *New York Times* 22 May 2014. Web. 3 Jan. 2015.

Macpherson, Karen. "Rowling Has Magic Touch with 'Prisoner.'" *New York Times*. 1 Oct. 1999. Web. 8 Jan. 2015.

McGinty, Stephen. "The J.K. Rowling Story." *The Scotsman*. 16 June 2003. Web. 9 Jan. 2015.

Nel, Philip. *J.K. Rowling's Harry Potter Novels*. London: Bloomsbury–Continuum, 2001.

_____. "You Say 'Jelly,' I Say 'Jell-o'? Harry Potter and the Transfiguration of Language." *The Ivory Tower and Harry Potter: Perspectives on a Literary Phenomenon*. Ed. Lana A. Whited. Columbia: U of Missouri P, 2002. 261–84.

Nexon, Daniel. "Terror, Counter-Terror, and Insurgency in Harry Potter, or Why Harry Won." *Duck of Minerva*. 21 Jul. 2011. Web. 15 Jan. 2015.

Nezol, Tammy. "Review of *Harry Potter and the Chamber of Secrets*." *About.com*. About.com, n.d. Web. 12 Jan. 2015.

Paolini, Christopher. "Review of *Harry Potter and the Half-Blood Prince*." *Entertainment Weekly*, 20 Jul. 2005. Web. 7 Jan. 2015.

Parravano, Martha V. "Harry Potter Reviews: Review of *Harry Potter and the Goblet of Fire*." *The Horn Book Magazine*. 76.6 (2000): 762.

Paul. "Review by Paul: Review of *Harry Potter and the Philosopher's Stone* by J.K. Rowling." *BookLore*. 1 Feb. 2002. Web. 4 Jan. 2015.

Paul, Annie Murphy. "Harry Potter Casts a Spell for Tolerance." *New York Times*. 14 Aug. 2014. Web. 15 Jan. 2015.

Pigott, Nick, ed. "Headline News: Red Livery for Taw Valley?" *The Railway Magazine* July 2000: 17.

"Potter-mania Sweeps Bookstores." *CNN*. 30 Jun. 2003. Web. 8 Jan. 2015.

"A Potter Timeline for Muggles." *Toronto Star*. 14 Jul. 2007. Web. 14 Jan. 2015.

"Record Print Run for Final Harry Potter." *BBC News*. 15 Mar. 2007. Web. 3 Jan. 2015.

"Revealed: The Eight-Year-Old Who Saved Harry Potter." *The Independent* 3 Jul. 2005. Web. 3 January 2015.

Rowling, J.K. *Harry Potter and the Chamber of Secrets*. New York: Scholastic, 1999.

_____. *Harry Potter and the Deathly Hallows*. New York: Scholastic, 2007.

_____. *Harry Potter and the Goblet of Fire*. New York: Scholastic, 2000.

_____. *Harry Potter and the Half-Blood Prince*. New York: Scholastic, 2005.

_____. *Harry Potter and the Order of the Phoenix*. New York: Scholastic, 2003.

_____. *Harry Potter and the Prisoner of Azkaban*. New York: Scholastic, 1999.

_____. *Harry Potter and the Sorcerer's Stone*. New York: Scholastic, 1998. Print.

_____. "Title of Book Six: The Truth." *J.K. Rowling Official Site*. 29 Jun. 2004. Web. 6 Jan. 2015.

Rozenburg, Liz. "A Founding Boy and His Corps of Wizards; Harry Potter and the Sorcerer's Stone." *The Boston Globe*. 1 Nov. 1998. Web. 6 Jan. 2015.

_____. "Prince' Shines Amid Growing Darkness." Review of *Harry Potter and the Half-Blood Prince* by J. K. Rowling. *The Boston Globe*. 18 Jul. 2005. Web. 8 Jan. 2015.

Safire, William. "Besotted with Potter." *New York Times*. 27 Jan. 2000: A27. Print. (Syndicated in many newspapers; rpt. in *The Roanoke Times* as "Adult Fare Harry Potter Is Not.")

Schillinger, Liesl. "*Harry Potter and the Half-Blood Prince*: Her Dark Materials." *New York Times*. The New York Times Company, 31 Jul. 2005. Web. 13 Jan. 2015.

Sexton, Colleen. "Pottermania." *J. K. Rowling*. Minneapolis: First Avenue Editions, 2007.

Stuart, Mary. "Review of *Harry Potter and the Chamber of Secrets*." *Curledup.com*, n.d. Web. 12 Jan. 2015.

Vezzali, Loris, et al. "The Greatest Magic of Harry Potter: Reducing Prejudice." *Journal of Applied Social Psychology*. 44 (2014). *Wiley Online Library*. 23 July 2014. Web. 15 Jan. 2015.

"Webchat with J.K. Rowling." *Bloomsbury.com*. Bloomsbury.com, 30 July 2007. Web. 14 Jan. 2015.

Weinraub, Bernard. "New Harry Potter Book Becoming a Publishing Phenomenon." *New York Times*. New York Times Company, 3 July 2000. Web. 6 Jan. 2015.

Whited, Lana A. *The Ivory Tower and Harry Potter: Perspectives on a Literary Phenomenon*. Columbia: U of Missouri P, 2002.

Wilde, Susie. "Harry Potter and the Sorcerer's Stone." *The Children's Literature Database*. CLCD, LLC, n.d. Web. 6 Jan. 2015.

Winerip, Michael. "Review of *Harry Potter and the Sorcerer's Stone*." *New York Times*. New York Times Company, 14 Feb. 1999. Web. 6 Jan. 2015.

Yagelski, Robert P. "Crisis of Sustainability: *Harry Potter* and Global Warming." *Computers, Literacy, and Being: Teaching With Technology for a Sustainable Future*. State University of New York at Albany, n.d. Web. 3 January 2015.

Zipes, Jack. Lecture. Hollins University (Va.) 27 July 2014.

_____. *Sticks and Stones: The Troublesome Success of Children's Literature from Slovenly Peter to Harry Potter*. New York: Routledge, 2000.N

The Once and Future Wizard: Arthurian (and Anti-Arthurian) Themes in the Harry Potter Series

Danny Adams

In May of 2001, about 3,000 medievalists and medieval enthusiasts met at Western Michigan University in Kalamazoo, Michigan, for the annual International Congress on Medieval Studies. "For an academic conference it is remarkably unstuffy," wrote the *New York Times*. "There is no vetting of papers, and a platform is open to almost anyone with an idea" (Kinzer). In fact K-Zoo, as participants call it, tends to be extremely casual, a place where participants look forward to non-professional gatherings, like the nightly get-togethers for drinks, as much as they do the multitude of presentations.[1] So it would be no surprise to anyone there (except perhaps the *New York Times*) that the conference would make immediate connections with Harry Potter and that, even so early in the life of the Harry Potter series, those attending welcomed it warmly.

"Early," of course, is relative. By spring 2001, four of the books had been released, with millions of copies sold, although the much-anticipated first movie was still six months away. Nevertheless, it was still early in academics' discovery of Harry Potter—anyone searching would be hard pressed to find a scholarly paper referring to Harry or his author J. K. Rowling prior to 2000. But right away medievalists in particular were among the first to find much to love about and mine from the books. In particular, they noticed early on that much of the series was descended from one of the oldest and certainly the most venerable characters in British folklore, King Arthur.

"If you look closely, you see a lot of Arthurian components," University of Cincinnati professor Heather Arden told the *New York Times*. "So much of it fits into wonderful ancient patterns" (Kinzer).

But to truly understand the connections between Harry Potter and the Arthurian stories, legends, and myths, one has to understand that there really is no single, monolithic King Arthur—and not just in the sense that the history of early medieval Britain is so fuzzy that no one is really certain whether Arthur existed at all. In fact, the ruler of Camelot has gone through many incarnations, some of them before there was even a Camelot in the tales at all. The oldest stories have come down to us from Wales—and the Welsh were still reciting them as late as the sixteenth century, a thousand years after the historical Arthur might have existed. These tales form the story of a man who was not a king at all, but a relentless warlord, a *Dux Bellorum*[2] as some called him. This Arthur led the Britons through a series of grueling battles (with many victories, but occasional defeats) against Saxons, Angles, Picts, and other raiders and despoilers until a final battle with an enemy host at a (still vague) place called Camlan around AD 537 or, according to the *Annales Cambriae* (*The Welsh Annals*), 539. Arthur's fate wasn't necessarily to die there—some stories say he did—others, only that the Saxons were driven back for a time. Whether this particular warlord existed or not, something made the Saxons lick their wounds for a few years, as they held off advancing further until the 550s. When Arthur's pessimistic contemporary Gildas, a British monk writing from Scotland, lamented the "ruin of Britain" and the destruction of the churches and Christian belief alike there among the former Roman cities, he didn't mention Arthur by name, but found a beacon of hope in a Roman-British leader named Ambrosius Aurelianus, who many scholars have speculated might have been the original Arthur. Ambrosius was said to wear a bearskin in the British fashion, for example, and *bear* in Welsh is *Arth*.

That Arthur/Ambrosius would have been a gritty, pragmatic, but possibly charismatic and Christian warrior. He went through a few more renditions in the early Middle Ages, but kept much the same character as that Welsh warrior: we see him in the *Canu Aneirin* (*Book of Aneirin*) in Scotland around 600 and Nennius' *Historia Britonum* (*History of the Britons*) in Wales around 800. Then there were, of course, the numerous Welsh poems and tales from an unknown time in the distant past up until the twelfth century, which gradually converted Arthur from a gritty leader into a gritty but occasionally mystical one. The Welsh storytellers gave us the original Excalibur (called Caledfwich), Guinevere (Gwenhwyfar), and Mordred (Medrod or Medraut).[3]

By that time, the Welsh had become known abroad as popular storytellers, and the Normans were looking for a historical British template for their chivalric ideas, which much of the native British— that is to say, Saxon and Celtic—population still regarded as foreign. Enter an Oxford-educated Benedictine monk and archdeacon named Geoffrey of Monmouth.

The King Arthur we know, the one of chivalry and romance, would finally emerge fully fleshed out by the late twelfth century, when his story really got rolling across Europe. The one major surviving Arthurian storyteller of the early 1100s, Geoffrey of Monmouth, introduced the Welsh stories to non-Welsh audiences in the 1130s with his *Historia Regum Britanniae* (*The History of the Kings of Britain*), which mixed them with Norman sensibilities and drew on Gildas, among others, as a source. He also wrote a biography of Merlin, as well as what he said was a translation from an unspecified language of Merlin's prophecies. Nowadays most scholars regard Geoffrey's "history" (written six centuries after Arthur) as little more than myth and less noble invention (though a few regarded it as such in his own time, too). Nevertheless, his book caused a literary explosion on both sides of the English Channel.

Geoffrey introduced the English and French to Caledfwich, Latinized to Caliburn and finally Excalibur, a sword Arthur wielded since many of the earliest Welsh tales. From Geoffrey we also get the tale of Merlin: the wise Meryddin, turned into the wild man of the woods through the grief of losing his family, then ultimately an adviser to kings even before Arthur, and a tale that may have been older than the first Arthur himself. Geoffrey tells us about Guinevere and of Mordred's betrayal. In 1155, not quite twenty years later, the Norman poet Wace did a French version of Geoffrey's history called the *Roman de Brut* in which he mentioned an egalitarian innovation called the Round Table.

France fell in love with the Arthurian stories and mixed them with their own folklore. In the 1170s the poet Chrétien de Troyes took an older folk hero, Lancelot, and made him one of Arthur's knights. As if that wasn't enough, Chrétien does double duty in his poem *Lancelot, the Knight of the Cart,* which gave us another of Arthur's most famous themes with the simple line "Upon a certain Ascension Day King Arthur had come from Caerleon, and had held a very magnificent court at Camelot as was fitting on such a day." Thanks to the Anglo-Normans and the French still living on the Continent, Arthur and his knights were no longer just magnificent, wise, and mystical warriors, but also chivalrous ones. And to crown the chivalry, it is from the French stories that the knights of Camelot are introduced to the Holy Grail.

Throughout the twelfth century, King Arthur was also attracting numerous other stories, which had been floating through British folklore for centuries, like a moor mist. Arthur became the guardian of the (Welsh) Thirteen Treasures of Britain—including a mantle that makes its wearer invisible, and a cauldron that can discern truth from lies, carried by Arthur's faithful servant, Hwgwydd. He was granted sacred weapons, like the Cutting Spear, Rhongomyniad. He encountered the Green Knight, who walked into Camelot wielding a holly club and challenged the Knights of the Round Table to cut off his head in a test proving whether or not the man accepting the challenge had honor.

Finally, two incarnations remained that would solidify King Arthur's identity to modern readers. While languishing in 1469 and 1470, Sir Thomas Malory took a 4,300-line fourteenth-century French poem titled *Morte Arthure* (*Arthur's Death*), which combined traditional stories and the anonymous author's imagination, edited it, combined it with other stories, translated this new work into English, and thus essentially codified the Arthurian elements in twenty-one books titled *Le Morte D'Arthur* (*The Death of Arthur*). Between its popularity in its time and British printer William Caxton making it one of his earliest books (along with the English Bible), it has been handed down to us with the legacy of being the primary story we know today.

And at last, in 1938, following a British imperialist wave of Arthurian nostalgia during the Victorian era—and perhaps as a reaction against it—T. H. White crystallized much of what we think about the elements surrounding Arthur in the first of his Arthurian cycle, *The Sword in the Stone*. (A generation later, Disney set those elements in stone, as it were, thanks to the movie of the same title, if not always the same story as White's.)

It was to White that J. K. Rowling often looked when she created Harry Potter. White was "Harry's spiritual ancestor," as she put it ("J. K. Rowling"). From White, we see "The Wart," the young future king, not starting out as the chosen one, raised to be a king, but an uncertain boy growing up under the tutelage of the wise, but often fumbling, white-bearded Merlyn with a 'y' (and Merlyn's owl, Archimedes). While Malory and other earlier French stories tell us that the infant Arthur was in danger and thus tucked away with Sir Ector and his wife, they then skip ahead to Arthur becoming king. In *The Sword in the Stone*, we see for the first time Arthur—whose real name is not even given until near the end—starting from scratch. We read him growing into his role and power, his successes and mistakes. And we observe that even his drawing the Sword from the Stone, though foreordained, was not necessarily a certain thing. Nor does The Wart stay a child in White's books (ultimately compiled into *The Once and Future King*), but he grows increasingly complex with age.

So thus we come to Harry Potter. In writing about the 2001 K-Zoo, the *New York Times* continued, "The professors . . . started by noting physical similarities like invisible doors, magical animals and the use of parchment, sealing wax and coats of arms. From there they turned to thematic devices like the ease with which characters move between normal and abnormal worlds" (Kinzer).

Quite honestly, these are all components of literary medievalism anyway. And it's certainly nothing new to say that Western fantasy has commonly used them, particularly since J. R. R. Tolkien's pervasive success with *The Hobbit* and *The Lord of the Rings* trilogy. Scholars have written about such medievalism for decades. So what is it about the Harry Potter series—beyond the setpieces—that leads the medievalists and Rowling's readers to keep connecting the seven chronicles of Harry and Hogwarts to King Arthur?

The Once and Future Wizard

Harry, like the Wart, is hidden and tutored early on, even if the Wart doesn't necessarily know that he was hidden or why he is being tutored. As Sybill Trelawney predicted obliquely that Harry, a child who was "born as the seventh month" dies (Rowling, *Order of the Phoenix*), was the one who could defeat Voldemort—thus saving Britain from the forces of darkness for both wizards and Muggles alike—Merlyn predicted that Arthur would be the one to conquer Britain's enemies. In the case of White's Merlyn, though, it's not exactly a prediction so much as a memory, as Merlyn moves backwards through time and remembers the adult Arthur (along with the twentieth century).

In both cases, then, Harry's opening defeat of Voldemort and Arthur's legacy as the son of an effective Saxon-fighter, along with their similar destinies, place both infants in grave danger. Dumbledore hides Harry with Lily Potter's sister, Petunia, and her family, the Dursleys, who out of spite (and being afraid of how "weird" magic is) throw Harry into the closet, literally and metaphorically. Yet as Dumbledore explains at the beginning of *Sorcerer's Stone*, when Professor McGonagall wonders how this can be better than Harry growing up among wizards and knowing his fame, "Can't you see how much better off he'll be, growing up away from all that until he's ready to take it?" (Rowling, *Sorcerer's Stone* 13). It is growing up in such mean and meager circumstances that will teach Harry compassion and instill in him a sense of justice—so much so that he won't even let Ron kick the wretched cat Mrs. Norris "just once" (Rowling, *Sorcerer's Stone* 274).

The bespectacled, white-bearded Merlyn, who likes to keep things tucked into his pointed hat because he finds it "most convenient," takes the baby Arthur to Sir Ector (as Merlin did in prior incarnations of the legend as well), a "passing true man and faithful" according to Malory (4), until he comes to claim Arthur for training many years later, as Hagrid does for Harry at Dumbledore's insistence. Sir Ector and his wife never mistreat Arthur, certainly not to the extent the Dursleys do Harry, although they never exactly regard him as their son. Their son Kay, two years older than the

Wart, is also not as bad as Harry's cousin Dudley, though Kay has his abusive and mocking moments with the young Arthur. In Dudley's case, the older Harry gets and the more Dudley realizes just how important (and truly good) a person Harry is, the more Dudley comes to respect Harry (if grudgingly), and Sir Kay does likewise. Eventually, Kay becomes one of Arthur's most trusted knights; one wonders if Dudley may have likewise come around if Rowling continued her series into Harry's adulthood.

Eventually, at the ages of ten and eleven (respectively), Arthur and Harry both are given to their tutors (though in the Wart's case, he has to slog his way through a beast-filled forest on his own to get there).

When the Wart enters Merlyn's chambers, he finds it "the most marvellous room that he had ever been in" (White 24). It is filled with "thousands of brown books in leather bindings . . . stuffed birds . . . and a reputed phoenix which smelt of incense and cinnamon." There are "a very lifelike basilisk" and numerous other animals magical and otherwise, "a guncase with all sorts of weapons that would not be invented for half a thousand years," an astrolabe and globes, "a gold medal for being the best scholar at Winchester," cauldrons, Bunsen burners, and numerous other sorts of intensively described wonders great and small that Harry might have found more than a little reminiscent of Dumbledore's office.

Despite Merlyn's occasionally fumbling appearance and Dumbledore's regular (and occasionally admitted) penchant for holding information back from Harry, Harry and Arthur thus have the best mentors that a young leader fraught with destiny could imagine. Rowling, however, is not content to have a direct one-to-one translation from Merlyn to Dumbledore, and the literary influence that was Merlin now fragments Horcrux-style into several characters. Harry, thus, is blessed multiple times by having Sirius Black and Minerva McGonagall—and Severus Snape as well, though he doesn't realize it until near the final battle with Voldemort—along with trustworthy friends in Hermione and Ron. This large alliance makes all the difference for both his fate and the fate of Britain. Sirius, indeed, matches up with the old tale of Merlin as the wild man of the woods—for Sirius himself certainly has the wild man's appearance when he first finds Harry again, after losing James and Lily Potter and spending over a decade in Azkaban—a dark forest in itself—for a crime he did not commit.

Ultimately, both leaders would suffer having their mentors taken from them—Dumbledore killed (though at his own behest, and occasionally able to return to Harry for a few moments) along with Sirius and Snape killed, and Merlin likewise removed, either locked away in a cave by Nimue (in the high medieval stories) or fading into the airy otherworld (as the Welsh often told), taking the Thirteen Treasures of Britain (including the invisibility mantle) with him. When Arthur faces Mordred, he does so alone in the end; Harry starts out by facing Voldemort alone in *Deathly Hallows*, but in the end has all of Hogwarts behind him.

Despite being kept in ignorance of their destiny to one degree or another, Harry and Arthur both take up their crowns of leadership early on. Arthur pulls the sword out of the stone as a young man—fifteen by White's reckoning, a "youth" according to Malory. In Arthur's case, his stepbrother Sir Kay had broken his sword in a tournament, and Arthur goes hunting for another one. Malory's Arthur happens upon the sword in the stone and "lightly and fiercely pulled it out of the stone" (Malory 5) without realizing the significance of the act. White's Wart has a bit more trouble retrieving it from an anvil, even imploring the sword itself that he wants the blade not for himself but Kay. When he calls to Merlyn for help, the very animals and banners around the Wart give him advice and encouragement until finally, on his third attempt, he "drew it out as gently as from a scabbard" (White 195).

Harry, meanwhile, earns his icons in trials by fire, but as barely more than a child nevertheless. Dumbledore's phoenix, Fawkes, brings Harry the Sorting Hat during the second battle with Voldemort in *Chamber of Secrets*, where "a gleaming sword had appeared . . ., its handle glittering with rubies the size of eggs" (320). Harry uses the sword to kill Salazar Slytherin's basilisk. This is, of course, the Sword of Godric Gryffindor, and "only a true Gryffindor could have pulled that out of the hat," Dumbledore explains to Harry (334).

Not all of the old Arthurian stories consider the Sword in the Stone and Excalibur to be the same blade, however. In fact, the French stories, particularly those from the Lancelot-Grail cycle, specifically say that they are different. In these versions, the Sword in the Stone (usually unnamed) is broken in a battle where Arthur is badly wounded. Afterwards, partly through the efforts of Merlin, the Lady of the Lake, whose arm rises above the surface of the water holding the sword, gives Excalibur to Arthur. Or as Ollivander might say, the wand chooses the wizard.

After Harry is bequeathed the Sword of Gryffindor in Dumbledore's will—and Rufus Scrimgeour asks Harry if he got the sword "because Dumbledore believed only the sword of Godric Gryffindor could defeat the Heir of Slytherin" (Rowling, *Deathly Hallows* 129)—circumstances become such that the sword must be retrieved from a lake, where it had been hidden—not dissimilarly to Excalibur, guarded by the Lady of the Lake. (However, it is Ron who does the retrieving in this case.)

Harkening to Malory and farther back to Geoffrey of Monmouth, Arthur thus becomes King of the Britons young. Geoffrey, like Malory, specifies that Arthur is fifteen at the time, and there is much rejoicing surrounding the event (Geoffrey 192). Harry does not become a king at the age of fifteen, but it is right around that time, in *Order of the Phoenix*, when he does become the leader of his first army: Dumbledore's Army. Dolores Umbridge has effectively wrested control of Hogwarts even from Dumbledore, apparently as a result of the Ministry of Magic's fearing that it would lose its grip on power over the wizarding world, and one major consequence for Harry and the other students is that Umbridge yanks the teeth out of the Defense of the Dark Arts class. The students know that all of the theory without practice won't help when Voldemort comes. And unlike Umbridge and the Ministry, Harry and the others know the Dark Lord *is* coming, just as the Britons knew that they needed a new king quickly after Uther Pendragron's death because "the Saxons . . . were aiming to expel the Britons" (Geoffrey 192). So Hermione suggests that Harry become their Defense of the Dark Arts teacher (Rowling, *Order of the Phoenix* 326).

It has a simple start—what he thinks will be just a handful of close friends learning both spells and how to face their fears. But when the first "class" shows up, there are quite a few more people than Harry expects. Nevertheless he wins them over and finds the Room of Requirement as a secret practice location, and as their numbers and confidence grow, Dumbledore's Army is born. While King Arthur was lauded, however, Harry is crucified by the newspapers, the Ministry, and Umbridge and must practice in secret.

Over the course of seven years and his battles with Voldemort, Harry is given more help as he proves himself, just as Arthur was. According to the poems and stories of the Welsh Triads, for instance, there were "sacred weapons that God had given [Arthur]," such as the Cutting Spear, *Rhongomyniad*, which in English fashion Geoffrey of Monmouth shortened to just "Spear," translated as *Ron*. "Hermione," writes the aforementioned Heather Arden, "resembles . . . the wise, active, clever women of Chrétien's romances . . . . Many women are also wise and learned in the ways of nature—to the point of appearing to have magical powers" (Arden 60). Hermione herself, Arden continues, "is brighter, more knowledgeable about magic . . . than her male counterparts, and she often provides a crucial piece of information or action for the completion of Harry's tasks" (60). Harry dates and eventually marries Ginny Weasley, whose real (if detested) name is Ginevra—the German form of Guinevere.

There were the Thirteen Treasures of Britain, such as the mantle, which Arthur found in Cornwall. According to the Welsh stories, the mantle was empowered so that "whoever was under it could not be seen, and he could see everybody" (Coe & Young 137). Around 1100 the Welsh story *Culhwch and Olwen* explained that the Cauldron of Diwnarch the Irishman could—like a flip side of Veritaserum— discern whether or not someone was telling the truth. When Arthur took the cauldron, he passed it along to a faithful follower named Hwgwydd (pronounced as if spelled Hagwid or Hoogwid). Whether that faithful servant is closer to Hagrid (who is certainly capable of hauling around cauldrons) or Hedwig (who carries Harry's most precious messages) is open to interpretation.

As Alessandra Petrina points out, it isn't just characters and events that reflect the Arthurian tradition, be that tradition old or modern, but also the spaces in the books, most notably Hogwarts and the Forbidden Forest. "A lake, a high mountain or a cliff, a castle with a dark secret entrance. These are recurring elements in Arthurian literature . . . . They are conventional signals for romance (the hero always has to cross water in order to enter the castle of adventures) . . . ." (Petrina 102). More specifically to the Arthurian authors we have met, "The lake, charged with mysterious meaning in Thomas Malory's last tale . . . is great and black, yet smooth as glass: this is romance in its initial, peaceful and entrancing stage . . . ." Yet the lake takes on more ominous meanings as the books proceed and the wizarding world itself grows darker. "In the fourth . . . volume of the series, instead, we have a 'storm-tossed, fathoms-deep lake' in which a very young student risks losing his life . . ." (Petrina 102).

Petrina draws parallels between the Forbidden Forest and the

> Syege Perelous, or the Waste Forest surrounding the Grail Castle, or even T. H. White's Forest Sauvage. The associations here are immediate: the forest of the hunt of the magical, half-human white stag in Chrétien de Troyes' *Eric et Enide* . . . the forest as the place of wilderness . . . in which the werewolf loses its human traits and is turned from an unfortunate hero into a figure of destruction, as in the anonymous *Arthur and Gorgalon* . . . ." (Petrina 105)

But it is there amid the dangers and the wildness and chaos of the Forbidden Forest, as Petrina further points out, that Harry meets his true self in *Prisoner of Azkaban* after initially thinking he saw his father.

It was also no coincidence that Harry has his penultimate confrontation with Voldemort in the Forbidden Forest, the one leading to Harry's death and the destruction of the Horcrux within him. This was the place where Voldemort initially came to hide close to Hogwarts, and where he still feels safe among its dark spaces. But Harry has been here many times, and he has come to terms with it and conquered his own fears of the place where so many people's fears were manifested. He doesn't overcome the wild and the dark there, but learns to adapt to it, and thus the forest becomes as much his ally as Voldemort thinks it is his. Harry no longer needs his Merlin in Dumbledore; he has learned what he needs from Merlin and escaped the cave that Merlin could not.

Not all of the Arthurian spaces need be dark, however. Petrina draws one far less threatening parallel: "Like the hall at Camelot, Hogwarts' Great Hall is also set with a high table for teachers and important guests and lower tables for the students; Dumbledore, king of the feasts like Arthur in [*Sir Gawain and the Green Knight*], can take all participants in a single glance" (Petrina 104).

As is becoming clear, though, Rowling only very rarely makes direct analog connections with Arthurian tradition. Like the variety of Arthurian authors themselves, she takes pieces here and there, reweaving them in different ways and melding them with parts of her own imagination. The Holy Grail, for instance, is split into two parts: the Sorcerer's Stone and the Goblet of Fire. The Sorcerer's Stone can grant extended life, as it does to Nicolas Flamel, or restore a lost form, Voldemort's hope. To get the stone, Harry, Hermione, and Ron have to pass through a series of ordeals ranging from the guardian, Fluffy, to a dangerous chess game and finally a bottle-laden riddle, just as Sir Galahad needed to penetrate a series of ordeals to reach the Grail. The Goblet of Fire, a more physically obvious parallel, likewise has the power to heal anyone drinking from it and includes its own sequence of trials.

Quite often in all seven books, Rowling specifically diverges from Arthurian tradition. The Sorcerer's Stone is destroyed rather than preserved or revered; in a twist to the Knights of the Round Table's Grail Quest becoming corrupted, Voldemort corrupts the Goblet of Fire in order to trap and kill Harry. These *anti*-Arthurian elements become more common as the books proceed. And heretical though it may seem, it is precisely in the places where Harry breaks the most from the Arthurian mold that he is allowed to succeed where Arthur failed.

*   *   *

It is our choices, Harry, that show what we truly are, far more than our abilities. (Albus Dumbledore, *Harry Potter and the Chamber of Secrets*)

Choices, those Arthur makes and those Harry makes, become critical in determining whether the heroes succeed or fail—and whether Britain will survive or fall into darkness as well. Harry and Arthur start out much in the same place, even with similar personalities: Geoffrey describes Arthur as a youth of "great promise and generosity, whose innate goodness ensured that he was loved by almost everybody" (Geoffrey 192). Harry is loved by almost everyone who knows him, except his enemies, for whom his innate goodness is anathema. "As newly-crowned king," Geoffrey continues, "[Arthur] displayed his customary open-handedness." And while Harry doesn't exactly dispense gifts in the medieval royal fashion, he does, whether it is training Dumbledore's Army or doing whatever it takes to save his friends, give everything of himself to those he loves and the wizarding (and Muggle) world at large.

Harry is far from perfect, of course. He becomes a "law unto himself" at times, as Edmund M. Kern puts it in *The Wisdom of Harry Potter*—particularly when the thirteen-year-old Harry is faced with far more difficult and complex choices in *Prisoner of Azkaban* than he ever faced before. As Kern points out, in that particular book, Harry eavesdrops on the Weasleys, lies often, and attacks a teacher. Professor McGonagall is already complaining by *Chamber of Secrets* that Harry has become known for "breaking a hundred school rules into pieces" (328). But Harry's bad behavior is rarely arbitrary. *The Prisoner of Azkaban* is "a single extended commentary upon the tensions between the rules and the moral principles they are intended to sustain" (Kern 72), and at this point, Harry must first figure out how doing right sometimes means doing what is wrong in a legalistic sense—yet without crossing lines that must never be crossed.

Arthur and Harry aren't the only ones with similarities; in *Chamber of Secrets*, Harry learns, to his grief, just how similar he is to Voldemort on a multitude of levels. But those similarities are what compel Harry to redouble his efforts not to be like or become another Dark Lord. And this makes the ultimate difference both for him and in drawing the anti-Arthurian parallels.

Harry and Arthur face the same sorts of choices, and the differences in the decisions resulting from those choices illuminate the differences between the two. We see signs of this all through Rowling's books. The aforementioned stag is one direct and contradicting parallel. In British, particularly Celtic, folklore, the stag (usually a white stag) represents a message from the other world (usually the spirit world) that people encountering it are about to experience a profound change in their lives. The stag could not be caught—though this fact never stopped Arthur. As we see in many stories, particularly Chrétien de Troyes' *Erec and Enide*, Arthur is an avid hunter of earthly stags, and he tries to pursue this less earthly white stag as well. For Harry the stag brings a similar message after a fashion, but he has a very different reaction to its presence. Instead of prey, it signifies protection, his Patronus. He doesn't need to chase after it as Arthur must. The stag comes to him.

One way or another, Harry goes on a quest in each book, including quests for the Hallows and Horcruxes that parallel both the search for the Holy Grail and Arthur's gathering the Thirteen Treasures of Britain. But the point of these quests for Harry is never self-aggrandizement or the achievement of power. When he seeks the Sorcerer's Stone, Harry gets it—and as easily as Arthur gets the Sword in the Stone—because he wants only to find the stone and not to use it, as Dumbledore explains (Rowling, *Sorcerer's Stone* 300). Harry enters the Triwizard Tournament and seeks the Triwizard cup not for glory and fame, but because Voldemort ensured that Harry's name was placed in the Goblet of Fire.

Arthur is lauded early on. Harry is raised in emotional squalor and at Hogwarts is often castigated by the press, the Ministry of Magic, the members of Slytherin House, and others. But instead of becoming bitter or outright turning to evil to seek vengeance against those who have wronged him, Harry's upbringing has taught him humility and given him a sense of justice, while Arthur felt entitled to use his power as he would, justifying it by the needs of the times. Arthur is often heavy-handed—or murderous, as we will see below—while Harry is only reluctantly dragged into becoming a leader and sometimes into using his abilities as well. His friends see him consistently choosing the right path, despite the obstacles thrown against him, and they accompany him on that path. As Ron sets the tone at the outset of the quest for the Sorcerer's Stone: "Oh, come off it, you don't think we'd let you go alone?" (Rowling, *Sorcerer's Stone* 271). By contrast, by the time Arthur meets Mordred at the fateful Battle of Camlan, the king is practically alone.

When Harry seeks the Horcruxes, these Treasures of the Wizarding World, he doesn't try to use them for his own ends or let them corrupt him as the Grail Quest corrupted Camelot, but instead he means to destroy them. Even the incredibly powerful Elder Wand itself offers little temptation. At the end of *Deathly Hallows*, Harry shocks Ron by admitting that he's not interested in keeping the Elder Wand for himself even though he is now its master—he prefers his own wand. Instead, Harry lays the Elder Wand back to rest with Dumbledore.

Harry knows almost from the beginning that Voldemort wants to kill him—in order for one to live, the other must die. But even so, he never strays from the path of his own innate goodness (though he often fears he will, even fretting about the Sorting Hat wanting to put him in Slytherin—hence Dumbledore's quotation opening this section of the essay), and never seeks to gather power about himself with the justification of fighting Voldemort. Arthur, on the other hand, takes a dark turn from the very beginning. When, according to Malory, he hears Merlin's prophecy that Arthur will fall at the hand of a child born on May Day, Arthur takes all of the children born that day and loads them on a ship, which is swept onto the rocks. The infant/child Mordred—Arthur's nephew in some stories, his cousin in others, but almost always a family member—survives the attempted drowning, though all the others perish. But rather than attacking others, Harry tries gathering people around him to help them and even to try winning over his enemies in many cases. For Harry, the result is that his friends stay close and have his back, while he finds allies in numerous unexpected places, including the

Forbidden Forest. For Arthur, the prophecy becomes self-fulfilling, and he loses Guinevere and Lancelot, and finally his kingdom and his life.[4]

Harry goes to face Voldemort in the Forbidden Forest, knowing he will have to die in order to destroy the Horcrux within him. And die he does, as did Arthur. But while some may still be awaiting Arthur's return at the time of Britain's greatest need, Dumbledore tells Harry that he does, in fact, have the choice to go back if he feels he is needed. Harry decides that now is the time of his world's and his friends' greatest need, so he returns to finish what he started.

Another specific example of Harry's directly breaking the Arthurian template is starkly clear in both *Half-Blood Prince* and *Deathly Hallows*. Despite Draco Malfoy's tormenting Harry for years, Harry (and Dumbledore) won't give up the hope of his long-time nemesis taking a turn towards the good. And even at the end, in his final duel with Voldemort, Harry tries helping the Dark Lord regain some of his humanity. "It's your one last chance," said Harry. "It's all you've got left . . . . Try for some remorse . . ." (Rowling, *Deathly Hallows* 741).

This has its own anti-Arthurian parallel: in the High Medieval stories of Arthur, the king wielded two swords, Excalibur and Clarent. Excalibur was Arthur's sword of war, while Clarent was the sword of peace, used for events such as knighting ceremonies. Mordred steals Clarent and uses it to mortally wound Arthur at the Battle of Camlan. When Harry defeats Draco in a wand duel in *Half-Blood Prince*, wherein Harry is not seeking to kill Draco or any other such nasty business, Harry becomes the Elder Wand's master. That mastery causes the Elder Wand to turn Voldemort's killing curse back on the Dark Lord himself during his final duel with Harry. So instead of slaying Harry as Clarent did Arthur, the weapon destroys Voldemort once and for all.

And thus are the wizarding world, England—and Harry—saved. Instead of witnessing a tragic death scene and Excalibur being thrown back to the Lady of the Lake, Harry Potter readers have an epilogue set nineteen years later, with the next generation attending a rebuilt and thriving Hogwarts. Harry even gets a subtle but world-telling nod from the saved Draco Malfoy.

Through the Trapdoor

Says Heather Arden, "The hero himself . . . shows us that a seemingly ordinary orphan child can turn out to be an exceptional person." Arden continues, "Perhaps the greatest quality shared by Harry and the Arthurian hero is to show us the power of imagination to transform the established boundaries between things and people, to show us the possibilities of other worlds" (qtd. in Kinzer).

Apparently so. All in all, what the scholars and Harry Potter's readers seem to be saying is that it doesn't really matter so much whether or not the Sword of Gryffindor is Excalibur, or the Sorcerer's Stone and the Goblet of Fire are the Holy Grail. What matters is that the *spirit* of Harry Potter is Arthurian at its best and anti-Arthurian to avoid the point when Camelot met its worst. And it is a reminder for us commoners or Muggles that, even if we aren't born to a king, we can do just as well as Harry if the need arises.

Notes

1. Presenter Heather Arden turned her own Arthurian K-Zoo presentation into "The Harry Potter Stories and French Arthurian Romance," co-written with Kathryn Lorenz and published in *Arthuriana* 13.2 (2003).
2. Roughly translated, "Lord of War." But rather than "warlord," this means someone who was a chief commander of forces. In Arthur's case, this could have meant many different groups.
3. Arthur is most definitely originally a Welsh/Celtic hero—the Welsh being descendants of the surviving original Britons—and they have far and away enough early Arthurian stories to back this up. Certainly, there are far more tales than can be listed here in any practical way.
4. Note how often Harry's magic involves self-defense: Expelliarmus, Protego, etc.

Works Cited

Arden, Heather, & Kathryn Lorenz. "The Harry Potter Stories and French Arthurian Romance." *Arthuriana* 13:2 (2003): 54–68.

Blake, Steve, & Scott Lloyd. *Pendragon: The Definitive Account of the Origins of Arthur*. Guilford, CT: Lyons, 2002.

Coe, John B., & Simon Young. *The Celtic Sources for the Arthurian Legend*. Somerset, UK: Llanerch, 1995.

Goodrich, Normal Lorre. *King Arthur*. New York: Harper & Row, 1986.

Harvey, Paul, ed. *The Oxford Companion to English Literature*. 2nd edition. Oxford: Oxford UP, 1944.

"J. K. (Joanne Kathleen) Rowling." *The Guardian*. 22 Jul. 2008. Web. 30 Aug. 2014.

Kern, Edmund M. *The Wisdom of Harry Potter: What Our Favorite Hero Teaches Us About Moral Choices*. Amherst, NY: Prometheus, 2003.

Kinzer, Stephen. "An Improbable Sequel: Harry Potter and the Ivory Tower." *New York Times* 12 May 2001. Web. 27 Apr. 2015.

Lacy, Norris J., ed. *The New Arthurian Encyclopedia, New Edition*. New York: Routledge, 1996.

Malory, Thomas. *Le Morte d'Arthur*. New York: Heritage Press, 1955.

Petrina, Alessandra. "Forbidden Forest, Enchanted Castle: Arthurian Spaces in the Harry Potter Novels." *Mythlore 93/94* 24:3–4 (2006): 95–110.

Rowling, J. K. *Harry Potter and the Chamber of Secrets*. Illus. Mary Grandpré. New York: Arthur A. Levine/Scholastic, 1999.

_____. *Harry Potter and the Deathly Hallows*. Illus. Mary Grandpré. New York: Arthur A. Levine/Scholastic, 2007.

_____. *Harry Potter and the Goblet of Fire*. Illus. Mary Grandpré. New York: Arthur A. Levine/Scholastic, 2000.

_____. *Harry Potter and the Half-Blood Prince*. Illus. Mary Grandpré. New York: Arthur A. Levine/Scholastic, 2005.

_____. *Harry Potter and the Order of the Phoenix*. Illus. Mary Grandpré. New York: Arthur A. Levine/Scholastic, 2003.

_____. *Harry Potter and the Prisoner of Azkaban*. Illus. Mary Grandpré. New York: Arthur A. Levine/Scholastic, 1999.

_____. *Harry Potter and the Sorcerer's Stone*. Illus. Mary Grandpré. New York: Arthur A. Levine/Scholastic, 1998.

White, T. H. *The Once and Future King*. New York: Putnam's, 1958.

Moral Ambiguity in Authority Figures in *The Hunger Games*, *Divergent*, and the Harry Potter Series

Crystal Wilkins

> *Perhaps those who are best suited to power are those who have never sought it.* (J. K. Rowling)

A walk through the young adult section of any local bookstore will tell you that dystopian books are one of the most popular forms of literature with that age group (and with quite a few adults as well). Though dystopian literature has long had a place among young adult readers, the last ten years have seen a significant rise in popularity, with many popular series also moving to successful screen adaptations. In addition, Linda Gann and Karen Gavigan note a trend in the increasing number of dystopian novels that have been awarded various literary prizes in young adult literature since the mid-2000's. While the initial popularity of certain series, such as The Hunger Games and the Harry Potter series, certainly led to other authors writing along a similar vein, perhaps it is a more specific event that has led to the increase in dystopian literature among young adult readers.[1] While there were spotty publications of one or two books a year during the early 2000s, it was after the bombings of the World Trade Center on September 11, 2001, that there was such a noticeable increase in dystopian fiction for young adults. The September 11 attacks marked a cultural turning point, and for millennials, reading dystopian literature can be a way of processing 9/11 and its impact, even if the storylines are not directly related to 9/11 itself. As Efraim Sicher and Natalia Skradol note, these darker dystopian novels "tend to reflect cultural anxieties of the present" (169), and while Karen Springen lists several recent current events that may contribute to an increase in the appeal of young adult dystopian literature, she acknowledges that "most editors and authors credit lingering unease from the World Trade Center attacks" (21). Melissa Ames argues that dystopian literature is a safe haven for millennials to explore topics and subjects, particularly around political themes, because engaging with these topics on a fictional level offers a certain distance; however, this does not mean that these young adults are politically disengaged. On the contrary, Ames and Anthony Gierzynski (in *Harry Potter and the Millennials*) both argue that dystopian fiction can be used as an educational tool and that it has a great impact on the political attitudes and behavior of those who read it.

One of the most significant ways in which these novels can impact the political views of young adults, particularly in the dystopian literature since 9/11, is through the use of moral ambiguity in characterizing authority figures. While political ads and Us-versus-Them propaganda have been used in the United States since the development of the predominantly two-party system, these have been more prevalent post-9/11, with the flooding of 24-hour news sources; "fake" news sources (*The Onion, The Daily Show with Jon Stewart, The Colbert Report,* etc.); big screen documentaries, such as *Fahrenheit 9/11*; and numerous social media outlets, like Facebook and Twitter, where people can post anything they like and call it the truth. Reading this dark, dystopian literature with authority figures who are bad, but may not always be bad, or seem good, but perhaps aren't as good as they seem, helps young adults understand that not everyone who does bad is evil and not everyone who seems good truly is. Take, for example, The Hunger Games, Divergent, and Harry Potter series (specifically *Harry Potter and the Order of the Phoenix, Harry Potter and the Half-Blood Prince, and Harry Potter and the Deathly Hallows*, as this essay focuses on dystopian literature post-9/11)—each of these series has characters in some position of power or authority who are neither entirely good nor purely evil.

The Hunger Games Trilogy
In Suzanne Collins' The Hunger Games trilogy, Katniss Everdeen finds herself repeatedly thrust into situations in which she is pitted

against authority figures who think they know what is best, not only for her, but for a nation. The most obvious of these is President Coriolanus Snow, the leader of Panem, who is perpetuating the seventy-five-year-long tradition of the Hunger Games. President Snow is the epitome of the despotic villain—Katniss even paints a picture of him that is redolent of Adolf Hitler and Nazi Germany in *Catching Fire*, when she imagines he "should be viewed in front of marble pillars hung with oversized flags" (18). Anthony Pavlik makes the comparison to Umberto Eco's theory of "Ur-Fascism" in his essay "Absolute Power Games," in which he discusses how "everyone must follow the party line or suffer" (32). Snow controls with an iron fist and absolute power. Anyone opposing him is disposed of in the most literal sense.

As the series progresses, President Snow and Katniss come to an understanding that they will not lie to each other. Still, he takes great pleasure in torturing her at least psychologically, particularly after she is taken from the arena at the Quarter Quell. First, he leaves her a single white rose at her home in the Victor's Village in District 12 when she returns for the first time after President Snow destroyed the district immediately after the games, killing over 700 people. Then again after the bombing of District 13, Snow leaves roses again—this time, as Katniss explains, "long-stemmed pink and red beauties, the very flowers that decorated the set where Peeta and I performed our post-victory interview. Flowers not meant for one, but a pair of lovers" (Collins, *Mockingjay* 161). These are roses meant to remind Katniss of Snow's power—power over her, over Peeta, and over the ongoing game between the two of them.

Finally, and worst of all, Snow gives Peeta back broken and damaged. Peeta's very first act on seeing Katniss is to try to kill her—Snow has taken what Katniss wants most of all and turned him into a weapon to destroy her. This is doubly painful both because Katniss cannot be near Peeta, who will try to kill her, and because Peeta was obviously tortured. The process of "hijacking," as described by Betee in *Mockingjay*, involves "ask[ing] you to remember something—either with a verbal suggestion or by making you watch a tape of the event—and while that experience is refreshed, giv[ing] you a dose of tracker jacker venom. . . . Just enough to infuse the memory with fear and doubt" (Collins, *Mockingjay* 181). Not only has Snow tortured Peeta; he has, possibly irrevocably, taken him away from Katniss.

Still, these are only specific instances against a single person over the arc of the series. The reader learns from Finnick Odair in his rebel broadcast to the entirety of Panem in *Mockingjay* that President Snow has a long history of eliminating his opposition and manipulating people in order to keep them in line. Finnick admits that Snow sold him for sexual favors after he won the Hunger Games, that sometimes his suitors would give him favors, but that his favorite trade was secrets. His best kept secret is President Snow's repeated use of poison on his adversaries—and Snow's frequent drinking from the same cup to remove any suspicion from himself. This results in continuously open sores in his mouth, which is why he always has strongly scented roses on his lapels.

While we expect and are not surprised by this level of tyranny and villainy from Snow, the reader hopes for more from President Alma Coin in District 13. It becomes clear fairly early, however, that this leader is cut from a similar cloth as Snow. Pavlik notes the similarity between the two leaders as well: "Coin, . . . like Snow, distrusts others and works to ensure that those she oversees are kept on a tight rein, ostensibly for their own safety" (33). Under the guise of their own protection, Coin forbids anyone from going aboveground and imprints their schedules on their arms. And while Snow tortures Peeta mentally, Katniss' prep team suffers in a different way in District 13:

> The stink of unwashed bodies, stale urine, and infection breaks through the cloud of antiseptic. The three figures are only just recognizable by their most striking fashion choices. . . . On seeing me, Flavius and Octavia shrink back against the tiled walls like they're anticipating an attack, even though I have never hurt them. . . . The preps have been forced into cramped body positions for so long that even once the shackles are removed, they have trouble walking. Gale, Plutarch, and I have to help them. Flavius' foot catches on a metal grate over a circular opening in the floor, and my stomach contracts when I think

of why a room would need a drain. The stains of human misery that must have been hosed off these white tiles . . . . (Collins, *Mockingjay* 47, 49)

Why this level of treatment for Katniss' prep team? For stealing one slice of bread. These three people who come from the Capitol—a place where bulimia is in fashion so that one can eat more at a party—are thrown into this room and left there for stealing a piece of bread. Coin's iron fist in dealing with the prep team shows an utter lack of compassion or understanding in dealing with anyone outside of her immediate circle and shows a level of secrecy, since even Coin's closest "allies" are unaware of the treatment of the prep team.

This, however, is Katniss' introduction to Coin, and Katniss is not fooled by the schedules and need for food rations or security. In fact, Katniss tells Fulvia, a former Capitol citizen, that the treatment of the prep team is a warning to them, "[a]bout who is really in control and what happens if she's not obeyed" (Collins, *Mockingjay* 50). President Coin only confirms this when she announces the agreement for the immunity of the captive victors she has made with Katniss—with the additional, undiscussed caveat that should Katniss step out of line as the Mockingjay, the deal is off and the victors, even Katniss, are no longer protected and under the jurisdiction of District 13.

While there is tacit cooperation between Katniss and Coin, when Katniss serves as the Mockingjay, Coin sees the arrival of Peeta as a solution to her biggest problem. When Katniss' military unit finds itself down a man, Coin sends Peeta in the hopes that he will be overcome by the "hijacking" started by President Snow and kill Katniss, which will serve Coin in two ways—creating a martyr for the rebel cause and eliminating any future difficulty from Katniss. There is no question that Katniss poses any type of threat by taking on a role as a political leader, but Boggs—up until this point Coin's right-hand man—asks if her support will be for Coin: "If your immediate answer isn't Coin, then you're a threat. You're the face of the rebellion. You may have more influence than any other single person" (Collins, *Mockingjay* 266). Coin has never planned on Katniss' surviving the war, but rather on her serving as the ultimate martyr for the cause. In the end, Katniss takes her shot intended for Snow's execution and kills Coin, choosing to save the future of Panem from another corrupt leader rather than exacting her own revenge on Snow by taking his life.

Readers expect President Snow to be evil, yet he keeps his word by always being honest with Katniss. Readers hope that President Coin will be a better leader; unfortunately, they are disappointed but not necessarily surprised when she turns out to be a different kind of evil—even calling for one final Hunger Games with the children of the Capitol when the rebellion is over, for the satisfaction of the people of the districts, of course. Both Snow and Coin have an Us-versus-Them approach—Snow has long ruled by fear, using the games as a means of controlling those in the districts. Coin, planning to step into that position of power, assumes that fear is how she will have to rule as well. Neither stops to think that there might be an alternative means to maintaining control or peace in the districts once the fighting is over.[2]

The Divergent Series

The Divergent books by Veronica Roth are a dystopian series set in a future Chicago, where society is split into factions—Abnegation (selfless), Erudite (intelligent), Dauntless (brave), Candor (honest), and Amity (peaceful). The novel is rich in complicated situations where the protagonist, Tris, has to deal with adults who are on the darker side of upright. These adversaries range from Jeanine in the Erudite Faction trying to control all of the factions and eradicating the Divergents (those who cannot be limited to one faction) altogether; to Marcus in the Abnegation Faction who may want what is best for the people, but abuses his family in private; to Evelyn in the factionless (those who have been banned by their Factions), who wants to destroy the whole system; and finally to those outside the walls of the city—the Bureau running the experiment and the rebels trying to infiltrate the Bureau and take it down.

Jeanine, like President Snow, is the first obvious oppressor the reader encounters. Leader of the Erudite Faction, she works diligently and tirelessly to continue the faction tradition and to develop the serums that would allow her to control the minds of everyone outside of Erudite. When that is threatened by the Abnegation Faction, Jeanine develops a serum for the Dauntless that forces them to eradicate Abnegation. Julia Karr writes of Jeanine's decision to murder Abnegation, "[S]he does so without mercy and with the coldhearted intention of removing anyone who might try to thwart her purpose—a purpose that included complete control over the factions and a government of her own design, over which she would rule" (131). Jeanine is willing to go to any lengths to stop those who stand in her way—turning other people into murdering machines against their will in the serum-induced simulation. While the Divergent are able to withstand the effects of the serum, Four—a Divergent, a Dauntless trainer, and Tris' love interest—is taken to Jeanine and given a specially formulated serum specifically for Divergents. Later under a truth serum, Four is able to describe what the simulation is like for him:

> When a simulation is running, your eyes still see and process the actual world, but your brain no longer comprehends them. On some level, though, your brain still knows what you're seeing and where you are. The nature of this new simulation was that it recorded my emotional responses to outside stimuli . . . and responded by altering the appearance of that stimuli. The simulation made my enemies into friends, my friends into enemies. I thought I was shutting the simulation down. Really I was receiving instructions about how to keep it running. (Roth, *Insurgent* 86)

Those under the serum's influence are cognizant of their actions, even if those actions feel justified at the time. Jeanine not only turns the members of Dauntless into murderers, every one of them will remember his or her actions.

As if controlling other people's brains and actions is not enough, Jeanine also conducts medical experiments on Divergents—studying their brains for as long as possible and then discarding them once the studies are complete. Tris, of course, finds herself as one of Jeanine's subjects. While Jeanine may be interested in maintaining power, Tris notes to herself that Jeanine's interest is also scientific:

> She wants to study my response. . . . I used to think that cruelty required malice, but that is not true. Jeanine has no reason to act out of malice. But she is cruel because she doesn't care what she does, as long as it fascinates her. I may as well be a puzzle or a broken machine she wants to fix. She will break open my skull just to see the inner workings of my brain; I will die here, and that will be the merciful thing. (Roth, *Insurgent* 192)

This callousness and sense of detachment may be behind much of what Jeanine does, but that does not serve as an excuse. She has been developing serums for years, and now a segment of the population is immune to them; it is natural for her Erudite sensibilities to want to study the Divergents and see what makes them able to withstand the serums.[3]

There may also be a skewed sense of protection at work as well, as Tris thinks after viewing the video from outside the gates—with the images of blood and death and gore—Jeanine may have just wanted to keep the factions safely and naively ensconced within the confines of the city no matter what the cost. Regardless of whatever motivates Jeanine at any given time, her decisions as a leader, or even as a human being, leave much to be desired; while there are still many power-hungry authority figures to deal with, everyone in the factions is better off when Jeanine is killed.

Marcus, Four's father, and a member of the Abnegation Faction would likely be an upright and just leader. Overall, he is looking out for the best interests of the people. His ultimate goal is to make sure that the truth comes out and people are made aware of what lies beyond the gates. However, Marcus is flawed on a much more personal level—Marcus abuses his wife and son to the point that his wife abandons him for the factionless, and his son transfers to another faction. While Tris knows the truth from Four, most of the stories about Marcus are simply whispers and gossip until Four is put under truth serum by the Candor Faction and tells an entire room of Candor, Dauntless, and Abnegation members that he left his faction to get away from his father.

How Marcus treats his wife and son may not appear to affect his ability to lead, as most see him as a just leader, but once this kind of secret is out, people do not quickly forget. Tris is able to see that, while Marcus is not a good man, he is working for the good of the people in this war against Jeanine and the Erudite. In a bold move that may cost her any relationship with Four, she goes with Marcus to find and protect the video that Abnegation wanted to release to everyone, but she openly expresses how she feels about his actions, letting him know that while she may not shoot him, she will not stop anyone else from doing so. After the two are separated in battle, at least one person notes that she wouldn't be surprised if he's been killed by either side. Like many political figures with dark personal secrets, Marcus has a private life that overshadows any good he has done and becomes the thing most people remember about him.

Four has poor luck with family. He has long thought his mother to be dead, only to find that she is the leader of the factionless, those living on the borders of society. While he does not quite trust her, he does want to get to know her. So, he works with her during the war to help destroy Jeanine. However, as he is trying to unlock the Erudite computer systems and access the video that Tris has found, his mother is moving to take Jeanine's place as the newest tyrant of the city. Evelyn wants to do away with the faction system—no more factions, just people. This sounds reasonable since the faction system created the factionless in the first place; without factions, there would be no one left on the outside and everyone would be included. Yet Evelyn's methods are just as violent as Jeanine's, if not more so. Even Four knows that what Evelyn is suggesting is not freedom—the new era she hopes to usher in is not one where people will get to choose what they want to be, but rather an era where everyone will remain factionless, stagnant, and under her control.

First, Evelyn tries Tris and several of her friends as traitors. While Tris' discovering of the video revealing the people outside of their city is an inconvenience to Evelyn, the trial is less about whether they are actually traitors than it is about getting Tris away from Four.

Luckily for Tris, she can withstand truth serum and comes up with a story to protect her friends. Still, Evelyn quickly lets Tris know that Evelyn is onto her: "I have known the truth far longer than you have, Beatrice Prior. I don't know how you're getting away with this, but I promise you, you will not have a place in my new world, especially not with my son" (Roth, *Insurgent* 191). While it is not unusual for political leaders to use their positions for personal gain or power moves, these moves are not typically so public or against teenagers.

Evelyn institutes rules that allow her factionless followers to seek out and target the smallest of infractions by former faction members—not unlike organizations such as the SS and Hitler Youth of Nazi Germany. In one instance, a former Erudite boy makes the mistake of not mixing colors from the different factions in his wardrobe. A group of factionless bullies are in the process of beating him when Tris discovers them and gives the boy a sweatshirt to alter his uniform, making it acceptable. These infractions and punishments that Evelyn creates work to breed fear and anger among her subjects. In the end, Four confronts Evelyn and tells her the truth about herself: "You . . . you remind me of *him*! . . . I don't care if you don't want to hear it. . . . He was a tyrant in our house and now you're a tyrant in this city, and you can't even see that it's the same!" (Roth, *Allegiant* 463). Four gives her a choice: the city where she can reign supreme but always with the threat of rebellion at her back, or him, a relationship with her son. For all her faults, for all that she has taken from the people and destroyed in the city, at least she chooses wisely in this instance. While this may not ameliorate all of her former actions, Evelyn's choosing Four, putting her relationship with her son first, does show that she has human compassion and empathy. In this way, she is the polar opposite of her husband, Marcus—while he is vested in the best interest of the city's people at the cost of all other relationships, even to the point of physical abuse, she is willing to put her family's needs before those of the city (even if her ideas of what is in the best interest of the city are misguided).

In *Allegiant*, Tris, Four, and several others make their way outside the city limits to see who needs the Divergents so badly.

Outside the gates, they find the Bureau of Genetic Welfare, a government agency whose intention is to rid the world of genetic damage. David, the leader of the Bureau, explains how the United States government manipulated the genes of its citizens with devastating effects, resulting in the Purity War, which he describes as a civil war. However, history is written by the victors, and Dan Krokos argues that "(almost) every conflict can be traced back to one group not liking what another group is doing, or wanting whatever that group has" (123). This war of the Genetically Pure against the Genetically Damaged and the subsequent targeting of the Genetically Damaged is the same Us-versus-Them dichotomy that is seen so often throughout history: the Crusades, Nazi Germany, Rwanda, etc. Essentially, the Purity War is the same war that has happened repeatedly for centuries in one form or another under different guises.

On the other hand, the Bureau of Genetic Welfare has a sculpture in its facility—a large slab of stone with a tank of water above it that releases a few drops every minute or so, slowly and steadily wearing a hollow in the stone's surface. This is symbolic to the bureau of the challenge it faces with healing the Genetically Damaged. Zoe, one of the members of the bureau, describes it: "The slab of stone is the problem we're facing. The tank of water is our potential for changing that problem. And the drop of water is what we're actually able to do, at any given time" (Roth, *Allegiant* 146). The sculpture is hopeful and elicits a feeling of faith in what the bureau is trying to accomplish, even if its methods are questionable.

Really, the bureau cannot be held too accountable for the beginning of the Chicago experiment. Each initial member of the experiment signed a consent form to have a genetic procedure to "heal" him or her, authorize any memory erasing as deemed necessary by the bureau, reproduce within the experiment's framework, and have all of their descendants continue in this way until the bureau deems the experiment no longer needed. The only thing the bureau is not authorized to do by these consent forms— and yet has done and plans to do again—is to reset the memories of future generations with the memory serum. A reset is exactly what

David plans to do after his attack simulation serum failed to work—yes, the serum Jeanine uses to control the Dauntless was provided by the bureau, the very people she was trying to avoid. Rather than having the Abnegation reveal the truth to everyone in Chicago before the bureau is ready, David provides this serum as a stopgap measure, justifying his action on the basis that it would be better to kill a single faction than have the whole experiment fail. Now that the serum hasn't worked and Jeanine is out of power, a reset is the only thing that will save the experiment.

The rebels, those Genetically Damaged living on the fringes between the governmentally controlled lands and the experiments, plan to stop the bureau from resetting the people of the Chicago experiment by stealing their memory serum and destroying it. At least that's what rebel Nita would have Four and Tris believe. In truth, they plan to steal a death serum and release it in aerosol form for wider killing range within the bureau. The rebels aren't wrong for wanting to be treated as equals rather than being labeled as "damaged" because of a genetic fluke generations ago. They even have allies on the inside of the bureau; Matthew, one of the scientists, helps Nita several times until he realizes exactly what it is she is up to: "All this 'genetic damage' nonsense is ridiculous. . . . I thought I was helping her with something smarter," Matthew says. "If I had known I was helping her start another war, I wouldn't have done it. . . . We may have a problem with the way we treat GDs in this country, but it's not going to be solved by killing a bunch of people" (Roth, *Allegiant* 280–1). It is their approach that is too extreme. It was a civil war that isolated and branded the Genetically Damaged several generations ago; more killing is not the solution—protests perhaps, but not killing.

Really, even if the rebels were successful in their attempt, they would only be living up to the expectations of their genetic limitations. As Dan Krokos writes in his essay "Bureaus Versus Rebels," "A person can't believe they're genetically damaged or not. The science is there. And by using deadly force, [Nita] and the rebels are reinforcing the deeply held (though extremely bigoted) belief that genetically damaged individuals are inferior" (126).

There are so many other ways that the rebels could bring about change without resorting to such a drastic level of violence. Their protest and actions will not change their genetic make-up—they cannot hope to be any less damaged or to be treated for a cure; their only hope is to be treated more fairly, and mass murder is probably not the best way to go about getting fair treatment.

The Harry Potter Series

While the characters in authority in *The Hunger Games* and *Divergent* series are primarily in positions of power within the government, Harry Potter encounters men and women with greater authority at every turn—each with the capacity for doing what is right or what is not. In the Harry Potter series, the reader correctly thinks of Voldemort as the primary evil; however, there are others within the novels who fall somewhere on the lower end of the moral spectrum—Rita Skeeter, the journalist who manipulates peoples' words to make the best story; Dudley Dursely, Harry's cousin, who is a bully simply because he was raised to believe that he is better than everyone else; even Draco Malfoy, who cannot bring himself to kill Dumbledore even after taking Voldemort's Dark Mark and knowing that failing means his own death. In order to isolate some of those characters in the Harry Potter series within a position of authority (and for the sake of time and space), the two Ministers of Magic and Albus Dumbledore are the focus here, with special attention to details within the final three novels of the series.[4]

In *The Order of the Phoenix*, when Harry is recovering from watching Cedric Diggory die at the hands of Lord Voldemort during the Triwizard Tournament, his return to the wizarding world makes it apparent that not everyone is keen to believe his story of the Dark Lord's return when his trial for underage magic results in a full hearing in front of the entire Wizengamot. This is a move by the Minister of Magic, Cornelius Fudge, in conjunction with slanderous stories in the wizarding newspaper, *The Daily Prophet*, to spread doubt about Harry's story. While Fudge should be looking out for the wizarding world's best interests and preparing for the return of Voldemort (since he has, in fact, already returned), Fudge is instead "infatuated with tedious ministry regulations and tak[ing] bribes in the form of 'donations' from families such as the Malfoys and then shows them favor over those who do not possess such bloodlines or money" (Gierzynski Ch.1). Fudge is so busy trying to make Harry a scapegoat and keeping Dumbledore from power that he completely overlooks his responsibility as Minister of Magic, and both the wizarding world and the Muggle world suffer for it.

Fudge is the kind of leader who operates just fine if things are running smoothly—he is personable and friendly, if a little befuddled most of the time; it is only when faced with a crisis that Fudge literally lives up to his name and mucks things up by responding in a completely unhelpful way. One of the ways that Fudge responds to the Voldemort Crisis (or in his mind, the Dumbledore Crisis) is to place Dolores Umbridge at Hogwarts as instructor for Defense Against the Dark Arts. This is an attempt to keep an eye on the goings-on at the school as well as to prevent Dumbledore from forming an army among his students to overthrow the ministry. Fudge's placement of Umbridge sets a foul taste for the ministry in Harry's mouth, as Umbridge repeatedly tortures him in detention with a magic quill that uses his own blood to write lines.

At the end of *The Order of the Phoenix*, Fudge is no longer able to deny the return of Voldemort, as Voldemort and his Death Eaters attack Harry and his friends within the very heart of the Ministry of Magic. As a result, Fudge is replaced as Minister of Magic at the beginning of *The Half-Blood Prince* by Rufus Scrimgeour, who was previously Head of the Aurors, which *should* mean that he is a little more prepared to handle the threat of Voldemort. Sadly, he seems more interested in turning Harry from a scapegoat, as Fudge attempted, into a poster boy for the ministry. Scrimgeour seeks out Harry repeatedly to see what he and Dumbledore have been up to, whether or not Harry is truly "the Chosen One" that can save the wizarding world from Voldemort, and to get Harry on Team Scrimgeour:

> "I don't want to be used," said Harry.
> "Some would say it's your duty to be used by the Ministry!"

"You never get it right, do you? Either we've got Fudge, pretending everything's lovely while people get murdered right under his nose, or we've got you, chucking the wrong people into jail and trying to pretend you've got 'the Chosen One' working for you!"

"So you're not 'the Chosen One'?" said Scrimgeour.

"I thought you said it didn't matter either way?" said Harry, with a bitter laugh. "Not to you anyway."

"I shouldn't have said that," said Scrimgeour quickly. "It was tactless—"

"No, it was honest," said Harry. "One of the only honest things you've said to me. You don't care whether I live or die, but you do care that I help you convince everyone you're winning the war against Voldemort. I haven't forgotten, Minister. . ."

He raised his right fist. There, shining white on the back of his cold hand, were the scars which Dolores Umbridge had forced him to carve into his own flesh: *I must not tell lies.*

(Rowling, *Half-Blood Prince* 346–7)

Luckily, Harry is smart enough to see that Scrimgeour wants his face and his name without actually wanting his help, and he is brave enough to point that out to Scrimgeour. This behavior from the minister is particularly disappointing because of his previous post as head Auror, which should have better prepared him for dealing with Death Eaters and the probable return of Lord Voldemort.

Scrimgeour's abuse of Harry and his friends continues in *The Deathly Hallows*, when he holds the items Dumbledore left for them upon his death so that the ministry can inspect them for dark magic, as though Dumbledore would be dabbling in the dark arts. He underestimates, however, Hermione's knowledge of the law as she challenges the ministry's right to withhold their inheritances. Scrimgeour knows that the items are somehow integral to defeating Voldemort, but he and the Aurors have not been able to figure out how, and he has held them illegally. Still, he continues to question Harry, Ron, and Hermione, hoping to find some clue as to the relics Dumbledore left them. They argue until Scrimgeour loses his patience and singes Harry's shirt with the tip of his wand:

"Remembered you're not at school, have you?" said Scrimgeour, breathing hard into Harry's face. "Remembered that I am not Dumbledore, who forgave your insolence and insubordination? You may wear that scar like a crown, Potter, but it is not up to a seventeen-year-old boy to tell me how to do my job! It's time you learned some respect!" "It's time you earned it," said Harry. (Rowling, *Deathly Hallows* 130)

Gierzynski addresses the importance of Harry's dealings with the ministry, and Scrimgeour in particular, explaining that the boy does not become cynical in his dealings with those in authority within the Ministry of Magic; instead Harry and his friends "try to get to the truth, to hold on to hope, to see the good in *most* everyone, and to trust those who have shown themselves trustworthy" (Chapter 1, emphasis mine). Harry's refusal to become jaded or cynical is hugely important as leadership changes—Fudge is not a good leader, and Scrimgeour is not a good leader; however, that does not mean there will never be a Minister of Magic who can be a good leader.

One of the people whom Harry trusts implicitly is Albus Dumbledore, headmaster of Hogwarts. Of course, there are moments when Harry is angry with Dumbledore (there are times he has every reason to be angry, such as each time Dumbledore withholds information from him). Dumbledore has a longstanding reputation for his great achievements and for being a wonderful wizard overall. His memorial in the newspaper, written by Elphias Doge, reads that Dumbledore "was never proud or vain; he could find value in anyone, however apparently insignificant or wretched, and I believe that his early losses endowed him with great humanity and sympathy" (Rowling, *Deathly Hallows* 20). However, shortly after his death, a biography is published that sheds light on some of Dumbledore's darker history.

In his youth, Dumbledore befriended Grindelwald, the very dark wizard that he would someday defeat, and shared in his schemes of a world where wizards ruled over Muggles. The biography even reprinted a letter that Dumbledore wrote to Grindelwald:

Yes, we have been given power and yes, that power gives us the right to rule, but it also gives us responsibilities over the ruled. We must stress this point, it will be the foundation stone upon which we build. Where we are opposed, as we surely will be, this must be the basis of all our counterarguments. We seize control FOR THE GREATER GOOD. And from this it follows that where we meet resistance, we must use only the force that is necessary and no more. (Rowling, *Deathly Hallows* 357, emphasis original)

Shortly after this, Dumbledore's sister, who suffered a traumatic attack as a child and could not control her magic, was killed by Dumbledore, Grindelwald, or Dumbledore's brother, Aberforth, after she tried to stop an argument among them and her magic got out of control. Following her death, Grindelwald departed Dumbledore's life until the two met again as enemies, and Aberforth and Dumbledore became estranged.

Dumbledore's history is important because it allows Harry to see that even the very best of us are flawed—it is all right to make mistakes. Dumbledore learns from the mistakes that he has made and spends the rest of his life making amends. As his memorial states, Dumbledore is able to find value in anyone, and he consistently encourages Harry to do the same, particularly in regard to Severus Snape, of whom Harry is distrustful. Dumbledore's view shifts from a wizard-controlled worldview to one of more equality, one where house-elves are free and centaurs can teach in wizard academies. Although Dumbledore teaches Harry a great many things, perhaps one of the most important is that people are capable of change for good.

Dumbledore, unlike any of the other characters discussed previously, is offered a chance to explain his choices when he meets Harry again at the ethereal King's Cross in *Deathly Hallows*. Dumbledore explains that, like Voldemort, he wanted to conquer death—when he was forced to return home to care for his sister, he was drawn in by Grindelwald and the tales of the Deathly Hallows. Dumbledore dreamed of power over death so that he could bring his parents back, and he then would be free of the responsibility of taking care of his siblings. Instead, Dumbledore lost his sister,

Ariana, and his relationship with his brother, Aberforth. He had great power and was offered the post of Minister of Magic several times, but Dumbledore also learned from his mistakes and "learned that [he] was not to be trusted with power" (Rowling, *Deathly Hallows* 717).

Dumbledore acknowledges that even late in life, he is still tempted by the idea of controlling death. In finding the Resurrection Stone that Voldemort had bound as a Horcrux, Dumbledore admits,

> I lost my head, Harry. I quite forgot that it was now a Horcrux, that the ring was sure to carry a curse. I picked it up, and I put it on and for a second I imagined that I was about to see Ariana, and my mother, and my father, and to tell them how very, very sorry I was. . . . I was such a fool, Harry. After all those years I had learned nothing. (Rowling, *Deathly Hallows* 719–20)

Dumbledore's honesty illustrates that even the very best of us struggle with doing what is right sometimes, and sometimes we fail. However, this never stops Dumbledore from continuing to try do what is right at the next step—what is right for him, what is right for the world, wizard and Muggle alike—by his willingness to sacrifice himself and asking Harry to be brave enough to do the same.

In most dystopian fiction, readers come to the story after the "end" has already happened—whether the war between the districts has led to the Hunger Games or manipulation of genetics has led to closed city experiments with the Genetically Damaged—readers are witnessing the fallout of the event rather than the event itself. For millennials, September 11, 2001, was the end event, and they lived through it. Gierzysnki writes "all stories contain lessons we may learn; all characters in those stories have traits and values we may try to emulate" (Conclusion). Millenials are looking to these young adult dystopian novels for context, for role models; however, there are also those characters who are, at times, morally corrupt that we could take a lesson from as well. When we see leaders or those in authority acting in such a way outside the pages of a novel, we should sit up, take notice, and keep a very close eye on the situation before real life becomes too much like fiction; this is especially true in a post-9/11 world.

Notes

1.   While the Harry Potter series is more specifically fantasy, there are enough elements of the dystopian genre to categorize the series as dystopian for the purposes of this essay, particularly within the last three novels when Voldemort's success would truly mean the end of the wizarding world as Harry knows it.

2.   Perhaps the most morally ambiguous character in The Hunger Games trilogy is Gale Hawthorne. While his passion for freedom and justice is in the right place, he is quick to take to developing ways to utilize his hunting and trapping skills for war. In fact, it is his bomb that ultimately ends the rebellion, killing many of the Capitol's children and Katniss' sister, Prim. A full discussion of Gale's moral character deserves its own essay.

3.   The use of serum is a fairly common motif in the history of the dystopian genre. Citizens are given a daily dose of serum in *The Giver* by Lois Lowry, and the use of serum is at least as old as Aldous Huxley's *Brave New World*.

4.   Discussion of Severus Snape would fit in ideally here, as he is an authority figure as an instructor, and he is rife with moral conflict; however, Snape's convoluted morals deserve their own essay.

Works Cited

Ames, Melissa. "Engaging 'Apolitical' Adolescents: Analyzing the Popularity and Educational Potential of Dystopian Literature Post 9/11." *The High School Journal* 97.1 (Fall 2013): 3–20. *One Search.* Web. 20 Nov. 2014.

Collins, Suzanne. *Catching Fire*. New York: Scholastic, 2009.

_____. *The Hunger Games*. New York: Scholastic, 2008.

_____. *Mockingjay*. New York: Scholastic, 2010.

Gann, Linda A., & Karen Gavigan. "The Other Side of Dark." *Voice of Youth Advocates* 35 (August 2012): 234–238. *One Search.* Web. 20 Nov. 2014.

Gierzynski, Anthony. *Harry Potter and the Millenials: Research Methods and the Politics of the Muggle Generation*. Baltimore: Johns Hopkins UP, 2013. Kindle edition.

Pavlik, Anthony. "Absolute Power Games." *Of Bread, Blood and The Hunger Games: Critical Essays on the Suzanne Collins Trilogy*. Eds. Mary F. Pharr & Leisa A. Clark. London: McFarland, 2012.

Roth, Veronica. *Allegiant*. New York: HarperCollins, 2013.

_____. *Divergent*. New York: HarperCollins, 2011.

_____. *Insurgent*. New York: HarperCollins, 2012.

Rowling, J.K. *Harry Potter and the Deathly Hallows*. New York: Scholastic, 2007.

_____. *Harry Potter and the Half Blood Prince*. New York: Scholastic, 2005.

_____. *Harry Potter and the Order of the Phoenix*. New York: Scholastic, 2003.

Sicher, Efraim, & Natalia Skradol. "A World Neither Brave Nor New: Reading Dystopian Fiction after 9/11." *Partial Answers: Journal of Literature and the History of Ideas* 4.1 (Jan. 2006): 151–179. *One Search*. Web. 20 Nov. 2014.

Springen, Karen. "Apocalypse Now." *Publishers Weekly* 15 Feb. 2010 (257.7): 21–24. *One Search*. Web. 20 Nov. 2014.

CRITICAL
READINGS

Mums Are Good: Harry Potter and Traditional Depictions of Women_____

Jeanne Hoeker LaHaie

Hermione Granger, Ginny Weasley, and even Luna Lovegood are brave, smart, nurturing and capable, and when the Harry Potter novels were first published, they were nearly unique in fantasy fiction, which tended to rely almost exclusively on male characters. As role models, they represent a wide range of possibilities for young women; however, the adult female characters in the series are more likely to be defined according to their ability to nurture or to be "motherly" than by their magical, intellectual, or leadership capabilities. This leaves readers with a generational disconnect and raises questions about the roles available to the adolescent characters when they reach maturity.

There are many aspects of Rowling's work that tend toward traditional depictions of women. Ann Alston notes, for example, that

> Rowling's texts have adhered to the conservative conventions of children's literature: Harry, the Cinderella-type orphan figure, is left with the 'bad' family as exemplified by the Dursleys, but escapes to Hogwarts School, which acts as an alternative family, and to the 'good' family epitomized by the Weasleys. (136)

The ideal of home as a place of safety and security is a common one in fantasy literature written for adolescents, and the symbol of this kind of home is the "good" mother. Alston also notes, "The home, like the idealized mother, is not bitter or angry, but patiently awaits the character/child's return; it is always there offering security and stability" (79). This may seem contradictory to what happens in the Harry Potter series, since Harry lives in a home in which the other occupants are nearly always angry with him, would prefer he did not return, and make Harry feel anything but safe. But Harry's lack of an adequate home with the Dursleys draws attention to the home Harry had before his parents died, which is mirrored, although not exactly duplicated, in Harry's Hogwarts "family" and also in his interactions with the Weasleys, who treat him like an adopted child.

The centrality of home, however, is not the only factor in Rowling's adherence to traditional representations of the feminine. The Harry Potter series combines the genre of the romantic hero fantasy with the school story and adds a satirical bent. These genres traditionally feature male protagonists, making other possibilities difficult to imagine, or at least not immediately apparent to writers working within the genre. In fact, Maria Nikolajeva argues, "It is not a coincidence that Rowling has chosen a male protagonist for her saga. The romantic narrative is by definition masculine, and any contemporary attempts to place a female character in a masculine plot merely results in a simple gender permutation, creating 'a hero in drag'" (137). Nikolajeva's assertion somewhat overstates the necessity of the male hero because, while the medieval romances to which she refers do feature men exclusively in the role of hero, children's fantasy draws from them rather than mimics them, making a female hero unlikely, but not impossible.[1] Tison Pugh and David Wallace further assert, "Hero stories are gendered as well as school stories, and the heroism demanded for the protagonist of these narratives typically depends upon an alpha-male model of masculinity that systemically marginalizes most other characters, especially in relation to gender and sexual orientation difference" (261). In other words, the hero story demands a male character who is traditionally masculine, and it rejects others. While critics often draw attention to the Harry Potter books as a modern reincarnation of the school story as it was made popular by Thomas Hughes' *Tom Brown's School Days* (1857),[2] few have made the connection between the use of these genres and the lack of diverse and empowered adult females in the series.

There are, of course, other reasons why the books are problematic in terms of gender, and critics have been quick to note them. Elizabeth Heilman, for example, argues that although the books can be read from multiple viewpoints, it's important to recognize the most dominant ones, and they are mostly traditional. She further argues that much of the popularity of the books can be attributed to the "comfort" of these stereotypes and that, while "any one gender stereotype would not be significant, repeated and varied examples of demeaning stereotypes are very significant. In addition, these gender ideologies are especially powerful because the books are pleasurable and popular" (Heilman 235). Pugh and Wallace concur, writing, "These texts invite readers to enter their fantastic world with considerable readerly pleasure, but the ultimately regressive gender roles bear the potential to harm readers as well" (263). Here, they essentially argue that the books support rather than challenge acceptable behavior for men and women, and the enjoyment readers derive from the series is potentially problematic because it may cause them to overlook troublesome gender representations. Additionally, the texts continually present readers with flashes of fully empowered female figures, girls and women, distracting readers from the more consistently traditional depictions of females. Rowling exclusively utilizes male characters within the main arc of the story, relegating even powerful female figures to support roles. The degree to which girl characters in the series are empowered varies, as do the adult female figures who provide diverse blueprints for adulthood.

Rowling creates girl characters who have a great deal more agency than their counterparts from earlier fiction. In "Hermione Granger and the Heritage of Gender," Eliza Dresang points out that "There is no unified one best way for a woman to be, no feminist ideal that can be articulated and applied. Instead the ideal for a female is to become what she wants to be with concern and respect for both self and others" (241). The girls who populate Rowling's work represent a wide variety of models for what it means to be a girl; Ginny is brave; Cho is athletic; Luna is what might generously be called intuitive; Fleur turns out to be loyal and brave; and Hermione is intelligent, resourceful, and talented. Nonetheless, even though Rowling's portrayal of these girls is more nuanced and positive than her portrayal of adult women, these characters still do not represent fully-empowered girls. Heilman points out, for instance, that girls are nearly always presented in groups rather than as individuals: "This repeated grouping [of girls] reinforces a tendency for readers to interpret females as types rather than individuals. It also reinforces the idea of the sociological construct of the communal and friendly girl compared to the individual and competitive boy" (228).

While there are certainly positive aspects to the idea that girls work in community rather than individually, the problem for Heilman is the fact that, "[t]hough they are portrayed as giggly, emotional, gossipy, and anti-intellectual, many of the girls are very hazy characters. Certain traits do not seem to be authoritatively owned by any one female character, but, instead, are presented in groups" (227). At issue here is the idea that most girls in the series are not clearly developed and are instead defined by stereotypes that are very often coded negatively, such as "giggly," "emotional," "gossipy," and "anti-intellectual."

Another issue with girls in the novels is the extent to which they exercise their own agency rather than simply supporting the patriarchal status quo. After describing the scene in *Chamber of Secrets*, when Harry fights the basilisk with the sword of Gryffindor, Andrew Blake argues, "[T]his episode indicates, whatever the gestures toward equality, in the end the stories represent a patriarchal world, in which power is exercised by individual males and transmitted to other males—whether they are 'good' (Dumbledore) or 'bad' (Voldemort)" (43). In this case, Harry's loyalty to Dumbledore leads Fawkes the phoenix to bring Harry the sorting hat, which in turn leads to Harry pulling Gryffindor's sword from the hat. The line from Gryffindor to Dumbledore to Harry Potter is an exclusively male one. Other critics have pointed out the fact that Hermione's intelligence and talents are generally used in support of Harry's adventures. Heilman has specifically noted, "Hermione is primarily an enabler of Harry's and Ron's adventures, rather than an adventurer in her own right....Hermione's knowledge is important, but it is primarily used for Harry's adventures, not her own" (224). While there are certainly some places in the books wherein Hermione acts on her own or in concert with other girls for aims other than male adventure,[3] the central fantasy plot concerns the exploits of men and boys with support from women and girls.

Girls

As the principal female figure in the series, Hermione Granger's example is the most crucial, and critics are divided on the topic of her empowerment or agency. While Nikolajeva states, "I see nothing sexist in [Hermione being Harry's helper], at least no more than any male heroic tale is by definition sexist. Hermione and her intelligence are simply part of Harry's entourage, alongside magic wands and flying brooms" (131). Other critics have pointed out serious issues with Hermione's role in the series; for example, Dresang argues that the language used to describe Hermione and her actions marks her as a girl stereotype. She notes, "Repeatedly Rowling has Hermione 'shriek,' 'squeak,' 'wail,' 'squeal,' and 'whimper,' verbs never applied to the male characters in the book" (Dresang 223), and as a result, "[t]he language that constructs the roles played by Harry and Ron is much calmer, more reasoned, despite the fact that Hermione is the problem solver" (223). Indeed, the moments in which Hermione is portrayed as a silly little girl are often at odds with her otherwise logical and intelligent persona. Dresang explains, "Her hysteria and crying happen far too often to be considered a believable part of the development of Hermione's character and are quite out of line with her core role in the book. They add nothing to an understanding of her persona or its individual caricature, nor, for the most part, anything to the story" (223). However, Dresang also points to empowered aspects of Hermione's character, noting that she "appears armed to withstand the most dangerous gender-related pitfall and not retreat into silence, intimidated by the masculine world" (229). This is in reference to Hermione's responding to Malfoy's teasing with a cutting remark, but there are several other instances where Hermione stands up for herself and for what she believes to be right. In fact, much of her value to the trio is her ability to see moral imperatives more clearly than either Harry or Ron is apt to while in the midst of a crisis or adventure. Ultimately, the character of Hermione is stereotypically feminine in many ways; however, that does not necessarily mean that her character is not also an empowered one, particularly given the dictates of the school story and heroic fantasy genres. Dresang sums this up concisely when she writes,

"Hermione is not a feminist model for engagement in sisterhood and is the antithesis of a strong female in the 'shrillness' with which Rowling has at times portrayed her. But Hermione is seeking what she wants to become with a healthy concern and respect for both self and others" (241). Hermione provides one model of female behavior that is valid, even as it is often traditional but also evolving.

Nonetheless, Rowling includes a very telling episode in *The Goblet of Fire* with Hermione's development of the Society for the Promotion of Elfish Welfare, or S.P.E.W.. In this storyline, not only do Harry and Ron censure Hermione, the narrator and the narrative structure combine to make Hermione seem ridiculous, which portends the shutting down of opportunity for Hermione as an adult woman who demonstrates volition. It is important to note here that Hermione's cause is a just one, a fact made clear when Hermione first becomes aware that Hogwarts meals are prepared by house-elves. She says, "Slave Labor… That's what made this dinner. *Slave Labor*" (Rowling, *Goblet of Fire* 182, emphasis original). Furthermore, at the end of *The Order of the Phoenix*, when Harry complains that Kreacher, a house-elf, had been the source of Sirius' death and Hermione had defended the elf, Dumbledore, whose voice is closest to Rowling's, tells Harry, "She was quite right… I warned Sirius when we adopted twelve Grimmauld Place as our headquarters that Kreacher must be treated with kindness and respect. I also told him that Kreacher could be dangerous to us. I do not think that Sirius took me very seriously, or that he ever saw Kreacher as a being with feelings as acute as a human's—" (Rowling, *Order of the Phoenix* 832). Dumbledore goes on to tell Harry, "[Kreacher] was forced to do Sirius' bidding, because Sirius was the last of the family to which he was enslaved" (832). These passages suggest that the house-elves could be seen as magical equivalents of the literary figure of the "Happy Darkie," who appeared in late nineteenth- and early twentieth-century American and British cultural artifacts. Edward Margolies explains in "The Image of the Primitive in Black Letters" (1970):

In popular literary terms a primitive usually connotes a dark-skinned person (most often an Indian or Negro) who lives close to nature, his emotions, or impulses, and is incapable of submitting himself to the restraints of reason and 'civilization.' Insofar as Indians or Negroes represented no immediate physical or psychic danger to the workaday white American they were frequently portrayed as noble savages or happy-go-lucky darkies. (67)

This closely coincides with Rowling's house-elf dialogue from *The Goblet of Fire*: "'Begging your pardon, miss," said the house-elf, bowing deeply again, 'but house-elves has no right to be unhappy when there is work to be done and masters to be served'" (538). The fact that Rowling depicts Hermione as a character who recognizes the connection between the status of the house-elves and the status of other oppressed peoples is seemingly counteracted by the manner in which Hermione's activism is treated by the narrator and her peers. What could be a place in the narrative where Hermione is not only rewarded for enlightened thinking, but also is laying the foundation for a career as a public advocate, becomes instead a site of frustration.

The problems with Hermione's activism become apparently immediately. The letters S.P.E.W. are naturally read as "spew," a fact that a highly intelligent young woman such as Hermione should have figured out before naming her group, particularly since the name suggests an irrational rant rather than an important social movement. When Ron complains about having to work hard and says that he feels like a house-elf, Hermione tells him,

> "Well, now that you understand what dreadful lives they lead, perhaps you'll be a bit more active in S.P.E.W.! . . . You know, maybe it wouldn't be a bad idea to show people exactly how horrible it is to clean all the time—we could do a sponsored scrub of Gryffindor common room, all proceeds to S.P.E.W., it would raise awareness as well as funds—." (Rowling, *Goblet of Fire* 159)

Ron makes fun of Hermione secretly when he whispers to Harry, "I'll sponsor you to shut up about *spew*" (Rowling, *Goblet of Fire*

159). This scene is typical of Hermione's friends' reactions to her activism. Also, the first adult Hermione tries to recruit, Hagrid, tells her, "It'd be doin' 'em an unkindness, Hermione . . . . It's in their nature to look after humans, that's what they like, see? Yeh'd be makin' 'em unhappy ter take away their work, an' insultin' 'em if yeh tried ter pay 'em" (Rowling, *Goblet of Fire* 265). This incident is especially worthy of note because Hagrid's mother is a giant, and he encounters great difficulties because many people believe by nature he must be blood-thirsty and untrustworthy.

In the following book, *Order of the Phoenix*, Hermione hatches a ridiculous scheme to free the house-elves against their will when she knits "misshapen wooly objects" (255) that are supposed to be hats. She hides them where the cleaning elves are likely to pick them up because house-elves can be freed only by being presented with clothes. Later Hermione begins to increase her output by using magic, and she branches off into socks. She is delighted when the garments disappear, but her lack of success is revealed when Harry sees Dobby, one of two free house-elves at Hogwarts, wearing "what looked like all the hats that Hermione had ever knitted; he was wearing one on top of the other, so that his head seemed elongated by two or three feet" (Rowling, *Order of the Phoenix* 384–385). Dobby tells Harry that none of the other house-elves "will clean Gryffindor Tower anymore, not with the hats and socks hidden everywhere, they finds them insulting, sir" (385). Hermione's project is not only ridiculed by her friends: it is completely ineffectual.

Even if one were to offer up a very charitable reading of Rowling's treatment of the house-elves in which Hermione's mistake could be seen as her attempt to impose Muggle values upon the magical world, this is still the only time Rowling depicts a young girl engaged in social activism, and it is an utter failure. In fact, Farah Mendlesohn writes, "Radicalism, as embodied in Hermione, is irrational, ignorant, and essentially transient. Stasis and a conformity to a certain status quo bolster success, justice, and peace, whereas positive action to change matters is always ascribed at best to foolishness and at worst to evil intent" (181). Hermione's inability to navigate effectively the important political process of agitating for change, particularly since Rowling portrays her as ridiculous, points to her likely lack of agency as an adult. This is further reinforced in Hermione's constantly care-giving and vigilant attention to Harry and Ron. In *Goblet of Fire*, Rowling writes, "Hermione began doling beef casserole onto each of their plates" (207). In *Half-Blood Prince*, after Hermione thinks she sees Harry giving Ron an illegal potion so he can win at Quidditch, she says, "Ron, I warn you, don't drink it!" (293), and in *Deathly Hallows* when she, Harry, and Ron are forced to go into hiding, she tells them, "It's okay...I've got clothes for both of you" (161). In fact, she packs everything they could possibly need. These examples are only a small sampling of the dozens in each book. Hermione's nurturing behavior is so consistent, when Rowling presents Hermione as a wife and mother of two in the postscript to the series, the depiction seems to be the only plausible choice. In this short section, Hermione is portrayed as a nurturing mother when she reassures her children about going to school, and readers also learn that as a wife she is either easily duped by her husband or that she humors him when Ron admits to Harry that he lied to Hermione about passing his driving test. Her position in the Department of Magical Law Enforcement, which Rowling has mentioned in interviews, is secondary to her motherly role and is not even included in the books. Although Rowling portrays a variety of adult women in her texts—career women, full time caregivers, and others—the defining characteristic for nearly all of them is the extent to which they follow the traditional stereotype of the nurturing woman.

Nurturing Women

Among the most conventional women in the series are Molly Weasley and Lily Potter. Both women sacrifice the entirety of their lives for their children, Lily because she literally gives her life and Molly because her life is consumed by taking care of her family. I would also include in this group Minerva McGonagall as a maternal substitute, who "is concerned that the students get enough sleep and stay well" (Heilman 225). Lily is separated from her child by death before the series begins, and McGonagall is separated from the children by the rules guiding student/teacher relations, so Molly Weasley becomes the role model for what a good mother should be. Molly Weasley derives a certain kind of power and authority from her relationship with her children and Harry, even while they might not always appreciate her overprotectiveness. One place where this is particularly apparent, although her nature remains consistent throughout all seven books, is in *The Order of the Phoenix*, when she tries to act like a parent to Harry and to forbid him information about the Order's activities. When Sirius overrules her, Rowling writes, "Harry did not look at Mrs. Weasley. He had been touched by what she had said about his being as good as a son, but he was also impatient at her mollycoddling" (Rowling, *Order of the Phoenix* 90). Sarah Fiona Winters points out that "Molly's coddling is, if not legitimized, eventually forgiven by the series because unlike Umbridge, and unlike the paranoid parents found in best-selling critiques of child raising, she at least fears the right danger" (224). Additionally, Molly tries to protect Harry by limiting his access to information and thus keeping him innocent, as she believes a child should be. Mrs. Weasley's fear and protective instincts for her children reach their apex in *Deathly Hallows* in the final battle, when Bellatrix is fighting Hermione, Ginny, and Luna at the same time, and she nearly hits Ginny with a killing curse. Before Harry, the hero, can save Ginny, Mrs. Weasley yells, "NOT MY DAUGHTER, YOU BITCH!'" (Rowling, *Deathly Hallows* 736) and begins dueling Bellatrix with skill unrevealed to that point. Bellatrix taunts Molly, asking, "'What will happen to your children when I've killed you?'" (736), but this allows Molly to draw even more heavily upon her motherly reserves of power. She screams, "'You—will—never—touch—our—children—again!'" (736) and curses Bellatrix to death. Under other circumstances, such fighting between two powerful and angry women might seem titillating, but Molly is so coded as "mother" that the scene rather emphasizes the power of the maternal. Ximena Gallardo and Jason Smith point out, "We are to understand that Lestrange does not stand a chance against Molly Weasley because the latter is fighting for more than herself: she is fighting for her children" (97). Unfortunately, this effect is somewhat spoiled when Voldemort tries to kill Molly in revenge, and Harry magically protects her with a shield charm, indicating that Mrs. Weasley's power is limited to motherhood, and she needs a male to protect her.

Not all critics see Molly Weasley so positively. In discussing the typical reactions of the Weasley children when they receive new hand-knit sweaters each Christmas, John Kornfield and Laurie Prothro argue that the "lack of respect that Mrs. Weasley receives from her children" is "[p]articularly disturbing" (189) because the sweaters "are a standing joke throughout the series, eliciting derision rather than appreciation for the care and love that they represent" (190). They further argue that the children, or rather the boys, constantly get into trouble and challenge authority, while Mrs. Weasley seems unable to stop it, and Mr. Weasley is rather more fascinated than upset by the things they do, when either parent is actually aware of the children's antics. If Mrs. Weasley's character represents a wholly negative stereotype, then Kornfield and Prothro's statement is undoubtedly valid; however, it fails to take into consideration that rather than being simply an outmoded character type, as she appears in the satirical sketches of her, Mrs. Weasley provides one kind of positive role model. Her children do sneak and get into trouble, but they are never openly disrespectful, and they are likewise unhappy when she is angry with them—not because they will be getting into trouble, but because she is their mother and they care about her. One example from *Chamber of Secrets* demonstrates this point. When George, Fred, and Ron rescue Harry from his aunt and uncle's house using their father's bewitched car, they come home to find their mother is aware that they have been gone and has been very worried. Rowling writes, "All three of Mrs. Weasley's sons were taller than she was, but they cowered as her rage broke over them" (Rowling, *Chamber of Secrets* 33). She sentences the children to de-gnoming the garden, which they do without much complaint. The children do not fear her anger because they are physically afraid of her or because she could force them to do chores; rather, they do not wish to make their mother unhappy, and they willingly do what she tells them to do in order to be restored to her good graces. The problem is not that Molly Weasley is stereotypically maternal—the greater issue is that she, and the other nurturing women in the series, provide the only positive models for what grown females should be. Rowling is harshly critical of almost every other kind of woman.

Non-Maternal Women

Rowling reserves her most critical treatment for those women who are not nurturing, including two mothers who do not actually appear in the series: the mothers of Sirius Black and Tom Riddle. Mrs. Black rejects her son when he chooses to go against family traditions, and Merope gives birth to Tom but is not strong enough to stay alive and raise him. The most despicable characters, however, are those who are not motherly at all, particularly Bellatrix Lestrange, Sybil Trelawney, Rita Skeeter, and Dolores Umbridge. Bellatrix is an uncomplicatedly evil character who resides in Azkaban prison for much of the series. In *Half-Blood Prince*, however, she is introduced to readers when she accompanies her sister, Narcissa Malfoy, on a visit to Professor Snape to beg him to protect Narcissa's son from having to carry out a task he has been assigned by Lord Voldemort. When Narcissa bemoans the fact that her son is being used for a task beyond his ability, Bellatrix "ruthlessly" says "You should be proud! . . . If I had sons, I would be glad to give them up to the service of the Dark Lord!" (Rowling, *Half-Blood Prince* 35). In Rowling's world, the worst that can be said for a woman is that she would choose anyone or anything over her own children. In the final book of the series, Bellatrix is labeled as Voldemort's "last, best Lieutenant" (Rowling, *Deathly Hallows* 737), a position that marks her as completely evil. Thus her lack of maternity or maternal feelings, even for her own nephew, seems a necessary component of her dark persona.

Rita Skeeter is another unpleasant adult female character, but rather than being motivated by dark purposes, she acts according to ambition. Most of her participation in the series happens in *Goblet of Fire*, when she comes to Hogwarts to cover the Triwizard Tournament. Rowling describes: "Her hair was set in elaborate and curiously rigid curls that contrasted oddly with her heavy-jawed face. She wore jeweled spectacles. The thick fingers clutching her crocodile-skin handbag ended in two-inch nails, painted crimson" (303). Her appearance is that of a worldly woman, and she lacks any positive characteristic, particularly the ability to nurture. She makes up sensational stories in order to sell newspapers and build her reputation as a writer, even when those stories cause great harm to others. One example of this is when she illegally utilizes her ability to become an animagus beetle and overhears Hagrid confess to his giant parentage. This leads to an outcry against Hagrid and a call for him to be fired. Likewise, she tells sympathetic stories about Harry before turning on him and calling him "Disturbed and Dangerous" (Rowling, *Goblet of Fire* 611). Rita Skeeter may not be on Voldemort's side, but she is still a thoroughly bad character who is selfish to the point of exclusively taking care of her own interests at the expense of nearly everyone she encounters.

Sybil Trelawney is quite different from either Bellatrix or Rita Skeeter because instead of seeking power in socially unacceptable ways, she is nearly powerless and mostly pathetic. Rather than nurturing the students in her care, she most often falsely predicts their untimely demise. When the students meet her in their third year, she looks like "a large, glittering insect" (Rowling, *Prisoner of Azkaban* 102). And in the very first class, she tells Parvati Patil to "beware a red-haired man," and Harry that he has "The Grim," the "giant, spectral dog that haunts churchyards! My dear boy, it is an omen—the worst omen—of *death!*" (107). Throughout the series, readers become aware that she is a terrible teacher, an inconsistent seer, and an alcoholic. In *Order of the Phoenix*, Professor Umbridge fires her, and Rowling writes,

> Professor Trelawney was standing in the middle of the entrance hall with her wand in one hand and an empty sherry bottle in the other, looking utterly mad. Her hair was sticking up on end, her glasses were lopsided so that one eye was magnified more than the other; her innumerable shawls and scarves were trailing haphazardly from her shoulders, giving the impression that she was falling apart at the seams. (294)

In this scene, Trelawney seems pathetic and helpless, a foil for the maternal Professor McGonagall, who comes to the rescue. Even so, while readers may be led to pity this character, Rowling does not encourage sympathy for her. In fact, Trelawney does deserve to be fired because she is a poor teacher, but Rowling also makes her unlikable because she does not nurture the students in her care. Trewlawney is particularly harsh with Hermione because, in contrast to nearly every other teacher in the school who all find Hermione particularly bright, Trelawney angrily tells her, "'I am sorry to say that from the moment you have arrived in this class, my dear, it has been apparent that you do not have what the noble art of Divination requires. Indeed, I don't remember ever meeting a student whose mind was so hopelessly mundane'" (Rowling, *Prisoner of Azkaban* 398). When Hermione acts disrespectfully toward Trelawney, the teacher reacts as might be expected from a fellow student rather than from an adult in whose care Hermione has been placed. Harry and Ron even feel pity for Trelawney after Umbridge has been horrible during a class inspection, "—until she swooped down on them a few seconds later" (315) and began to predict Harry's "gruesome and early death . . . .at the top of her voice" (315). Lestrange, Skeeter, and Trelawney are all marked as negative characters, not only because of their actions, but also because of their inability to nurture or to be motherly. None of them, however, is designed to discomfit readers in the same way as Dolores Umbridge.

Rowling introduces Umbridge in *The Order of the Phoenix*, and before readers are given more than her name, she is described:

> [S]he looked just like a large, pale toad. She was rather squat with a broad, flabby face, as little neck as Uncle Vernon, and a very wide, slack mouth. Her eyes were large, round, and slightly bulging. Even the little black velvet bow perched on top of her short curly hair put [Harry] in mind of a large fly she was about to catch on a long sticky tongue. (146)

Shortly thereafter, she speaks "in a fluttery, girlish, high-pitched voice" (Rowling, *Order of the Phoenix* 146). I would argue that the reason Umbridge repulses readers is not only because she is unattractive, power-hungry, racist, and cruel, but most of all because all these unpleasant aspects of her are paired with an overt femininity. Together these traits are at odds with lingering Victorian expectations for proper behavior in women. Gallardo and Smith argue,

> Umbridge's most obvious pretense is her disquieting performance of femininity. Her soft, "girlish" voice, demure manners, feminine attire, and collections of plates decorated with mewling kittens are all props in her crusade for power and control. Tricked out in fluffy pink sweaters and hair bows, Umbridge mimics the ideal of the proper, ultraconservative woman who consolidates her power behind the scenes. (94)

The critics' analysis assumes that Umbridge's gender performance is "pretense"—presumably to a greater extent than other women and girl characters in the series "perform" as female. In *Gender Trouble*, Judith Butler argues that gender identity is formed through the performance of deeds: "There is not gender identity behind the expressions of gender; that identity is performatively constituted by the very 'expressions' that are said to be its results" (34). A person's actions rather than his or her body, then, create gender identity. Therefore, the reason that Umbridge seems unpleasant is not so much that she performs in a way that is coded as distinctly feminine, but rather that this performance is coupled with other acts that are coded as "male"—particularly her quest for power, her penchant for violence and even torture, and her unwillingness or inability to nurture. Umbridge's performance, therefore, controverts the concept of nurture.

The first instance in which Rowling depicts Umbridge combining a girlish persona with a performance that is coded as traditionally masculine is during Harry's hearing for underage use of magic in *The Order of the Phoenix*. The Minister of Magic, Cornelius Fudge, is quite flustered by Dumbledore's defense of Harry. During the hearing he "snapped," "snarled," "blustered," and "shouted" (Rowling, *Order of the Phoenix* 147–148). Umbridge, however, responds quite differently: "'I'm sure I must have misunderstood you, Professor Dumbledore,' she said with a simper that left her big, round eyes as cold as ever. 'So silly of me. But it sounded for a teensy moment as though you were suggesting that the Ministry of Magic had ordered an attack on this boy!'" (147). This passage contrasts the emotional outbursts of the male authority figure with Umbridge's firm control, which seems at once both feminine (simper) and masculine (cold). Her quest for power also leads her to Hogwarts, where she goes from being a professor to high inquisitor to headmistress. In each instance, she utilizes power she derives from her position to carry out her own agenda, while positioning herself for further advancement. As a teacher, she punishes Harry by making him use a special quill to write lines that "cut into his skin as though traced there by a scalpel" (267). As high inquisitor, she initiates a series of "Educational Decrees" designed to ensure her total control over the students at Hogwarts and ending with 'Educational Decree Number Twenty-Eight," which reads, "Dolores Jane Umbridge (High Inquisitor) has replaced Albus Dumbledore as Head of Hogwarts School of Witchcraft and Wizardry" (624). Gallardo and Smith note, "The combined effect of Umbridge's genteel, moralistic mannerisms and perverse methods makes her one of the downright nastiest and creepiest adversaries of the whole series" (95). Pugh and Wallace further find that

> What is disturbing about the depiction of Umbridge's character is that she is one of the few women who acts [*sic*] in a way that directly affects the plot of the books, and these independent actions are cast as outside the bounds of civilized behavior. Thus, . . . Umbridge is a "bad" woman in large part because she acts according to her personal desires (272).

Umbridge is problematic, not only because she is evil, but because her actions are at odds with her hyper-feminized performance of gender. She is a gendered oxymoron consisting of stereotypically feminine traits and traits completely at odds with the feminine, and as such, she makes readers uncomfortable. However, as Butler explains, "If one 'is' a woman, that is surely not all one is; the term fails to be exhaustive, not because a pregendered 'person' transcends the specific paraphernalia of its gender, but because gender is not always constituted coherently or consistently in different historical contexts" (4). In other words, what it means to be a woman or a man is not uniform and changes over time, and it is precisely because current cultural norms dictate that Umbridge should be womanly in a uniformly stereotypical way that the character is a difficult one. Readers are led to connect her lack of physical attractiveness with her unpleasant behavior and to assume that her femininity is the part of her that is consciously performed. The fact that her performance does not include any kind of nurturing behavior further reinforces Rowling's linking of good, female and nurturance.

Liminal Women

There are three adult female characters who do not fit neatly into one of the above categories, but because they do not, they offer further proof that Rowling's adult female characters are identified more by their maternal ability than by the side they choose in the battle of good and evil. The first to appear in the series is Petunia Dursley, whose hyper-maternal actions seem largely to be the reason her son is a spoiled bully. Narcissa Malfoy, Draco Malfoy's mother, is a similar character. Although she has not been the subject of much criticism, Mrs. Malfoy plays a key role in the latter part of the series. Some critics have compared the Malfoy family to the Dursleys because the families consist of an authoritarian father figure, a stereotypical mother figure and a spoiled male child.[4] However, there is a distinct difference between the two. Mrs. Dursley's actions lead to strictly negative consequences for her son and for Harry, while Mrs. Malfoy risks herself to save her son's life and, in doing so, saves Harry. The first instance where Rowling describes Mrs. Malfoy's devotion to her son is in *Half-Blood Prince*, when she goes to Snape and begs him to save her son. Her sister, the evil Bellatrix, argues that she should not trust Snape and that she is going against the Dark Lord's wishes by confiding in Snape, but Narcissa willingly does whatever she must in order to save her son. Upon hearing that her son might well be a sacrifice to Voldemort's anger at Mr. Malfoy, Mrs. Malfoy, "crumpled, falling at [Snape's] feet, moaning on the floor" (Rowling,

Half-Blood Prince 35). She does everything in her power to get Snape to try to protect her son, even if it means her own torture or death at the hands of a displeased Voldemort. Narcissa's love for her child eventually leads her to lie about Harry Potter's death in the final installment of the series because she "knew that the only way she would be permitted to enter Hogwarts, and find her son, was as part of the conquering army. She no longer cared whether Voldemort won" (Rowling, *Deathly Hallows* 726). Furthermore, when she goes to Harry to see if he still lives after he confronts Voldemort, Rowling writes, "Hands, softer than he had been expecting, touched Harry's face, pulled back an eyelid, crept beneath his shirt, down to his chest, and felt his heart" (726). Narcissa is gentle with Harry and risks her life for the chance to find her son, demonstrating that she is a mother first and a part of Voldemort's Army second. Because of this, Narcissa Malfoy is essentially a sympathetic character, and readers are encouraged to think more highly of her than of any other member of Voldemort's group. It's worth noting here, however, that Narcissa differs from Molly Weasley in that her nurturing does not include discipline, and it leads to a spoiled, horrible child.

Nymphadora Tonks, the other character who falls outside clearly defined groups in the series, is on the side of good. When Tonks is first introduced in *Order of the Phoenix,* she acts very much like a girl rather than a grown woman, in spite of the fact that she is of age and is working as an Auror when she meets Harry. Rowling describes her: "She looked the youngest there; she had a pale heart-shaped face, dark twinkling eyes, and short spiky hair that was a violent shade of violet" (Rowling, *Order of the Phoenix* 47). Tonks helps Harry pack, and Rowling reveals that not only does she look like a girl, but she also lacks womanly housekeeping skills. She makes a half-hearted attempt to clean Hedwig's birdcage and tells Harry, "I've never quite got the hang of these sort of householdy spells" (53). Gallardo and Smith argue:

> Overall, Tonks seems to embody the very notion that being different and complex is not necessarily a bad thing. She is descended from a noble family and yet is a 'cop'; she is beautiful and a tad vain but also tough in battle; she is concerned and brave; she is a woman who

speaks bluntly with men, and so on. In all, Tonks seems to live a constructive, happy life in juxtaposition, and this gives us hope for Harry's increasingly grim future. A radically different female than we have previously seen in Rowling's magical world, Tonks embodies a liminal position that is nonetheless powerful—like Harry, she is in between. (93)

I would agree with their assessment that Tonks is unique in the world Rowling has created, but only as long as she remains a girlish figure who is most at home among young people, often comically transforming her appearance for their amusement. Unlike the stereotype of the young woman improving her appearance through makeup, Tonks' outward appearance reflects her emotional state. When she becomes lovesick at the beginning of *Half-Blood Prince*, she completely changes to the point that Ron notes she "hasn't been much of a laugh lately" (94) because she acts both serious and depressed. When she rescues Harry from the Hogwarts Express at the beginning of this sixth year, Harry notes, "Last year she had been inquisitive (to the point of being a little annoying at times), she had laughed easily, she had made jokes. Now she seemed older and much more serious and purposeful" (Rowling, *Half-Blood Prince* 158). She emerges from this dark period at the beginning of the final book, now sporting hair that is "her favorite shade of bright pink" (45) and showing Harry the ring on her left hand as evidence that she and Lupin have been married. Tonks' development into an adult woman is complete when her husband reveals that she has given birth to a son, and both are happy and well. When the final battle begins at Hogwarts, Lupin tells the others, "Tonks is with [the baby]—at her mother's" (605), which is apparently exactly where a new mother should be, with her child, keeping him safe; however, Tonks cannot stay away from her husband, and presumably the action at Hogwarts, and she leaves her son to join the fight. When Harry asks why she is not at her mother's, she replies, "I couldn't stand not knowing—" (624). Although the specifics of her part in the battle are not revealed, when it is over Harry finds "Remus and Tonks, pale and still and peaceful-looking, apparently asleep beneath the dark, enchanted ceiling" (661). Gallardo and Smith have argued both that

Tonks' "... death challenges expected roles: when she joins the final battle against Voldemort, we are to understand that her active role in the fighting is appropriate even though she is a new mother" (94) and also, "Tonks is, in her life and untimely death, a good Auror and a good mother who makes the ultimate sacrifice as both: she takes positive action to help save the world and thereby saves her son" (94). However, in the context of what I have discussed thus far, I would argue it is more likely that Tonks' death is the logical result of her failure as a mother. Instead of staying to guard, protect, and nurture young Teddy, Tonks chooses to be with her husband, and in doing so she leaves her son an orphan. Tonks provides a foil for Harry's mother because while both sacrifice their lives for the greater good, Lily dies to protect Harry, and Tonks dies with her husband.

Conclusion

In spite of the inclusion of strong girl characters, who have been common in adolescent fantasy since the late nineteenth century, and even a few strong women, such as Minerva McGonagall, the Harry Potter series closely follows its traditional predecessors. In the epilogue to the series, readers learn that Harry and Ginny have married. Together with their youngest child, Lily, they reenact Harry's first trip on the Hogwarts Express when Ginny begged to accompany her brothers. Lily, who also watches her brothers go off to school before she is old enough, echoes her mother, saying, "I want to go *now*!" (Rowling, *Deathly Hallows* 753). Readers also learn that Ron and Hermione have married and created a family, as have Draco Malfoy and his wife. Other than the participants in this scene, little has changed since Harry, Ron, and Hermione first boarded the train. Gallardo and Smith observe, "Although this ending fills in the lack left by the loss of 'Lily and James'—the heterosexual couple at the center of all events in Harry Potter—it has unfortunate repercussions . . . , as it suggests that the real quest of the main characters was to restore the traditional nuclear family" (104). Similarly, Alston notes, "The family at the end of the twentieth century is as central as ever, as children's texts attempt to guide their readers through the complexities of family relationships, which continually advocate and privilege the traditional, clearly outdated, conventional nuclear ideal" (64). The entire series revolves around the sacrifice of Harry's mother, Lily Potter, who became a true Victorian angel through her death, which, in this world of magic, does not prevent her from giving support when Harry most needs it. Harry's father likewise died to save him, but his sacrifice does not carry the same weight as Lily's; he is not the mother.[5] Winters explains,

> James' death also protects Harry, but at two removes from Lily's; the Invisibility Cloak which James leaves him protects Harry only when he himself takes action to walk into danger, and it can be forgotten or misplaced or deliberately set aside. The mother's love protects Harry all the time; the father's only when he wants it. The mother's love allows Harry to be passive; the father's love requires him to be active. (225)

Thus the series is built around the idea that a woman's primary purpose is to sacrifice for her children and that the only appropriate role for an adult female is one in which her principal function is to nurture. Essentially at issue is not only whether the series provides strong characters with whom girls can relate, but also that there exists only one acceptable path for those girls to follow. Given that Hermione lacks empowered adult female role models, the fact that the ending depicts her as a wife and mother, and nothing else, should not be surprising. Hermione practices maternal behavior throughout the series by taking care of Ron and Harry and seems to accept this role willingly. Therefore, although Rowling explores new roles for girls and even women, the influence of stereotypes from earlier literature endures.

Notes

1. Examples include contemporary series, such as The Golden Compass as well as earlier works by J. R. R. Tolkien, C. S. Lewis, and Susan Cooper.

---

2. See, for example, David Steege's essay "Harry Potter, Tom Brown, and the British School Story: Lost in Transit" and Karen Manners Smith's essay "Harry Potter's Schooldays: J. K. Rowling and the British Boarding School Novel."

3. For example, in *The Prisoner of Azkaban*, Hermione utilizes the Time-Turner in order to enact justice for Buckbeak.

4. Kornfeld and Prothro assert, for example, "the Malfoy family seems like a magical world version of the Dursleys" (191).

5. Rowling is most specifically invested in the heteronormative family. In part, Voldemort is a foil for Harry because he has no desire to perpetuate traditional values, while Harry wants nothing but normalcy, which Rowling defines as heteronormative and mostly conservative.

Works Cited

Alston, Ann. *The Family in English Children's Literature*. New York: Routledge, 2008.

Blake, Andrew. *The Irresistible Rise of Harry Potter*. London: Verso, 2002.

Butler, Judith. *Gender Trouble*. New York: Routledge, 1990.

Dresang, Eliza T. "Hermione Granger and the Heritage of Gender." *The Ivory Tower and Harry Potter: Perspectives on a Literary Phenomenon*. Ed. Lana A. Whited. Columbia: U of Missouri P, 2002. 211–242.

Gallardo, Ximena C., & Jason Smith. "Happily Ever After: Harry Potter and the Quest for the Domestic." *Reading Harry Potter Again: New Critical Essays*. Ed. Liza Anatol. Santa Barbara: Praeger, 2009. 91–108.

Heilman, Elizabeth. "Blue Wizards and Pink Witches: Representatives of Gender Identity and Power." *Harry Potter's World: Multidisciplinary Critical Perspectives*. Ed. Elizabeth E. Heilman. New York: RoutledgeFalmer, 2003. 221–239.

Hughes, Thomas. *Tom Brown's Schooldays*. Ed Andrew Sanders. New York: Oxford UP, 1989.

Kornfield, John, & Laurie Prothro. "Comedy, Conflict, and Community: Home and Family in Harry Potter." *Harry Potter's World: Multidisciplinary Critical Perspectives*. Ed. Elizabeth E. Heilman. New York: RoutledgeFalmer, 2003. 187–202.

Margolies, Edward. "The Image of the Primitive in Black Letters." *Midcontinent American Studies, American Studies Journal*.11.2. (1970): 67–77.

Mendlesohn, Farah. "Crowning the King: Harry Potter and the Construction of Authority." *The Ivory Tower and Harry Potter: Perspectives on a Literary Phenomenon*. Ed. Lana A. Whited. Columbia: U of Missouri P, 2002. 159–181.

Nikolajeva, Maria. "Harry Potter—A Return to the Romantic Hero." *Harry Potter's World: Multidisciplinary Critical Perspectives*. Ed. Elizabeth E. Heilman. New York: RoutledgeFalmer, 2003. 125–140.

Pugh, Tison, & David Wallace. "Heteronormative Heroism and Queering the School Story in J. K. Rowling's Harry Potter Series." *Children's Literature Association Quarterly* 31.3 (2006), 260–281.

Rowling, J. K. *Harry Potter and the Chamber of Secrets*. New York: Scholastic, 1999.

_____. *Harry Potter and the Deathly Hallows*. New York: Scholastic, 2007.

_____. *Harry Potter and the Goblet of Fire*. New York: Scholastic, 2000.

_____. *Harry Potter and the Half-Blood Prince*. New York: Scholastic, 2005.

_____. *Harry Potter and the Order of the Phoenix*. New York: Scholastic, 2003.

_____. *Harry Potter and the Prisoner of Azkaban*. New York: Scholastic, 1999.

_____. *Harry Potter and the Sorcerer's Stone*. New York: Scholastic, 1997.

Smith, Karen Manners. "Harry Potter's Schooldays: J. K. Rowling and the British Boarding School Novel." *Reading Harry Potter: Critical Essays*. Ed. Giselle Liza Anatol. Westport, CT: Praeger, 2003. 69–87.

Steege, David K. "Harry Potter, Tom Brown, and the British School Story: Lost in Transit?" *The Ivory Tower and Harry Potter: Perspectives on a Literary Phenomenon*. Ed. Lana A. Whited. Columbia: U of Missouri P, 2002. 140–156.

Winters, Sarah Fiona. "Bubble-Wrapped Children and Safe Books for Boys: The Politics of Parenting in Harry Potter." *Children's Literature* 39 (2011): 213–234.

Rock Cakes and Reciprocity: Food and the Male Performance of Nurturing in Harry Potter_____

Danielle Bienvenue Bray

Have you ever chosen your outfit because you wanted to send a certain message? Or chosen your words more to shock or impress someone than for their meaning? In the 1950s, the sociologist Erving Goffman wrote a book called *The Presentation of Self in Everyday Life* that talked about how, whether we know it or not, whenever we're around even just one other person, we're putting on a performance: we're acting like the version of ourselves we want that person to know. Goffman was building on the work of another sociologist, Émile Durkheim, who wrote about how people behave in communities. Durkheim theorized that the everyday activities people perform within their communities are really "ceremonies" that celebrate their being in community with one another and having shared "values" (qtd. in Goffman 35). One of the ceremonies that particularly interested Durkheim was what he called "alimentary communion," that is, sharing food with one another to reinforce being in a community together. Durkheim wrote that when members of a community share food with one another, they're making themselves a family; even if they're not blood relatives, "those who share the same meal [are made] 'the same flesh and the same blood'" (qtd. in Hasratian 59).

The school of gender studies theory has found Goffman's and Durkheim's ideas about performance particularly valuable. Judith Butler, an early gender studies theorist, published a book called *Gender Trouble* in 1990, in which she argues that our gendered behavior is not something we're born with, but instead is something we learn and do, a performance. Another gender studies theorist, Michael Mangan, builds on this idea by arguing that "[g]ender . . . is always a relationship" (9). For Mangan, gender exists not just in performance, but in relationship, which means that gender isn't something a person does alone, but is instead expressed in how that person interacts with others.

One way that we perform our gender in our relationships with others is by sharing food. In contemporary American culture, we generally perceive preparing and serving meals to be part of the mother's gender role. Women and mothers are the main food-sharers in a wide swath of our popular culture; during every presidential election for the last twenty years, *Family Circle* magazine has even held a cookie bake-off between the two main candidates' wives. Because food-sharing is so important to how we understand motherhood, observing what characters share food and with whom can be a useful way of identifying mother-characters in the books we read, even when those characters aren't female or the biological mothers of children.

In the Harry Potter series, because Harry is an orphan, one of his chief tasks as he grows up over the course of the series is to form surrogate family bonds to provide the nurturing he was not able to receive from his biological parents. He forms new, performed family relationships both in and out of school with a variety of characters, many of whom do not conform to conventional expectations. Many of the mother- or nurturer-figures Harry bonds with as he grows up are not female, and most function as part of a community of nurturers rather than as individuals. For students who need it, Hogwarts offers a performed family through the sharing of food in group settings, as at school feasts, as well as in one-on-one interactions with various faculty members. Many Hogwarts faculty members fulfill complementary functions as nurturer-figures in Harry's life, and none of them functions as a stand-alone, ideal mother-figure. Beyond his school life, Harry engages with other food-sharing surrogate families, including those like the family comprised of Sirius Black and Remus Lupin, which do not "do gender" in a traditional way. Approaching the Harry Potter books with a particular focus on food-sharing as an alimentary communion that forges performed families can help a reader to identify the maternal contributions of many of Rowling's characters, including several biologically male characters who demonstrate their traditionally feminine nurturing instinct through motherly acts, such as food-sharing. The characters of Hagrid and Lupin serve as exemplary mother-figures, following patterns of food-sharing and nurturing behavior that can also be identified in the actions of other characters in the books.

Performing Family at Hogwarts

Harry's first contact with Hogwarts School is through Hagrid, who comes to rescue him from his unfit Muggle biological family, the Dursleys, by inviting him into the wizarding community. Aunt Petunia Dursley, in particular, demonstrates her unfitness as a mother-figure in that she starves Harry and overfeeds her biological son, Dudley, and in that she is more often depicted disinfecting her kitchen than cooking in it. When Hagrid bursts in on the Dursleys with Harry's Hogwarts acceptance letter, he gives Harry his first-ever birthday cake and then cooks for the two of them, producing from his pockets "a copper kettle, a squashy package of sausages, a poker, a teapot, [and] several chipped mugs" (Rowling, *Sorcerer's Stone* 47–48); he then gives to Harry "the first six fat, juicy, slightly burnt sausages from the poker" and "[takes] a gulp of tea" before finally starting to explain the wizarding world to the boy (48–49). The following morning, Hagrid again prioritizes food over other concerns, instructing Harry to have breakfast before taking him to Diagon Alley for the first time to buy school supplies (63). Hagrid and Harry continue their food-sharing activities during this outing first by entering Diagon Alley through the Leaky Cauldron, "a tiny, grubby-looking pub" (68), and then by having "large ice creams together" (78).

At the end of Harry's first week of school, Hagrid again takes up the role of food-sharer when he invites Harry for tea (Rowling, *Sorcerer's Stone* 135–36). Much of the narration that describes Hagrid in his own home focuses on his serving tea and rock cakes to Harry, Ron, and Hermione. Even when the three appear on his doorstep the night he returns from a diplomatic mission to the giants, he immediately starts making them tea, although he has not yet even had time to unpack (Rowling, *Order of the Phoenix* 421–23). Hagrid continues his tradition of having students to tea even after Harry is grown, inviting Harry's son Albus Severus to tea at the end of his first week of school in the epilogue to *Deathly Hallows* (758).

In addition to using tea for social, relationship-building time, Hagrid is also able to use it to fulfill a variety of other ends. It provides comfort and healing when he makes Harry "a cup of strong black tea," apparently as a restorative after his broomstick is cursed at his first Quidditch match (Rowling, *Sorcerer's Stone* 191–92). After the fight at the Ministry of Magic during which Sirius Black is killed, Harry goes to see Hagrid, who again offers Harry a comforting beverage, inviting him in for "a cup o' dandelion juice" (Rowling, *Order of the Phoenix* 853). During this visit, though, Harry rejects Hagrid's comfort; Hagrid tries to talk to Harry about Sirius, but the result is that Harry gulps down half of his dandelion juice to shorten the visit and then ends it abruptly, leaving the remaining half unfinished (854). Hagrid again pairs appropriate food-sharing with appropriate first aid in *Chamber of Secrets*, when Harry and Hermione bring Ron, who is vomiting slugs from a backfiring curse, to Hagrid's house. Hagrid "d[oes]n't seem perturbed," but instead puts "a large copper basin in front of [Ron]" while serving tea and treacle fudge to Harry and Hermione (Rowling, *Chamber of Secrets* 116–17). Hagrid is also able to use food-sharing as an occasion for parental instruction, as in *Prisoner of Azkaban*, when he invites Harry and Ron over for tea to scold them for giving Hermione the silent treatment when they believe her cat has eaten Ron's pet rat (272–75).

As much attention as Hagrid shows to motherly food-sharing for Harry, Ron, and Hermione, he is at his most motherly with Norbert, his pet baby dragon, in *Sorcerer's Stone*.[1] Hagrid procures Norbert when he[2] is still an egg, and so is responsible for his gestation and hatching, as well as his first feedings (Rowling, *Sorcerer's Stone* 233).[3] Hagrid calls himself Norbert's "mommy,"[4] and like many mothers of newborns, finds "beautiful" the infant that is to other eyes awkward and alien (235–36, 240). When it is time to smuggle Norbert out of the country, Hagrid makes sure he is well-supplied with food and "his teddy bear in case he gets lonely" (240).

Hagrid likewise fusses over other animal child-surrogates, including the acromantula Aragog, whom he also raises from an egg, "feeding [him] on scraps from the table" (Rowling, *Chamber of Secrets* 277). Perhaps his most effective performance mothering a non-human creature, though, is with his half-brother, Grawp, a giant who, under Hagrid's ministrations, matures from his role as mostly a danger and then a weapon in *Order of the Phoenix,* to concerned brother by the end of *Half-Blood Prince* (643, 651), and finally, to fully socialized member of the Hogwarts community when the celebrating defenders "[throw] food into his laughing mouth" following the Battle of Hogwarts (Rowling, *Deathly Hallows* 745). Hagrid's interactions with Grawp show, at its best, his power to nurture surrogate children as they grow to the point of being able to participate appropriately in the wholesome food-sharing, or "alimentary communion" (Hasratian 59), that marks them as members of the Hogwarts community.

It is interesting to note that at the end of *Sorcerer's Stone*, Hagrid and Harry's mother-child relationship is essentially inverted when Hagrid, having realized that he leaked information that nearly resulted in Harry's death, breaks down, and Harry comforts him by giving him a Chocolate Frog (Rowling, *Sorcerer's Stone* 303–4). While Hagrid continues his food-sharing connection with Harry throughout the series, often giving Harry gifts of food, such as the "vast box of sweets" he gives him for Christmas in *Goblet of Fire* (410), the occasional reversal of his and Harry's roles points to another important facet of "alimentary communion" as Avak Hasratian theorizes it: reciprocity. As Hasratian describes it, an act of alimentary communion binds people together in performed kinship by placing them under "reciprocal obligation" to one another; that is, the ceremony isn't in one person's offering food to another, but in that person's returning the gesture (58). Under this model, it is when Harry offers the despondent Hagrid a Chocolate Frog at the end of *Sorcerer's Stone*, and not when Hagrid first gives him a birthday cake at the beginning, that the two truly become part of a performed family. This opportunity to reciprocate food-sharing shows Harry his own role in the performed family, thus investing him in it. An important facet of the food-sharing relationship within a performed family is that it affords opportunities for the child to reciprocate food-sharing in communion with adults as he ages. The importance of this reciprocity is demonstrated through the strength of Harry's relationship with Sirius Black and Remus Lupin, discussed at more length below.

The performed family of Hogwarts School relies, furthermore, on the participation of more than one member to function well, and all its members are flawed when taken individually as mother-figures; Hagrid is perhaps the member of the Hogwarts staff who most frequently shares food and maternal attention with Harry, and it is thus unsurprising that his offerings are also the most frequently flawed. As early as his first meeting with eleven-year-old Harry, Hagrid's propensity for strong drink is present in the "amber liquid" he "swig[s]" before making Harry's dinner (Rowling, *Sorcerer's Stone* 48), and in his leaving Harry alone his first time in Diagon Alley so that he can go "fer a pick-me-up in the Leaky Cauldron;" during this time, Harry meets Draco Malfoy, who tells him that Hagrid is known for being a "drunk" (76–8). Hagrid also wins Norbert's egg playing cards in a pub, where he has apparently had too much to drink and reveals secret information that nearly allows Voldemort to get his hands on the Sorcerer's Stone (Rowling, *Sorcerer's Stone* 266, 303–4). Hagrid's tendency to overindulge in alcohol continues throughout the series.

Hagrid's relationship with food is also problematic in that he is not a particularly good cook; in fact, after the "slightly burnt" dinner on the night of their first meeting (Rowling, *Sorcerer's Stone* 48–9), his cooking grows steadily worse, ranging from the strange—"stoat sandwiches" (Rowling, *Sorcerer's Stone* 231) and a casserole containing "a large talon" (Rowling, *Goblet of Fire* 265)— to the inedible, perhaps best characterized by his famous rock cakes (Rowling, *Sorcerer's Stone* 140; *Goblet of Fire* 28; *Half-Blood Prince* 232). Harry thinks little enough of Hagrid's cooking that on two occasions, he politely refuses the food Hagrid offers because, in the same words of narration each time, "he had had too much experience with Hagrid's cooking" (Rowling, *Prisoner of Azkaban* 273; *Goblet of Fire* 28).

The Performance of Family in Transition

Filling in where Hagrid's attempts at food-sharing and nurturing do not succeed, other Hogwarts staff members also figure as potential mother-surrogates for Harry, many of them unlikely in a traditional sense because, like Hagrid, they are male. One such figure is Albus Dumbledore, host of Hogwarts' lavish school feasts and frequently associated with candy. Severus Snape, whose position as potions master consists largely of combining ingredients and cooking them in a womb-like cauldron[5] is another such figure. One female Hogwarts staffer who fits the bill is Professor McGonagall, who often uses offers of food to temper punishments, as when she leaves Harry and Ron a self-refilling plate of sandwiches to eat when their fate is being decided after they crash Mr. Weasley's car onto school grounds (Rowling, *Chamber of Secrets* 80–3) and who later barks at Harry to eat some ginger newts while she lectures him about the importance of watching what he says about Dolores Umbridge (Rowling, *Order of the Phoenix* 247–49). A number of other figures and even the Hogwarts Castle itself also function as food-sharing parent-figures for Harry, but one other representative Hogwarts staffer is Remus Lupin, who nurtures Harry both at school and in a more domestic setting when Harry is older.

The first time he meets Harry, Ron, and Hermione, Lupin shares food with them, giving them chocolate to counter the effects of the Dementors on the Hogwarts Express (Rowling, *Prisoner of Azkaban* 84–87). Lupin must urge the children several times to eat the chocolate, but when Harry finally does, it instantly counteracts the cold of the Dementors' attack (86–87). Even Madam Pomfrey, the school nurse, is impressed by Lupin's knowledge of "remedies" (90), which ties him to other healing mother-figures such as Snape and Mrs. Weasley. Another benefit of Lupin's distribution of chocolate to the children is that when he breaks the chocolate to share with them, it makes a loud noise and distracts the others from fussing over Harry, who is embarrassed to have fainted (84). While Hagrid can accomplish a number of ends through food-sharing, Lupin, one of the more effective nurturers in Harry's life, can accomplish several goals through a single performance of food-sharing.

Lupin again offers Harry food as comfort by inviting him for tea when Ron and Hermione go on a trip into the village of Hogsmeade and Harry, without a signed permission slip, must stay behind (Rowling, *Prisoner of Azkaban* 153–57). Harry is so comfortable during this visit that he finds the courage to ask Lupin a question about his perception that Lupin sees him as weak, and Lupin is able to reassure Harry by dispelling it (155). Lupin's use of food-sharing as part of an occasion for Harry to talk about his feelings continues during their private Patronus-conjuring lessons. Rather than the nondescript "enormous slab" of chocolate he produced on the train (84), during these sessions, Lupin goes in for celebratory variety, giving Harry a Chocolate Frog on one occasion (239) and "a large bar of Honeydukes' best chocolate" on another (242), a sign of these food-sharings as symbolic of the close familial bond they are forging, rather than merely medicinal.[6] Further marking these sessions as a special bonding time, when Harry has made some progress with his Patronus, Lupin rewards him with butterbeer (246). As during their conversation over tea, Harry feels comfortable enough while sharing butterbeers with Lupin to ask him a troubling question: "What's under a Dementor's hood?" (246–7).

Despite the many positive aspects of Lupin's relationship with Harry at Hogwarts, ultimately, Lupin is not a completely nourishing mother-figure for Harry there, symbolized by the type of food he shares with Harry, which, though comforting, is not nutritious. Just as the chocolate heals after a Dementor attack but is not the stuff of a steady diet, so Lupin in *Prisoner of Azkaban* is not a fit mother-figure without the complementary gifts of the other members of the Hogwarts community. Fittingly, Lupin's appearance in the book is frequently described in terms of malnutrition, with narration from Harry's point of view regularly focusing on his thinness and reflecting that even though he seems to "ha[ve] had a few square meals" (Rowling, *Prisoner of Azkaban* 130), "[h]is old robes were hanging more loosely on him" (185). Even his departure from Hogwarts is coupled with an absence of food where food is customary; when Lupin has had to leave Hogwarts, Black is on the run, and Harry "had never approached the end of a school year in worse spirits" (429), the end-of-term feast, usually described in voluminous detail, is dashed off in two sentences (430).

While Lupin is not able to be an ideal nurturer-figure to Harry at Hogwarts, his attentions to Harry continue in life outside the school as a family friend to Harry and de facto domestic partner to Sirius Black, whom Harry's parents chose as his godfather (Rowling, *Prisoner of Azkaban* 204). Sirius and Lupin, who is generally called by his first name, Remus,[7] once he is no longer a teacher at the child protagonists' school, often appear together as parent-surrogates for Harry. They frequently perform this role in contrast to the Weasleys, a more conventional and arguably more obvious set of surrogate parents. In her quest to become Harry's primary mother-surrogate, Mrs. Weasley becomes hostile toward overtures from Sirius and Remus, holding against Sirius motherly behaviors they have in common, such as opening their tables to everyone they know: though she happily feeds anyone who is nearby when she is about to serve a meal, including, on one occasion, breakfast for the disembodied head of Amos Diggory in the Burrow's fireplace (Rowling, *Goblet of Fire* 160), she blames Sirius for Mundungus "Dung" Fletcher's bad influence on the children because Sirius invites Dung to stay for dinner after the Order of the Phoenix meetings (Rowling, *Order of the Phoenix* 86–7).

The most vivid moment of controversy between Mrs. Weasley and Sirius occurs shortly after her complaint about Dung's coming to dinner, when she and Sirius have an argument over what Harry should be told about Voldemort and the Order, during the course of which Mrs. Weasley calls on her spouse, and Remus comes to Sirius' aid, establishing Remus as a spouse-equivalent and parenting partner in relationship with Sirius and Harry (Rowling, *Order of the Phoenix* 87–90). The argument takes place after a meal, when Sirius invites Harry to ask questions about what the Order is doing, and his invitation prompts Remus to pause in the act of "tak[ing] a sip of wine" (87); that Sirius' invitation interrupts Remus' consumption of a drink would seem to undermine his role as a food-sharer, but it also draws a connection between Sirius and Remus and signals that Sirius is not the food-sharing mother-figure in the pairing. During this turf war between two sets of surrogate parent-figures, the two mother-father pairings become clear when Mrs. Weasley turns to her husband for support:

> "Arthur!" said Mrs. Weasley, rounding on her husband. "Arthur, back me up!"
>
> Mr. Weasley did not speak at once. He took off his glasses and cleaned them slowly on his robes, not looking at his wife. Only when he had replaced them carefully on his nose did he say, "Dumbledore knows the position has changed, Molly. He accepts that Harry will have to be filled in to a certain extent now that he is staying at headquarters—"
>
> "Yes, but there's a difference between that and inviting him to ask whatever he likes!"
>
> "Personally," said Lupin quietly, looking away from Sirius at last, as Mrs. Weasley turned quickly to him, hopeful that finally she was about to get an ally, "I think it better that Harry gets the facts—not all the facts, Molly, but the general picture—from us, rather than a garbled version from . . . others." (Rowling, *Order of the Phoenix* 89)

In this portion of the argument, Remus marks himself as a mother-surrogate contrasted with Sirius' serving as father-figure by entering it after Mrs. Weasley has gone to her own spouse for support,[8] and by mirroring Mr. Weasley's body language when he does so, "looking away from Sirius," as Mr. Weasley is "not looking at his wife." Mrs. Weasley further identifies Remus as specifically a wife-figure to Sirius by assuming that, since the two husband-figures have banded together, Remus will function in the argument as her "ally."

The battle over the role of surrogate parent to Harry peaks when Sirius claims the role outright, telling Molly that she may decide what to tell or not to tell the Weasley children, but does not have this right with Harry, concluding, "He's not your son" (Rowling, *Order of the Phoenix* 88–90). Mrs. Weasley counters by referring to herself as "someone who has got Harry's best interests at heart,"

---

implying that Sirius does not, bringing up his jail time, and finally saying Harry is "as good as" her son (90). Ultimately, though, Mrs. Weasley concedes defeat, echoing the words of this argument in a later message to the children, sent through Sirius, forbidding Ron to participate in their planned covert Defense Against the Dark Arts club and dissuading Harry and Hermione from going forward, "though she accepts that she has no authority over either of them and simply begs them to remember that she has their best interests at heart" (370–71). Although her wording, especially its echo of the earlier, humiliating argument, may invoke some motherly guilt, Mrs. Weasley ultimately cedes parental authority over Harry to Sirius and Remus.

Once the question of who should serve as Harry's primary parent-surrogates is settled, the relationship among the four adults becomes much more nourishing, marked by Sirius and Mrs. Weasley cooking a meal together: When Mr. Weasley is attacked while on guard duty in the Department of Mysteries, Sirius invites the Weasley family to stay with him in Grimmauld Place, near the hospital, "with such obvious sincerity" that Mrs. Weasley reconciles with him by immediately "beg[inning] to help with breakfast" (Rowling, *Order of the Phoenix* 480). Sirius and Remus seal their position as joint parent-figures to Harry shortly after this reconciliation by giving Harry a Christmas gift together (501). Sirius' and Remus' roles as a father-mother pairing for Harry continue even after their deaths; at the conclusion of *Deathly Hallows*, when Harry uses the Resurrection Stone, his two closest, deceased pairs of parent-figures appear to him: his biological parents and Remus and Sirius (699); though Tonks, Remus' wife, has also died, she does not appear. Remus is the mother-figure here, to Sirius' father-figure.

Thus Harry's most direct surrogate parent relationship is with perhaps the least heteronormative mother-father coupling presented to him in the series. Gender is at times problematic even for Sirius, ostensibly the appropriately gendered father-figure in the pairing. He is troubled by the feminizing effect of having to stay in his family home and clean—it has stood vacant for a decade—while others, including Snape, go out on assignment for the Order (Rowling,

Order of the Phoenix 83). When Harry looks into Sirius' bedroom in Grimmauld Place in *Deathly Hallows*, he discovers signs that Sirius used his sexuality to make his parents uncomfortable, decorating with "posters of bikini-clad Muggle girls" (179); while his interest in Muggles would certainly bother the pureblood Black family, Sirius seems also to be asserting his masculinity by showing so much "nerve" (178) in proclaiming interest in pictures of scantily-clad women.

Remus seems to be more comfortable than Sirius with his non-traditional gender expression. He holds Harry as they watch Sirius die, and afterward, he openly goes through the grief of a man who has just lost his lover, speaking to Harry "as though every word was causing him pain" (Rowling, *Order of the Phoenix* 806–8). In fact, Remus is a more effective mother-figure to Harry than he is a father to his biological son, whom he abandons twice: once when he first learns Tonks is pregnant and leaves her, and then again when Teddy is an infant and Remus goes off to fight and be killed in the Battle of Hogwarts (Rowling, *Deathly Hallows* 212–16, 661). Despite this attitude toward his own son, Remus has, before his marriage to Tonks, presented himself as a willing mother-surrogate not only to Harry: When Mrs. Weasley expresses her fear that she and Mr. Weasley will be killed and their youngest children left orphans, he chides her, "[W]hat do you think we'd do, let them starve?" (Rowling *Order of the Phoenix* 177), offering himself and Sirius, through use of the plural pronoun, as potential surrogate parents and food-sharers to Ron and Ginny.

Sirius likewise presents himself as an enthusiastic food-sharer and surrogate parent, though his offers are more impulsive and less nutritious. He first offers to take Harry in while he is still standing in front of the rubble of the Potters' house, from which Hagrid has just rescued baby Harry (Rowling, *Prisoner of Azkaban* 206–7), and he renews the offer to thirteen-year-old Harry the moment it seems likely the godfather's name will be cleared (379). Sirius is not able to make good on either of these offers, though, and his food-sharing is likewise sweet and tempting, but not nourishing enough to last; for example, Sirius sends Harry one of the "four superb birthday cakes" the boy gets when he turns fourteen (Rowling, *Goblet of Fire* 28), but seldom gives him nutritious food. Sirius again shares treat food, butterbeer, with Harry and the Weasley children to keep them occupied while they await word about Mr. Weasley's condition after he has been attacked. When he summons the bottles, though, they "[scatter] the debris of Sirius' meal," the nutritious food he was eating before they arrived, and when it is time for him to offer the children a substantial meal, Mrs. Weasley helps him prepare it (477–80).[9]

Sirius' performance as a parent is complicated by his difficulty demonstrating affection for Harry. He places "a hand on Harry's shoulder" as the boy tells the difficult story of Voldemort's return and Cedric Diggory's murder at the conclusion of *Goblet of Fire* (694), but though he first presents himself as a parent-figure to Harry in the third book of the series, he does not hug him until the fifth, and when he does so he is in dog form (Rowling, *Order of the Phoenix* 183). Later in the same book, when Sirius in human form finally hugs Harry the morning the boy returns to Hogwarts after Christmas break, it is "a brief, one-armed hug," accompanied by an admonition to "Look after yourself, Harry," that cuts off whatever Harry might have wanted to say to him (524).

Despite this difficulty with physical affection, Sirius and Remus seem to be the parent-figures of Harry's choice. When "he really want[s] . . . someone like a *parent*: an adult wizard whose advice he could ask without feeling stupid, someone who cared about him" (Rowling's emphasis), Harry writes to Sirius, not Mr. or Mrs. Weasley (Rowling, *Goblet of Fire* 22); much later, after Sirius dies, Harry mourns the loss of "someone outside Hogwarts who cared about what happened to him, almost like a parent" (Rowling, *Half-Blood Prince* 77). The gender-neutral "parent" instead of "father" or "mother" in both of these instances stresses the gender-ambiguity of Sirius and Remus as nurturer-figures in Harry's life.

Perhaps one aspect of his relationship with Sirius and Remus that is attractive to Harry as a young adult is its reciprocity, the establishment of "reciprocal obligations" Hasratian deems essential to a performed kinship group (58). At an age where he is beginning to practice adult behaviors, more than many other children his age as a result of his being "the Chosen One," Harry is drawn more strongly toward those adults whom he can nurture as well as from whom he can receive nurturing. In one of his first face-to-face interactions with Sirius after his escape from the Dementors at the conclusion of *Prisoner of Azkaban*, Harry meets Sirius in Hogsmeade, obeying Sirius' instruction to "[b]ring as much food as [he] can" (Rowling, *Goblet of Fire* 510). Sirius does address Harry's needs, but first, he ravenously consumes the food Harry has brought (520–28); even as he accepts nurturing from Harry, though, Sirius also nurtures another, feeding his table scraps to Buckbeak, the hippogriff on whose back Harry helped him to escape to freedom and with whom he is now in hiding (523, 528). In this context, both food-sharing and problem-solving are mutual: Sirius receives food from Harry and gives food to Buckbeak; Harry helped Sirius escape on Buckbeak in the previous book, and now Sirius helps Harry with his problems. This pattern of reciprocal nurturing comes even more full-circle when Remus appoints Harry godfather to his own son, placing Harry in the same role Sirius filled for him and also requesting from him a significant gift of nurturing (Rowling, *Deathly Hallows* 514). By inviting Harry to offer nurturing as well as to accept it, Sirius and Remus provide Harry with an adult role he can grow into, an idea of the man he is to become, and this role gives him both a clear, necessary position in the performed family and a direction for his growth into an adult.

Conclusion

Through his connection to Hogwarts, Harry finds the first surrogate family that truly nurtures him: the school itself and its staff. But while Hogwarts serves as "the first and best home" many of the wizarding world's "abandoned boys" have the privilege of "know[ing]" (Rowling, *Deathly Hallows* 697), its nature as an educational institution prevents it from being an ideal long-term family unit. Because he can follow Harry outside of school and interact with him in a setting that invites reciprocal nurturing and the shouldering of more adult family responsibility, Remus is ultimately able to shepherd Harry out of his Hogwarts home and into performed kinship with himself and Sirius, creating the family that nurtures Harry into adulthood and into the formation of a new family group with his own wife and children.

Notes

1. Hagrid is not the only male mother-figure and Hogwarts staff member in the series to mother a baby animal. In the fifth book of the series, during the battle at the Ministry of Magic between the Death Eaters and the Order of the Phoenix, Albus Dumbledore's phoenix Fawkes swallows an Avada Kedavra curse, dies, and is reborn from his own ashes (Rowling, *Order of the Phoenix* 815). Dumbledore carries the baby bird home and, as soon as he returns to his office at Hogwarts, places him in a bank of "soft ashes" under the adult Fawkes' perch (822). While space does not permit a full exploration of Dumbledore as a male mother-figure here, such a study yields a number of interesting examples of food-sharing, and of Hasratian's principle that performed families should share in "reciprocal obligations," a principle that will be discussed here in relation to other characters (Hasratian 58).

2. In *Sorcerer's Stone*, Hagrid uses masculine pronouns to refer to Norbert, though we later learn from dragon expert Charlie Weasley that Norbert is, in fact, a female dragon (Rowling, *Deathly Hallows* 120).

3. Hagrid is also connected with childbirth in that it is his responsibility to conduct Hogwarts' first-year students across the lake and into their school lives every year (Rowling, *Sorcerer's Stone* 111–2).

4. In addition to his use of this feminine appellation to define his relationship with Norbert, Hagrid also marks himself as traditionally feminine in other ways, such as his tendency to burst into tears at emotional times, often blotting his eyes with table linens (*Prisoner of Azkaban* 93, 94, 422), and his participation in needlework, knitting to pass the time on the train to London (*Sorcerer's Stone* 65) and darning socks (Rowling, *Goblet of Fire* 265). Hagrid's interest in needlecrafts again aligns him with Dumbledore, who remarks to Horace Slughorn, "I do love knitting patterns" (Rowling, *Half-Blood Prince* 73). A fondness for needlework may also be found in male mothers in other works, such as the pirate bo'sun Smee, who, in the 1911 novel version of *Peter Pan*, keeps a sewing machine on board

the ship (Barrie 183). I have argued elsewhere that Smee is a more fitting mother-figure for the pirates than Wendy, despite his sharing the other pirates' wish to have Wendy for a mother (Bienvenue 24).

5.	Voldemort is even reborn in a large cauldron at the conclusion of *Goblet of Fire* (640–43).

6.	This familial bond between Harry and Lupin is complicated by the ulterior motives each seems to bring to the Patronus lessons. Lupin appears to be trying to re-live his friendship with James by seeking to bond with his son, while Harry secretly wants the Dementors to get to him because when they do, he relives his memory of his mother's murder and thus gets to hear her voice (Rowling, *Prisoner of Azkaban* 239, 243).

7.	It is interesting that Remus favors his first name once he becomes a more prominent surrogate parent for Harry because it refers to a pair of twins in Roman mythology: Remus and Romulus, who are perhaps best known for their own surrogate mother, a wolf.

8.	Rowling recalls this moment to establish another pairing as a husband-and-wife equivalent later in the book when Hermione appeals to Ron for support in an argument, "and Harry was forcibly reminded of Mrs. Weasley appealing to her husband during Harry's first dinner in Grimmauld Place" (Rowling, *Order of the Phoenix* 658). By referring to Mr. Weasley not by name, but as "her husband," Rowling underscores the importance of the relationship role of the person being called upon; Hermione is looking to Ron as a husband-figure who should, for that reason, come to her aid in the argument.

9.	After Sirius' death, when there is another Weasley family crisis— the fall of the Ministry during Bill and Fleur's wedding, resulting in everyone having to flee for fear Death Eaters will arrive—Lupin mimics Sirius' comforting gesture, bringing "a few butterbeers" to Harry, Ron, and Hermione, again at Grimmauld Place (Rowling, *Deathly Hallows* 204).

Works Cited

Barrie, J. M. *Peter Pan*. 1911. Illus. Elisa Trimby. New York: Puffin-Penguin, 1986.

Bienvenue, Danielle R. "Serial Mom-nogamy: *Peter Pan* and the Search for a Mother-Figure." *Shawangunk Review* XVI (2005): 22–6.

Butler, Judith. *Gender Trouble*. New York: Routledge, 1990.

Hasratian, Avak. "The Death of Difference in *Light in August*." *Criticism* 49.1 (2007): 55–84. *Project Muse*. Web. 26 Oct. 2011.

Goffman, Erving. *The Presentation of Self in Everyday Life*. New York: Anchor-Doubleday, 1959.

Mangan, Michael. *Staging Masculinities: History, Gender, Performance*. New York: Palgrave-MacMillan, 2003.

Rowling, J. K. *Harry Potter and the Chamber of Secrets*. Illus. Mary Grandpré. Harry Potter. New York: Arthur A. Levine-Scholastic, 1999.

_____. *Harry Potter and the Deathly Hallows*. Illus. Mary Grandpré. Harry Potter. New York: Arthur A. Levine-Scholastic, 2007.

_____. *Harry Potter and the Goblet of Fire*. Illus. Mary Grandpré. Harry Potter. New York: Arthur A. Levine-Scholastic, 2000.

_____. *Harry Potter and the Half-Blood Prince*. Illus. Mary Grandpré. Harry Potter. New York: Arthur A. Levine-Scholastic, 2005.

_____. *Harry Potter and the Order of the Phoenix*. Illus. Mary Grandpré. Harry Potter. New York: Arthur A. Levine-Scholastic, 2003.

_____. *Harry Potter and the Prisoner of Azkaban*. Illus. Mary Grandpré. Harry Potter. New York: Arthur A. Levine-Scholastic, 1999.

_____. *Harry Potter and the Sorcerer's Stone*. Illus. Mary Grandpré. Harry Potter. New York: Arthur A. Levine-Scholastic, 1997.

Mentoring in the Wizarding World: Dumbledore and His Literary Ancestors_____

Christina Vourcos

α Lumos: Beginning

If it weren't for Professor Albus Dumbledore, headmaster of Hogwarts (school for wizards and witches), Harry wouldn't have survived. With the help and guidance of Dumbledore, Harry grows as a student and as a hero. But Dumbledore wasn't the first wizard in literature to guide a great hero. There have been others, such as Merlin and Gandalf, and what makes them so similar is that their actions as well as words make the difference in the success of the literature, far more than great magic. By looking through Dumbledore's literary ancestors, we can understand why his character exemplifies a great mentor and how his impact extends to more than just the hero of the story. The relationship that Dumbledore has with his protégé Harry not only helps the main character become who he is meant to be, but also helps the reader have a better understanding of the concepts of the books.

β Mythological and Archetypal Approach

Myths are more than just early fictions. These stories were our first ways of being aware of the universe and how we fit within history. Myths are communal and collective by nature, so they can bind a culture, nation or group together. These stories can have unique ties within their cultural environments, but all of them have something universal, which explains why there are similar motifs or themes found throughout different myths and images that recur no matter where the myth originates. "It has always been the prime function of mythology and rite to supply the symbols that carry the human spirit forward, in counteraction to those other constant human fantasies that tend to tie it back," writes Joseph Campbell, author of *The Hero with a Thousand Faces* (11).

When we look at images and motifs, we find universal symbols and archetypes. The archetype most relevant to the mentor is "The Wise Old Man," who represents someone with knowledge, insight, wisdom, cleverness, and intuition, as well as moral qualities, such as readiness to help and goodwill. This is one of many common archetypes in literature. There is something within the familiar that keeps us willing to explore a similar story over and over again, just like a favorite book that we can't help but re-read for comfort. Umberto Eco explains this phenomenon in his essay "The Myth of Superman." There is a psychological connection when it comes to the attraction of a certain book, where the reader wants to know what he already knows. Yet at the same time, the reader is drawn to concluding some kind of meaning or purpose that helps him or her have a better understanding of the world. There will be aspects that the reader doesn't know, but the familiar universal archetypes and plot devices keep the story going.

⌐ Merlin's Background and Lasting Influence

This kind of repetition can be seen when it comes to the well-known wizard Merlin. Not only has his character continued long after the medieval ages, but Merlin can also be seen as a linchpin, the main source from which all the modern wizards have come. He is also shadowed in mystery by the mixture of different tales about him, even possibilities of others with the same name, as well as stories that have evolved through the generations, but in the end, his presence still exists in our creative imagination and inspires curiosity for knowledge.

"There's something about you, Merlin," Arthur Pendragon eventually admits on the BBC show *The Adventures of Merlin*; "I can't quite put my finger on it." He isn't the only one who is mystified. Michael A. Torregrossa, in his essay "The Way of the Wizard: Reflections of Merlin on Film" from the book *The Medieval Hero on Screen: Representations from Beowulf to Buffy,* says that "many scholars have noted the interrelationships between Merlin and his fellow wizards" and that it has been "shown that the medieval legend of Merlin and its modern adaptations still have an enormous influence on how creative artists choose to represent the idea of the wizard in popular text" (182). Torregrossa adds that there are many wizards that "serve their protégés in the pivotal role of guide and mentor, either aiding or inspiring their charges as they fulfill their pre-destined tasks" (182). This shows that there is a connection between Merlin and Dumbledore, as they both make their own decisions to become mentors to their protégés.

We can learn more about this connection by understanding Merlin's influence. Charlotte Spivack claims in her text "Medieval Merlins: Emergence of the Monomyth," part of *Merlin: A Thousand Heroes with One Face*, that each age has its own version and derivatives of Merlin. Before Spivack makes this claim, she asserts that the reason Merlin seems multiple is that he is "not a hero with a thousand faces: he is a thousand heroes with one face, that of the 'wise old man'" (1). Therefore, it is stories that have made this character last, much more than history will. Merlin's story brings hope. In the chapter "Merlin as Psychological Symbol: A Jungian View," in *Comparative Studies in Merlin from the Vedas to C.G. Jung*, James Gollnick mentions that Merlin in Geoffrey of Monmouth's *Historia Regnum Britanniae (History of the Kings of Britain)* is seen as a prophet who "calls the people to their true identity;" while the character "paints a very dark picture of the evil times, the terrible suffering and the hours of war, . . . [Merlin] also reminds them that the human spirit still retains its nobility and that human destiny must be fulfilled even though the current situation appears hopeless" (qtd. in Goodrich 116). This is very much like the way that Dumbledore reassures Harry, as well as the Wizarding World, during dark times relating to Voldemort.

Even in the recent version of BBC's *Merlin* (2008–2012), Merlin inspires those who are around him to be the best they can be when times are tough. Since there are many versions of Merlin's character, we have made him into a legend that is more extraordinary than ourselves. Merlin is much like the character Superman, who has been remade with multiple versions of his story. Any characters become extraordinary because we make them so. In the BBC show, Merlin always stands his ground that the use of magic must be for good and not evil purposes, and he works to enlighten Arthur about the value of magic, as well as helps Arthur grow to be better than his father. He does this by his actions, as well as his words.

Merlin has inspired other fantasy characters, as well as the wizard archetype that keeps his presence alive in our minds. Many would picture Merlin as an older man with a long beard, wearing a cap and robes, as well as someone who looks as though he is full of wisdom because he has lived for a long time. This look, even the personality, is very similar to J. R. R. Tolkien's character Gandalf and, more recently, Professor Dumbledore, the headmaster of Hogwarts School and advisor to Harry Potter. According to John Matthews, who wrote the book *Merlin: Shaman, Prophet, Magician*, "It is as tutor and guide to the young king that we know [Merlin] best, and as such he appears again and again in modern retellings" (134). The earlier tales of Merlin mention that he had a demonic father and a human mother. This might have been a way during the time of the growth of Christianity to explain his powers, and it is his mother's choice to baptize him that saves him from becoming evil. Yet Harry Potter inherits his skills from his parents, as if these abilities were just another genetic trait. Matthews says, "Reading the accounts of Harry's adventures we get a glimpse of what Merlin's own youthful exploits might have been like if we knew more of them" (136). Here the repetition happens again, but this time, it shows a way to see Merlin as more than just a legendary character.

If we can do that for Merlin, then we can also do the same for Dumbledore. We can remove them both from the pedestal and see them as human with flaws, just as we are. This is important because all characters come from the human condition. They aren't divine; therefore, we need to see them as who they are, even if they have magic, unlike us. According to Peter Goodrich, who has written Arthurian texts as well as edited the book *The Romance of Merlin*, "The increasing rate of change in science and society also encouraged Merlin's adoption into two apparently contradictory ways: as an icon of fantasy, the prototypal magician; and as the forerunner of technological innovation, the scientist and inventor" (xv). This is a clear example of how we have made the image of

Merlin our own. In recent times, besides Harry Potter, the wizard Gandalf of J. R. R. Tolkien's *The Hobbit* and *The Lord of the Rings* trilogy can be compared to Merlin.

Several scholars, such as Nikolai Tolstoy, who wrote *The Quest for Merlin*, have made the comparison between these two characters. Tolstoy explains why, "Like Merlin, Gandalf is a magician of infinite wisdom and power; like Merlin, he has a sense of humor by turns impish and sarcastic; and like Merlin, he reappears at intervals, seemingly from nowhere, intervening to rescue an imperiled cosmos" (19). According to Tolstoy, Merlin's "enchantments have secured him a permanent place" in human consciousness and he becomes "an archetype to which the race turns for guidance and protection" (19–20). So if we explore Dumbledore's literary ancestors, Gandalf and especially Merlin have a large impact on the creation of the character as well as his decision to become a mentor.

Δ Mentoring the Incredible Heroes

While many people know, or think they know, what a "mentor" is, according to Anthony W. Lee in his introduction to the book *Mentoring in Eighteenth-Century British Literature and Culture*, he finds it strange that little attention has been focused on relating to mentoring within the field of literary studies. He suggests that most would agree "mentoring refers to a relationship between an older and younger person, in which the elder imparts to the younger one his or her greater experience, knowledge, and expertise" (Lee 2). This isn't the only possibility though; for example, mentoring can involve young mentors and older protégés. Even with these possibilities, we mostly focus on the first, especially the "presence of authority and the presence of influence," (Lee 2) which marks the classic mentoring relationship. The mentor's authority comes from his or her experience and ability to instruct the protégé, but the responsibility for what to transmit also factors. Influence is a force that "transfers from mentor to protégé the articles of authority and tradition, thus charismatically reshaping and refashioning the protégé's outlook and identity" (3). Afterwards, there comes a point where the protégé chooses to leave. Some protégés don't have the choice, for life forces them to move on. Yet the trace of the mentor still lingers, whatever the reason for the separation of the mentor and the protégé.

The mentors we see in fantasy stories aren't quite like what we expect in the real world, with career experience, but they do hold some other aspects that help us relate to these characters because they support their heroes with moral and sometimes emotional encouragement and sources of information and aid somehow in their success. According to Lynnette R. Porter, who wrote the book *Unsung Heroes of the Lord of the Rings*, Merlin and Gandalf are seen as mythical because their powers and abilities surpass those of humans. Porter mentions the difference between those characters: "Whereas Merlin, in most versions of the Arthurian legend, uses his powers to assist Arthur, teach him a lesson, or influence events, Gandalf seldom uses magical power. He prefers to counsel leaders and to become directly involved in events as they unfold" (8). There seems to be a move towards using words over power when it comes to these powerful wizards, especially in relation to Dumbledore.

These wizards use magic sparingly, unlike what is expected of them, but their actions trump dramatic feats. Charles W. Nelson in the article "From Gollum to Gandalf: The Guide Figures in J.R.R. Tolkien's *Lord of the Rings*" suggests that Gandalf, after his transformation, doubts his power. This makes him seem to be a good character because he possesses humility and realizes the extent of his abilities and how they can affect others. This is similar to Dumbledore, but different from some portrayals of Merlin. So these characters might look at first glance like copies, but Gandalf and Dumbledore have been distanced from Merlin because they realize how to use power appropriately, which leads them to be good, whereas Merlin is seen as more evil, or evil in intent with his use of his powers to change things. Nelson mentions that there is no doubt with Gandalf because from the beginning, in *The Hobbit*, the character "assumes control and leads the other characters with assurance and confidence" (58). Gandalf also protects, rallies, counsels, and inspires courage. According to Frank P. Riga, who wrote the article "Gandalf and Merlin: J.R.R. Tolkien's Adoption and Transformation of a Literary Tradition," Gandalf is strongly linked to the role of teacher. Even though Merlin figures have been portrayed in the past as teachers and counselors, they didn't quite resemble the best because these figures "seldom explained themselves, seldom asked questions, and seldom showed patience with those they counseled. Those who doubted the wisdom of their worlds and advice suffered, or even died, as a result" (Riga 39).

Gandalf is more like the teacher we expect, as he has no access to the past or future, and in ordinary ways, he discovers and shares knowledge so that others can help themselves. He understands the context of individuals and cares for them with that in mind. Gandalf and Dumbledore both value friendship over wisdom and knowledge, which benefits their charges because the protégés hold up that value as well, and it helps them on their journey. That can help when magic or technology isn't available; then we have to resolve to use our own natural resources. Gandalf teaches those who don't have magic, and he demonstrates how to overcome with words and deeds. According to Riga, "Unlike Merlin figures that are profligate in their use of magic, Gandalf not only uses magic sparingly, but he goes so far as to deflect attention from wizardry in order to emphasize the importance of working through ordinary human means" (40). He teaches those around him how to choose wisely and gives them courage to persevere in their choices. When these lessons are taught well, Gandalf is no longer needed in the mentoring role, just as at the end Harry no longer needs Dumbledore.

Dumbledore is a good mentor to Harry, even if he isn't perfect. Michael W. Austin, in the essay "Why Harry and Socrates Decide to Die," explains why: Dumbledore is humble in recognizing his own faults and honest as much as necessary; he commends his protégé's qualities, such as his courage and unselfishness, and encourages him during difficulties (267). If Harry didn't have a good mentor like Dumbledore, maybe his story would have turned out completely different. Especially since Harry lost his parents at such a young age, he needs others to fill that void. They wouldn't be able to completely replace Harry's parents, but they could give him guidance, instruction, and encouragement. Harry, like us, has had many different mentors (such as his professors, his godfather Sirius, Arthur Weasley, and Molly Weasley) who have made an impact, but there will always be one that is more significant than the others. Marcus Schulzke, in his essay "Politics and Political Activation in *Harry Potter*," suggests that some of Dumbledore's actions come from the understanding that political life could have corrupted his character. Dumbledore is seen throughout most of the series as very noble, honorable, and worthy of trust, but there is a time when Harry begins to doubt and question Dumbledore. This happens when Dumbledore's past is explored in *Deathly Hallows*. It brings a critique of authority, but according to Schulzke, Harry accepts Dumbledore despite his flaws because Dumbledore has earned respect and overcome his past errors (116).

Even this critique shows the human side of Dumbledore, which makes him more relevant and draws on real life, because not every mentor will always make the right choices. Even with his faults, what is most important is that Dumbledore grew to not let those mistakes define his legacy and began to do things that would be best for others. Being a mentor to Harry was one of Dumbledore's greatest accomplishments, even though it might not show up on a chocolate frog card. Lykke Guanio-Uluru, in the essay "Dumbledore's Ethos of Love in *Harry Potter*," explains how Dumbledore used his role as Harry's guide and teacher: as mentor, Dumbledore points out to Harry Voldemort's weakness and prepares Harry for his journey to defeat the greatest evil. So in these ways, Dumbledore becomes "an agent for Harry's moral growth" (Guanio-Uluru 85–86).

There is a point where the protégé can't be completely protected, and the mentor's trying to provide complete protection might leave the protégé in a worse position than if the mentor were honest. Dumbledore realizes that holding back information might not have been quite the right thing to do, but he has tried to do his best to protect Harry, and he had felt to a point that withholding information was in Harry's best interest. Dumbledore wanted to protect Harry from pain and worry, as the boy already had enough of those in his life. He tries to explain this to Harry:

"I cared about you too much," said Dumbledore simply. "I cared more for your happiness than your knowing the truth, more for your peace of mind than my plan, more for your life than the lives that might be lost if the plan failed. In other words, I acted exactly as Voldemort expects we [sic] fools who love to act.

Is there a defence? I defy anyone who has watched you as I have—and I have watched you more closely than you can have imagined—not to want to save you more pain than you had already suffered. What did I care if numbers of nameless and faceless people and creatures were slaughtered in the vague future, if in the here and now you were alive, and well, and happy? I never dreamed that I would have such a person on my hands." (Rowling, *Order of the Phoenix* 743)

I agree with Guanio-Uluru that this passage shows that Dumbledore has realized this shortcoming when it comes to his feelings relating to Harry. There is a line between caring for someone and doing what is best for everyone. Dumbledore thought that being impartial would have been better than letting his emotions direct his actions. This is another flaw to which readers can connect: the normal internal battle between emotions and logic. Dumbledore's imperfections might help him in his interactions with his students, even if the headmaster's emotions might sometimes interfere with his best judgment. We need to be reminded when it comes to mentors that they aren't without their flaws and their humanity.

This is important to see when we look at Dumbledore because his flaws might make it seem as if he wasn't a good mentor to Harry. However, there is much that he has done right as a mentor, and that is what should be remembered. Rusmir Musić and Lyndsay J. Agans, who wrote the article "Five Lessons of a Dumbledore Education: What Harry Potter's Mentor Knows," mention that there are several good educational practices at Hogwarts related to Dumbledore's philosophy that could be concepts exercised in real life. In their article, they present five simple but powerful concepts: information, empowerment, self-care, empathy, and choice. Dumbledore believes in giving information necessary for students to make their own decisions. As mentioned before, he struggled with finding the "balance between providing students with necessary information and potentially hurting them" (Musić & Agans 22). Dumbledore also believed in student empowerment. As Harry says,

> "He's a funny man, Dumbledore. I think he sort of wanted to give me a chance. I think he knows more or less everything that goes on here, you know. I reckon he had a pretty good idea we were going to try, and instead of stopping us, he just taught us enough to help." (Rowling, *Sorcerer's Stone* 302)

Dumbledore trusts his own instincts when it comes to conflicts over his choices. He tells Harry to share important information with his best friends, Ron and Hermione, so as a group they can learn and support each other, even in the toughest times. Dumbledore helps make Harry aware of the importance of love and feelings. Even though Harry questions Dumbledore, he still appreciates the wisdom that Dumbledore has given him, especially related to the importance of empathy. According to Musić and Agans, "Effective mentors teach students to recognize, manage, and communicate emotions, so that they can ultimately learn from them" (23). This is the protégé's greatest power. Even after everything Harry has experienced in his life, he is still able to love, and learning how to use that power is just as important as, or even more important than, learning or knowledge.

The final lesson Dumbledore gives is choice. He makes this powerful statement to Harry: "It's not our abilities that show what we truly are, it is our choices" (Rowling, *Chamber of Secrets* 333). Every time Harry's life is tough, he questions his abilities. Dumbledore teaches Harry the importance of choice and of using that opportunity well. Musić and Agans additionally write, "The educator's responsibility is to support students in making good choices, even if they sometimes lead to mistakes. Like the greatest wizard of all time, effective educators invite their students to choose to feel; everything else will fall into place, as if by magic" (23).

Now it can be seen that Dumbledore is an effective mentor when we look to his literary ancestors and his techniques, but why is he a good mentor to Harry? Dumbledore sees Harry as a child, unlike Voldemort, who sees Harry as an enemy. Mentoring Harry gives Dumbledore a chance to finally be the father that he wished his father could have been. At the end of each school year, Dumbledore talks to Harry to help him understand what he has gone through. This gives a chance for Dumbledore to have a more paternal concern for Harry, to understand himself what happened, and gradually to give necessary information. I believe that Dumbledore struggled when deciding to give information to Harry because, like a father, the headmaster didn't want to burden Harry. Yet Dumbledore knew as time went on that certain information was necessary to give to Harry, especially when Harry needed it the most.

The readers can see early on what kind of mentor Dumbledore will be in chapter twelve of *Sorcerer's Stone*, "The Mirror of Erised":

> "Let me explain. The happiest man on earth would be able to use the Mirror of Erised like a normal mirror, that is, he would look in it and see himself exactly as he is. Does that help?"
> Harry thought. Then he said slowly, "It shows us what we want . . . whatever we want . . ."
> "Yes and no," said Dumbledore quietly. "It shows us nothing more or less than our deepest, most desperate desire of our hearts [...] Men have wasted away before it, entranced by what they have seen, or been driven mad, not knowing if what it shows is real or even possible . . . . I ask you not to go looking for it again. If you ever do run across it, you will now be prepared. It does not do to dwell on dreams and forget to live, remember that. Now, why don't you put that admirable cloak back on and get off to bed?" (213–14)

In this scene, we see Dumbledore's kindness and willingness to help Harry understand this special magical object. This lesson is more than just knowledge of the object, but a way for Harry to remember not to "dwell" on the past and "forget to live." Dumbledore could have easily disciplined Harry for being out of bed, but he didn't. When Harry asks this personal question, "What do you see when you look in the mirror?" Harry realizes later that Dumbledore's answer might not have been truthful. This doesn't deter Harry from trusting Dumbledore, especially when Harry realizes he has asked a personal question. At this moment, there isn't a lie in what

Dumbledore said; he just doesn't give the full truth. Harry comes to realize that Dumbledore might not always give the full truth, but he will give enough of it to keep Harry going. Harry also realizes much later that this is one of the moments where Dumbledore held back from explaining his own past, partly because it is painful but also because it is something that Harry didn't need to know, at least in that moment.

In chapter eighteen of the book *Harry Potter and the Chamber of Secrets*, Dumbledore not only teaches Harry the importance of choices, but also reassures Harry about who he is. Throughout his second year at Hogwarts, Harry questions his identity. When Harry talks to Dumbledore about being similar to Riddle (Voldemort), they are not talking about which house Harry really should be in, but the fact that no matter what powers were transferred from Voldemort to Harry, it is who Harry is that stands out. Dumbledore helps Harry focus on who he is not only with words, but also with proof, because it is important for Harry to understand the differences as well as the similarities to make Voldemort not as mysterious. This action from Dumbledore is similar to many he takes with Harry that step out of the normal teacher-student relationship. He is acting like a father reassuring his son that he is on the right path.

We can see this action again in chapter twenty-two of the book *Prisoner of Azkaban*, when Harry feels as though he didn't make a difference. Dumbledore explains to Harry why he has made a difference with uncovering the truth and saving "an innocent man from a terrible fate" (425). Afterwards, Dumbledore helps Harry feel better about his mistake of thinking his father was alive.

> "You think the dead we loved ever truly leave us? You think that we don't recall them more clearly than ever in times of great trouble? Your father is alive in you, Harry, and shows himself most plainly when you have need of him. How else could you produce that *particular* Patronus? Prongs rode again last night" (Rowling, *Prisoner of Azkaban* 427–428).

Dumbledore reminds Harry that his parents are still with him, even though they have died, because a large part of who Harry is comes from his parents. They live through him. In this instance, Dumbledore doesn't need to tell Harry this, but he knows it would not only help Harry feel better at that time, but also help in the future when Harry confronts the resurrection stone, one of the Deathly Hallows.

In *Goblet of Fire*, Harry's curiosity causes him to find Dumbledore's Pensieve filled with a memory. This is the first opportunity of many where Dumbledore shows Harry the importance of understanding memories. Yet Dumbledore still points out to Harry that, even though "curiosity is not a sin," they should "exercise caution" with their curiosity (Rowling, *Goblet of Fire* 598). Dumbledore gives Harry wisdom for the future. It can be seen that Dumbledore acts more like a father than Harry's godfather Sirius, such as the moment in the chapter "Parting of the Ways," when Sirius wants to let Harry sleep off the traumatic moment while Dumbledore knows it will help Harry to discuss it right away. This is how Dumbledore responds to Sirius' words, but he directs his remarks towards Harry "gently":

> "If I thought I could help you . . . by putting you into an enchanted sleep and allowing you to postpone the moment when you would have to think about what has happened tonight, I would do it. But I know better. Numbing the pain for a while will make it worse when you finally feel it. You have shown bravery beyond anything I could have expected of you. I ask you to tell us what happened." (Rowling, *Goblet of Fire* 695)

This shows Dumbledore's wisdom, as well as a hint to his past. He's experienced pain, and he "knows better." It isn't just because he is superior in intellect, but because his wisdom comes from his own experience. When death happens, Dumbledore teaches Harry that it needs to become real so that one can move on from it. So discussing it and telling others help as part of an on-going process. Later, Dumbledore tells the school what happened so that moment can become real for them as well. Dumbledore does this not to hurt them, but for them to realize the truth and move on the best way that they can. He is willing to be honest with them, instead of protecting their innocence, as others might do. Ignoring that death happens just makes facing it worse later.

These moments when Harry is dealing with death are important, since death is such a large part of what influences and impacts the series. It affects Harry, Dumbledore, and Voldemort in completely different ways. The way they react to it defines the persons they become, just as much as the past does. When Sirius dies, Harry shouts at Dumbledore, frustrated and hurt. Dumbledore allows him to release his anger, but also reveals his weaknesses to Harry. Dumbledore understands that some aspect of what happened was his fault and tries to explain enough for Harry to handle. That can be seen when Dumbledore explains why he didn't choose Harry as a prefect: "I must confess...that I rather thought...you had enough responsibility to be going on with" (Rowling, *Order of the Phoenix* 884). Additionally, it's very important to notice that Harry "saw a tear trickling down Dumbledore's face into his long silver beard" (844). Both what Dumbledore says and his actions show that he cares for Harry, and this affection has grown over time.

Even though Dumbledore still cares for Harry in *Half-Blood Prince*, his mentoring shifts towards teaching Harry more about what he is up against because Dumbledore knows his death is imminent. In Harry's sixth year, we see far more of Dumbledore interacting with Harry than ever before. Every moment now is important for each of them, even if Harry doesn't quite understand all that Dumbledore is teaching him at first. It isn't simple defensive spells, but actually something far superior. He's teaching him to understand one's enemy through memories. Dumbledore gives him enough clues through this year and the next to help Harry search for the Horcruxes and destroy them. Dumbledore believed that Harry would be able to figure it out, but we're left to wonder why he chose to leave Harry clues instead of telling him exactly what he needed to do to destroy Voldemort. Ron even brings this up in *Deathly Hallows*. Dumbledore was giving Harry a chance to make those decisions. Dumbledore couldn't give him everything, and he also couldn't know everything. He hoped he was right. There is some point at which the mentor has to trust and hope for the best because he or she can't hold the protégé's hand forever. By some point, the protégé has to decipher solutions without his or her mentor's assistance.

When Dumbledore appears again at the end of *Deathly Hallows*, during a limbo moment that looks very much like King's Cross, it is to give Harry comfort and reassurance, as well as the additional information that only Dumbledore could give to Harry before they said their "goodbyes for the present" (722). Dumbledore even asks forgiveness for not telling Harry the truth about the Hallows because he feared that Harry would make his own mistakes. Dumbledore was finally able to confess to Harry about his past so that Harry could understand why Dumbledore had originally been drawn to the Hallows. Even though Harry doubts Dumbledore in the beginning of this book, he doesn't lose faith in what Dumbledore taught him. Afterwards, Harry was ready to continue on his journey. Dumbledore leaves perfect advice from a mentor to a protégé: "It's a curious thing, Harry, but perhaps those best suited for power are those who have never sought it. Those who, like you, have leadership thrust upon them, take up the mantle because they must, and find to their own great surprise that they wear it well" (Rowling, *Deathly Hallows* 718).

Ω Nox: Ending

Much remains to be discovered about the fascinating mentor protégé relationship. I've only touched the surface of what I believe that scholars can explore not only with these characters, but with other literary mentors in fantasy and other genres. Dumbledore wasn't only a great wizard; he was a great mentor because he chose to help Harry as best as he could. That's all the protégé could ever wish for.

Works Cited

Ackroyd, Peter, & Thomas Malory. *The Death of King Arthur: Thomas Malory's* Le Morte D'Arthur: *A Retelling.* New York: Viking, 2011.

Bassham, Gregory. *The Ultimate Harry Potter and Philosophy: Hogwarts for Muggles.* Hoboken, NJ: Wiley, 2010.

Campbell, Joseph. *The Hero with a Thousand Faces.* Princeton, NJ: Princeton UP, 1968.

Eco, Umberto. "The Myth of Superman." *The Critical Tradition: Classic Texts and Contemporary Trends*. Ed. David H. Richter. Boston: Bedford/St. Martin's, 2007. 950–61.

Goodrich, Peter. "Introduction." *The Romance of Merlin: An Anthology*. Ed. Peter Goodrich. New York: Garland Pub., 1990. xiii–xix.

Gollnick, James. "Merlin as Psychological Symbol: A Jungian View." *Comparative Studies in Merlin from the Vedas to C.G. Jung*. Ed. James Gollnick. Lewiston: Edwin Mellen, 1992. 111–131.

Guanio-Uluru, Lykke. "Dumbledore's Ethos of Love in Harry Potter." *J.K. Rowling: Harry Potter*. Eds. Cynthia J. Hallett & Peggy J. Huey. Houndmills, Basingstoke, Hampshire: Palgrave Macmillan, 2012. 82–96.

Guerin, Wilfred L., Earle Labor, Lee Morgan, Jeanne C. Reesman, & John R. Willingham. "Chapter Four: Mythological and Archetypal Approaches." *A Handbook of Critical Approaches to Literature*. Third ed. New York: Oxford UP, 1992. 147–81.

Hallett, Cynthia J., & Peggy J. Huey. *J. K. Rowling: Harry Potter*. Houndmills, Basingstoke, Hampshire: Palgrave Macmillan, 2012.

Lee, Anthony W. *Mentoring in Eighteenth-Century British Literature and Culture*. Surrey, England: Ashgate Publishing Limited, 2010.

Malory, Thomas, & Keith Baines. *Le Morte D'Arthur; King Arthur and the Legends of the Round Table*. New York: C.N. Potter, 1962.

Matthews, John. "The Return of Merlin." *Merlin: Shaman, Prophet, Magician*. London: Mitchell Beazley, 2004. 121–144.

Musiæ, Rusmir, & Lyndsay J. Agans. "Media Montage: Five Lessons of a Dumbledore Education." *About Campus* 12.5 (2007): 21–23. *Academic Search Complete*. Web. 27 Feb. 2014.

Nelson, Charles W. "From Gollum to Gandalf: The Guide Figures in J. R. R. Tolkien's Lord of the Rings." *Journal of the Fantastic in the Arts* 13.1 [49] (2002): 47–61. *MLA International Bibliography*. Web. 24 May 2014.

Porter, Lynnette R. *Unsung Heroes of the Lord of the Rings: From the Page to the Screen*. Westport, CT: Praeger, 2005.

Riga, Frank P. "Gandalf and Merlin: J.R.R. Tolkien's Adoption and Transformation of a Literary Tradition." *Mythlore* 27.1/2 (2008): 21–44. *Literary Reference Center*. Web. 27 Feb. 2014.

Rowling, J. K. *Harry Potter and the Philosopher's Stone.* London: Bloomsbury, 1997.

_____. *Harry Potter and the Chamber of Secrets.* New York: Arthur A. Levine/Scholastic, 1999.

_____. *Harry Potter and the Prisoner of Azkaban.* New York: Arthur A. Levine/Scholastic, 1999.

_____. *Harry Potter and the Goblet of Fire.* New York: Arthur A. Levine/Scholastic, 2000.

_____. *Harry Potter and the Order of the Phoenix.* New York: Arthur A. Levine/Scholastic, 2003.

_____. *Harry Potter and the Half-Blood Prince.* New York: Arthur A. Levine/Scholastic, 2005.

_____. *Harry Potter and the Deathly Hallows.* New York: Arthur A. Levine/Scholastic, 2007.

Schulzke, Marcus. "Wizard's Justice and Elf Liberation: Politics and Political Activation in Harry Potter." *J.K. Rowling: Harry Potter.* Eds. Cynthia J. Hallett & Peggy J. Huey. Houndmills, Basingstoke, Hampshire: Palgrave Macmillan, 2012. 111–21.

Spivack, Charlotte. "Chapter 1—Medieval Merlins: Emergence of the Monomyth." *Merlin: A Thousand Heroes with One Face.* Lewiston: E. Mellen, 1994. 1–16.

Tolkien, J. R. R. *The Hobbit, Or, There and Back Again.* Boston: Houghton Mifflin, 1966.

_____. *The Fellowship of the Ring.* Boston: Houghton Mifflin, 1993. The Lord of the Rings.

_____. *The Two Towers.* Boston: Houghton Mifflin, 1965. The Lord of the Rings.

_____. *The Return of the King.* Boston: Houghton Mifflin, 1965. The Lord of the Rings.

Tolstoy, Nikolai. "The Matter of Britain." *The Quest for Merlin.* Boston: Little, Brown, 1985. 1–20.

Torregrossa, Michael A. "The Way of the Wizard: Reflections of Merlin on Film." *The Medieval Hero on Screen: Representations from Beowulf to Buffy.* Eds. Martha W. Driver & Sid Ray. Jefferson, NC: McFarland, 2004. 167–191.

The Dark Lord and the Prince: Machiavellian Elements in Harry Potter_____

Todd J. Ide

In his book *The Irresistible Rise of Harry Potter,* Andrew Blake argues that England in the late 1990s was in the midst of an identity crisis, unsure of who it was and where it fit in an increasingly global economy. England, Blake asserts, had only its past, which was no longer sufficient to drive the economy, attract tourists, or define itself. Enter Tony Blair and New Labor, who were viewed as forward thinkers who would both honor and build on the past. New Labor was able to unseat the Conservative party of Margaret Thatcher and Tony Major, whom the public saw as defenders of the status quo. This "retrolution," as Blake called it, was successful because it "present[ed] aspects of the future through terms set by the past, in order to make [the future] seem more palatable" (8–9).

According to Blake, J. K. Rowling's *Harry Potter and the Sorcerer's Stone*, reflects the optimism felt by many British citizens with the election of Tony Blair (23). With the publication of *Harry Potter and the Prisoner of Azkaban* in 1999, a political thread begins to emerge from the storyline. Yet, some argue that, despite the appearance of this theme, it would be "foolish to try and glean precise real-life parallels between Potter's world and ours" (Taylor). This assertion is flawed. While *Harry Potter and the Sorcerer's Stone* and *Harry Potter and the Chamber of Secrets* do reflect the optimism to which Blake refers, it is slowly replaced with a darker view of the world.

The political thread found in these two works does not fade over the course of the series, but instead becomes one of its main themes. What does slowly fade is the optimism expressed within the books. It begins to fade in *Harry Potter and the Prisoner of Azkaban* and is replaced with a growing sense of disillusionment with political leaders and politics alike. The last four novels of the Harry Potter series draw clear parallels both to events that are happening within our reality and to modern political practices used therein. These parallels clearly can be read as a reflection on the political climate within the United States and how it has become more cynical and pessimistic.

Misfortune and Gain

The most obvious of these references is the opening of *Harry Potter and the Half-Blood Prince.* Chapter one opens in the office of an unnamed British prime minister who is busy trying to "suppress [the] unpleasant memories of" a very long and frustrating week and waiting for a phone call from "The President of a far distant country" (Rowling, *Half-Blood Prince* 1). While it is arguable that these two characters represent Tony Blair, the British prime minister at that time, and George W. Bush, then president of the US, what is not arguable is the political predicament in which the prime minister finds himself. Rowling describes his preoccupation with newspaper accounts that not only "enumerate[d] all of the terrible things that had happened that week" but pointed out how each was the fault of the current government (1). The news stories included several quotations from and a picture of one of his political opponents that "barely concealed his own broad grin" (2). The prime minister is interrupted from his thoughts when a painting in his office speaks to request a meeting between himself and Cornelius Fudge.

Fudge's appearance and conversation with the prime minister allow Rowling to give the reader back-story of various events that have transpired since the close of the last installment in the series. It also allows the reader to learn that the waning political fortunes of the unnamed Muggle prime minister reflect events and fortunes in the wizarding world as well. Fudge explains how Lord Voldemort has indeed returned and is behind the various murders, bridge disasters, hurricanes, and other events that have plagued the Muggle prime minister and damaged his approval ratings. Fudge's own fate is the most interesting and useful for our purposes.

After explaining the state of war the wizarding world is in with the return of Voldemort and how these events are spilling over into the Muggle world, the prime minister demands that Fudge has a "responsibility as Minister of Magic" to act. To which Fudge replies, "My dear Prime Minister, you can't honestly think I'm still Minister of Magic after all this? I was sacked three days ago! The whole Wizarding community has been screaming for my resignation for a fortnight" (Rowling, *Half-Blood Prince* 15). Later in the chapter, the reader is introduced to the new minister of magic, Rufus Scrimgeour.

This section illustrates a basic truism of modern politics—the misfortune of one is another's opportunity. Regardless of whether a political leader can control events or not, events do influence the popularity and support that leader enjoys, and if he or she is seen to stumble in response to those events, the result can damage a politician beyond the ability to recover. Modern examples abound. President George H. W. Bush enjoyed approval ratings of over 89 percent following the first Gulf War (Kagay); yet, because of a faltering economy and a perception of being out of touch with the American people, he lost his bid for reelection a little over a year later, drawing just under 38 percent of the popular vote (Leip).

Indeed, the second President Bush experienced a similar drop. George W. Bush enjoyed a job approval rating similar to that of his father following the terrorist attacks on September 11, 2001; however, his decision to go to war with Iraq, the mishandling of that war, his poor response to Hurricane Katrina in 2005, and a lagging economy damaged both his ability to lead and his popularity. British prime minister Tony Blair faced similar problems at home because of his decision to support Bush and send troops to fight in Iraq (Travis & Black). These stumbles resulted in the political fortunes of both faltering. With falling poll numbers, some in his party began to view George W. Bush as a potential liability in the 2006 off-year Congressional elections (Balz). Tony Blair experienced a similar drop in popularity and faced pressure from within his own party to resign as prime minister (Adams). Both of these real-world situations mirror the situation faced by the Muggle prime minister and Fudge in the *Half-Blood Prince.*

Wealth and Fame

While political references are most prominent in *Half-Blood Prince*, they neither start nor end there. The earliest reference to the political landscape that exists within the wizarding world occurs in *Prisoner of Azkaban* when the Minister of Magic, Cornelius Fudge, meets Harry for the first time. Harry has escaped from his uncle's house aboard the Knight Bus after accidentally inflating his Aunt Marge like a balloon, and he heads toward the Leaky Cauldron. As he exits the bus, Harry is greeted by Fudge and quickly escorted into a private room, where Fudge expresses his relief that Harry is safe.

When Harry asks what his punishment is going to be for breaking The Decree for the Restriction of Underage Wizardry, Fudge declares, "Oh, my dear boy, we're not going to punish you for a little thing like that. . . . It was an accident! We don't send people to Azkaban just for blowing up their aunts!" (Rowling, *Prisoner of Azkaban* 45). Harry explains to the prime minister that he had been warned by the ministry the previous summer, after magic had been detected in his home, that he would be expelled from Hogwarts if it occurred again. To this, Fudge looks awkward and explains, "Circumstances change, Harry. . . . We have to take into account . . . in the present climate . . . . Surely you don't *want* to be expelled?" (45, emphasis Rowling's).

In this exchange, Rowling begins to call attention to the often cynical nature of politics. It could be argued that the minister's decision was based on concern for Harry's safety given the fact that Sirius Black had escaped Azkaban. This assessment, however, would fail to take into account Harry's fame. Fudge's decision not to pursue disciplinary action against Harry is based not on any concern for safety, but entirely on Harry's celebrity within the wizarding world. Throughout the series, we are continually reminded that *everyone* in the wizarding world knows Harry Potter's story and that the public believes Voldemort's reign of terror came to an end because of Harry. One can only imagine the backlash that would result from Harry's arrest and expulsion from Hogwarts. It would be seen as a punishment far exceeding the crime, especially given that the perpetrator, Harry, has already suffered tremendous personal losses. Fudge, realizing this, opts instead to intervene on Harry's behalf to ensure that there will be not only no punishment, but also no official record of the event.

Wealth, like fame, warps the political and legal system of the magical world. This is made evident in *Harry Potter and the Goblet of Fire* and *Harry Potter and the Order of the Phoenix.* The reader sees how money can buy access to those in power. One of the first examples is the Minister of Magic inviting the Malfoy family to be his personal guests at the Quidditch World Cup. This is not something that the vast majority of those in the magical world could ever expect to experience. Later, we see how the Malfoys' money and support of the ministry and its causes buys them the benefit of the doubt, when toward the end of *Goblet of Fire,* Harry returns from the graveyard after battling Voldemort and accuses Lucius Malfoy of being a Death Eater. "'Malfoy was cleared!' said Fudge, visibly affronted. 'A very old family—donations to excellent causes—'" (Rowling, *Goblet of Fire* 706). The power of money to derail the wheels of justice can also be seen in *Order of the Phoenix* when Mr. Weasley asserts that Willy Widdershins wasn't prosecuted for creating regurgitating toilets as a form of Muggle-baiting because money changed hands (Rowling, *Order of the Phoenix* 489–90). The wizarding world appears to be no different from our own when it comes to the corrupting influence of money and our infatuation with fame to alter the course of justice.

In our own world, it is not hard to see how the power of money and celebrity is used to circumvent or bend the legal system to favor the rich and famous. For example, musician Kid Rock (Robert Ritchie) was stopped by Nashville police in 2005 for suspected drunk driving (Clarke). Rock was also wanted for punching a DJ at a strip club earlier that night. The officer neither administered a field sobriety test nor arrested him for the alleged assault. He opted instead to let him go after getting his autograph. This is not an isolated incident. Rap artist Dr. Dre (Andre Young) received a five-month jail sentence for a DUI conviction in 1994, despite already being on probation for a battery conviction after he broke a rival's jaw (Clarke). While in jail, he was allowed work release to shoot a music video. Many of the rich and famous, such as actresses Lindsay Lohan and Michelle Rodriguez and socialite Nicole Richie, do not even see the inside of a jail cell despite convictions for illegal drug use, DUI, and reckless driving (Clarke; Winton).

In addition, various correctional institutions in the United States now offer inmates who can *pay a premium*, the opportunity to stay in better facilities, have private rooms, use cell phones and computers, and eat restaurant meals (Groden, Clarke). Clearly, as Bethany Barratt writes in *The Politics of Harry Potter*, "money itself, without title or old connections, [is] . . . now sufficient to gain access to positions of power, which would have been inaccessible in the past" (14). As a result, those who can afford to, are able to manipulate the system to avoid punishment altogether or to substantially soften any consequences for bad behavior.

Control of Information and the Message

Money, however, is not the only factor that can twist the political systems of both our own and Harry's world. As Barratt notes in *The Politics of Harry Potter*, "[It is] in fact, information, and access to it, [that has] always been the currency of creating and maintaining political power" (118). The wealthy and political elites work hard to control not only the way information is presented, but also what information is disseminated for public consumption. In doing so, these elite individuals are able to manipulate public opinion to fit their agenda, a phenomenon described by Noam Chomsky and Edward Herman as "manufactured consent." In both Harry's world and ours, we see the results of manufactured consent.

One tool politicians in both worlds use to sway public opinion and, as a result, to manufacture consent, is to attempt to control the message presented by the government and its representatives. This desire to speak with one voice is illustrated in *Half-Blood Prince* through Fudge and his actions. In the first chapter, Fudge is shown repeatedly downplaying potential problems to the Muggle prime minister. When Fudge informs him that there has been a mass breakout from Azkaban and the prime minister reacts with fear, Fudge reassures him, saying, "No need to worry, no need to worry! . . . We'll have them rounded up in no time—just thought you ought to know!" (Rowling, *Half-Blood Prince* 9). As Barratt argues, "Elites seek to affect the public's understanding of the nature of political problems [and] the causes behind them. . . . [In order] to gain office or stay in office" (22).

As ministers of magic, Cornelius Fudge and Rufus Scrimgeour strive to control and spin events by exerting control over the media in order to manage public opinion. An early example is the issuing of various educational decrees by Fudge and the ministry throughout Harry's fifth year in school. Fudge announces, in the middle of the night, his appointment of Dolores Umbridge as the first-ever Hogwarts High Inquisitor under the guise of responding to the concerns of "anxious parents" about "falling standards" at the school (Rowling, *Order of the Phoenix* 306–7). This, of course, receives extensive coverage by *The Daily Prophet,* which has clearly been notified of the decision in advance. These actions are merely an extension of the efforts by Fudge, through *The Daily Prophet* and Rita Skeeter, to orchestrate a smear campaign against Harry and Albus Dumbledore as headmaster in *Order of the Phoenix.*

Scrimgeour continues along this path. He uses *The Daily Prophet* to promote his and the ministry's efforts to protect the students at Hogwarts and report the arrests of supposed Death Eaters, all in an effort to put the ministry in the best possible light (Rowling, *Order of the Phoenix* 41, 221). Scrimgeour even tries to convince Harry, in a cynical attempt at spin for the media, to drop by the ministry to give the public the impression that "the Chosen One" is working with, and supports the efforts of, the ministry in this second war with Voldemort (344–48, 649).

Politicians in our world are as media savvy as their wizarding counterparts. George W. Bush and his handlers made a concerted effort to control the media and, as a result, control the message. Bush rarely held press conferences where he had to face unscripted questions (Drum). Instead, Bush preferred the staged photo op complete with a crowd of handpicked supporters and questions that had all been prescreened by his handlers. President Barack Obama is only slightly better. Like Bush, Obama rarely holds press conferences,[1] and even when he does, he seldom takes questions (Koffler). The White House closely controls "access to Obama" preferring "one-on-one settings" that, because of time limitations, force the reporter to stick to planned questions (Koffler). In addition, because of the intimidating nature of a one-on-one interview environment with the President and the reporter's desire for future access, few challenge Obama (Koffler).

Efforts to control both the message and the flow of information coming out of a given administration in the Muggle world go even further. Unlike Fudge and Scrimgeour, who appear to exert considerable influence over *The Daily Prophet* and what it reports, presidents and prime ministers are unable to exert the same level of control or censorship. This is not for lack of trying. Both President George H.W. Bush and George W. Bush controlled the media during both Gulf Wars by not allowing independent news coverage. Instead, reporters were embedded with various military units, and reporters identified by the administration and the military as potential "troublemakers" were not selected for these positions (Hutchinson). Those who were selected and who violated the rules established by the military were expelled from Iraq and barred from any US military base in the world (Kamber & Arango).

George W. Bush's administration also provided ready-made video news releases to various media outlets and paid Iraqi newspapers to publish positive stories about the US presence (Mazzetti & Daragahi; Chaddock). President Obama and his administration have also taken various measures in an attempt to control their message. Obama's administration has used the Espionage Act to pursue criminal prosecutions of anyone who leaks information that contradicts the administration's narrative to the media (Kreig). Obama has investigated and prosecuted whistleblowers at a greater rate than any previous president. According to ProPublica, an investigative news service, the US government has used the Espionage Act eleven times since 1945 to prosecute government workers who leaked classified information to journalists (Greenberg). Of those eleven occasions, seven have been at the behest of the Obama administration (Greenberg). These actions have had a "chilling effect" on the media (Mitchell).

Alternative media sources and many reporters' refusal to identify their sources despite prosecution have stymied these efforts, to an extent (Mitchell; Kreig). For example, despite the ministry's best efforts to discredit the story that Lord Voldemort has returned, Harry manages to get the facts out by using *The Quibbler* (Rowling, *Order of the Phoenix* 566–67). In our world, there are many alternative media outlets. These come in the form of a multitude of digital media sites (see this chapter's bibliography). Alternative sources for raw information include other websites such as WikiLeaks. These media outlets see it as their duty not only to challenge the official narrative presented both by politicians and in the mainstream media, but also to provide access to information that allows members of the public to draw their own conclusions.

Political leaders in both worlds demonstrate their belief in another basic truism about politics—that perception is reality. People are convinced not by data, but by what they see and hear. These are the things that people put their faith in, regardless of what the facts may say to the contrary. This explains the lengths to which politicians in both worlds will go in order to craft and control the message that the public receives. Scrimgeour readily acknowledges this to Harry when he states that the question of Harry's being "the Chosen One" is largely irrelevant to him except as it relates "to the Wizarding community at large" because to them "it's all perception" and what is important is "what people believe" (Rowling, *Half-Blood Prince* 344). We can see the belief that perception is reality play out in the Muggle world almost daily.

The confusion between perception and reality occurs because, as Barratt notes, "political elites can control information without actually misrepresenting it," (22). The political elite can do this because of their position and title. With the American public's ever-shrinking attention span, the decline of newspapers, and the need to get higher and higher television ratings, media producers must make decisions about where to focus their attention. Those that have the bully pulpit command the media's attention. This attention, allowing politicians and others in positions of power and influence to control the message the media present and, as a result, to influence what we believe. For example, 38 percent of Americans still doubt that President Obama was born in the United States despite all of the evidence to the contrary.

Pushing an Agenda

The *Harry Potter* series also comments on the willingness of wizard and Muggle political leaders alike to use the power of their office to pursue their own political and ideological agenda in an effort to increase or shore up their own political power. The first instance of the ministry's taking actions to satisfy the political and personal agendas of ministry officials occurs toward the end of *Prisoner of Azkaban* when the ministry declares its intention to have the Dementors administer the ultimate punishment to Sirius Black upon his capture, the sucking out of his soul. This action is decided not by the courts or by legal decree, but on the order of the minister of magic himself because of Sirius' being the first to successfully escape from Azkaban. A public failure such as this causes the electorate to question their elected leaders and the competency of the government.

Additionally, the willingness of public officials to ignore laws for political advantage can be seen later in *Prisoner of Azkaban*, when Fudge recalls how only "trained hit wizards" could have taken down Black after he killed Pettigrew (Rowling, *Prisoner of Azkaban* 208). Fudge's word choice clearly indicates that these are not Aurors, but something different. This reference to hit wizards is the only one in the novels. The term "hit" in this usage can only have one possible meaning,[2] and that is the murder or killing of an individual on the order of another. This is not within the purview of normal law enforcement or military activities. Such an action, the murder or "hit" of someone on the orders of a government, is illegal and undertaken to advance the political and/or ideological agenda.[3]

This theme is developed further in *Goblet of Fire*. Fudge is not the only ministry official willing to ignore laws or abuse the power of his office in order to pursue a personal agenda. The extent of the actions taken by the ministry to round up Death Eaters and Voldemort supporters is developed in greater depth when Sirius tries to explain to Harry, Ron, and Hermione what life was like before and after Voldemort's first defeat. Sirius tells of how he and others were thrown into Azkaban without trial on the orders of Bartemius Crouch, Sr. (Rowling, *Goblet of Fire* 526–27). Black goes on to explain how Crouch enjoyed wide support for his "very harsh measures against Voldemort's supporters," including giving the Aurors the power to kill rather than just capture and to use the other Unforgivable Curses on suspects as well (527). Black says, "Crouch fought violence with violence" and "became as ruthless and cruel as many on the Dark Side" (527).

The willingness of the Ministry to bend or ignore the law in pursuit of political gain extends beyond the pursuit or punishment of alleged criminals to include also those that oppose or contradict the government's official line. We see this in the early chapters of *Order of the Phoenix* as the ministry begins its efforts to discredit Harry and Dumbledore for claiming that Voldemort is back. When Harry uses magic to defend himself and his cousin Dudley from Dementor attack, the ministry ignores established due process rights by unilaterally expelling Harry and ordering the destruction of his wand (Rowling, *Order of the Phoenix* 26–27). This is in sharp contrast to the actions taken by Fudge in *Prisoner of Azkaban*, when Fudge viewed Harry as a potential ally. The ministry goes even further in its efforts to circumvent due process by changing the time of the hearing at the last minute without notifying the accused, by saying that the hearing is only a formality, and by trying the matter before the entire Wizengamot (Rowling, *Order of the Phoenix* 32–33).

The efforts of the minister and his supporters to shore up their power can be seen later in *Order of the Phoenix* when Dolores Umbridge, through the actions of Fudge and the Ministry, increases her power dramatically as the Hogwarts High Inquisitor. This office gives Umbridge the power to discipline students, dismiss faculty (306), and ban student organizations (Rowling, *Order of the Phoenix* 351–52). Both Fudge and Umbridge admit that the Ministry of Magic under Fudge's leadership is consciously changing or ignoring laws in an effort to achieve its political agenda (149, 416). Umbridge's torture of Harry through her use of the blood quill and her vendetta against both him and other Hogwarts students who are seen to be opponents of the ministry and herself demonstrates the ministry's willingness to violate both ministry rules and the law to achieve their goals.

Once again, numerous parallels exist between Harry Potter's world and ours. George W. Bush authorized the indefinite imprisonment of "enemy combatants" in Guantánamo Bay. Nearly 800 such individuals have been held by America, with 136 still being detained as of December 11, 2014 (Crapapple). This, despite the assertion of Major General Michael Lehnert, Guantánamo's first commander, "[that] many of the detainees should never have ended up there at all" (Crabapple).

The Bush administration also embraced the use of torture (which it euphemistically termed "enhanced interrogation techniques") by US intelligence agencies and the military in an attempt to gain information from suspected terrorists. The study on the CIA's use of torture, released by Senate Select Committee on Intelligence, indicated that these techniques included sleep deprivation, extreme temperatures, mock executions, threats to have detainees' families killed, waterboarding, and sexual assault ("Senate report"; "Techniques Used in Guantánamo"; Crabapple). These techniques led to the death of at least one detainee ("Senate report").

Both President Bush and Vice President Cheney repeatedly defended these practices, often citing a US Justice Department memo that claimed such practices are legal. This claim is legally questionable, given the fact that the US has signed international treaties outlawing torture, including the International Convention Against Torture (Shane). Such techniques, according to a US Senate report, "yielded no significant intelligence," despite claims to the contrary by the Bush administration and the CIA.

President Obama, despite criticizing these violations of law as a candidate, has extended the ability of intelligence and security agencies to ignore basic rights. His administration has issued opinions that allow individuals, including US citizens, to be questioned by officials without counsel or without being advised of their Miranda rights (Perez). Additionally, Obama's administration has expanded the use of drone strikes, which again are legally questionable under international law (Memmott). Targets of these strikes include US citizen Shaykh Anwar Aulaqi (also spelled al-Awlaki), who had never been charged with a crime (Ratner). Aulaqi, who was living in Yemen, was a radical cleric associated with Al-Qaeda and had made speeches calling for the destruction of America, but he was also an American citizen (Friedersdorf; Ratner). Despite knowing Aulaqi's whereabouts, the Obama administration did not capture him, but instead had him killed. Many see Obama's decision to order the execution of a US citizen through drone strikes as a direct violation of "the Fifth Amendment, an executive order that forbids assassinations, and a federal statute that prohibits murdering American citizens abroad" (Friedersdorf; Ratner).

Mistakes

Actions such as the ones listed above are, more often than not, viewed in hindsight as mistakes. However, seldom do politicians admit their mistakes, and if they do, they attempt to downplay their significance. Neither Fudge nor Scrimgeour is different from Muggle politicians in this regard. Fudge, for example, when asked by the prime minister if Sirius Black has joined forces with Voldemort, replies, "'Merlin's beard, no. Black's dead. Turns out we were— er—mistaken about Black. He was innocent after all . . .' he added defensively" (Rowling, *Half Blood Prince* 11). Scrimgeour is no different. In chapter sixteen, Scrimgeour meets with Harry to try to enlist his help in a publicity ploy. When Harry accuses him of being no better than his predecessor was because he has "chuck[ed] the wrong [person] into jail,"[4] Scrimgeour neither denies Harry's claim nor admits that the action or charges were a mistake (347).

George W. Bush and his administration are no different from the leaders presented in *Half-Blood Prince.* They, too, had a difficult time accepting responsibility for their actions, decisions, or statements. The Bush administration repeatedly denied that it misled or misrepresented the evidence that Iraq had terrorist ties or was pursuing weapons of mass destruction, despite reports and evidence to the contrary ("How the Bush Administration Sold the Iraq War"). In response to Hurricane Katrina, the President did no better. He spent weeks trying to shift blame and deny inaction, making statements that FEMA and its then director, Mike Brown, were doing an excellent job (McGreal; Diemer).

The efforts to deny the mistakes made by the Bush administration relating to the Iraq war have continued. Vice President Dick Cheney and his daughter penned an opinion piece that made every effort to rewrite the facts of history (Baragona). Cheney writes, "Rarely has a U.S. president been so wrong about so much at the expense of so many" (Cheney & Cheney). Ironically, it is not the second Bush presidency to which he refers. Cheneys blame the instability of Iraq on Obama, citing his decision to withdraw American troops in 2014. Both Cheneys seem to forget that it was the Bush administration that signed the agreement requiring American troops to withdraw in 2014 (Bishop). They also seem unaware that the Iraqi government refused to negotiate with the US to keep troops there (Bishop). Finally, neither seems to grasp that it was the Bush administration, as Secretary of State John Kerry says, "who blundered into Iraq on false intelligence, with no endgame," and that the blame for Iraq's predicament solely belongs to them (qtd. in "'Please'").

Control, Don't Be Controlled
Politicians, whether wizard or Muggle, attempt to minimize the damage these mistakes cause by working to appear to control events, rather than be controlled by them. Within the pages of the Harry Potter series we see this several times. Fudge flatly states this fact in *Harry Potter and the Chamber of Secrets* as he is explaining the necessity of arresting Hagrid. "'Look at it from my point of view,' said Fudge, fidgeting with his bowler. 'I'm under a lot of pressure. Got to be seen to be doing something. If it turns out it wasn't Hagrid, he'll be back and no more said. But I've got to take him in. Got to. Wouldn't be doing my duty—'" (Rowling, *Chamber of Secrets* 261). Fudge implies that Hagrid's arrest and imprisonment in Azkaban

could become permanent if no one else is charged with the attacks that occur in the novel (261).

This concept is further supported through Fudge's conversation with the Muggle prime minister. Fudge mentions that he had "every Auror in the Ministry" trying to capture Voldemort and his followers (Rowling, *Half-Blood Prince* 12). One can assume that these efforts were heavily publicized in order to try to calm the wizarding public. Part of these efforts include the publication and distribution of a pamphlet entitled "Protecting Your Home Against Dark Forces" that list steps and suggestions those in the wizarding community should take in order to help ensure their safety (42–3), suggestions that both Dumbledore and Harry and, by inference, the majority of the wizarding community, did not find particularly useful or valuable (61).

In the *Half-Blood Prince*, Scrimgeour, as minister of magic, also wants to be seen in control. He does this by "set[ting] up several new offices in response to the present situation" (Rowling, *Half-Blood Prince* 84) and publicly announcing unnamed "tough new measures ... to ensure the safety" of Hogwarts students (41). The Ministry even arrests innocent people in order to appear to be winning the war against Voldemort and the Death Eaters (221).

Again, the events described in *Half-Blood Prince* have a ready counterpart in the real world. The Bush and Obama administrations, like Fudge and Scrimgeour, desperately want to be portrayed as in control of events. After the September 11 attacks, President Bush reorganized several governmental departments and created the Department of Homeland Security whose job it is to protect Americans from the dark forces that want to do America and her citizens harm (Gerstenzang). In addition, Bush created an Intelligence Czar, who would oversee the various intelligence agencies and coordinate their efforts so information like the type that could have prevented 9/11 would not fall through the cracks again (Branigin). Homeland Security Secretary Tom Ridge even went so far as to appear on national television urging the public to buy duct tape and plastic sheeting to seal their windows with in case of a chemical or biological terrorist attack (Reaves). These efforts in particular were considered inane and laughable by most of the public.

During daily press briefings and public speeches, both presidents and various administration officials have outlined efforts, preparations and plans that they have implemented or are implementing to ensure the safety of the public at large. They even mention that a number of terrorist plots have been foiled, numbers which are impossible to confirm or deny (Sculietti). This is further supported by evidence cited in the Senate Report on the CIA's use of torture which disproves the claim that the use of the torture prevented terrorist plots ("Senate report"). The American government has arrested and imprisoned American citizens and, in the process, denied them due process guaranteed under the Constitution. Sami Al-Arian, a University of South Florida professor who was arrested and charged as a terrorist under the Patriot Act, was found innocent on December 6, 2005 (Lichtblau). In a similar case, lawyers for the Justice Department reversed their position that American citizen José Padilla was an enemy combatant and therefore not entitled to Constitutional protections after he was held for three years without being charged with any crime (Levy). Each of these actions, whether committed by wizards in *Harry Potter* or Muggles in our world, is designed to try to reassure the public that the leaders are in control and "they're doing something" (Rowling, *Half-Blood Prince* 221).

Spying

The desire of politicians to be seen in control of events often goes hand in hand with increased efforts at intelligence gathering. Where the *Harry Potter* series and our world parallel each other is the decision by both the Ministry of Magic and the government of the United States to intensify spying on their own citizens. Within the wizarding world, governmental spying takes two primary forms. The first is the interception and reading of Owl Post. This action is first mentioned in *Goblet of Fire* when Sirius warns Harry not to use Hedwig again to send him letters because she is so recognizable (Rowling, *Goblet of Fire* 240). The interception and reading of Owl Post by government officials also occurs on at least two different occasions in *Order of the Phoenix*. All of the letters that Harry receives from Ron and Hermione in the beginning of the novel comment on how they are unable to give many details about what they're up to in case the letters are intercepted (Rowling, *Order of the Phoenix* 8).

While it could be argued that the both Ron and Hermione are referring to Voldemort and his supporters with these references, I would argue that it is the Ministry of Magic and its officials that they are attempting to evade. It is the ministry that is actively seeking to discredit both Dumbledore and Harry in this installment of the series. This is also supported by the later injury to Hedwig, when she was intercepted and her message was read (Rowling, *Order of the Phoenix* 336). The surveillance put in place by Umbridge and the Ministry at Hogwarts even extended to the Floo Network, which was monitored to ensure that there could be no unknown communication. This monitoring is made evident when Sirius is nearly captured by Umbridge in the Gryffindor common room's fireplace in chapter seventeen of the *Order of the Phoenix*. The monitoring of the Floo Network is also demonstrated by Harry's need to break into Umbridge's office later in the novel to contact Sirius, as it is the only space that is unmonitored—a fact that Umbridge herself admits.

The ministry and its officials employ the time-honored technique of utilizing human spies as well. This is evidenced in a couple of different ways within the series. The first is when Fudge promotes Percy to be his assistant, despite his failure as the senior Barty Crouch's assistant (Rowling, *Order of the Phoenix* 71). This is widely seen in the novel as an attempt by Fudge to keep tabs on members of the Order of the Phoenix. This theme is further carried through when Umbridge, as headmaster, creates the Inquisitorial Squad, which is "a select group of students who are supportive of the Ministry of Magic, [and] handpicked" (626). One of the main purposes of the Inquisitorial Squad is to spy on fellow students and report back to Umbridge.

The parallels to spying by both American and British governments on their own citizens is readily apparent. One of the best known programs is code–named PRISM. This program allowed the National Security Agency, FBI and British intelligence to "extract audio and video chats, photographs, e-mails, documents, and connection logs" from various Internet sites and service providers including Microsoft, Apple, Google and Facebook (Gellman & Poitras). The United States also pursued a program of collecting metadata on the cell phone calls of American citizens without obtaining search warrants (Nakashima). These actions are seen by civil libertarians as illegal despite "an independent executive-branch board" finding that because the program "target[ed] foreigners overseas [it was] lawful and effective but that certain elements push 'close to the line' of being unconstitutional" (Nakashima). Just as in the wizarding world, politicians in our world use spies to keep tabs on perceived enemies ("Surveillance of Citizens by Government").

Attack Opponents

The final example involves the willingness of the Ministry of Magic and political leaders in our own world to smear their political enemies and to seek retaliation against those who oppose them. Again, we see this clearly in *Harry Potter and the Order of the Phoenix* when, as has been mentioned earlier, the Ministry is orchestrating a public campaign to discredit both Dumbledore and Harry, and, as a consequence, the wizards' claim that Voldemort has returned (Rowling, *Order of the Phoenix* 74–75, 95, 184). Within these pages, it becomes clear that ministry employees are not free to oppose or contradict official ministry positions without fear of losing their jobs (95).

Fudge demonstrates a willingness to use whatever means are at his disposal to either silence his critics or discredit them. As has been previously mentioned in *Order of the Phoenix*, Fudge attempts to paint Harry in the wizarding world as a delusional lunatic who cannot be believed. Fudge then tries and fails to have Harry expelled. Finally, he uses dubious political means to appoint Umbridge to the faculty at Hogwarts. These efforts by the ministry to silence Harry do not end with the start of the school year. For example, when Harry announces in Umbridge's class that Voldemort has returned, she

---

publicly declares that to be a lie and issues immediate punishment for this offense (Rowling, *Order of the Phoenix* 245). This form of retaliation is designed to chill and prevent others from publicly challenging the Ministry's version of events lest they, like Harry and Dumbledore, find themselves the victims of a smear campaign in *The Daily Prophet.*

Scrimgeour is not above using the same tricks to maintain his grip on power. He circumvents Dumbledore and drops in unexpectedly on Harry at the Weasleys' during the Christmas holiday (Rowling, *Half-Blood Prince* 341–48). During his visit, he attempts to convince Harry to use his regained fame and credibility in the wizarding world to boost the image of the ministry by making it appear as if "the Chosen One" (346–47) is involved and approves of the ministry's activities. Scrimgeour also uses this visit with Harry to try to gain information that may be useful in keeping Dumbledore in line or forcing him to be supportive of the ministry. The desire to smear and destroy one's political enemies, at least in the case of the Ministry of Magic, even extends to those who, like Dumbledore, have died.

Harry Potter and the Deathly Hallows demonstrates the animosity that political opponents can inspire. I would argue that Rita Skeeter's biography of Dumbledore and the articles that appear in *The Daily Prophet* are, in large part, an effort at continued retaliation by Scrimgeour and others within the Ministry for Dumbledore's refusal to publicly support their course of action and to convince Harry to do likewise (Rowling, *Deathly Hallows* 4, 152). Skeeter and the ministry, I believe employ many well-worn tricks to boost the effectiveness of thier attacks on Dumbledore in her biography of him. First, Skeeter claims that the biography is factual and based on extensive research, but insists on keeping secret many of her sources (24). Second, Skeeter uses innuendo to call into question the character of both Dumbledore and Harry. She does this within the biography and *The Daily Prophet* interview when she states that the relationship between headmaster and student has "been called *unhealthy*, even *sinister*. . . . There is no question that Dumbledore took an *unnatural* interest in Potter from the word go" (27, emphasis added).

Politicians in our world use the same tactics. Bush and his allies were not above running smear campaigns against their political opponents. Again, there is ample evidence to support this claim. The administration and its proponents repeatedly branded as unpatriotic, uninformed, ill-advised, wrong, even traitorous anyone who criticized or questioned its policy on Iraq, the evidence used to justify the country's invasion, or its refusal to support an outright ban on torture (ACLU; Gertz). A prime example of this was the Dixie Chicks, who after criticizing President Bush publicly, found their careers nearly destroyed and their lives threatened ("Dixie Chicks"). Both Bush and Obama have used with regularity secret sources to justify their actions (Warren).

The Bush and Obama administrations have also sought retaliation against their opponents. An obvious example of this was the outing, by Bush administration sources, of Valerie Plame as a CIA operative after her husband, former ambassador Joe Wilson, criticized the Bush administration and its handling of the Iraq War ("Key Players"). This action was taken as a form of political payback, despite its illegality. Within the Obama White House, retaliation takes the form of efforts to fire or imprison those who would leak contradictory information to the media (Kreig; Mitchell). Prosecuting leakers is, perhaps, a safer political option, since these whistleblowers are technically violating the law. If administrations can manage to slow or stop the leak of information, they can deprive opponents of potential ammunition and thereby strengthen their position.

Throughout *Half-Blood Prince*, J. K. Rowling expresses her feelings about modern politics and politicians through her descriptions of those in the world of her creation. For example, she describes the unnamed Muggle prime minister's first encounter with Fudge and the wizarding world: "He had been standing alone in this very office, savoring the triumph that was his after so many years of dreaming and scheming" (5). The choice to use the word "scheming" in her description of how he rose to power not only makes a clear value judgment about this particular politician, but also implies that any person who reaches that level of power will be like-minded.

This idea is supported further by the text when the prime minister is informed that the Dementors have abandoned Azkaban and are breeding throughout the countryside. The prime minister is not concerned that they are attacking people, but that they are "spreading despair and hopelessness among his voters" (Rowling, *Half Blood Prince* 14–5). Again, the implication is clear: The prime minister is more concerned about how this will affect his ability to stay in power than the potential death and destruction the Dementors may cause.

Conclusion

Karin E. Westman writes that Rowling's writing "marks the Wizarding community as an echo of and commentary on both the Muggle world of the novels and the contemporary world of post-Thatcher England—a connection Rowling herself has acknowledged in a Canadian Broadcasting Corporation interview" (306). Others, such as Alfonso Cuaron, director of the film adaptation of *Harry Potter and the Prisoner of Azkaban*, state that Rowling "reworked the fifth book in the series to incorporate—and decry—current events and trends" (Hersh). Additionally, in an interview posted on *The Leaky Cauldron,* Rowling gave this response to a question about the significance of the year a character died. "It amuses me to make allusions to things that [are] happening in the Muggle world so my feeling would be that while there's a global Muggle war going on, there's also a global Wizarding war going on" (Anelli).

With each installment of the Harry Potter series, the tone becomes increasingly darker and more complex. Rowling's presentation of the political forces within Harry's world reflects the growing cynicism that many in our own world feel toward governments and politicians. We are reminded that government, any government, is only as good or as bad as the people that serve in it. These elements mark a departure from Blake's claim that political optimism fueled the initial installment of the series. Clearly, Rowling has become more cynical and mistrusting of the politicians in our world, and this mistrust has carried over into Harry's world as well. Some, including Jazk Zipes, criticize Rowling and this shift in tone, claiming it reflects too much of the paranoia of our time (181).

This shift in the novels, though, is not negative, but should be seen instead as positive. Rowling's incorporation of current events and modern political practices has added another layer of complexity to the series and created a political universe that avoids the cookie-cutter 'black vs. white' approach often found in children's books. This relevance provides yet another reason to continue reading the series (Hersh). Several critics including Shira Wolosky Weiss argue that the "most prominent allegory in Harry Potter . . . is a political one" (34). The political elements of the novel are a vital theme that should demand our attention. David Nexon and Iver Neumann note that popular culture is not "merely [a] passive mirror" that reflects the culture that creates it, but popular culture "also play[s] a crucial role in constituting [and shaping] the social and political world" of that society (6).

The events of September 11, 2001, accelerated the growth of this cynicism. The public, and those elected to represent them, were shaken and scared. This environment helped to create the environment that allowed for drastic measures to be taken. Like Barty Crouch, Sr. and his actions to round up Death Eaters after the first war with Voldemort. George W. Bush and his successors took actions that were and are illegal; they passed laws that limit privacy, erode rights, and go against our democratic ideals. Like Crouch's actions these were and, to an extent, are still popular. It seems that we may have, consciously or unconsciously, accepted Barry Goldwater's idea that "[e]xtremism in the defense of liberty is no vice. And moderation in the pursuit of justice is no virtue." Readers can only hope that we here in the Muggle world can follow the lead of Harry and the wizarding world, who managed to find their way back from the precipice where Fudge, Scrimgeour, Crouch, and Umbridge had taken them.

Notes

1.	According to Martha Kumar, a presidential historian, President Obama finished his first term having the fewest number of press conferences of any president since Reagan. The numbers are as follows: Reagan—27, G. H. W. Bush—143, Clinton—133, G.W. Bush—89, Obama—79 ("Obama").

2.	Rowling attempted to sanitize her use of the term "Hit Wizard" in a classified ad that appeared in *The Daily Prophet* newsletter. ("'Hit-Witch or Wizard' for the Magical Law Enforcement Squad." *The Daily Prophet*, 8 Feb. 1999.) This was a newsletter written by Rowling and distributed by Bloomsbury Publishers to members of its Harry Potter Fan Club in Great Britain. The ad states that Hit Wizards are members of the Department of Magical Law Enforcement charged with the capture of dangerous witches and wizards. This does not fit in the context of the novels. Throughout the series, it is clear that it is the job of the Aurors to battle the Dark Arts and capture dangerous witches and wizards. For example, Aurors and the Auror office are shown throughout the series heading up efforts to recapture Sirius Black, battle Death Eaters, and bring Voldemort to justice. If this is the responsibility of Hit Wizards, then it would follow that they should be carrying out these activities and not the Aurors. Instead, this is the sole mention of Hit Wizards within the series. This supports my contention that the term "Hit Wizards" refers to government-sanctioned murder/assassination to achieve a political end.

3.	This argument draws on the works of Foucault (1972), Saussure (2000), and Langer (1979) and their contributions to semiotics.

4.	Harry is referring to the arrest and imprisonment of Stan Shunpike, conductor on the Knight Bus.

Works Cited

ACLU. *Freedom Under Fire: Dissent in Post-9/11 America*. New York: American Civil Liberties Union, 2003.

Adams, Christopher. "Blair's Popularity Hits All Time Low." *Financial Times*. 30 Jul. 2006. Web. 11 July 2014.

Anelli, Mellissa & Emerson Spartz. "The Leaky Cauldron and MN Interview Joanne Kathleen Rowling." *The Leaky Cauldron*. The-Leaky-Cauldron.org, 10 Sept. 2007. Web. 26 Apr. 2015.

Balz, Dan. "Campaigner in Chief Has Limited Reach." *The Washington Post*. 1 Nov. 2006. Web. 12 Aug. 2014.

Baragona, Justin. "Dick Cheney Rewrites History and Blames Iraq Violence and Obama and Discussing Op-Ed." *Politics USA*. 15 July 2014. Web. 1 Sept. 2014.

Barratt, Bethany, & Ebooks Corporation. *The Politics of Harry Potter*. New York: Palgrave Macmillan, 2012.

Bishop, Thomas. "Rewriting History: Conservatives Attack Obama For Withdrawing All Troops from Iraq." *Media Matters*. 10 Aug. 2014. Web. 12 Sept. 2014.

Blake, Andrew. *The Irresistible Rise of Harry Potter*. New York: Verso, 2002.

Branigin, William. "Bush Backs Creation of Intelligence Czar: New Position Would Be Placed Outside the White House." *The Washington Post*. 2 Aug. 2004. Web. 1 Sept. 2014.

Chaddock, Gail Russell. "Bush Administration Blurs Media Boundary." *Christian Science Monitor*. 17 Feb. 2005. Web. 2 Sept. 2014.

Cheney, Dick, & Liz Cheney. "The Collapsing Obama Doctrine: Rarely Has a U.S. president Been So Wrong about So Much at the Expense of So Many." *The Wall Street Journal*. 17 June 2014. Web. 2 Sept. 2014.

Clarke, Matt. "Celebrity Justice: Prison Lifestyles of the Rich and Famous." *Prison Legal News*. 15 July 2010. Web. 30 Sept. 2014.

Crabapple, Molly. "Today Marks the 12th Anniversary of America's Guantánamo Prison Disgrace." *The Guardian*. 11 Jan. 2014. Web. 2 Sept. 2014.

Diamond, Jeremy, & Michael Martinez. "Shutting Down Guantanamo: Who's Left and What's in the Way." *CNN Politics*. 11 Dec. 2014. Web. 12 Dec. 2014.

Diemer, Tom. "Hurricane Katrina: 'Brownie' Winced at Bush's 'Heck of a Job' Line." *Huffpost Politics*. 18 Mar. 2011. Web. 1 Sept. 2014.

"Dixie Chicks Pulled from Air after Bashing Bush." *CNN.com*. 14 March 3003. Web. 1 Sept. 2014.

Drum, Kevin. "Scripted Press Conferences?" *Washington Monthly*. 20 Apr. 2004. Web. 12 Jan. 2013.

Fitsanakis, Joseph. "Senate Report: CIA Misled Us Government About Torture." *Intelnews.org: Expert News and Commentary on Intelligence, Espionage, Spies, and Spying.* 2 Apr. 2014. Web. 12 July 2014.

Fletcher, Michael A., & Richard Morin. "Bush's Approval Rating Drops to New Low in Wake of Storm." *The Washington Post.* 20 Apr. 2004. Web. 13 Sept. 2005.

Foucault, Michel. *The Archaeology of Knowledge and the Discourse on Language.* Trans. A. M. Sheridan Smith. New York: Pantheon Books, 1972.

Friedersdorf, Conor. "7 Pages That Gave President Obama Cover to Kill Americans." *The Atlantic.* 18 Aug. 2014. Web. 18 Aug. 2014.

Gellman, Barton, & Laura Poitras. "U.S., British Intelligence Mining Data from Nine U.S. Internet Companies in Broad Secret Program." *The Washington Post* 7 June 2013. Web. 30 June 2014.

Gerstenzang, James. "Bush Proposes a Cabinet-Level Homeland Security Department." *Los Angeles Times.* 7 June 2002. Web. 30 Jan. 2014.

Gertz, Matt. "O'Reilly: 'I Respect Dissent on the Iraq War.'" Research. *Media Matters for America.* 23 Sept. 2007. Web. 15 July 2014.

Greenberg, Jon. "CNN's Tapper: Obama Has Used Espionage Act More than All Previous Administrations." *Tampa Bay Times.* 10 Jan. 2014. Web. 30 Sept. 2014.

Groden, Claire. "Want a Jail Cell Upgrade? That'll Be $155 a Night." *Time.* 31 July 2012. Web. 12 Aug. 2013.

Herman, Edward S. & Noam Chomsky. *Manufacturing Consent: The Political Economy of the Mass Media.* New York: Pantheon Books, 1988.

Hersh, Mike. "Harry Potter Lessons in Action". *MikeHersh.com: Political Commentary and Analysis.* 24 Sept. 2003. Web. 5 March 2005.

"How the Bush Administration Sold the Iraq War." *MSNBC.* 14 Sept. 2013. Web. 15 July 2014.

Hutchinson, William. "Media, Government and Manipulation: The Cases of the Two Gulf Wars." *Proceedings of the 9th Australian Information Warfare and Security Conference: Ninth Australian Information Warfare and Security Conference. Perth, Western Australia. 1 December 2008.* Perth: School of Computer and Information Science, Edith Cowan University, 2008.

Kagay, Michael R. "History Suggests Bush's Popularity Will Ebb." *New York Times*. 22 May 1991. Web. 30 July 2014.

Kamber, Michael & Tim Arango. "4,000 U.S. Deaths, and a Handful of Images." *New York Times*. 26 July 2008. Web. 2 Sept. 2014.

"Key Players in the CIA Leak Investigation." *The Washington Post*. 3 July 2007. Web. 15 July 2014.

Koffler, Keith. "Obama Abolishes the Press Conference." *White House Dossier*. 4 May 2012. Web. 9 Sept. 2014.

Kreig, Andrew. "Press Probes 'Obama's War on Leaks.'" *Justice Integrity Project*. 2 May 2012. Web. 15 July 15 2014.

Langer, Susanne K. *Philosophy in a New Key: A Study in the Symbolism of Reason, Rite, and Art*. 3rd ed. Cambridge, MA: Harvard UP, 1979.

Larson, Leslie. "'Please:' John Kerry Answers Dick Cheney's Criticism on Iraq." *New York Daily News*. 19 Jun. 2014. Web. 30 Sept. 2014.

Leip, David. "1992 Presidential General Election Results." *David Leip's Atlas of U.S. Presidential Elections*. 15 May 2014. Web. 10 Mar. 2014.

Levy, Robert A. "Jose Padilla: No Charges and No Trial, Just Jail." *Chicago Sun-Times*. 11 Aug. 2003. Web. 30 Sept. 2014.

Lichtblau, Eric. "Professor in Terror Case May Face Deportation." *New York Times*. 8 Dec. 2005. Web. 2 Sept. 2014.

Mazzetti, Mark, & Borzou Daragahi. "U.S. Military Covertly Pays to Run Stories in Iraqi Press." *Los Angeles Times*. 30 Nov. 2005. Web. 1 Sept. 2014.

McGreal, Chris. "Decision Points: Katrina Response Was 'Flawed', but I Wasn't to Blame—Bush." *The Guardian*. 8 Nov. 2010. Web. 15 July 2014.

Mitchell, Greg. "Obama's War on Leaks: Already Having 'Chilling Effect' on the Media?" *The Nation*. 22 May 2013 . Web. 15 July 2014.

Memmott, Mark. "Us Drone Strikes Violate International Law, Reports Allege." *The Two-Way: Breaking News from NPR*. National Public Radio, 22 Oct. 2013. Web. 12 Aug. 2014.

Nexon, Daniel H. & Iver B. Neumann. *Harry Potter and International Relations*. Lanham, MD: Rowman & Littlefield, 2006.

"Obama Finishes First Term with Fewest Press Conferences since Reagan." *HuffPost* 15 January 2013. Web. 30 Nov. 2014.

Parry, Robert. "Bush's 'Perception Management' Plan." *Consortiumnews*. Consortiumnews.com, 18 Nov. 2004. Web. 12 Jan. 2014.

Perez, Evan. "Rights Are Curtailed for Terror Suspects." *The Wall Street Journal*. 24 March 2011, sec. Law.

"'Please:' John Kerry Answers Dick Cheney's Criticism on Iraq." *Daily News*. DailyNews.com, 19 June 2014. Web. 5 Jan. 2014.

Ratner, Michael. "Anwar Al-Awlaki's Extrajudicial Death." *The Gaurdian*. 30 Sept. 2011. Web. 1 Dec. 2014.

Reaves, Jessica. "Living with Terrorism: A How-to Guide." *Time*. Time, Inc., 12 Feb. 2003. Web. 25 July 2014.

Rowling, J. K. *Harry Potter and the Chamber of Secrets*. New York: Scholastic, 1999.

_____. *Harry Potter and the Goblet of Fire*. New York: Scholastic, 2000.

_____. *Harry Potter and the Half Blood Prince*. New York: Scholastic, 2005.

_____. *Harry Potter and the Order of the Phoenix*. New York: Scholastic, 2003.

_____. *Harry Potter and the Prisoner of Azkaban*. New York: Scholastic, 1999.

_____. "'Hit-Witch or Wizard' for the Magical Law Enforcement Squad." Advertisement. *Daily Prophet Newsletter* 8 Feb. 1999, sec. Classified Advertisements: 1.

Saussure, Ferdinand de. *Course in General Linguistics*. Trans. Roy Harris. Peru, IL: Open Court, 2000.

Scuiletti, Justin. "NSA Surveillance Doesn't Stop Terrorism, Report Claims." *The Rundown: A Blog of News and Insight*: PBS NewsHour. 14 Jan. 2014. Web. 25 July 2014.

"Senate report on CIA torture program." *CNN*. 9 Dec. 2014. Web. 11 Dec. 2014.

Shane, Scott. "US Engaged in Torture after 9/11, Review Concludes." *The New York Times*. 16 Apr. 2013. Web. 25 July 2014.

"Surveillance of Citizens by Government." *The New York Times*. 14 Aug. 2014. Web. 20 Aug. 2014.

Taylor, Justin. "Harry Potter and the War on Terror." *Counterpunch*. 30 Jul.–1 Aug. 2005. Web. 26 Apr. 2015.

"Techniques Used in Guantánamo." *The Justice Campaign*. The Justice Campaign, 16 July 2014. Web. 25 July 2014.

Travis, Alan, and Ian Black. "Blair's Popularity Plummets." *The Guardian*. 17 Feb. 2003. Web. 25 Sept. 2014.

Warren, Vincent. "The 9/11 Decade and the Decline of Us Democracy." *Center for Constitutional Rights*. Center for Constitutional Rights, 16 July 2014. Web. 25 July 2014.

Whited, Lana A. *The Ivory Tower and Harry Potter: Perspectives on a Literary Phenomenon*. Columbia: U of Missouri P, 2002.

Winton, Richard. "Richie's 82 Minutes in Jail." *Los Angeles Times*. 24 Aug. 2007. Web. 25 Sept. 2014.

Wolosky Weiss, Shira & Palgrave Connect (Online service). *The Riddles of Harry Potter: Secret Passages and Interpretive Quests*. New York: Palgrave Macmillan, 2010.

Zipes, Jack David. *Sticks and Stones: The Troublesome Success of Children's Literature from Slovenly Peter to Harry Potter*. New York: Routledge, 2001.

Morals vs. Christianity: How Harry Potter Goes Beyond Goodness to Godliness_____

Jenn Coletta

The Harry Potter series as a collective whole is ranked number one on the list of most banned or challenged books from 2000–2009, according to the American Library Association. The biggest issue raised against J. K. Rowling and her books is the potential indoctrination of readers into witchcraft, inspired by Harry and his friends at Hogwarts School of Witchcraft and Wizardry. This perspective tends to be professed most strongly by Christians who oppose the occult, claiming Harry Potter to be anti-Christian and anti-Bible. Informed or not, enough Christian parents have been enraged to cause a debate exacerbated by the extreme popularity of the Harry Potter books and movies. There is irony in the conservative Christians' perspective, however; many are protesting the series without widening their focus enough to recognize the morals and Christian symbols used throughout Rowling's work. On top of the many ethical values that are demonstrated in Harry Potter, the direct parallels to the Bible debunk the conservative Christian argument that good morals do not condone the witchcraft within the novels. The Christians against Harry Potter may be able to ignore moral teachings alone, but when morals are combined with the exploration of direct Christian themes, Harry Potter can no longer be viewed as anti-Christian without creating a double standard. If Christians against these books had exerted as much energy to understand Harry Potter as they did to rebuke it, the argument likely would not have been sustained. In the Harry Potter series, Rowling successfully intertwines both morals and Christian themes, thereby rendering the Christian argument ironic because those opposed on religious grounds to Rowling's books are vying to ban the exact messages they purportedly preach.

The main issue some conservative Christians have against Harry Potter is the use of witchcraft, which is expressly forbidden in the Bible. Scientist and Christian Rich Deem argues there are numerous passages in Christian doctrine that leave no doubt that "for both the one who practices [the occult] and the one who hires the one who practices, the penalty is death." A few examples of such doctrine are shown in the twentieth chapter of the Old Testament book of Leviticus, stating "as for the person who turns to mediums and spiritualists . . . I will also set my face against that person and will cut him off from among his people . . . [and] a man or a woman who is a medium or a spiritualist shall surely be put to death" (*New International Bible* Leviticus 20:6 27). Despite the use of witchcraft, many people—including some Christians—claim that Harry Potter is an innocent novel about a good wizard whose story should be viewed solely as fiction. It is important to note that the majority of current, mainstream Christians do not adhere to the majority of the commandments stated in Leviticus, such as "do not wear clothing woven of two kinds of material" (19:19) or "do not clip off the edges of your beard" (19:27). However, conservative critics such as Deem—who tend to be literalists—seem to suggest that Harry Potter cannot be taken as innocent fiction, saying "doing evil to accomplish good ends is not acceptable." The problem for such critics remains that Harry practices magic, regardless of his intentions.

Michael O'Brien at *Life Site News* accuses Harry Potter of being "anti-Gospel, a manifesto for behavior and belief embodied by loveable, at times admirable, fictional characters who live out the modern ethos of secular humanism to its maximum parameters." Further exacerbating the problem for such critics is that Harry's power source is unknown; we see him discover his power at age eleven when he is invited to Hogwarts School of Witchcraft and Wizardry, but his power just exists. There is no God mentioned behind the power; it is simply something one is born with or one is not. Speculatively, there would have likely not been as large an uproar if the characters' power was given by God and ultimately belonged to God; however, that is not the case. Arguing that Harry Potter supports humanism, O'Brien explains that the characters' powers are "never referred to as god-like powers because that would be a tacit admission of some kind of higher authority, and Potterworld will admit no absolute hierarchy in creation." This is a problem for many conservative Christians because the doctrine clearly states there is "but one God, the Father, from whom all things came and for whom we live" (1 Corinthians 8:6) thereby disallowing any other mortal to access the same types of power without being inherently unequal and blasphemous. The humanistic view is in itself problematic to some because Christian theology argues humans were never created to succeed apart from God. Richard Abanes in *Harry Potter and the Bible* observes the inconsistency for someone to "settle for inferior spiritual power when the most potent of spiritual power rests with God the creator, with whom anyone can have a relationship" (198). Critics such as Deem, O'Brien, and Abanes are at least informed regarding the book series as well as the Bible; unfortunately, the argument that the Harry Potter series is evil has been spurred on unnecessarily by many who are grossly uninformed.

In July of 2000, *The Onion,* a satirical "news" source, published an article entitled *"Harry Potter* Books Spark Rise in Satanism Among Young Children." The article, to the informed and unbiased reader, is obviously satire, stretching the boundaries of reality to call attention purposefully to the ridiculous claims made about Rowling's "evil" novels. Various fictional children are quoted in the article as denouncing religion and desiring witchcraft instead. One girl is quoted as saying, "I used to believe in what they taught us at Sunday School, but the *Harry Potter* books showed me that magic is real, something I can learn and use right now, and that the Bible is nothing but boring lies" (*"Harry Potter* Books"). *The Onion* goes on to create statistics that would later be the exact "proof" for which some Christians were searching. The article claims that "in 1995 it was estimated that some 100,000 Americans, mostly adults, were involved in devil-worship groups. Today, more than 14 million children alone belong to the Church of Satan," stating the Harry Potter series to be the leading cause (*"Harry Potter* Books"). Most readers recognized *The Onion* by name and understood the context of this "news source," chuckled at the obvious satire, and moved on; however, those Christians desperately trying to make their case against Rowling overlooked the satirical nature of the source, thereby leading to masses of chain emails and warnings, attempting to rally parents to ban the books and pray for Rowling's soul. This excessive paranoia coupled with the seemingly legitimate arguments from ostensibly informed theologians created a controversy that remains unsettled. However, the Harry Potter books contain an overall positive message, teaching the exact ethics and morals portrayed by modern Christianity.

Although many people are quick to argue about whether Harry Potter is innately evil or innately Christian, few have paused to consider the overall moral compass Harry Potter teaches, independent from theology. The main exception is Lana A. Whited and M. Katherine Grimes' essay "What Would Harry Do? J. K. Rowling and Lawrence Kohlberg's Theories of Moral Development," in which they show how Harry and his friends exceed the moral reasoning level typical for their respective ages. They discuss abstract concepts, such as innocence and justice, and explain that Rowling equips her characters with the moral sensibility to understand these ideas quite young. While the resounding theme that love conquers all is prevalent in each of the seven Harry Potter books, as will be discussed in further detail later, it is first important to begin with ethics, which have received less attention. One of the main moral lessons shown throughout the series is the idea that character—that is, correct choices, courage, and perseverance—is more important than status. Whited and Grimes show how Dumbledore prioritizes and teaches character by explaining that "in preparing the young wizards for the battle ahead, Dumbledore focuses on how to conduct oneself at the moment of moral decision-making" as opposed to winning for glory's sake (199). We first see Harry's character developing when, friendless and unfamiliar with the wizarding world, he still rejects Draco's invitation into his circle. Draco warns Harry of the dangers of "making friends with the wrong sort," claiming he can "help [him] there" (Rowling, *Sorcerer's Stone* 108). Despite potential status, Harry adamantly discards Draco's offer, saying, "I think I can tell who the wrong sort are for myself, thanks" (109). Harry has only just met Ron and Hermione, and yet he is already choosing friends without consideration for status, immediately showing the goodness of his character. In *Goblet of Fire*, Harry desperately wants to win the Triwizard Cup when he and Cedric Diggory come face to face at the end of the maze during the third task. Having already been able to surpass the expectations of the faculty and students in the prior tasks, Harry briefly sees "himself holding the Triwizard Cup aloft, hear[s] the roar of the crowd . . . and then the picture fade[s], and he [finds] himself starting at Cedric's shadowy, stubborn face" (Rowling, *Goblet* 634). Because neither can convince the other to rush ahead, claiming the glory, Harry does the noble thing—he suggests a tie between them, proposing they grasp the Cup at the same moment. Although the Cup ends up being a trap to deliver the boys to Voldemort, Harry's intentions are still pure; even after Cedric is killed, Harry risks his own life to ensure that Cedric's body is returned to his parents.

Similarly, in *The Order of the Phoenix*, instead of vying for the opportunity to lead a group of students in Defense Against the Dark Arts, Harry exhibits humility, claiming his proficiency was mostly "a load of luck" (331). Although he may not be the most skilled wizard at Hogwarts, he certainly possesses a high moral character. Dumbledore's philosophy is that "our choices . . . show what we truly are, far more than our abilities" (Rowling, *Chamber* 333). Throughout the series, we see the power of choices and how Harry often makes the difficult ones for the greater good.

Harry is undoubtedly courageous, valuing the wellness and well-being of others above his own comfort, convenience, and at times, his life. In *Harry Potter and Philosophy,* Tom Morris explains that courage is "doing what's right, not what's easy. It's doing what seems morally required, rather than what seems physically safe or socially expected. It's doing what's best, overall, rather than necessarily what's best for you" (13). Making good choices takes courage, and Harry demonstrates that by often denying himself to aid other people. Catherine and David Deavel of *Logos Journal* explain that "magic is not half as powerful as human virtue" (60). One of the first courageous moments is when Harry, not yet friends with Hermione, nevertheless risks his safety by going into the bathroom to save her from the troll. Repeatedly, we see this type of selfless courage: when he faces the Voldemort/Quirrel duo alone; when he enters the Chamber of Secrets to save Ginny; when he risks the Forbidden Forest to protect Hagrid's innocent reputation; when he defies the limits of time and faces Dementors to save Sirius Black and Buckbeak; when he proclaims the truth about Voldemort's rise to power, despite communal scorn; when he takes on a league of Death Eaters to keep vital prophecy information away from Voldemort; when he defies Professor Umbridge, insisting on speaking the truth; when he accompanies Dumbledore to try to destroy a Horcrux; when he resolves to uncover all Horcruxes and destroy them; when he saves his enemy Draco from a fire; and when he volunteers himself as a martyr, defenseless, to save the rest of his friends and family. In her article "Love Bears All Things: Thomas Aquinas, Harry Potter, and the Virtue of Courage," Rebecca De Young suggests that in order to have courage, "your love has to be greater than your fear of death" (5). Harry's love and selflessness are present in all the aforementioned examples of his courage and perseverance. Shira Wolosky explains Harry's morality in her article "Harry Potter's Ethical Paradigms: Augustine, Kant, and Feminist Moral Theory," positing that Harry's "moral constitution is fundamentally that of commitment to others, in pursuit of their common good: not to contempt of self . . . but as a pledge of engagement of the self outside itself, to joint growth, gaining its own strength and realization in community" (194). Harry does not engage in risky situations because he is looking for trouble. Instead, he accepts potential trouble, seeing the communal gain as more important than himself. If he had not sought a greater cause than his own glory, he would not have had the endurance to fight Voldemort again and again. Luckily, however, even when Harry almost reaches his breaking point and "wants out . . . wants it to end," claiming he "doesn't care anymore," he quickly regains composure and continues fighting evil (Rowling, *Order of the Phoenix* 824). It is not just about Harry, but about his moral compass that cannot willingly allow harm to befall innocent people.

Further perpetuating the moral integrity of the Harry Potter series are the aspects of loyalty to family and friends as well as a cry for equality among all creatures. Lily Potter sets a precedent of loyalty and family values when she sacrifices herself to save the infant Harry. From that point, we are shown the continued importance of family through the way the Weasleys take Harry in and care for him as if he were a blood relative. In *Sorcerer's Stone*, Harry receives a traditional Weasley sweater from Mrs. Weasley, initiating him into their family. Although Harry finds refuge in this alternative family, his yearning for his parents is portrayed throughout the series. When he encounters the Mirror of Erised, which shows the onlooker's deepest desire, Harry sees not fame and glory, but his family surrounding him. This message of the importance of family continues through the final book, in which Harry's most coveted Hallow is the Resurrection Stone. Instead of having the unbeatable wand, he explains his desire for the Stone by saying, "'Well, if you could bring people back, we could have Sirius . . . Mad-Eye . . . Dumbledore . . . my parents . . .'" (Rowling, *Deathly Hallows* 416). Again, he seeks not to be the most powerful or clever, but values familial ties over all else. Because this is his priority, he quickly bonds when he discovers Sirius Black is his godfather. Sirius acts as a father-figure, mentor, and friend to Harry, providing him with the closest thing he can have to his biological father. Finally, the Harry Potter series teaches about forgiveness within families, as Percy Weasley betrays and abandons his family but, like the prodigal son, is accepted and forgiven fully upon his return.

Beyond family, Harry also teaches readers the importance of remaining loyal to friendships. From the first book to the last, friends—despite inevitable trials—always stick together. In *Sorcerer's Stone*, Harry is willing to face the trouble alone; however, Ron incredulously asks, "You don't think we'd let you go alone?" to which Hermione replies, "Of course not" (271). This moment sets the standard within the group dynamics that no one will struggle alone. In *Goblet of Fire*, Hermione remains consistent, helping Harry prepare to overcome the life-threatening tasks. Although Ron strays for a time, he nonetheless returns and is forgiven, and the three are in harmony again. The books teach not of a perfect world in which friendships are not tested, but of a realistic world in which they are tested and still remain strong. Discussing the trials and perseverance of friendships, Harald Thorsrud explains in *Harry Potter and Philosophy* that "we see another example of the positive moral effects of friendship as Ron wrestles with his jealousy of Harry. . . . But, although their friendship is occasionally strained to near the breaking point, they always reconcile" (47). This reconciliation is possible because "they care for something more than the pleasure of benefits to be had from hanging out together. They care about each other . . . [which] reaffirms their commitment to the pursuit of common good" (47). Luna Lovegood, Neville Longbottom, and Ginny Weasley are able to enter the unity of the trio by proving their loyalty and friendship in *Order of the Phoenix*. Even when Harry is being persecuted for announcing Voldemort's return, Luna, Neville, and Ginny remain faithful. They trust Harry, and according to Wolosky, "trust is a gift, a pledge: in one sense a risk, in another, an active constitution, defining the terms of mutual relationship" (199). They stand up for Harry and the truth as well as risk their lives fighting Death Eaters to prevent the prophecy from reaching Voldemort. Yes, they take a risk, but in doing so, they create the foundation on which successful friendships are built, spanning from three, to six, to an entire room of loyal friends calling themselves Dumbledore's Army. A group of students dedicated to eradicating evil, Dumbledore's Army is led by Harry and ultimately assists in vanquishing Voldemort. The students are unafraid to fight and willingly take risks because they trust Harry and believe in the cause. They are more easily able to be loyal because "Harry's leadership directs the community to trust. In doing so, he strengthens the very commitment he relies upon" (Wolosky 199). The last element of loyal and lasting friendships is equality among them.

Beyond character, correct choices, courage, and loyalty values, *Harry Potter* also conveys messages of equality, balancing gender, race, and class hierarchies. Mimi Gladstein in *Harry Potter and Philosophy* notes that women "are anything but second-class citizens. J. K. Rowling depicts a world where equal opportunities among the sexes is a given" (49). Hermione is a perfect example of gender equality—she is an essential aspect of Harry's life at Hogwarts, and it is evident he would not fare well without her.

Throughout the series we see her guiding both Harry and Ron through homework assignments as well as helping them unlock clues to Voldemort's plans. Hermione is just as much a part of the search for Horcruxes as the boys—in fact, more so than Ron, not only because of her brilliance, but also because Hermione remains constant whereas Ron falters. Similarly, although Hogwarts is headed by Dumbledore, Professor McGonagall stands strongly as his right hand and is the only professor to stand against Umbridge in *Order of the Phoenix*. Gladstein observes further that McGonagall is the leader of Gryffindor, the house in which the main characters reside. Surpassing gender roles, there is another cry for the freedom and equality for all creatures and all people, despite their heritage. In *Goblet of Fire*, Hermione starts a house-elf liberation organization entitled Society for the Promotion of Elfish Welfare, or S.P.E.W. She wishes to free house-elves because they "are slaves" and have feelings despite their not being human (Rowling, *Goblet of* Fire 139). At first, this liberation movement is met with indifference or scorn; however, in *Deathly Hallows* we see this transform, especially with the treatment of the house-elf Kreacher and Ron's plea to dismiss the Hogwart's elves before the battle commences. Similarly, when Dobby is killed, Harry insists on burying him without magic, digging "with a kind of fury, relishing the manual work, glorying in the non-magic of it, for every drop of his sweat and every blister felt like a gift to the elf who had saved their lives" (Rowling, *Deathly Hallows* 478). Griphook, a Goblin whose race also struggles for equality, admires Harry for viewing other species as equal, admitting Harry is "a very odd wizard" for doing so (Rowling, *Deathly Hallows* 486). Harry never discriminates against creatures because of their heritage; he remains close to Hagrid despite the common prejudice against half-giants. While his openness might make Harry "odd," it also allows him to have meaningful relationships with a myriad of beings.

Finally, there is the ongoing battle to prove that lineage is irrelevant to the quality of a good witch or wizard. Voldemort, the Malfoys and various other Death Eater families stress the importance of pure blood. They claim that mating with Muggles—non-magical people—taints the heritage. However, this prejudice is shown to be ridiculous, as Hermione, coming from no magical genealogy, surpasses everyone in school, even those with the purest blood. Furthermore, Harry—the hero—has Muggles in his family tree. Wolosky discusses the idea of morality and equality by observing that the

> *Potterwatch* broadcast specifically focuses on the equality and value of all persons: that is, on the Kantian imperative of ends . . . in the novel's moral imperative, the principle of absolute value of each individual equally as end is then directly educed, as Kingsley appeals to all listeners to try to protect the Muggles around them. (202)

Kingsley Shacklebolt, the future Minster of Magic, condemns the segregation of wizards and Muggles, warning it is "one short step from 'Wizards first' to 'Purebloods first,' and then to 'Death Eaters.' We're all human . . . [and] every life is worth the same, and worth saving" (Rowling, *Deathly Hallows* 440). This principle is similarly supported in Christian doctrine when Paul claims, "there is neither Jew nor Gentile, neither slave nor free, nor is there male or female, for you are all one in Jesus Christ" (Galatians 3:28). Morally, Rowling is explicit in her ideas that everyone is equal—an ethic Christians should be hard-pressed to reject.

The last moral lesson is the largest theme woven throughout the Harry Potter series: love conquers all. The idea of sacrificial love consistently defeating evil is present in every book. *Sorcerer's Stone* begins with the discovery that Lily Potter died to save Harry, which protected Harry with her love and sacrifice so completely that Voldemort could not even touch him. At the end of the first book, the Voldemort/Quirrel parasite attempts to grab Harry, but his "fingers were blistering" from the touch (Rowling, *Sorcerer's Stone* 294). Dumbledore explains that Voldemort cannot understand love and, therefore, experiences "agony to touch a person marked by something so good" (Rowling, *Sorcerer's Stone* 299). We see this again in *Order of the Phoenix* when Voldemort is unable to possess Harry—he cannot inhabit a soul that desires goodness. Love conquers evil consistently. A perfect example is how Severus Snape, previously committed to Voldemort, risks his life and reputation to be a spy for one reason: his love for Lily. Snape never has an affinity for Harry personally, yet he sacrifices greatly to save Harry because the teacher had never stopped loving Lily, even after her death. Finally and more climactically, Harry—channeling his mother's sacrifice—gives himself up for the greater good. In her article on the courage of Harry Potter, Rebecca De Young explains that our "natural response to the threat of death (the ultimate form of human vulnerability) is to aggressively defend ourselves against it at all costs" (4). However, Harry goes to Voldemort with his wand in his robes instead of his hand to ensure he will not fight—his sacrifice is clear and intentional. He is scared, yes; he does not "seek death, and does not glory in it . . . . What enables [him] to conquer [his] fear of death is not faith in [his] own power, but the power of love" (De Young 5). And again, love triumphs over evil as Harry's parents and deceased loved ones surround him and support him until the end.

For the more liberal minded, the aforementioned argument of moral reason should likely be enough to prove that Harry Potter books teach desirable lessons. However, despite the explicit ethical integrity, some Christians may remain grounded in one simple doctrinal truth: morals and Christianity are not mutually inclusive. True, Christians should have strong morals. The Bible teaches upstanding characteristics, including honesty, goodness, self-control, peace, gentleness, purity, etc. However, Christian theology is also very clear that morals do not automatically make one a Christian. In the book of John, Jesus is quoted as saying "No man can come to the Father except through me" (John 14:6). Similarly, Paul explains in Ephesians that we are "saved by grace ... [and] cannot take credit for this; it is a gift from God. Salvation is not a reward for the good things we have done, so none of us can boast about it" (Ephesians 2:8–9). Harry Potter is one of the most moral characters in all literature, but that does not make him innately Christian and, therefore, does not preclude the concerns of conservative Christian parents. However, their argument becomes moot when one uncovers the direct Judeo-Christian parallels and connects them to the previously established morals.

Morals aside, the Christian critics' opposition to Harry Potter is ironic because of the many Christian overlays present in the novels. Most notable is Harry's parallel to Jesus. Harry is certainly not a perfect match for the image of Jesus because he "is limited, imperfect, feeling anger, envy, and frustration" (Wolosky 211). However, there are significant similarities worth mentioning. In both the story of Jesus and the story of Harry Potter, prophecies are made about their vanquishing evil. Talking to Satan, God alludes to someone who will "strike [Satan's] head, and [Satan] will strike his heel" (Genesis 3:15). This prediction is generally interpreted to show that Satan will harm Jesus, but Jesus will ultimately prevail. Similarly, Professor Trelawney prophesies, "The one with the power to vanquish the Dark Lord approaches . . . and either must die at the hand of the other for neither can live while the other survives" (Rowling, *Order of the Phoenix* 841). This prediction marks Harry as "the Chosen One," who is ultimately responsible for the well-being of mankind. We see the story of Jesus manifested through Harry as he is destined to die. Christian theology teaches that Jesus "bore our sins in his body" and "was made to be sin" (2 Corinthians 5:21, 1 Peter 2:24). Much like Jesus taking sin onto his body, "part of Lord Voldemort lives inside Harry . . . and while that fragment of soul . . . remains attached to and protected by Harry, Lord Voldemort cannot die" (Rowling, *Deathly Hallows* 686). Both Jesus and Harry are required to take evil into their bodies and die to expunge it. Before either character is killed within his story, however, there is one man who stands against the ruling, one man who wishes to be disconnected from any involvement. In the Bible, we see Pontius Pilate wash his hands of any guilt in Jesus' crucifixion, making it clear he "find[s] Him not guilty" (John 19:4). Paralleling Pilate, Snape is indignant that Dumbledore "kept [Harry] alive so he could die at the right moment," accusing Dumbledore of "raising [Harry] like a pig for slaughter" (Rowling, *Deathly Hallows* 687). Pilate does not always support Jesus, and Snape certainly does not favor Harry; however, in the end, both men stand up for the hero's right to live. The final allusion to the story of Christ found in Harry Potter is his death and resurrection. John Granger, a Christian author in support of the series, explains that the "climax of Harry's hero journey invariably turns out to be a strong image of the Christian hope: that death is followed by resurrection in Christ" (23). The resurrection of Harry is the most explicit Christian device in the books. It seems impossible to ignore because "martyrs give us a picture of . . . courage, and the martyrs in turn are imitating Christ" (De Young 6).

When looking at the parallels of the protagonists, it is equally important to compare the antagonists. In Harry Potter and the Bible, evil looks identical. Voldemort is described as having "wide, livid scarlet eyes and a nose as flat as a snake's with slits for nostrils" (Rowling, *Goblet of Fire* 643). From the beginning of the Judeo-Christian story in the Garden of Eden, Satan is described as a serpent. It is not a coincidence that Voldemort can speak with snakes and controls them with unnatural charisma. Just as Satan loves only himself, isolated in his power except for his minions, so is Voldemort with his Death Eaters. Rowling portrays good as good and evil as evil, maintaining similarities familiar to many people and commonplace in Christian imagery and symbolism.

Stepping away from the direct parallels of Harry to Jesus and Voldemort to Satan, there are further elements of Rowling's books that echo Christian beliefs. Rowling suggests there is more to this life than we may realize. In *Sorcerer's Stone*, Dumbledore tells Harry that "death is but the next great adventure to the organized mind," suggesting life—at least as far as the soul or mind is concerned—does not end with death (297). Wolosky agrees that Rowling "suggests some kind of immortality of the soul, as seen in the ghosts, the portraits of the headmasters, the whispers behind the veil, the Resurrection Stone, and of course, Harry's own sojourn in the uncanny interregnum space between death and life of King's Cross" (193). This is the exact message Christians preach—"the world and its desires pass away, but whoever does the will of God lives forever" (1 John 2:17). Eternal life is a key element of Christian theology, thereby matching the themes of Harry Potter accurately. Tying directly to the idea Rowling creates of an immortal soul is the idea that the soul is infinitely more important than the flesh and bone of our bodies. In the Harry Potter series, the soul is weighed so heavily that sin (particularly murder) literally splits the soul into pieces. In *Half-Blood Prince*, Professor Slughorn explains Horcruxes and the idea that the only way to split the soul is to damage it irrevocably with sin against mankind. This is considered such a high offense that the books discussing matters of destroying the soul are locked away in Dumbledore's office, forbidden even in the restricted area of the library. The soul is again valued over mortal life in regards to Dementors. Their "Kiss" is described as "a fate worse than death . . . [because] you can exist without your soul, but you'll have no sense of self anymore, no memory, no . . . anything. There's no chance at all of recovery. You'll just—exist. As an empty shell. And your soul is gone forever . . . lost" (Rowling, *Azkaban* 247). Harry fears this emptiness so greatly that he risks breaking the "no magic in the presence of Muggles" law to save Dudley—his enemy—from the Kiss in *Order of the Phoenix*. Christianity similarly explains the irrelevance of the body as compared to the soul because "though outwardly we are wasting away, yet inwardly we are being renewed day by day . . . so we fix our eyes not on what is seen, but on what is unseen, since what is seen is temporary, but what is unseen is eternal" (2 Corinthians 4:16–18). Unpacking Rowling's work to see such direct Christian parallels throws the old argument into new light. Catherine and David Deavel agree that "to the extent that the Harry Potter books promote true moral principles and bring them to life for children, these books further Christian teaching and a culture of life. The Potter books do in fact promote such principles—and to no small extent" (62). It would be hypocritical to maintain that the *Harry Potter* books elicit evil when they so clearly reflect—both morally and doctrinally—what is good.

There is no denying the immense popularity of the *Harry Potter* series, which is reason enough to look at the books more closely. Granger posits that "the fundamental reason for the astonishing popularity of the Harry Potter novels is their ability to meet a spiritual longing for some experience of the truths of life, love, and death taught by Christianity but denied by secular culture" (2). Although this is purely his speculation, it is an interesting theory, and it would be a shame to deny children the opportunity for such experiences because of misinformation or hasty judgments. Although parents should certainly observe what their children are absorbing, the Christian parent should logically applaud Harry Potter. Many people look either at morals or at Christian themes; however, they work better in tandem to reach a broader, more diverse group of people. Not all Christians will be satisfied with the moral elements alone. Similarly, those adhering to different religions—or none at all—may find it difficult to relate to theological didacticism. While all parents should use their judgment to decide what is appropriate for their children, anyone searching for a set of novels that will teach important values, while simultaneously paralleling Christian ideology, need look no further than Harry Potter.

Works Cited

Abanes, Richard. *Harry Potter and the Bible: The Menace Behind the Magick.* Camp Hill, PA: Horizon, 2008.

Deavel, David Paul & Catherine Jack Deavel. "Character, Choice, and Harry Potter." *Logos: A Journal of Catholic Thought and Culture* 5.4 (2002): 49–64. *Project MUSE.* Web. 29 June 2013.

Deem, Rich. "Harry Potter: Is It Something That Christian Children Should Read?" *God and Science.* 20 Aug. 2007. Web. 4 July 2013.

DeYoung, Rebecca Konyndyk. "Love Bears All Things: Thomas Aquinas, Harry Potter, and the Virtue of Courage." *Calvin College.* Virtual Library of Christian Philosophy. 12 Sept. 2007. Web. 30 June 2013.

Duran, Mike. "Guest Post: Kat Heckenbach on 'Magic in Christian Fiction.'" *deCompose.* Mikeduran.com, Nov. 2011. Web. 20 Jul. 2013.

Gladstein, Mimi R. "Feminism and Equal Opportunity: Hermione and the Women of Hogwarts." *Harry Potter and Philosophy: If Aristotle Ran Hogwarts.* Eds. David Baggett & Shawn E. Klein. Vol. 9. Chicago: Carus, 2004. 49–60. Popular Culture and Philosophy Series.

Granger, John. *Looking for God in Harry Potter.* Wheaton, IL: SaltRiver, 2004.

"*Harry Potter* Books Spark Rise in Satanism Among Children." *The Onion.* 26 Jul. 2000. Web. 30 Jun. 2013.

Holy Bible: New International Version. Grand Rapids, MI: Zondervan, 2005.

Morris, Tom. "The Courageous Harry Potter." *Harry Potter and Philosophy: If Aristotle Ran Hogwarts*. Eds. David Baggett & Shawn E. Klein. Vol. 9. Chicago and La Salle: Carus, 2004. 9–21. Popular Culture and Philosophy Series.

O'Brien, Michael. "*Harry Potter* and 'the Death of God'." *LifeSiteNews*. Campaign Life Coalition, 20 Aug. 2007. Web. 30 Jun. 2013.

Rowling, J[oanne] K[athleen]. *Harry Potter and the Chamber of Secrets*. New York: Scholastic, 2000.

_____. *Harry Potter and the Deathly Hallows*. New York: Scholastic, 2009.

_____. *Harry Potter and the Goblet of Fire*. New York: Scholastic, 2002.

_____. *Harry Potter and the Half-Blood Prince*. New York: Scholastic, 2006.

_____. *Harry Potter and the Order of the Phoenix*. New York: Scholastic, 2004.

_____. *Harry Potter and the Prisoner of Azkaban*. New York: Scholastic, 2001.

_____. *Harry Potter and the Sorcerer's Stone*. New York: Scholastic, 1999.

Thorsrud, Harald. "Voldemort's Agents, Malfoy's Cronies, and Hagrid's Chums: Friendship in Harry Potter." *Harry Potter and Philosophy: If Aristotle Ran Hogwarts*. Eds. David Baggett & Shawn E. Klein. Vol. 9. Chicago and La Salle: Carus, 2004. 38–48. Popular Culture and Philosophy Series.

"Top 100 Banned/Challenged Books: 2000–2009." *American Library Association*. American Library Association, n.d. Web. 30 June 2013.

Whited, Lana A. & M. Katherine Grimes. "What Would Harry Do? J. K. Rowling and Lawrence Kohlberg's Theories of Moral Development." *The Ivory Tower and Harry Potter: Perspectives on a Literary Phenomenon*. Ed. Lana A. Whited. Columbia: U of Missouri, 2002. 182–208.

Wolosky, Shira. "Harry Potter's Ethical Paradigms: Augustine, Kant, and Feminist Moral Theory." *Children's Literature* 40.1 (2012): 191–217. *Project MUSE*. Web. 29 June 2013.

J. K. Rowling: Author(ing) Celebrity_____
Saradindu Bhattacharya

J. K. Rowling rose to literary and cultural superstardom concurrently
with the phenomenal success of the Harry Potter books she authored.
The construction and effects of Rowling's persona can be examined
in the critical framework of celebrity culture studies. Rowling's
fame draws upon the traditional romantic notion of the artist as a
unique and inspired individual; simultaneously, it feeds into the more
contemporary media culture of the circulation and consumption of
details of a celebrity's private life and work in the public domain.
Through the strategic circulation of information about her "self" and
her work, Rowling has created a public persona that elicits feelings
of both intimacy and suspense in her audience. By exercising her
authorial agency over the generation of popular knowledge about
the Harry Potter series, Rowling has sustained public interest in her
own life as its creator and has actively partaken of and contributed
to its celebrity status. Popular media representations of Rowling in
journalistic reports and television interviews, as well as her own
official website and press statements, demonstrate how her celebrity
both depends on and adds to the plotting of a confessional life-
narrative of struggle and success. In addition, Rowling's celebrity
depends upon the public performance of her role as the arbiter of
meaning within the fictional world she has authored/authorized. The
extension of her role as a public figure goes beyond, as well as being
implicated in, the context of the Harry Potter series.

Rowling's celebrity status is constructed, first and foremost,
through the romantic discourse of the creative artist as a uniquely gifted
individual. In what has now become almost legend, the inception of
the story in Rowling's mind is represented as a momentous event, in
the sense of both a hugely significant occurrence in the evolution of
the text and of being traceable to a single point in time. In Rowling's
own oft-quoted words, Harry Potter "just strolled into [her] head

fully formed" (Gleick). Bloomsbury, Rowling's British publisher, charts the birth and evolution of the idea of the Harry Potter books:

> J. K. Rowling first had the idea for Harry Potter while delayed on a train travelling from Manchester to London King's Cross in 1990. Over the next five years, she began to plan out the seven books of the series. She wrote mostly in longhand and amassed a mountain of notes, many of which were on scraps of paper. She arrived in Edinburgh in 1993 with three chapters of *Harry Potter and the Philosopher's Stone* in her suitcase. By now she had a baby daughter, Jessica, but she continued to write in every spare moment she could find. ("Biography")

The origin of the Harry Potter books is thus traced back to a single transcendental moment that marks the burst of creative genius in the mind of an author who seems to be completely beyond her mundane surroundings. We may draw a parallel here between Wordsworth and Coleridge's practice of recording the date and the occasion of the composition of several of their poems in their headnotes and the way in which the Harry Potter books are made the subject of a similar originary discourse. Rowling's train journey is on its way to acquiring the kind of fame that Coleridge's opium-induced, visitor-interrupted composition of "Kubla Khan" has attained in the annals of literary history. Rowling embodies the romantic notion of the author as an inspired individual—one who is the human instrument for the expression of a creative impulse that renders her *more than human* and is, therefore, worthy of awe and admiration. This elevation of the individual, through a popular perception of her exceptional artistic talent, puts her at a certain critical distance from her audience and demands their admiration.

This official history of the books is plotted exclusively in terms of the author's concentrated efforts at writing, completely bypassing the possibility of the literary influences on her work of other writers she must have already read. Such an account of the genesis of Harry Potter, however faithful it might be to fact, takes us beyond the question of factual accuracy—it projects Rowling as an author who harks to the call of art with single-minded devotion, and the books as an expression and a product of such dedication. The significance of this schematic history is not suggested in terms of the books' intrinsic literary merit; rather, it is on the basis of pre-existing cultural notions of creative writing as a special kind of labor that Rowling's story of struggle is configured. It also presupposes a work of art as being unlike any other commodity, and it is thus that both the author and the text are rendered valuable. This conception the creative labor represented by Rowling functions as both the source and the marker of the exceptional cultural value ascribed to art. As Roland Barthes observes,

> [T]he function of the man of letters is to human labour rather as ambrosia is to bread: a miraculous, eternal substance, which condescends to take a social form so that its prestigious difference is better grasped . . . [T]his prepares one for the same idea of writer as superman, as a kind of intrinsically different being which society puts in the window so as to use to the best advantage the artificial singularity which it has granted him. (30)

Since uniqueness enjoys immense rarity-value in a general atmosphere of standardization, the special labor of artistic creation that Rowling performs marks her out for celebrity. As Joe Moran points out in *Star Authors*, celebrity culture's preoccupation with the "unique" individual seems to "tap into general anxieties in postmodern mediatised culture about the replacement of the 'real' with the surface image, and the subsequent blurring of boundaries between reality and fiction, public and private, high and low culture" (3). In fact, the literary celebrity, like the sports star, is primarily distinguished from other kinds of mass-marketed, mediatized celebrities through his or her commonly-accepted, genuine difference from the rest of the society. The literary celebrity becomes, in a sense, a personification of real value for audiences exposed increasingly to simulations of fame and achievement. Therefore, the domain of art and the artist is appropriated by the culture of celebrity not *in spite of*, but *because of* its perceived difference from ordinary mass-scale production of goods and services in a capitalist society.

Rowling is not merely the subject of this discourse of art as unique labor: she is an active participant in the creation of a romantic aura around herself and her work. By revealing exactly *when* and *where* she first came up with the idea of Harry Potter, Rowling not only asserts the original status of her work, but also claims for herself the privileged position as the authority from whom such a textual history must originate. Simultaneously, by maintaining an air of mystery about exactly *how* Harry Potter came into being (he just "strolled into" her head), Rowling seems to suggest that the recesses of the author's mind are ultimately inaccessible. Thus, the process of charting the genesis of the series does not really unravel its mystery—it only creates and reinforces the aura surrounding its origin. Such an aura is based on and reinforced by the assumption that the nature of artistic creation can never be fully known; yet, paradoxically, it is created and sustained through the selective disclosure of information about the text and its author and is, therefore, essentially "informatic." Rowling also becomes the self-conscious subject of the popular struggling-artist-in-the-garret myth by revealing the arduous process of writing the books and getting them published. Stories of her writing furiously on paper napkins in Edinburgh cafés (where she supposedly sat in order to escape from the chill of her unheated apartment), while her infant daughter slept in a pram nearby, have by now assumed legendary proportions within the Harry Potter fandom. Though Rowling has clarified that she did have paper to write on and that her flat did have heating (Thøgersen), she nevertheless posits her art as a kind of escape or release from the severely oppressive conditions under which she worked on the manuscript of the first Harry Potter book— penury, single parenthood, her mother's death, unemployment, and depression. This romantic notion of art—one that enables the artist to endure and overcome challenging external circumstances—encodes Rowling's "story" as being exceptional and extraordinary. The act of writing the books is itself deemed, almost independently of the quality of writing, as being heroic and, therefore, sets the author up for celebrity.

We must remember here that Rowling's story of struggle and success is essentially a retrospective account of events and can, therefore, be interpreted as a *confessional* life narrative. In *Seeing Stars*, Pramod K. Nayar identifies the confessional mode as one that employs a "hyper-mediated" but "self-effacing and invisible" setting that "makes the celebrity ordinary, one of us, but all the while emphasizing their uniqueness too" (53). One of the chief instances of the author's own participation in the construction of a confessional "self" in popular media is ITV's 2007 documentary *J.K. Rowling: A Year in the Life*. The documentary offers a behind-the-scenes glimpse into the private life and work of the author, following her through the intimate space of her home to investigate "the secret of J. K. Rowling's success." Thus, the narrator begins by asking Rowling a series of "direct questions" about her favorite virtue, biggest strength, greatest fear and so on, appearing to look for the "real" person behind the fame and success she has achieved. The narrator follows Rowling to the house where she grew up, the church where she was baptized and worked to earn extra pocket money, and the woods she frequented as a child, revisiting the sites of her personal memories as a means of understanding "where it has all come from." The establishing of a link between the author's own life and her literary output is a form of biographical criticism that is hardly unique to the case of the Harry Potter series. However, the degree to which Rowling's life has been scrutinized to explain the phenomenal success of the series is certainly unprecedented in media history. Thus, when the camera follows Rowling into the hotel room in Edinburgh where she finishes work on the final chapters of the last book, the audience is made privy to an activity that is normally not publicly visible and, in this particular case, also reportedly confidential. The documentary offers an "eyewitness" account of the author at work at a manuscript that is as eagerly awaited as it is fervently screened from readers. Such a strategy combines elements of both revelation and mystery, rendering the author and the book paradoxically familiar yet distant from the audience. The narrator's presence at the very site and moment of the completion of the book gives him (and through him, the audience) a seemingly unmediated access to a supposedly secret activity, making him and the audience *intimate* witnesses to the very act of artistic creation. This sense of intimacy is also generated through Rowling's asides on the notes she had earlier written on the margins of the draft, the declaration of her feelings upon finishing the book, and even the furnishing of ordinary details, such as the music she plays once she is done writing. Yet, we are also informed about the intense security measures adopted at every stage leading up to the production and release of the book to prevent a leak, which creates an aura of suspense around the act and product of Rowling's work. On the one hand, the audience is informed about the official embargo on information about the book; on the other, the documentary itself functions as a media tool to retrospectively publicize this embargo. This sets up a paradox between the twin elements of disclosure and secrecy about the author and her work.

In a similar instance, Rowling herself reveals to Jonathan Ross, the celebrity chat show host, that the manuscript of the last three books of the series had been stolen and recovered at the stage of printing.[1] Such an insider's revelation serves as an index of the intense hype created around the release of the books. At the same time, it also adds to this hype by reasserting their status as valuable objects that need to be defended against unlawful distribution. The generation of suspense and curiosity, essential to the production of a celebrity, is achieved here through the strategic, carefully calculated insight into Rowling's life and work. Rowling's celebrity is constructed as a familiar, yet miraculous rags-to-riches story of an extraordinary writer who is also an ordinary woman. This is perhaps most evident at the point in the documentary when she revisits her old apartment in Edinburgh and breaks into tears. This display of emotion exposes the ordinary, human aspect of Rowling's personality, one that is vulnerable to hardship and pain in spite of wealth and glory. Rowling consciously discloses as well as defines herself on camera as an ordinary individual who has managed to achieve extraordinary fame and success, which constitutes a public act of the *humanization* of the celebrity. This intimate, confessional "'moment before' fame," argues Jo Litter in "Making Fame Ordinary," legitimizes and authenticates celebrity. In following Rowling to sites that hold personal as well as professional significance to her life and work, the documentary also enables the audience to participate in a form of (mediated) literary tourism, a process of celebritization usually witnessed in the case of authors who are already dead, but in this case, marking the canonization of the writer during her lifetime.[2]

Significantly, the documentary also establishes a set of correspondences between Rowling's childhood and that of Harry, projecting each as an extension of the other and effectively conflating the real and the fictive. Thus, at the very outset, the narrator informs us that Rowling, "like her ophaned hero," had a difficult childhood, grew up on a suburban British street in a house that had a cupboard under the stairs, and even shares her birthday with Harry. The narrator also comments subsequently that the Harry Potter books are full of idealized father-figures because Rowling's own relationship with her father has always been strained. By thus establishing a correspondence between the author's life and the fictional world she has created, the documentary lends to the text a life-like credibility that reinforces its value as authentic art.[3] This mode of comparison between the author and her protagonist plots the former's life as though it were a story and describes the latter as though he were a real person. In other words, the documentary *fictionalizes* Rowling's life and *humanizes* Harry's story. It thereby renders them identifiable (and in some senses identical) in terms of one another and to the audience as familiar personae whose private lives become the subject of public knowledge. This transformation of the private into the public, the real into the fictive, is crucial to the creation of a celebrity. The stories of Rowling and Harry Potter are narrated here in terms of one another and combined to create what is essentially a celebrity text.

In a similar instance, Rowling herself offers a personal "Biography" on her official website, in which she charts her life-story, starting from her humble beginnings in a middle-class family (complete with very domestic childhood photographs), through her many professional and personal struggles, until the moment when she finally got the news that Bloomsbury had agreed to publish her first book. "And you probably know what happened next," she concludes. Not only does this selective biography give the eager fan a sneak peek into hitherto unknown facts of the author's life, but it also configures her story, in spite of its many mundane elements, as a progressive movement towards the publication of her books. It is noteworthy that Rowling ends this account of her life precisely at the point of the birth of her public persona as an author. This indicates her conscious attempt to plot her life-story in the popular format of a-star-is-born narrative that defines contemporary celebrity. Moreover, Rowling, the "biographer" who narrates her own life, seems to stand at a critical distance from Rowling, the author, which signals her participation in of a process of self-celebritization. It is thus that she transforms ordinary details of her personal life into the extraordinary tale of her famous public persona.[4] As Nayar observes, "A celebrity is one whose private life acquires as much public importance, and into which people want sights and insights, as her or his public one" (5). This is especially true of literary celebrities such as Rowling, whose life and work are confused to an extent that their perceived merits become interchangeable, and the celebrity status earned by one accrues to the other as well.

The conflation of the public and the private domains of an individual's life, which Chris Rojek identifies in *Celebrity* as both a necessary precondition and an inevitable effect of his or her "celebrification" (11), is an integral aspect of Rowling's self-projection as an author who nurtures and defends her readers' interest in the Harry Potter series. As part of this strategy, Rowling deliberately shares her personal experiences with her fans through her official website, inviting them, as it were, to look into her household through a virtual "window." In the link called "News," she keeps readers updated about the latest developments in her life, which she presents as being inseparable from the existence of Harry Potter. Here is an instance from a post she put up on December 12, 2004: "[T]he distance between the keyboard and yours truly increases day by day as my third child races Harry's next adventure into the world. I will soon need extendable fingers to type." In posts following this one, she gives readers an account of her anxieties, frustrations, and excitements as she writes the sixth book of the series during her third pregnancy. Thus, Rowling shrewdly combines the discourse of ("procreative") gestation and motherhood with that of writing as a "creative" process. She thereby implicitly ascribes to the latter the organic unity of creator/creation conventionally associated with the "labor" involved in the former. In other words, writing the book becomes comparable to birthing a child. In the post "JKR gives birth to a baby girl" (25/01/05)," Rowling says, "I was planning to do a few more updates to this site when events overtook me on Sunday, so when I've got past the next feed or two, and maybe caught up on a little sleep, I shall make a few more tweaks. In the meantime, I hope you're all having as good a week as I am." Here, she lets her fans into her most intimate experiences as a new mother who also happens to be an artist responsible to her fans, feeding (in an almost parodic version of feeding her own child) their voyeuristic desires by deliberately breaching the distinction between the public and the private. The books and the fans seemingly occupy nearly as close a place to Rowling's heart as her newborn baby, all vying for her time, energy and attention. By inviting her fans to share her happiness at the birth of her baby, Rowling makes a symbolic gesture of emotional intimacy towards her fans. However, such a gesture is possible precisely because and through the intervening presence of the medium of the website. The free and open nature of the medium effectively glosses over the fact that it is still entirely up to Rowling how much of her life and work she wishes to display to the public. This indicates that a clear distinction between the author and her work is no longer possible or desirable in a context where the celebrity status of one rubs off on the other.

The updates on her website perform a function similar to blogs and Twitter accounts maintained by contemporary film stars, in which they share their professional as well as personal experiences and opinions with their audiences. Thus, when Rowling recently retorted to homophobic comments made by an ex-fan on Twitter, defending Dumbledore as "a brave and brilliant man [who] could love other men," she seamlessly extended the fictional world of Harry Potter into the domain of real issues of public morality and human rights (Denham). Rowling's "virtual" presence thus offers her fans a sneak peek into her work and her life, a medium that creates the illusion of unmediated insight into what she does and who she is. Such a privileged perspective on the author's life and work tends rather conveniently to blend the two together. As a result, an interest in knowing about the personal details of the author's life becomes indistinguishable from an appreciation or even awareness of her art. This leads to an overlap between her image as a celebrity and that as an artist. As James F. English and John Frow note in "Literary Authorship and Celebrity Culture,"

> Romantic authorship requires a persona, and literary texts are, accordingly, read as kinds of performance, the acting out of the inner life of the author. Celebrity, we could say, is the production of persona in secondary performances . . . as though they were merely supplements or reflections of the "real" performance of persona in the book. (52)

Rowling actively creates an authorial persona that depends on the constant circulation and updating of information about her life and work in the public domain and thereby establishes herself as the ultimate arbiter of popular knowledge about all things Potter. For instance, she responds to rumors about Harry Potter in a link called "Rubbish" on her website, in which she classifies them as "starting to smell," "excessive addictives," "recycled," "mouldy," "pure garbage" and "toxic." By offering a typology of such rumors, Rowling not only manages to discredit them with her trademark humor, but also reinforces her position as the supreme authority over the textual world of the series. Moreover, a lively discussion on these rumors also serves as an effective instrument of generating and circulating discourses about the world of Harry Potter, perpetuating and adding to its celebrity status. Rowling seeks to exercise an unusual amount of control over the meanings that her audiences make of her work and of her status as the ultimate "authority" in the Harry Potter world. She justifies her position of supremacy within the Harry Potter industry by repeatedly playing upon her image as the protector of the rights of her fans and defender of art. For instance, prior to the release of *Deathly Hallows*, she stated,

> I am staggered that American newspapers have decided to publish purported spoilers in the form of reviews in complete disregard of the wishes of literally millions of readers, particularly children, who wanted to reach Harry's final destination by themselves, in their own time. I am incredibly grateful to all those newspapers, booksellers and others who have chosen not to attempt to spoil Harry's last adventure for fans. (qtd. in Reynolds)

It is interesting to note here that Rowling's attack on "spoilers" is presented here as a conscientious, almost maternal, writer's love and concern for her fans rather than an intellectual property owner's anxious safeguarding of her own economic interests. After all, book previews are not such an unheard-of thing in the literary world, and given the immense media hype created around the release of the last book, the kind of unmediated journey to the final book that Rowling seems to envision for her fans here is really only an illusion. Reading as a sacred act, one that involves direct communion between the reader and the text, is only a myth in the age of celebrity marketing, where the publicity machinery actively brings down the barriers between the actual act of reading a text and the intervening context of advertising and distribution. In a sense, readers are always already familiar with a text even before they have actually read it. In fact, during the publication of the books, Rowling managed to exert a degree of control over information about the plot that not only matched, but also fueled, the intense suspense surrounding them.[5] Thus, in her promotional interview with Jonathan Ross, Rowling disclosed that the last book was going to be a "bloodbath" and that she had altered the phrasing of the last sentence. Such authorial revelations constitute a strategy of deliberate and controlled release of information about the series and effectively establish Rowling as an oracle, the source of all knowledge about the world of Harry Potter. To use Ross' apt phrase, Rowling is a "literary tease," one who can express righteous indignation over unauthorized information leaks about the books as a benevolent defender of her audience's reading pleasure. Simultaneously, she also exercises supreme control over the nature and extent of information that she is willing to disclose to her audience. Thus, Rowling combines the role of a benevolent author genuinely concerned for her readers with that of a media-savvy entrepreneur very well aware of her own intellectual property rights.

In fact, Rowling is able to establish and perpetuate her absolute authority over the fictional world of Harry Potter by means of constantly adding to its details even after the books have been published. Whereas Rowling maintained a calculated level of secrecy about her fictional characters during the publication of the books, she now supplies a surfeit of additional information about them through her new website *Pottermore*. Not only does Rowling expand the world of Harry Potter by offering background stories and trivia about various characters, but she also extends its domain by giving her fans opportunities to participate in it virtually. Thus, the website offers its users features such as quizzes that determine which Hogwarts house one belongs to, links to be chosen by a magic wand and cast spells, and a selection of Harry Potter merchandise for sale. The continuation of the fictional world of Harry Potter beyond the limits of the series and into the virtual experience of fans blurs the distinction between literature and life. Thus, when she "outs" Dumbledore or declares that Ron and Herminone would have needed marriage counselling, she effectively gives her characters an extra-textual life that spills over the boundaries of the series itself and renders them identifiable to the audience almost as *real* human beings with a past and a future. Such additional knowledge about the books functions as a Derridean *supplement*[6]—both necessary and excessive to the popular interpretation of and response to the series. It also effectively establishes Rowling's own position as the ultimate insider in the world of Harry Potter and reiterates her authority over the "afterlives" of her fictional characters. It is significant to note here that the immense body of online fan-fiction dedicated to the series is essentially also an extension of the lives of these fictional characters beyond the limits of the official narrative. Unlike authors such as Anne Rice who discourage fan-fiction, Rowling has not only been tolerant of such unofficial appropriation of her work, but has even awarded some of the major fan websites with her seal of approval, thereby extending her authority over those domains of the Harry Potter world that she has not authored herself. Yet, underlying this populist strategy of benevolent indulgence towards her fans is the tension between Rowling's position as a liberal artist and a shrewd businesswoman. Thus, when in 2008, Steve Vander Ark sought to publish the material on his fan website *HP Lexicon* as a book, Rowling took preventive legal action against him on grounds of copyright infringement, arguing that such a publication would possibly eat into proceeds from the sale of an encyclopedic glossary she might herself pen at some point. It is evident that, while Rowling encourages her fans to participate in generating and circulating the cultural currency of the series through non-commercial means, she is acutely aware and in control of the economic capital it generates.[7] In this context, it is significant to note that in spite of the expansion of the Harry Potter series as a brand across various media formats—film, merchandise, and even a theme park—Rowling continues to maintain her authorial rights over each avatar in which her characters appear.

It is her ability to integrate seamlessly the economic and the cultural values of the Harry Potter series that has enabled Rowling to emerge as an *author-entrepreneur,* one whose public performance of her celebrity derives from her literary fame and success, but also goes beyond it. Rowling's celebrity is, in fact, a symptom of what Joe Moran describes as "the continuing integration of literary production into the entertainment industry" (41). Thus, the fact that her literary achievements are often described in statistical terms—she has been appearing regularly on the *Forbes* "Top 100 Celebrities" list since 2004 and was hailed by *Time* magazine in 2007 for being, the author of the fastest-selling book ever (15,000,000 copies of *Deathly Hallows* sold within twenty-four hours of its release), the second richest woman in the entertainment industry, and the first billionaire author in the world—points to the literary celebrity's implication in the media-driven processes of publicity and branding that transform the artist and her creation into marketable commodities. The celebrity that accrues to both Rowling and her work results from what John Frow describes in "Signature as Brand" as "the commercialization of art and the aestheticization of commerce in contemporary times" (56). In fact, Rowling has been successful in extending her celebrity beyond her immediate role and position as the author of the Harry Potter series precisely because of the economic and cultural value the series has acquired. Thus, it was on the basis of the massive success of the first three books of the series that Rowling authored two companion books, *Fantastic Beasts and Where to Find Them* and *Quidditch Through the Ages*, the profits from which she donated to Comic Relief, a British anti-poverty organization. In this case, Rowling has been able to translate the cultural meanings associated with her fictional world (the "books" are reading material for Hogwarts students) into real economic currency and then extend the values of both into the domain of social responsibility. In fact, through her various charitable contributions for the aid of children, single parents and patients with multiple sclerosis, Rowling has emerged as what might be termed a "civic celebrity"—one whose domain of public activity goes beyond, but is also materially connected to, her fame and success as a literary celebrity. In putting her phenomenal economic success to philanthropic uses, Rowling, like Bill Gates, represents the inherent potential for the extension and diversification of the celebrity persona and its impact beyond his or her original context.

Yet, Rowling's identity as the author of the Harry Potter books continues to be the paradigm for the popular response to her subsequent forays into the public domain. Thus, *The New Statesman* reported that following the news "leak" that it was Rowling who had authored the detective novel *The Cuckoo's Calling* under the pseudonym of Robert Galbraith, the sales of the book soared exponentially (Hern). While the public response to the book has clearly been influenced by the knowledge about the real identity of its author, Rowling's stated intent to "go back to the beginning of a writing career in this new genre, to work without hype or expectation and to receive totally unvarnished feedback" (*jkrowling.com*) indicates, on her part, an attempted withdrawal into a creative space independent of the trappings of her status as a literary celebrity. Yet, it is precisely the immense amount of economic and cultural capital she has amassed as the author of the Harry Potter books that now enables Rowling to write from a secure, private space, one where concerns of commerical failure become immaterial. Thus, it is Rowling's celebrity that puts Rowling in the privileged position of writing for creative satisfaction and publicly performing the role of an author committed to her art. In spite of—and ultimately even because of—her self-conscious distancing of her latest literary output from the celebrity that has accrued to her as the author of the Harry Potter books, Rowling's public persona is inevitably and irretrievably perceived and consumed by her audience as reflecting the values of the brand she represents. As Wenche Ommundsen observes in "Sex, Soap and Sainthood," "Celebrity, or rather, the processes of celebrification, [is] curiously circular in nature. Once famous, or imbricated in the discourse of celebrity, writers are subjected to (or subject themselves to—they're not all innocent bystanders) practices, meanings and manipulations acted out in public culture" (50–51).

It is evident from this discussion that Rowling and the Harry Potter series function as mutually defining, co-dependent and intersecting "stories" that circulate across media and render both of them together into popular "texts." Rowling's celebrity is essentially intertextual in nature and is predicated on her public performance of her private life and work with relation to Harry Potter. Her roles as a creative writer and a socially-aware citizen derive their meanings from the constant reiteration of her position as the authorial source of meaning within the world of Harry Potter; at the same time, the series itself derives its cultural and economic currency from the construction and perpetuation of the author's public persona as an embodiment of artistic merit. Thus, Rowling and Harry Potter function as mutually-constitutive elements of a celebrity brand—one that represents unique, but replicable, value. While the equivalence between the author's life and her creation is part of a long literary tradition, the convergence of the cultural and material values of the two results from contemporary market forces that commercialize individual personae and individualize commercial products. It is this interchangeability of value, achieved through the creation of a popular image representing both the author and her work, which renders Rowling and the Harry Potter series into a composite celebrity.

Notes

1. The popular anticipation of the books' release has been cross-referenced in the 2006 film *The Devil Wears Prada*, where the protagonist manages to achieve the seemingly impossible by procuring a copy of the yet unpublished Harry Potter book for her domineering boss's daughters through her contacts in the publishing industry.

2. This is evident from the fact that Nicolson's cafe, one of the coffee shops in Edinburgh that Rowling often used to visit to write the early drafts of Harry Potter, now has a plaque that declares its association with the genesis of the series and thereby participates in a mode of literary tourism that contributes to immortalizing the author during her own lifetime. This semblance of immortality, as Rojek points out, is the hallmark of the contemporary celebrity (78).

3. The conflation of the literary celebrity's persona with his work dates back to the nineteenth century, when Mark Twain and Charles Dickens became prominent figures in the American lecture circuit. The popular press of the time publicized these lecture tours and created for these authors a textual "image" that "stimulated a desire to meet the 'real' celebrity in person" (Moran 17–19).

4. Rowling is, in fact, acutely aware of the dynamics of celebrity culture in the age of mass media. Thus, within the Harry Potter books, she critiques the vain and obsessive pursuit of fame and gossip through the characters of Gilderoy Lockhart, the handsome but inept wizard, and Rita Skeeter, the intrusive, unscrupulous journalist. Both of these characters are, like Rowling herself, celebrity writers. However, both lack real merit and misuse their fame. By portraying these characters as ridiculous and sometimes even dangerous, Rowling self-reflexively alerts her audience to the pitfalls of celebrity culture.

5. In the build-up to the final book of the series, speculations about the ultimate fate of the characters in the books reached frenzied levels

on legions of fan-sites and even led to publications such as John Granger's *Who Killed Albus Dumbledore?* (2006).

6.   Jacques Derrida (1930–2004) was one of most influential literary theorists of the twentieth century. He emphasized the textual nature of all representation and challenged the very notion of fixed meanings and binaries (such as mind/body, sacred/profane, original/copy) on which the Western intellectual tradition is based. Derrida theorized the "supplement" in *Of Grammatology*, defining it as a "sign" that adds to as well as substitutes for another one.

7.   It is useful, however, to remember that in December 2000, soon after it acquired merchandising rights over the Harry Potter series, Time Warner/Warner Bros. issued legal notices to unofficial fan websites asking them to explain their intent and transfer their domain names to it within twenty-eight days. The controversy that ensued received a good deal of media coverage and forced Time Warner/ Warner Bros. to backtrack on its legal notice and defend its own stance as resulting from a concern about infringement of the Harry Potter trademark by some web users (Borah 353–54). It is obvious that the popularity and success of the Harry Potter series results from a process of negotiation between its legal "owners" and the audience who participate in making their own meanings out of the official narrative.

Works Cited

Barthes, Roland. *Mythologies.* Trans. Annette Lavers. London: Jonathan Cape, 1972.

"Biography: Joanne Rowling—The Girl Who Grew Up to Write Harry Potter." *Harrypotter.bloomsbury.com.* Bloomsbury Publishing, n.d. Web. 20 Aug. 2014.

Borah, Rebecca Sutherland. "Apprentice Wizards Welcome: Fan Communities and the Culture of Harry Potter." *The Ivory Tower and Harry Potter: Perspectives on a Literary Phenomenon.* Ed. Lana A. Whited. Columbia: U of Missouri P, 2002. 343–64.

Denham, Jess. "J. K. Rowling Hits Back at Twitter User Who Attacked Her for Revealing 'Dumbledore Was Gay.'" *The Independent*, 7 Sept. 2014. Web. 24 Sept. 2014.

Derrida, Jacques. *Of Grammatology.* Trans. Gayatri Chakraborty Spivak. Baltimore: Johns Hopkins UP, 1976.

English, James F. & John Frow. "Literary Authorship and Celebrity Culture." *A Concise Companion to British Fiction*. Ed. James F. English. Oxford: Blackwell, 2006. 39–57.

Frow, John. "Signature and Brand." *High-pop: Making Culture into Popular Entertainment*. Ed. Jim Collins. Oxford: Blackwell, 2002. 56–74.

Gibbs, Nancy. "Person of the Year 2007: Runners Up—J. K. Rowling." *Time* 19 Dec. 2007. Web. 11 May 2014.

Gleick, Elizabeth. "The Wizard of Hogwarts." *Time*. Time, Inc., 4 Apr. 1999. Web. 28 Sept. 2014.

Hern, Alex. "Sales of *The Cuckoo's Calling* Surge by 150,000% after JK Rowling Revealed as Author." *The New Statesman*, 14 July 2013. Web. 28 Sept. 2014.

Litter, Jo. "Making Fame Ordinary: Intimacy, Reflexivity and 'Keeping it Real'." *Mediactive 2: Celebrity* (2003): 8–25.

Moran, Joe. *Star Authors: Literary Celebrity in America*. London: Pluto, 2002.

Nayar, Pramod K. *Seeing Stars: Spectacle, Society and Celebrity Culture*. New Delhi: Sage, 2009.

Ommundsen, Wenche. "Sex, Soap and Sainthood: Beginning to Theorize Literary Celebrity." *Journal of the Association for the Study of Australian Literature* 3 (2004): 45–56. Web. 11 Apr. 2014.

Pilkington, Ed. "The Strange Case of Harry Potter and the Battle of US District Court 24A." *The Guardian*, 15 Apr. 2008. Web. 12 May 2014.

Reynolds, Nigel. "Harry Potter Spoilers Anger J. K. Rowling." *The Telegraph*, 20 Jul. 2007. Web. 23 Sept. 2014.

Rojek, Chris. *Celebrity*. London: Reaktion, 2001.

Ross, Jonathan. Interview with J.K. Rowling. *Friday Night with Jonathan Ross*. BBC One. 6 Jul. 2007. Web. 19 Apr. 2014.

Rowling, J. K. *JKRowling.com*. Web. 10 April 2014.

_____. *Pottermore*. Web. 4 September 2014.

Runice, James. *J. K. Rowling: A Year in the Life*. ITV. 30 Dec. 2007. Web. 25 April 2014.

Thøgersen, Jimmi & 'Marvelous Marvolo.' *Harry Potter and Me*. BBC. 28 Dec. 2001. Web. 28 Sept. 2014.

Growing Up with Harry Potter: What Motivated Youth to Read the Harry Potter Series?_____

Colette Drouillard

What is it about Harry Potter that motivates so many young readers to follow his adventures? Since 1997, when J. K. Rowling's *Harry Potter and the Philosopher's Stone* was first published in the United Kingdom, more than 450,000,000 copies have been sold, and the seven Harry Potter books have been translated into seventy-three languages (Dammann). As a result of the popularity of the Harry Potter books, one would expect to find numerous studies looking at why young readers are motivated to read the books and to what factors researchers attribute their motivations to begin and to continue reading as this series was published over an eleven-year period.

In 2009, a review of the literature found that over 800 peer-reviewed essays on the subject of Harry Potter had been published; however, very few of these included noteworthy focus on young readers and their response to Harry Potter; instead, focus was primarily on adult perceptions of young readers' responses (Drouillard). While each of these studies strove to contribute to better understanding the appeal of the Harry Potter series for young readers, almost all the conclusions were constructed from adult perceptions of young readers' responses rather than derived from descriptions of reading experiences from young readers themselves.

Sales demonstrate the popularity of the Harry Potter books, but the question remains: why do young readers think this series of books motivated them to read? In order to learn from the youth themselves, researchers implemented a project designed to systematically collect and analyze the opinions of young readers. This study explored the influence of the Harry Potter books on young readers. Explanations developed using responses drawn from the young readers themselves provide greater understanding of the reading interests and motivations of young readers than documented in previously existing explanations of Harry Potter's appeal.

The focus of this study was young readers who grew up in the United States, were born between 1984 and 1990, began reading Harry Potter between the ages of eight and thirteen and continued reading the series as the books were published until they had read each of the seven books one or more times. The selection of readers between eight and thirteen years old when the first book was published in the US in 1998 and between eighteen to twenty-three years of age when the seventh book was published in 2007 ensures that the participants' ages roughly parallel those of the main characters in Rowling's series.

The goal of this research project was identification of factors young readers report as motivating them to read Harry Potter and the development of themes in order to expand current knowledge and understanding of their reading interests, habits, and attitudes. The experience of growing up alongside Harry Potter and maturing as both adolescents and readers while the books became longer and the characters, themes, and plots increased in complexity was an experience unique to this group of readers.

Claims that the Harry Potter books motivate children to read more were present regardless of whether the article was published in the popular press or in a peer-reviewed academic journal. In his book, George Beahm described J. K. Rowling and her contribution to literacy in this way:

> She is of outstanding distinction and has an international impact in her own field. She had an impact in reversing the worldwide trend in decreasing literacy. Her writing has attracted a huge number of children who previously had difficulties in beginning to read, and her work has dispelled the myth that children lack the attention span to engage with longer books. (72)

Motivation theory impacts this research as the lens through which the young readers' responses were analyzed. Identification and rich descriptions of what young readers believe these motivations are, how their interests and preferences and self-efficacy relate to their choice of Harry Potter to read, and how this relates to current research on reader interests all contribute to expansion of current research on reading interests of children in several ways: they preferred reading adventure and fantasy over horror or science fiction, read for pleasure more frequently, and were more likely to perceive themselves as having strong reading skills (Drouillard 8).

Adult perceptions alone don't fully account for the books' success with readers. To gain a better understanding of young readers' motivations and preferences, it is essential to let the readers speak in their own voices, using sound methodological practices— something that is currently missing from the research base. Findings and conclusions derived from this study more fully inform us about the multidimensional factors impacting reading motivation and engagement.

Methodology

Exploration of the overarching question "What motivated youth to read the Harry Potter series?" was addressed through three research questions:

1. What are the general reading interests, habits, and attitudes towards reading of the young readers who participated in this study?
2. What factors do young readers identify as initially attracting them to Harry Potter?
3. What factors do young readers identify as motivating them to continue to read Harry Potter?

Reading motivation researchers have employed a variety of research designs and methods in the past, but a mixed-method design that utilizes a survey or questionnaire in conjunction with some other type of data collection has been shown to be most effective in previous studies with research questions focused on aspects similar to those of this study. Linda Baker and Allan Wigfield examined several dimensions of reading motivation related to students' reading activity and achievement by using a questionnaire in combination with interviews of students, while Gay Ivey and Karen Broaddus utilized a questionnaire to collect data from 1,765 sixth-grade students and to identify participants for follow-up interviews to facilitate collection of more detailed, in-depth data.

Consequently, the exploration of Harry Potter readership was conducted in two distinct phases: Phase One, administered using an online questionnaire to collect both quantitative and qualitative data, addressed the relationship of young readers who grew up with Harry Potter and the factors these readers identified as affecting their motivation to continue reading Rowling's series during the ten years the books were published, while Phase Two involved qualitative interviews to explore more fully themes and data derived in the first phase.

Data were sought from subjects who were identified as most capable of providing detailed descriptions of their motivations and experiences while they were young readers of the Harry Potter series. The population represented by the results of this research consisted of readers who grew up in the United States and met specified criteria: (a) a birth date between 1984 and 1990; (b) initial reading experience with Harry Potter during or prior to 1999; and (c) completion of all seven books in the Harry Potter series.

Purposeful non-probabilistic self-selection sampling[1] was used to collect Phase One data. An online survey was selected as the initial data collection instrument for this research in order to maximize access to the most diverse audience possible. Data collection began on July 28, 2008, and closed on August 18, 2008. Participants were recruited via an invitation posted on select Harry Potter websites: *HPANA*, *MuggleNet*, *The Leaky Cauldron*, and *Harry Potter Fan Fiction*. An article about the request for participation was posted on the *Harry Potter Automatic News Aggregator* (HPANA) by the editor-in-chief, Jeff Guillaume, on August 12, 2008, stimulating diffusion of the survey information via a wide variety of additional websites, discussion boards, and list serves and resulting in many more than the minimum numbers of responses necessary to obtain data saturation. A total of 2,170 survey responses was received, with 649 submitted by subjects meeting the research criteria: young readers who lived in the United States during the time they read

Harry Potter, were born between 1984 and 1990, began reading the series during or prior to 1999, read each of the seven books at least one time, and agreed to participate in the study.

Phase Two data collection builds on the results of Phase One data analysis. John Creswell and Vicki Plano Clark recommend that the same subjects should be included in both phases of data collection. The intent of this method is to use qualitative data to provide more detail about the quantitative results by selecting "participants that can best provide this detail" (Creswell & Clark 122). Use of purposeful sampling makes it possible to select participants who can best provide information about the phenomenon or concept being explored (112). Reliability of qualitative data analysis during Phase Two was established by means of member checking. Responses were analyzed and additional interviews conducted until data saturation occurred, with subject responses confirming previously identified results without identification of additional aspects of the motivating factors.

The question of reader motivation over the period of time the Harry Potter series was published was complex and required consideration of many facets identified in responses of this group of readers' reading experiences. The young readers who submitted questionnaire responses were motivated to read the Harry Potter books by a wide array of people and reasons. Aspects considered in this discussion reflect not only reasons these readers were initially motivated to read Harry Potter, but also the changing perspectives, interests, and motivations of this group of readers as they continued to read the Harry Potter books over the eleven years of publication.

Preliminary review of the open-ended question responses led to development of thirty-five initial concept nodes. A concept node is an abstract representation of an event or reason a young reader initially read or continued to read Harry Potter. After coding was complete, all passages of text associated with each concept node were reviewed and the concept node titles revised as necessary to describe most clearly the abstract representation associated with the event or reason that particular young reader described. Factor categories were developed to model different combinations of concept nodes into groups, in order to identify combinations with a distinct theme.

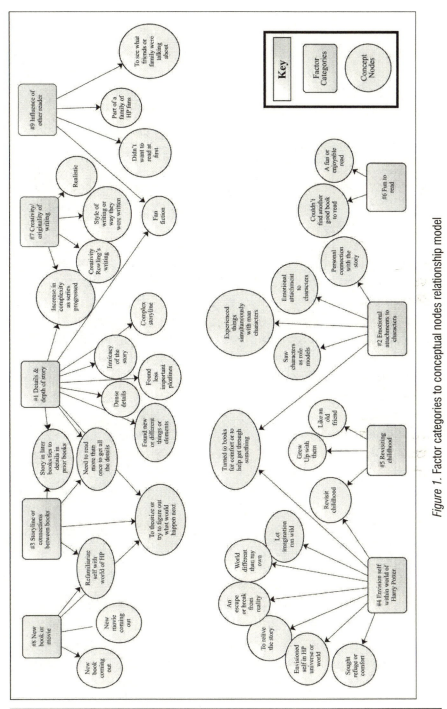

Figure 1. Factor categories to conceptual nodes relationship model

Nature of These Harry Potter Readers

The conclusion of the Harry Potter series provided a unique opportunity to explore reading motivation with those young readers who grew up at approximately the same pace and in the same time as Harry Potter and his friends. Many of Rowling's devoted readers began to read Harry Potter between 1997 and 1999 when they, like Harry in the early books, were eight- to ten-year-old children. Ten years later, as the series reached its conclusion, these readers had matured alongside Harry, Ron, and Hermione, and while their lives may not have exactly paralleled Harry's near-constant life-or-death battles, they too found themselves on the verge of adulthood and entry into the "real world."

This group of young readers had the singular opportunity to grow up at approximately the same pace and in the same time period as Harry Potter and his friends. As each book was published, these readers found a richly detailed world of magic with a hero near their own age. Then, along with the rest of the world, they had to wait a year, or two, or three for the next book to come out. By the time the true nature of evil was revealed through the deaths of beloved characters and as Harry and his reader friends were forced to accept the fact that the world is not a particularly safe place, the original eight- to ten-year-old readers were in their teens. As the books grew in length and complexity, these readers grew and matured as well.

Today's eight- to ten-year-old readers no longer have to wait for publication of the next book, but rather have the opportunity to read all the books in the series at a pace they determine. This means that the experience of growing up with Harry Potter was truly a unique one, and the opportunity to collect the reactions, experiences, and memories of these readers one that will never occur again.

Other Characteristics

About three-fourths of the readers in the current study were white (Figure 2). This is approximately the same proportion of whites found in the general population of the United States. However, the percentage of readers who identified their ethnicity as Black/African American or Hispanic/Latin American was less than half the proportion found in the United States. The less-than-representative number of Hispanic and African American youth may be explained by data that demonstrate less at-home access to the books for these two demographic groups (Scholastic Corporation & Yankelovich *2008 Kids & Family Reading Report*).

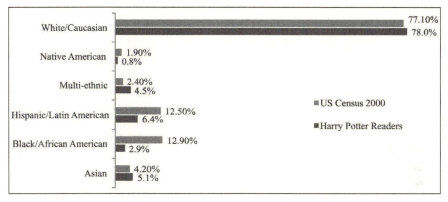

Figure 2. Ethnic background of Harry Potter study readers compared to US population

When readers identified in other Harry Potter studies are considered alongside this study's readers, this group reflects the ethnic background of the United States more closely than samples described in all but the studies conducted by Harry Potter's American publisher (Scholastic Corporation & Yankelovich, *Kids & Family Reading Report*; *2008 Kids & Family Reading Report*). The Scholastic studies collected data from twenty-five regions of the United States and weighted final data with variables such as region, race, and religion from the US Census Bureau and the current population survey.

Females were more than twice as likely to respond to this survey. A total of 622 responses meeting the study criteria were received, with the designation of "male" selected by 190 subjects (30.5 percent) and "female" by 432 subjects (69.5 percent). Observations of gender divides forming around reading practices and fan community construction are by no means new or unexpected. In 1986, reader-response critic David Bleich surveyed how male and female students read canonical literary texts. He concluded that the men he studied tended to read for authorial meaning, noting a "strong narrational voice" shaping the text, whereas the women "experienced the narrative as a world, without a particularly strong sense that this world was narrated into existence" (Bleich 239). Bleich also observed that female readers saw their own "tacit inferences" as part of the story, whereas men disregarded such inferences and focused more on textual "accuracy" (239).

Henry Jenkins suggests that the two communities' activities parallel one another, as each engages in repeated re-readings of common narratives and draws on secondary texts for added information. Women read "associationally," looking for interrelationships between their lives and the characters' lives, while men read texts linearly, looking for additional information from characters and their relationships to "resolve their own syntagmatic questions concerning plot development" (Jenkins 108). Jenkins' and Bleich's foci, while dissimilar, converge at describing gendered differences in fans' applications of texts. While male and female fans tend to read texts differently, what they have in common is the interest in developing deeper or better understandings about characters and relationships in order to answer questions about the text.

Because of the way the sample was drawn, it may be skewed towards females, as they may be more likely to participate in the online communities in general or the Harry Potter communities specifically, because they may be more willing to complete an online questionnaire, or because they may be more willing to share personal experiences.

Interpretation of Key Findings
Research Question One: What are the general reading interests, habits, and attitudes towards reading of the young readers who participated in this study?

Reading Interests
Researchers have studied children's reading interests and prefer-ences using a variety of methods, such as surveys and interviews.

Katherine Spangler clarified the distinction by defining preference studies as those that look at children's expressed attitudes toward reading—in other words, what children might read if given the opportunity. Reading interest studies, on the other hand, examine actual reading behaviors of children by analyzing the books children have actually read.

	Very Often	Often	Sometimes	Rarely	Never
Adventure		181	142	36	5
Fantasy	249	151	74	28	9
Historical Fiction	92	83	140	136	58
Horror	44	54	102	140	166
Humor	50	113	191	112	40
Mysteries or detective fiction	88	122	163	101	34
Non-fiction	55	75	122	190	67
Romance novels	31	40	76	124	228
Romantic fiction	55	68	86	119	174
Science fiction	88	97	118	120	74

Table 1. Frequency with which each kind of book was read by subjects as they grew up

Harry Potter readers identified "Fantasy" and "Adventure" as the kinds of books they most often read while growing up (Table 1). These interests differ from those found in other studies. Horror and science fiction have been identified as the most frequently selected kind of book by readers between twelve and eighteen years of age (Children's Literature Research Centre; Hopper; Snellman; Sturm; Whittemore), yet were selected "Sometimes" or "Rarely" by Harry Potter readers. A British study (Clark, Torsi, & Strong, 23,

38, 92), found a difference in genre-preference between reluctant and enthusiastic readers. This study established that enthusiastic readers preferred adventure most frequently, while reluctant readers preferred horror most often.

Reading Habits

Over a quarter of the Harry Potter readers (134 or 26.3 percent) reported that they read for pleasure every day, with another quarter (131 or 25.7 percent) reporting reading for pleasure four to six days a week. This differs greatly from national statistics that show only 22 percent of young Americans "Read almost every day," while 19 percent of young Americans "Never or hardly ever read" (Iyengal, Ball, & National Endowment for the Arts, 8).

One frequently mentioned aspect of the Harry Potter reading phenomenon has been the perception that the books are often read more than one time. This was strongly supported by those responding to this survey, with 596 (97.5 percent) selecting "Yes" when asked if they had read any of the Harry Potter books more than once.

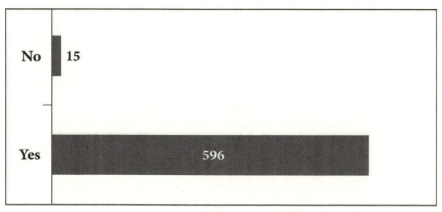

Figure 3. Have you read any of the Harry Potter books more than one time?

When the Harry Potter survey subjects were asked to identify the number of times they had read each of the books in the Harry Potter series, a clear trend was visible. Books published earlier in the series were re-read more often than books published later in the series.

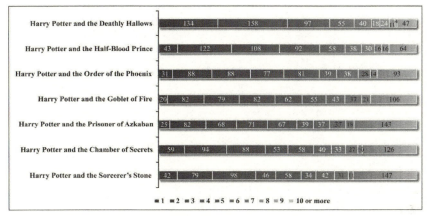

Figure 4. The number of times subjects have read each of the books

This can be seen in Figure 4, in which the lightest colored squares show the number of subjects reading that book in the Harry Potter series ten or more times and the number in the darkest box identifying the number of subjects who read the book one time.

When readers were asked if they were likely to read a book other than Harry Potter more than one time, the probability of repeat readings was much lower. While only fifteen (2.5 percent) of those responding said they had not read any of the Harry Potter books more than one time, 189 (32 percent) said they rarely or never read other books more than one time (Drouillard 51–52). This increased probability of reading the Harry Potter books more than one time is yet another piece of evidence that readers are finding something uniquely different in the way they are interacting with these books that is motivating them to return repeatedly to the world of Harry Potter.

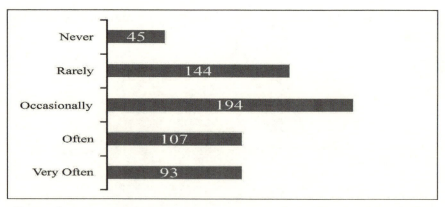

Figure 5. Frequency survey subjects read books other than Harry Potter more than one time.

Attitudes toward Reading

The Harry Potter readers were more likely than readers in other studies to perceive themselves as having strong reading skills. A positive self-concept as a reader is one aspect of considering oneself an able reader. The exception to the overall positive attitude toward reading expressed by these readers was their less-than-positive perception that their close friends thought reading was fun, which, although less obvious, is also considered as a component of self-concept as a reader. The readers' response to the question about friends' thinking reading was fun indicates only a moderate degree of self-concept as readers, which was not consistent with either the results for other questions related to self-concept as readers or responses to open-ended survey questions.

Because the Harry Potter readers spend more time reading than an average reader in the United States, it is expected that they demonstrate a higher positive perception of themselves as readers than the average student in the United States does. The way readers perceive their ability does not explain whether positive attitudes correlate with high achievement differences or vice versa; however, research suggests an association between reading attitudes and achievement (McKenna, Kear, & Ellsworth; Wigfield & Guthrie), which is consistent with results from these readers.

Research Question Two: What factors did young readers identify as initially attracting them to Harry Potter?

As might be expected, when asked to describe their first encounter with Harry Potter, most of the readers shared experiences relating to the joy of discovering the wizarding world and the extraordinary experience of a story so spellbinding that it transports them to another time, another place, or another adventure involving extraordinary people, extraordinary creatures, and extraordinary occurrences. This section considers three factors identified as initially motivating this group of readers to read Harry Potter: Factor #6, Books are fun or easy to read; Factor #8, New book or movie release; and Factor #9, Influence of others reading the books.

Factor #6: Books are fun or easy to read

The first books in the Harry Potter series were often described to readers as appealing because they were enjoyable and easy to read and featured a main character who shared many traits with the young readers, even though he was a wizard. The initial reading experiences were often depicted as joyful adventures into a new world and the first time many readers became lost in a story or between the pages of a book.

The age of the readers in this study when they read the first series book ranged from eight to thirteen years old. This may be one of the reasons why these readers were more apt to describe the reason they first read Harry Potter as parent-, family-, or teacher-focused. Interest in exploring what was causing the hype or reading in order to join in the fun of discussing the books with friends were other reasons identified for first reading Harry Potter; however, these latter reasons are found much more frequently when readers describe motivations for continuing to read Harry Potter.

Factor #8: New book or movie release

The first Harry Potter movie was not released until 2002. Within the parameters of this study, this would have been three to four years after these young readers read their first Harry Potter novel; however, news about the sale of movie rights to Warner Bros. in

1999 increased media coverage and was identified by several readers as a reason for first opening a Harry Potter book. The release of a new Harry Potter book was less often identified by these readers. Reference to media as motivating an initial reading of Harry Potter was more likely to occur after Bloomsbury and Scholastic began to release the books in the United Kingdom and the United States simultaneously in 2000, which was subsequent to the range of years readers in this study began reading the series.

Factor #9: Influence of others reading the books

Family and friends most often introduced these Harry Potter readers to Rowling's books for the first time. Harry Potter readers often learned about the books from other readers, who felt compelled to share their joy in the series with others by describing the books and trying to convince friends to join them in the reading experience (Figure 6). Equally convincing was the observation of a young person totally absorbed in reading one of the books, particularly in places or at times not typically associated with reading, often stimulating conversation.

A reader sub-category that must be recognized includes readers who initially were determined not to read Harry Potter because they did not want to follow the crowd or did not think the books could possibly be that interesting, but eventually found themselves drawn into reading the series. Other than friends, parents most often led to the first reading of Harry Potter. Parents who banned or restricted access to the Harry Potter books were identified by several readers as having the unintentional result of increasing interest in reading Harry Potter in order to see just what was in the books.

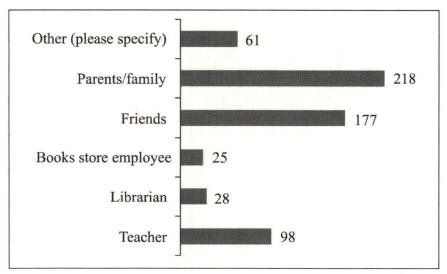

Figure 6. The person who first introduced the reader to the Harry Potter series

In this study, 87 percent of the Harry Potter readers did not find it was important to read Harry Potter in order to feel "in" with their friends (Table 2). These readers, on the other hand, were very likely to encourage their friends to read Harry Potter. As a group, they perceived themselves to be early mavens of the books and, therefore, were less likely to have felt it was important to read the series to feel "in" with their friends because they were already reading Harry Potter.

Question asked and aspect of reading evaluated (self-concept or value of reading)	Very Often	Often	Sometimes	Rarely	Never
I encouraged my friends to read Harry Potter (Value of Reading)	294	108	79	25	7

I think the Harry Potter books motivated me to read more than I did before I read them (Self-Concept as Reader)	185	85	95	63	51
I read books for fun before I started reading Harry Potter (Self-Concept as Reader)	224	89	86	68	44
I thought it was important to read Harry Potter to feel "in" with my friends (Value of Reading)	8	19	33	73	328
Reading Harry Potter increased my interest in reading other books (Value of Reading)	132	103	128	69	48
After reading Harry Potter I felt more confidence in my reading ability (Self-Concept as Reader)	116	78	104	64	78

Table 2. Attitudes toward reading Harry Potter books

The introduction to Harry Potter by friends or family members rather than through academic instruction and the act of initiating other readers "into the club" or family of readers was reflected in this study's readers. One reader described her experience as evolving from "just a girl reading a book to being Part of a Phenomenon" and enjoying the experience of participating in a "community of people doing this ultimately solitary thing (reading) together" (Drouillard 81).

Research Question Three: What factors did young readers identify as motivating them to continue to read Harry Potter?

According to the readers in this study, the Harry Potter books were about more than entertainment; they formed an independent universe, peopled with characters that readers grew to care for and worry about. As nine- or ten-year-old children, many Harry Potter readers found pleasure in the novels as simple outlets of escape. As these readers matured, they recognized, appreciated, and became engaged with many different literary and cultural elements in Rowling's books.

Factor #1: Detail and depth of storylines

The dense detail and complex intricacy of the storyline across the seven Harry Potter books enhanced the reading experience, particularly when the books were read multiple times. The suspense of finding out what would happen next kept interest high until the final book was published, while the complexity and detail in the final story motivated many readers to return and read earlier books in the series yet again.

> Those books were so big and indepth [*sic*] that I felt rereading them would make the new books better reads, because I had forgotten so much from them.
>
> I just loved them, and there was so much information to them that I felt I really needed to reread them to be fully ready to read the next one. Plus, they were such an easy read and really entertaining. (Drouillard 78)

The way the books were read changed as readers matured and developed increased awareness and interest in subtext and themes. Readers described differences in the way they read the books depending upon their mood, changes in life experiences, or differences in personal circumstances. They described reading the same book in very different ways at different times. Sometimes they chose to read a certain book to lose themselves, luxuriate, or relax in Rowling's world, while other times—such as with a newly released book—they read fast and furiously just to find out what would happen next.

Factor #2: Associations with and emotional attachments to characters

More than anything else, it was the very real human faults and foibles along with the magical abilities and heroic inclinations of characters that readers described as the foundation for developing attachments with these characters as deeply personal and emotionally intense as with their real friends and family. Not only Harry, but also each of the main characters was described as having a unique, yet universal, personality that was able to transcend the pages of the books. It may be this combination of each character's heroic abilities along with his or her equally evident faults and mistakes that caused so many readers to develop such personal attachments

Readers described these characters as being as familiar and real as actual people. Situations in the books were described as "more real" by some readers than actual events occurring in distant parts of the world. Personal engagement was found to be particularly strong in readers who shared difficult experiences such as the loss of a friend or a parent.

> For awhile my age was actually the same or almost the same as Harry's in the series. As Harry's life got more difficult as the series went on, so did mine, though in different ways. I grew to relate to Harry even more than I had previously.
>
> As I grew with the series I grew to be very invested in the characters. I was much more emotionally attached to them as I grew because they were a part of me.
>
> It was the attachment to the characters that drove the urge to read, and continue to read, and re-read to see what information was missed. It was the characters. (Drouillard 67)

Readers described finding role models in the characters, citing values they believe were developed while reading Harry Potter that shaped the young adults they were becoming. Characters also filled an important role as a friend to some readers, particularly those who felt they were alone in the world. The ability to open the books and

---

return to the world of Harry Potter meant access to friends they felt were able to relate to their struggles.

Rowling's connections between aspects of the real world and those in the magical world are details that many readers identified as enjoyable. Harry and his friends do many of the same everyday tasks as these young readers: buying school supplies, going to classes, doing homework, and playing sports; however, these activities could be considered from a new and novel perspective when classes are in subjects such as potions instead of chemistry, sports are played on brooms in the sky, and letters are delivered by owl rather than a mailman.

Strong feelings of personal connections with characters was the most frequent aspect of the stories identified as compelling these young readers to continue reading the Harry Potter books. Harry's uncertainty and crises of self-confidence were familiar experiences for adolescent readers who themselves often experienced similar moments of angst and frustration. Many readers found Hermione's intelligence and belief in herself characteristics they felt were reflected in themselves or that they aspired to develop.

> As Harry's life got more difficult as the series went on, so did mine, though in different ways. I grew to relate to Harry even more than I had previously. I grew up with Harry. If there was something wrong that happened in my life, Harry had it worse and there was a story to read.
> I think growing up in school where I was an outcast, and going through the horrible time period of life and all the troubles, it was like having friends when reading the books, because they were experiencing much of the same problems.
>
> My best friend died in 5th grade and my teacher, who considered me one of the top readers in the class, insisted I read Harry Potter for an escape from my grief. (Drouillard 68)

Factor #3: Storylines and connections among books

The detail in the books, particularly aspects linking storylines across volumes in the series, was identified as an important reason many readers not only continued reading until after the final book was published, but reread earlier books in order to identify details and clues that weren't evident initially. Many readers became active in online communities in search of elusive aspects of secondary storylines or information about the myths, legends, and literary antecedents Rowling wove into her books.

Factor #4: Envisioning self within world of Harry Potter

Readers not only described finding characters who shared experiences they were able to relate to their own lives; they also explained the experience of reading the books as giving them a sense of losing themselves in the story. Several readers described their experience while reading Harry Potter as going to a place where they were able to escape from the real world.

> When I first started I wanted it to be real and I wanted it to be my life so bad. As I grew up I realized that Harry Potter could never happen, but I could still escape to Hogwarts in my head while I was reading.

> I know for the first couple books, I used to fantasize about owls delivering my late admission letter to Hogwarts—"Sorry, the ruddy owls got lost on the way!" (Drouillard 71)

Descriptions of readers' feeling that they were "in" the text were frequent. Readers explained the feeling of being immersed so deeply in the world Rowling created they could "lose themselves within the story," in essence co-creating the text and inserting themselves into the books. The feeling of having "inside" knowledge about the world Rowling created was found in many responses of readers who felt they were within the world of Harry Potter while reading the books.

> I read them because I could live in that world for a time and really feel with the characters, I fell in love with the fantasy and the magic.

> It was my way of leaving the real world that was full of stress.

When I read the series I did so to escape reality, escape my life for a bit and live in Harry's much cooler world. (Drouillard 72–73)

The importance of these books as a way to escape reality during periods of trauma or stress was identified by readers experiencing many different challenges. Whether contemplating an unpleasant incident, such as appearing in front of a judge or dealing with the aftermath of a fight with a close friend, readers found related situations in the books that provided them with the opportunity to consider their own situations from another perspective.

Harry Potter became much more important to me as each book was realesed [*sic*] because the books became my only known and comforting resource to help guide me through my grief of losing loved ones. The 5th book was one of the most important because it was released a meer (*sic*) two weeks after I watched my mother die. Harry, in the 4th book, watched Cedric die and after I lost my mom I imagined myself being able to see Thestrals [the magical creature visible only to those who have seen death]. (Drouillard 73)

Factor #5: Revisiting a piece of childhood
The relationship of childhood and Harry Potter was one that the readers found strongly associated. The feeling of returning to visit old friends and being able to recall a simpler time in their lives was identified by many readers. Reading one of the Harry Potter books often triggered memories and provided a bridge to childhood memories.

When I think back on childhood, Harry Potter is my defining experience.

Harry became a part of me. I grew up with him, and it was easy for me to step into his shoes. Growing up with Harry made every new book feel like getting to talk to an old friend again after a long time apart. (Drouillard 74–75)

Factor #6: Books are fun or easy to read

Many readers identified the fact that these books were just plain fun to read as motivating them to return to Harry Potter and read these books again, even if reading books multiple times wasn't something they usually did. This was also reflected in several other factors; the feeling of becoming lost in a book, revisiting old familiar friends, and revisiting an aspect of childhood were also mentioned as reasons readers found the Harry Potter books fun to read again.

Factor #7: Creativity and originality of writing

Aspects of the way Rowling constructed her stories were reflected in a range of reasons identified as motivating young readers. The originality of names and places and almost constant introduction of new aspects and elements of the wizarding world were all reasons readers described as initially intriguing them and as keeping them interested and motivated to read more about the world Rowling created.

> The world she created was so intricate that I wanted to be submersed in it as much as I could.

> J. K. Rowling's writing style is so different than any other style I've become familiar with. Written simply, it was still able to call to mind a world like no other, one that many authors would need to go into immense detail to describe.

> I enjoy a multitude of books, but this series is so great at grabbing the reader's attention. It really brings you into a world you feel is magical . . . . Rowling does a fantastic job creating tones and really stretches the imagination.

> The universe that was created was so complete it was easy to envision yourself in it. The creativity involved really intrigued me. (Drouillard 77)

Factor #8: New book or movie release

The release of a new Harry Potter book or movie often provided the stimulus for readers to return for a visit with old friends in the world of Hogwarts. Some began again with the first book and reread the entire series, while others revisited only the prior book. Regardless of whether they returned to the beginning or only refreshed their memory of recent events, they most often sought the details foreshadowing the plot of the anticipated book.

Refamiliarize self with world of Harry Potter
[I wanted] to compare the movie vs the book. And when a new book came out—I wanted to be refreshed on what happened previously. The story is complex and pieces from book one are explained in other books—same goes with each book.

To theorize or try to figure out what would happen next
As the stories became more grown up and intricate, I became more and more excited about each new book and read the books with different points of view to try to figure out what would happen next.

New book coming out
As the later books came out, I reread the earlier books to refresh my memory about the plot and to get excited about the new release.

New movie coming out
I loved the stories and wanted to compare the books to the movies as they came out. (Drouillard 78–79)

Factor #9: The influence of others reading the books
This factor has a slightly different focus when considered from the perspective of motivations to continue reading the books. The communities of readers that often developed among those reading Harry Potter were often identified as important aspects of the continued reading experience.

The truth is, what changed the most was that I went from being just a girl reading a book to being Part of a Phenomenon. Which was kind of neat—by the fourth book there was this community of people doing this ultimately solitary thing (reading) together, and I really enjoyed that. (Drouillard 81)

These nine factors, some of which explain the motivation for the initial reading of Harry Potter and more of which explain the motivation to continue reading Harry Potter, provide strong evidence that these avid young readers are far more intrinsically than extrinsically motivated. All but one of the nine factors refer to elements of intrinsic motivation. The analysis of collected data demonstrates how these intrinsic motivations emerged from the perspectives of these young readers and how they compare to the perspectives of adults thinking about them.

The extrinsic motivation factor, "Influence of friends reading the books," resides in our socially networked world and in the community from which these readers were drawn. These readers chose to be a part of an online community discussing and theorizing about Harry Potter—even a year after the last book was published and a year before the next movie was due to appear. So it would be expected that a community of readers emerging around Harry Potter would be the one extrinsic motivating factor. Friends, parents, teachers might have motivated them to start reading, but it was largely the intrinsic motivations that kept them reading.

One unanswered question in the discussion of these factors is how they are weighed one against the other. Is any one of the nine factors more important than the others? The only appropriate way to answer this question seems to be one that reflects the lens through which the responses were considered, and as reader-response theory would predict, "it depends." It depends on the reader, on the situation of that reader, on the needs of that reader, on an infinite list of factors that may impact the way in which an individual reader interacts with a text. The reader who is depressed and needing solace might find one factor the most important in motivating his or her reading, while a film buff is more likely to identify aspects of another factor as more important. So the answer seems to be that there are really nine most important factors, with the determination of which factor ascending as the most motivating for any reader at a given moment dependent upon . . . well, it depends.

Conclusion

While a definitive answer to the overarching research question remains somewhat elusive, this study deepened understanding of the reading motivations of this group of long-term and enthusiastic Harry Potter readers. Many of the findings verify what had already been established through prior research. They expand the scope, emphasis, and meaning of literary critical analysis by validating those themes with carefully elicited responses from young readers. They demonstrate that reader response provides insights into which factors are most important in motivating young readers, into how these readers express those factors (often not in the same language as that of scholars), and into the depth of emotion that lies behind the largely intrinsic motivations.

The study also validates reader-response theory in that many of the motivating factors reflect a personal transaction that occurs between an individual reader and the text. What was thought or assumed before about young people reading Harry Potter can now be discussed with more certainty and with more insight. In addition, a few previously unresearched motivations surfaced. Most of the Harry Potter readers in this study did not feel it was important to feel "in" with their friends, although they were very likely to encourage friends to read the books. As a group, they perceived themselves to be early adopters of the books, and therefore, while reading the books to feel "in" was not identified as a motivating factor for this group, it may be because they felt they were part of the group before everyone else was. The previously unresearched motivations of most interest, however, were those describing how this group of young readers' responses changed as they matured from children into young adults.

When reflecting on first reading the Harry Potter novels at the age of eight or nine years old, many readers described them as simple outlets of escape. The first few books were described as adventures into Rowling's extravagantly-imagined universe, tempting readers to lose themselves in the pages of the books. However, as Harry's world grew increasingly dark, readers began to compare the often harsh aspects of reality reflected within the story instead of discussing the books' enchanting flights of fantasy. The Death-Eater attacks ravaging Harry's world were identified by readers as having frightening similarity to the 9/11 terrorist attacks. Harry's struggles with loss and betrayal as the wizarding world became a war zone and scenes where Hermione scans the daily paper for the latest casualty toll were identified as being sadly familiar to readers with family or friends serving in Iraq.

> I grew up with Harry Potter, who was as real to me as the war in Iraq, or perhaps even more real. He and his friends (and enemies) aged as I aged, experienced some things as I experienced them; this was great motivation to keep reading the book when I needed fictional solace. (Drouillard 67)

So why did these readers keep reading? Considering the international atmosphere of fear and terror, where every week seemed marked by heightened security alerts and suicide bombings, it seems counterintuitive for these readers to seek escape in a world that often mirrored their own increasingly worrisome reality. Yet somehow, readers found enough hope within the pages to sustain a sense of belief that, in the end, good really would triumph over evil, and justice would be granted to those who deserve it. Harry was described as an endearingly normal hero, enduring the same romantic insecurities, pressures of friendship, and mood swings or irritability that these young readers experienced, and these readers found the shared challenges heartening.

Elizabeth Schafer found that Harry Potter fulfills many of the criteria of mythical heroes, including acquisition of self-knowledge, maturing during an ordeal, and the ability of readers to "identify with Harry's experiences and recognize parallels in their own lives" (130). If a rather ordinary boy, not so very different from themselves, was able to achieve such extraordinary things, readers are able to see that they also may have potential to make positive changes.

The scope of this project was limited to young readers who grew up in the United States at least 90 percent of the time while they were reading the Harry Potter series. A total of 2,170 survey responses were received, with 649 submitted by readers meeting the research criteria and who agreed to participate in the study. An additional 383 responses were received from readers who did not grow up in the United States at least 90 percent of the time while they were reading Harry Potter. They were not included in the analysis and results of this study because they were outside the scope of the research criteria; however, these young reader survey responses will be analyzed in the future and compared to the responses of the young readers who grew up in the United States.

Although this study identified and explored a number of factors influencing young readers to read the Harry Potter series, more research is needed. Future studies should expand the scope of young readers considered and expand understanding of factors motivating young readers. Findings from the present study raise important questions and provide the groundwork for future research examining Harry Potter reader motivation as well as other aspects of young children's reading motivations.

It would be fascinating to follow some of these young readers into the future to see what happens to their motivations and interests as they mature even more. A longitudinal study could provide even more insight into growing up with Harry Potter. What about new young readers, those who did not grow up with the books and now have the ability to read the books one after another. How does their experience and motivation differ from this group of young readers?

The extent of future Harry Potter reading has yet to be determined. It seems likely that the enthusiasm for this series will continue. The extrinsic motivation of new books in the series may no longer exist, but the intrinsic motivations remain, and it is these intrinsic motivations and readers' interactions with the text that seem likely to keep young readers happily reading Harry Potter for many years to come.

Note

1. Purposeful sampling allows a researcher to hone in on particular people or events instead of examining a cross-section of the entire population, allowing the research to concentrate on instances that illuminate the research question at hand (Descombe; Dane).

Works Cited

Baker, Linda & Allen Wigfield. "Dimensions of Children's Motivations for Reading and Their Relations to Reading Activity and Reading Achievement." *Reading Research Quarterly,* 34 (1999): 452–477.

Beahm, George W. *Fact, Fiction, and Folklore in Harry Potter's World: An Unofficial Guide.* Charlottesville, VA: Hampton Roads, 2005.

Bleich, David. "Gendered Interests in Reading and Language." *Gender and Reading: Essays on Readers, Texts and Contexts.* Eds. Elizabeth A. Flynn & Patrocinio P. Schewickert. Baltimore: Johns Hopkins UP, 1986.

Children's Literature Research Centre. *Young People's Reading at the End of the Century.* London: Book Trust; British National Bibliography Research Fund, 1996.

Clark, Christina, Stephen Torsi, & Julia Strong. *Young People and Reading: A School Study Conducted by the National Literacy Trust for the Reading Champions Initiative.* London: National Literacy Trust, 2005.

Creswell, John W., & Vicki L. Plano Clark. *Designing and Conducting Mixed Methods Research.* Thousand Oaks, CA: SAGE Publications, 2007.

Dammann, Guy. "Harry Potter Breaks 400m in Sales.*" The Guardian* 18 Jun. 2008. Web. 25 Apr. 2015.

Dane, Francis C. *Research Methods.* Pacific Grove, CA: Brooks/Cole, 1990.

Descombe, Martyn. *The Good Research Guide: For Small-Scale Social Research Projects.* London: Guildford & Kings, 1998.

Drouillard, Colette. "Growing Up With Harry Potter: What Motivated Youth to Read?" Diss. Florida State University. Ann Arbor: UMI, 2009.

Guillaume, Jeff C. "College-aged 'Potter' Fans Needed for FSU Survey." *Harry Potter Automated News Aggregator.* 12 Aug. 2008. Web. 25 Apr. 2015.

Hopper, Rosemary. "What Are Teenagers Reading? Adolescent Fiction Reading Habits and Reading Choices." *Literacy* 39.3 (2005): 113–120.

Ivey, Gay, & Karen Broaddus. "'Just Plain Reading': A Survey of What Makes Students Want to Read in Middle School Classrooms." *Reading Research Quarterly, 36*.4 (2001): 350–377.

Iyengar, Sunil, Don Ball, & National Endowment for the Arts. *To Read or Not To Read: A*

Question of National Consequence. Washington, DC: National Endowment for the Arts, 2007.

Jenkins, Henry. *Textual Poachers: Television Fans & Participatory Culture.* New York: Routledge, 1992.

McKenna, Michael C., Dennis J. Kear, & Randolph A. Ellsworth. "Children's Attitudes Toward Reading: A National Survey." *Reading Research Quarterly,* 30 (1995): 934–956.

Rowling, J. K. *Harry Potter and the Chamber of Secrets.* New York: Arthur A. Levine, Scholastic, 1999.

_____. *Harry Potter and the Deathly Hallows.* New York: Arthur A. Levine, Scholastic, 2007.

_____. *Harry Potter and the Goblet of Fire.* New York: Arthur A. Levine, Scholastic, 2000.

_____. *Harry Potter and the Half-Blood Prince.* New York: Arthur A. Levine, Scholastic, 2005.

_____. *Harry Potter and the Order of the Phoenix.* New York: Arthur A. Levine, Scholastic, 2003.

_____. *Harry Potter and the Philosopher's Stone.* London: Bloomsbury, 1997.

_____. *Harry Potter and the Prisoner of Azkaban.* New York: Arthur A. Levine, Scholastic, 1999.

_____. *Harry Potter and the Sorcerer's Stone.* New York: Arthur A. Levine, Scholastic, 1998.

Schafer, Elizabeth D. *Beacham's Sourcebooks for Teaching Young Adult Fiction: Exploring Harry Potter.* Osprey, FL: Beacham, 2002.

Scholastic Corporation & Yankelovich. *The Kids and Family Reading Report™.* Scholastic.com, 2006. Web. 25 Apr. 2015.

_____. *The 2008 Kids & Family Reading Report™: Reading in the 21st Century: Turning the Page with Technology.* Scholastic.com, 2008. Web. 25 Apr. 2015.

Snellman, Leena M. *Sixth Grade Reading Interests: A survey.* Charlottesville: University of Virginia, 1993. *ERIC.* ED358415. Web.

Spangler, Katherine L. "Reading Interests Versus Reading Preferences: Using the Research." *The Reading Teacher* 36 (1983). 876–878.

Sturm, Brian W. "The Information and Reading Preferences of North Carolina Children." *School Library Media Research*, 6a (2003), 1 MURL: E-Journal Link. Web.

Whittemore, Shirley. *Reading Interests of North Ridgeville High School Students.* Kent, OH: Kent State, 1992.

Wigfield, Allan, & John T. Guthrie. *Dimensions of Children's Motivations for Reading: An Initial Study.* College Park: University of Maryland, 1995.

Zimmerman, Barry J., & Manuel Martinez-Pons. "Student Differences in Self-regulated Learning: Relating Grade, Sex and Giftedness to Self-efficacy and Strategy Use." *J of Educational Psychology* 82 (1990): 51–59.

"Splinched": The Problem of Disability in the Harry Potter Series

Leigh A. Neithardt

> *"It's not easy, Apparition, and when it's not done properly it can lead to nasty complications. This pair I'm talking about went and splinched themselves." Everyone around the table except Harry winced. "Er—splinched?" said Harry. "They left half of themselves behind," said Mr. Weasley, now spooning large amounts of treacle onto his porridge. "So of course, they were stuck. Couldn't move either way." (Harry Potter and the Goblet of Fire 66–67)*

J. K. Rowling's septology provides ample opportunity to discuss disability. In the exchange above from *Harry Potter and the Goblet of Fire*, Mr. Weasley, the father of one of Harry Potter's best friends, Ron, is explaining the physical consequence of not being able to Apparate properly—when a witch or wizard disappears from one location and reappears in another. Mr. Weasley's description of "splinching" is an apt metaphor describing the author's treatment of disability throughout the series. Rowling's narratives engage with ideas about difference and the tension between magical characters and non-magical ones. Disability is often understood in our world as an impairment—whether congenital or acquired—that should be mitigated, if not cured, so that the person with a disability can be "normal," or as close to that state as possible. In the series, being magical is considered "normal," and an absence of magical capabilities is considered problematic. Rowling includes in her books characters with impairments and characters unable to perform magic. Alastor "Mad-Eye" Moody has one artificial eye and one prosthetic leg. Arabella Figg and Argus Filch are both Squibs who lack powers. Both states of being are analogous to "being disabled" in the actual world.

Together with creating distinctions between the "disabled" and "abled" individuals in the Harry Potter series, Rowling repeatedly calls attention to bodily difference. These constructions are sometimes associated with the actual world's understanding of disability. The corporality of some of Rowling's characters deviates from what readers would consider "average" or "normal." In addition to Moody, George Weasley loses an ear, and Albus Dumbledore severely injures his right hand. Harry is often subjected to stares because he has a lightning-bolt-shaped scar on his forehead, the result of Voldemort's attempt to kill him when he was an infant. Rubeus Hagrid is a half-giant whose size and parentage repulse many wizards.

The septology's participation in the fantasy genre allows Rowling to create characters and circumstances that are impossible in the real world: for example, wizards and witches and half-giants. These impossible creations extend to notions of disability. Moody's glass eye is magical and can see through objects. Prior to the start of the series, Remus Lupin was bitten by a werewolf; the same creature bites Bill Weasley in *Harry Potter and the Half-Blood Prince*. Whereas certain animals in our world might transmit rabies through bites, Remus and Bill both acquire wolfish tendencies, and Remus turns into a werewolf during the full moon if he has not taken an antidote beforehand.

Disability studies scholar Simi Linton writes, "[T]he medicalization of disability casts human variation as deviance from the norm, as pathological condition, as deficit, and, significantly, as an individual burden and personal tragedy" (11). These remarks resonate with the attitudes about difference that permeate Rowling's series: the disgust that some wizarding families have for Muggles and the contempt that pure-blood families have for wizards who are born into Muggle families or into families of mixed parentage. In *Harry Potter and the Sorcerer's Stone*, Harry overhears Draco Malfoy commenting that he believes that only pure-blood children should be allowed to attend Hogwarts. Likewise, in *Harry Potter and the Chamber of Secrets*, Draco uses the offensive term "Mudblood" to describe Hermione Granger. However, because these differences are biological rather than social, the reactions that others have to them are similar to reactions that people outside her text have toward disability. To be a wizard of "mixed parentage" (like Harry) or to be a witch whose parents are Muggles (like Hermione) is a "variation" that is seen by some as "deviance from the norm" and as a "deficit." Rowling's depiction of the differences between wizards and Muggles is a metaphor for the real-world juxtaposition of able-bodied and able-minded people with those who have disabilities. In both cases, the former state is preferable. From the opening line of the first book, the series engages with a central concept of disability studies: normalcy. "Mr. and Mrs. Dursley . . . were proud to say that they were perfectly normal . . ." (Rowling, *Sorcerer's Stone* 1). Disability studies scholar Lennard J. Davis, exploring the beginnings of the idea of "normal," wrote, "[T]he concept of disability is a function of a concept of normalcy" (2). The two ideas are inextricably linked. The repeated claims throughout the septology about what is "normal"— as described by Rowling—encourage readers to consider what is figured as "not normal" in Harry's world and in their own.

Rowling, a Muggle, occasionally "splinches" herself as she writes about wizards who are not "normal." She writes supportively about disabled characters yet also perpetuates stereotypes. According to the website of her American publisher, "The Harry Potter books are distributed in over two hundred territories, are translated into sixty-eight languages and have sold over four hundred million copies worldwide" ("Meet Author J.K. Rowling"). Countless readers receive these worrisome messages about individuals who are "different." The problematic aspect of Rowling's own "splinching" is apparent in the differences between her portrayals of two characters who can be viewed as "disabled": Argus Filch, the Hogwarts caretaker, and Alastor "Mad-Eye" Moody, a respected Auror, a "Dark wizard catcher" (Rowling, *Goblet of Fire* 161). Although most of the characters in the series are different from actual readers because they are witches or wizards, Rowling demonstrates that, magical abilities aside, Harry, Hermione, and Ron share qualities with actual children. By contrast, readers may have little or no experience with disability, and the novels could serve as an introduction to people whose bodies and minds are not typical. It is therefore worth considering how Rowling has written these characters and what messages she communicates (intentionally or not) about people with disabilities.

Argus Filch

Exploring the representation of disability in the Harry Potter books must begin by examining the Hogwarts caretaker, because his disability is contingent on living in Rowling's storyworld. Argus Filch is not someone whom actual readers would consider disabled. Like them, he lacks magical abilities. Judged by the norms of the extratextual world, he is one of the series' most "normal" characters. Yet Rowling writes his "ordinariness" as a disadvantage: to have magical abilities is typical. To be born to wizards yet lack those abilities, to be a Squib, is atypical, disabling, and problematic. This non-magical condition is invented by Rowling, who depicts characters' responses to it in ways that align with the norms of her magical universe. She compounds Filch's unenvied state by often surrounding him with negative commentary from the narrator or other characters.

The series' introduction to Filch is Harry's first start-of-term feast. Dumbledore comments, "'I have also been asked by Mr. Filch, the caretaker, to remind you all that no magic should be used between classes in the corridors'" (Rowling, *Sorcerer's Stone* 127). Many of Rowling's characters have names whose meaning offers insight into the characters. One definition of "filch" offered by the *Oxford English Dictionary* is, "To steal, *esp.* things of small value; to pilfer." Readers aware of the definition of "filch," and its synonyms, may bring a dislike for the character to their reading, even though his job is to look for people who "filch." The name "Argus" also has noteworthy connotations. The *Oxford English Dictionary* notes that Argus was, "A mythological person fabled to have had a hundred eyes."

The "all-seeing" descriptor is apt for a caretaker and is a quality at odds with the behavior of "filching." Rowling constructs him as a paradoxical figure who is important to the functioning of Hogwarts yet is disliked by most of the castle's inhabitants. Since Filch is first mentioned in a reminder about following a rule (a recurrence throughout the series), this behavior will endear him neither to students nor to readers.

Harry Potter and the Sorcerer's Stone includes descriptive commentary from the narrator on the layout of Hogwarts and its various inhabitants, so that readers may begin imagining Rowling's magical world. The narrator says of Filch:

> Even worse than Peeves [the resident poltergeist], if that was possible, was the caretaker, Argus Filch. Harry and Ron managed to get on the wrong side of him on their very first morning. Filch found them trying to force their way through a door that unluckily turned out to be the entrance to the out-of-bounds corridor on the third floor. He wouldn't believe that they were lost . . . and was threatening to lock them in the dungeons . . . (Rowling, *Sorcerer's Stone* 132)

Filch is described as being so extremely awful that his terribleness borders on incomprehensibility. Moreover, the point of comparison is not another human, but a poltergeist. Readers, like Harry and Ron, will imagine themselves on his "wrong side," too. Harry and Ron accidentally tried to open a forbidden door. The audience, sympathizing with their honest mistake, will become angry that Filch "didn't believe" the boys and think that his response is unwarranted and extreme. Rather than threaten to report them to Professor McGonagall, head of Gryffindor House, Filch wants to lock them in the dungeons.

Filch seems even more inhumane in the series' fifth book. He is thrilled when Dolores Umbridge is appointed headmistress by the Minister of Magic.

> Rowling describes him as "in an extremely good mood," humming to himself as he conducts Harry, Ron, Hermione toward Professor McGonagall's office. He notifies the trio that his power over them will soon increase: . . . .
> ". . . You filthy little beasts would never have dropped Stinkpellets if you'd known I had it in my power to whip you raw, would you, now? . . . . when Educational Decree Twenty-nine comes in, Potter, I'll be allowed to do them things." (Rowling, *Order of the Phoenix* 628–629)

Umbridge has given Filch permission to use corporal punishment. This occurrence is problematic in the storyworld, certainly, but, in thinking about disability, it is problematic both because of the way that Rowling has written it and the fact that she has written the incident at all. What has caused Filch's "good mood" is horrific: he is excited about the "power" he will soon be granted "to whip [students] raw," and he gleefully tells students that he will do this. He has aligned himself with Umbridge, another character whom readers have grown to despise because of the horrible way she treats the students, faculty, and staff. Until this book, the central detail Rowling has shared about Filch is that he is a Squib, that he has a disability. Now the character with a disability becomes evil and potentially dangerous.

Filch identifies himself as a Squib during Harry's second year at Hogwarts. The caretaker brings Harry to his office for tracking mud indoors and, distracted by a noise, leaves the boy alone. Harry snoops and reads a letter on Filch's desk: "KWIKSPELL: A Correspondence Course in Beginners' Magic," and wonders, "Why on earth did Filch want a Kwikspell course? Did this mean he wasn't a proper wizard?" (Rowling, *Chamber* 127, 128). Harry does not guess, for example, that Filch's memory for how to perform magic might be fading, and he needs assistance. Harry immediately assumes that Filch is deficient in some way. There is something "improper" about a wizard needing to take a course in magic, just as there is something "improper" with a disabled person's body. Filch returns to his office and sees that Harry has read the letter and sends him away: "'Very well—go—and don't breathe a word . . .'" (128). Filch abandons his beloved pastime of punishing a student because he is terrified, seeming to affirmatively answer Harry's question about whether the caretaker "wasn't a proper wizard."

In *Sorcerer's Stone*, Filch's introduction is coupled with that of his cat, Mrs. Norris. She prowls the school, seemingly looking for students to report to Filch. "The students all hated [Filch], and it was the dearest ambition of many to give Mrs. Norris a good kick" (Rowling 133). In *Chamber of Secrets*, Mrs. Norris is petrified by someone or something in the castle. Filch believes that Harry is responsible, that he attacked Mrs. Norris because he had seen Filch's KWICKSPELL letter and, disgusted with Filch's inability to perform magic, decided to harm his cat. Harry, Ron, and Hermione have the misfortune to find the petrified Mrs. Norris. Filch yells at Dumbledore, "'You saw what he wrote on the wall! He found—in my office—he knows I'm a—I'm a—'. . . . 'He knows I'm a Squib!' . . ." (Rowling, *Chamber of Secrets* 142). Harry asserts his innocence and later asks Ron what a Squib is:

> To his surprise, Ron stifled a snigger.
> 'Well—it's not funny really—but as it's Filch. . . . A Squib is someone who was born into a wizarding family but hasn't got any magic powers. Kind of the opposite of Muggle-born wizards, but Squibs are quite unusual. If Filch's trying to learn magic from a Kwikspell course, I reckon he must be a Squib. It would explain a lot. Like why he hates students so much.' Ron gave a satisfied smile. 'He's bitter.'
> (Rowling, *Chamber of Secrets* 145)

Filch is pained by having to admit that he is a Squib. Even though readers, like Harry, do not know what one is, they likely guess that it is something negative. Filch believes that it is the reason for the cruelty inflicted on Mrs. Norris. Ron's amusement at Filch's condition demonstrates an immaturity that actual people may have when discussing someone's disability. Likewise, Ron's assumption that Filch is bitter is akin to the assumption that people without disabilities may make about those who have them—that they wish that they were like "everyone else," and are bitter toward those who are "normal." It is difficult to say whether Filch wishes he had magical capabilities, or is nonplussed except during situations when he is embarrassed because he knows that society thinks poorly of Squibs. Though Filch is a minor character, his position of caretaker seems to be similar to that of Hagrid, who is the keeper of the keys and grounds, yet Rowling writes the two characters very differently. Rowling gives the caretaker two small plotlines in the series, neither of which is flattering. The first is centered on the discovery that he has a disability, one that is incredibly limiting because he is incapable of doing what comes naturally to others. Rowling doesn't just "make him" a Squib, however. She makes him despised by most of the students. She then has Ron attribute bitterness and, perhaps, jealousy to Filch because of his disability.

Hagrid's function as a paternalistic figure for Harry is a partial explanation of why Rowling has written him differently than she has written Filch. Readers know more about Hagrid's personal life and his personality than they do about Filch. One the other hand, Hagrid has flaws, that, thought comical, are dangerous. One of his worrisome tendencies is to make foolhardy decisions. In *Sorcerer's Stone*, he illegally procures and hatches a dragon's egg. He cares for a vicious three-headed dog, Fluffy, that Dumbledore uses to protect the Sorcerer's/Philosopher's Stone, then carelessly tells a stranger how to get past Fluffy. In *Chamber of Secrets*, Harry and Ron are nearly eaten alive by the offspring of an enormous spider that Hagrid had raised from the time it was small. Ron exclaims, "'That's exactly Hagrid's problem! . . . He always thinks monsters aren't as bad as they're made out . . .'" (Rowling, *Chamber of Secrets* 280–281). Though Ron swears, "'I'll never forgive Hagrid,'" (280) he does. Readers follow his lead because Rowling has written Hagrid as kind and well-intended.

In contrast, she never gives Filch the same reprieve. Readers, including those who are the same age as the students that the caretaker terrorizes, will dislike him because the students do, and the only substantive pieces of information that they get about him are that he has a disability and a nasty temper. The introduction to Filch that the narrator offers in *Harry Potter and the Prisoner of Azkaban* shares both of these damning pieces of information at once: "Filch was the Hogwarts caretaker, a bad-tempered, failed wizard who waged a constant war against the students . . ." (Rowling, *Prisoner of Azkaban* 131). Perry Nodelman suggests that a narrator of a children's book often "seems to see more and know more" than the young characters (20). The narrator is an adult figure. Rowling's narrator here offers a harsh judgment—Filch is a "failed wizard"— which readers may incorporate into their own thoughts about the character. It is disturbing to think of an adult saying something exceptionally cruel about Filch to children, who have taken these comments as fact. "Bad-tempered, failed wizard" is then joined with Filch's second plotline, which, as mentioned earlier, begins in *Order of the Phoenix*, when he works with Dolores Umbridge.

Readers learn that Mrs. Figg, one of Harry's neighbors in Privet Drive, is also a Squib, as is, possibly, Ariana Dumbledore, the headmaster's young sister, although it is more probable that Ariana was just unable to control her magical abilities. Dumbledore explains that Merope, witch and mother of the man who would become Lord Voldemort, had problems using her magic. Although Merope's father calls her a "disgusting little Squib," (Rowling, *Half-Blood Prince* 210), it is not clear that she was one; in fact, the assertion that Merope used a magical love potion would argue that she was not. Rowling wrote these women sympathetically, but the Squib whom the characters and the audience get to know is Filch. Ron has pointed out that being a Squib "isn't funny," yet he laughs because "it's Filch," a character whom the author has not written positively, but as a bitter and merciless man, who has no patience for children.

Rowling always has Dumbledore accord the caretaker respect by addressing him as "Mr. Filch." The headmaster knows more about Filch than any of the students do. Perhaps he knows that the caretaker has redeeming qualities that would change students' (and readers') minds about him. Unfortunately, the audience is able to form an opinion of Filch only based on what is in the books. It is troubling that Rowling paired an extreme, nasty temperament and the aforementioned stereotype of bitterness with Filch's lack of magical abilities. When readers are told that students "hated Filch" in the first book, the only justification for this might be his threatening Harry and Ron. There has been no mention of what the caretaker has done to other students. The audience also does not know whether it was an empty threat—would Filch have put them in the dungeons? Further reading suggests "yes," but the audience cannot draw that conclusion definitively yet. Rowling initially defines the caretaker by his quick agitation, a love of enforcing rules and an unsubstantiated hatred by the students. It is enough that her protagonist and his best friend have run afoul of Filch. If readers dislike the man, this animus may be compounded by learning that he is a Squib. More troubling is the idea that they may believe that Filch deserves this "punishment."

Alastor "Mad-Eye" Moody

Rowling establishes parallels between Argus Filch and Alastor Moody and then disrupts them to positively portray the Auror more positively. In contrast to the troublesome ways that she writes about Filch, she addresses disability in welcome ways through her writing of Moody. However, she also uses the powerful wizard to perpetuate stereotypes.

Like Filch, Moody has disabilities. He has a wooden leg and a glass eye. Readers may be familiar with individuals who have these prostheses; the latter of these lends itself to Moody's nickname, "Mad-Eye." Two of the *Oxford English Dictionary*'s definitions for "mad" are, "uncontrolled by reason or judgement; foolish, unwise" and "insane, crazy; mentally unbalanced or deranged; subject to delusions or hallucinations." As Rowling did when naming "Argus Filch," she juxtaposes the two halves of Moody's nickname, and "sight" is highlighted. The *Oxford English Dictionary* notes that the etymology of "Alastor" is from the "ancient Greek ἀλάστωρ[,] avenging deity, of uncertain origin." "Avenger" is an apt description of an Auror. Many in the wizarding community respect Moody. Unlike Filch's, Moody's disabilities are not hindrances. The narrator tells readers, "One of [his eyes] was small, dark, and beady. The other was large, round as a coin, and a vivid, electric blue. The blue eye was moving ceaselessly, without blinking, and was rolling up, down, and from side to side, quite independently of the normal eye . . ." (Rowling, *Goblet of Fire* 184–185). Moody's prosthetic eye enables him to have 360-degree sight: he is able to see behind himself and through objects, even those that ordinary sight cannot detect, such as Harry's invisibility cloak.

The Auror is introduced in the fourth book in the series, *Harry Potter and the Goblet of Fire*. Harry is with the Weasleys when Mr. Weasley is summoned to help Mad-Eye after he uses magic in front of Muggle policemen. George calls him a "nutter."

"He's an old friend of Dumbledore's, isn't he?" said Charlie.

"Dumbledore's not what you'd call *normal*, though, is he?" said Fred. "I mean, I know he's a genius and everything . . ." (Rowling, *Goblet of Fire* 161; italics and ellipsis in orig.)

It is interesting that Fred counters with a question about Dumbledore's "normalcy." Lennard J. Davis points out that "[t]he word 'normal' as 'constituting, conforming to, not deviating or differing from, the common type or standard, regular, usual' only enters the English language around 1840" (24). The term is ubiquitous in the actual world; people like to think of themselves as "normal," and many have a clear idea of who is "not normal," including those with disabilities. The same can be said of characters in the Harry Potter universe, who use the word to different ends—what is "normal" for the Dursleys is not for wizards and vice versa. Fred's suggestion that Dumbledore isn't "normal" "even though he's a genius," allows readers to think about how subjective the term is and how it can be loaded with personal prejudice: Fred's oddly incongruous qualification about Dumbledore is similar to how able-bodied people often speak of people with disabilities—"Dan has a disability, but he's very nice." If readers who like Dumbledore recognize that he is "not normal," they will consider that there is nothing wrong with being "not normal" and assume that they also will like his friend Moody.

Rowling used the context of rule-breaking to introduce both Moody and Filch and the invocation of Dumbledore to opposite effect. In the first instance, Dumbledore shared a rule, at Filch's request. Even though the caretaker's being a Squib makes him similar to readers, being linked with rule-enforcement distances him from the audience. In the second instance, Moody allows himself to be seen by Muggles, perhaps the gravest transgression in the wizarding world, as the audience knows. Harry and Ron uses Mr. Weasley's enchanted Ford Anglia to get to Hogwarts for their second year and are spotted by Muggles. Dumbledore warns them, "'[I]f you do anything like this again, I will have no choice but to expel you'" (Rowling, *Chamber of Secrets* 81). Though the audience understands that Moody did something illegal and dangerous, it overlooks Moody's behavior because he is Dumbledore's ally and a character with significant agency. Readers are also predisposed to like Moody because Mrs. Weasley, Bill, and Charlie speak well of him. Charlie tells Harry, "'He was an Auror—one of the best. . . . Half the cells in Azkaban are full because of him'" (Rowling, *Goblet of Fire* 161–162). Readers are not yet aware of Moody's physical disabilities, but already believe that he is "different" in some way. Respectable characters assure each other and the audience that Moody is a good person, despite his breaking the law. In contrast, in any discussion of Filch, both before and after it is revealed that he is unable to perform magic—and therefore is "different"—the caretaker is never given routine, strong support by the narrator or other "good" characters, with the notable exceptions of Dumbledore and Remus Lupin, who also respectfully refers to Filch as "Mr. Filch." Filch is not a major character, and that accounts for the lack of character development, but Rowling could have easily had people briefly speak thoughtfully of him.

While Moody is eccentric, he is well-liked by the staff and most of the students at Hogwarts, where Dumbledore hires him as professor of Defense of the Dark Arts during Harry's fourth year. He became disabled, ostensibly, in his line of work, one of the most respected jobs in the wizarding world. In *Goblet of Fire*, readers learn about the heavy price that Aurors may pay: Dumbledore tells Harry that Frank Longbottom, the father of Harry's classmate Neville, was also an Auror. He and Neville's mother, Alice, had been "tortured" into mental incapacitation by Lord Voldemort (Rowling, *Goblet of Fire* 603). Subsequent novels introduce readers to other Aurors, including Nymphadora Tonks, and Kingsley Shacklebolt, who eventually becomes Minister of Magic. During his fifth year, Harry decides that he wants to become an Auror. Moody's clear link to the protagonist demonstrates Rowling's respect for him, and she has Moody protect Harry during the Triwizard Tournament. (Of course, readers and characters discover after the tournament that a follower of Lord Voldemort had disguised himself as Moody and behaved as the real Moody would have so as not to arouse suspicion.) Harry's career plans and the inclusion of other Aurors in the series encourage readers to think about Moody's gifts, rather than to think about him as "different" or "disabled."

When Moody arrives at Hogwarts, "Everyone else seemed too transfixed by [his] bizarre appearance to do more than stare at him" (Rowling, *Goblet of Fire* 185). There is a lengthy description of his entrance and appearance, which reads, in part: "Every inch of skin [on his face] seemed to be scarred. The mouth looked like a diagonal gash, and a large chunk of the nose was missing. But it was the man's eyes that made him frightening" (184). Unlike Filch, who was born without powers, Moody has retained his, but has lost a leg and an eye, both of which would make him "disabled" by Muggle (and extratextual) standards. As she did with Filch, Rowling uses stereotypes associated with disabled people to describe Moody and the students' reaction to him: He looks "bizarre" and "frightening," and the students "stare." However, because Moody's entrance comes *after* Rowling has given her audience information about his strengths, readers, unlike the students, might not be as fazed by Moody's appearance. If nothing else, they will know that Moody is powerful and respected, so their own visualizations of him will be tempered by this knowledge.

Moody's abilities and the reverence that he is afforded unintentionally and subtly invoke one of the most criticized concepts in disability studies: the "Overcoming Narrative." Simi Linton begins her critique of it by explaining,

> The popular phrase *overcoming a disability* is used most often to describe someone with a disability who seems competent and successful in some way, in a sentence something like 'She has overcome her disability and is a great success.' One interpretation of the phrase might be that the individual's disability no longer limits her or him, that sheer strength or willpower has brought the person to the point where the disability is no longer a hindrance. Another implication of the phrase may be that the person has risen above society's expectation for someone with those characteristics. (17 italics in original)

Moody is not "limited" by his disabilities. They make him more powerful. Linton points out, "The idea that someone can *overcome* a disability has not been generated within the community; it is a wish fulfillment generated from the outside. It is a demand that you be plucky and resolute, and not let the obstacles get in your way" (18). In effect, Rowling, as an "outsider," has "generated" both the disabilities and the "wish fulfillment" of "overcoming" for Moody. What saves her from falling completely into the "Overcoming Narrative" trap is that no character ever makes a comment about the Auror's capabilities "even though" or "despite" his prostheses. This also saves him from being a stereotypical "Super Crip," a person with a disability who has extraordinary talents (Biklen & Bogdan 8). Moody is talented, certainly, but in J. K. Rowling's universe, this does not make him unique.

Rowling succumbs to the problematic use of visual markers of disability, however. Moody's eccentricities—namely his wariness that Dark wizards are always nearby—are mirrored physically. Mary Anne Prater and Tina Taylor Dyches note,

> Historically, many authors have used physical disabilities metaphorically to represent a character's inner traits, both positive and negative. In their folktales, the Grimm brothers portrayed witches with physical deformities and poor eyesight to represent evil. *Pinocchio*'s nose grew as his integrity diminished. (ix–x)

Rowling tries to shape Moody's character over the second half of the series in ways that dismantle these stereotypes. While Moody may be eccentric, he is also capable and respected, and he does not complain about his wooden leg or prosthetic eye, though in *Order of the Phoenix*, he grumbles that the latter has been "'sticking—ever since that scum [Bartemius Crouch, Jr.] wore it—'" (50).

Conclusion

One of the Harry Potter series' themes is about difference, the importance of recognizing and respecting—or at least tolerating—it and then learning from it. In the final book, Harry reads an unauthorized biography of Dumbledore. One of the less-than-flattering stories in that book is that, when younger, Dumbledore and his best friend, Gellert Grindelwald, wanted to control Muggles, as well as wizards:

> Gellert—
> Your point about Wizard dominance being FOR THE MUGGLES' OWN GOOD—this, I think, is the crucial point. (Rowling, *Deathly Hallows* 357)

Harry is incensed because this contradicts what he knew of Dumbledore. When he tells Hermione, she replies,

> "He changed, Harry, he changed! . . . Dumbledore was the one who stopped Grindelwald, the one who always voted for Muggle protection and Muggle-born rights, who fought You-Know-Who from the start, and who died trying to bring him down!" (Rowling, *Deathly Hallows* 361)

These lessons—and the abilities to grow and change and become accepting and appreciative of others—apply to wizards and Muggles, and to real people. One hopes that Rowling's emphasis on these beliefs and her location of these sentiments in the character of Hermione, who is known for her insight, will have some effect on the way Rowling's Muggle readers think about others.

These books feature a diverse group of characters along with Filch and Moody who might be considered "disabled." Remus and Bill live with the consequences of werewolf bites. After George Weasley loses his ear in the seventh book, thanks to an errant curse from Snape, he jokingly later tells Fred, "'I'm holy. *Holey,* Fred, geddit?'" (Rowling, *Deathly Hallows* 74). In the final novel, readers learn that Dumbledore touched a fatally cursed ring, but on the night Harry notices the injury a year earlier and asks about it, the headmaster tells him, "'I have no time to explain now. . . . It is a thrilling tale, I wish to do it justice'" (Rowling, *Half-Blood Prince* 61). None of Rowling's characters with disabilities ever expresses self-pity, which is useful for a nondisabled audience to read.

Rowling uses these injuries along with their lasting (and, in Dumbledore's case, deadly) effects to explore disability issues, even if not by name. It is, unfortunate, however, that the first "disabled" character readers meet, Argus Filch, is stereotypically negative. It seems that Rowling splinched herself, like numerous unfortunate witches and wizards, and inadvertently brought stereotypes into the writing of the caretaker before writing characters like Alastor Moody. People do not always register the ways in which details about a character may shape their perception of that character and may influence their view of real people who are reminiscent of that character. Disability studies scholar Rosemarie Garland-Thomson writes about the representation of disabilities in literature:

> Literary conventions even further mediate experience that the wider cultural matrix, including literature itself, has already informed. If we accept the convention that fiction has some mimetic relation to life, we grant it power to further shape our perceptions of the world, especially regarding situations about which we have little direct knowledge. (10)

Garland-Thomson argues that an adult's understanding of and interaction in the world is "mediated" by reading. She suggests that people need to be aware of the "power" that literature has and that the resultant perceptions of the world might not be positive. Ellen Rubin and Emily Strauss Watson, writing in an early essay about disabilities in children's literature, felt similarly. Children's literature might perpetuate disability bias, "the attitudes and practices that lead to unequal and unjust portrayals of people with disabilities in children's literature" (Rubin & Strauss Watson 60). Related to the potency of "unjust portrayals," Garland-Thomson explains, "The very act of representing corporeal otherness places [these characters] in a frame that highlights their differences from ostensibly [able-bodied] readers" (10). The unavoidable "highlighting" of disability is a reason to pay attention to its representation in the successful Harry Potter series. If an adult can allow her "perceptions of the world" to be "shaped" by what she has read, surely the same can be said of a child. We must be aware of how disability is represented here because it may be the first exposure that many children have to disability, rather than the more ideal relationship with another person.

Works Cited

Bilken, Douglas and Robert Bogdan. "Media Portrayals of Disabled People: A Study in Stereotypes." *Interracial Books for Children Bulletin* 8.6 & 7 (1977: 4-9)

Davis, Lennard J. *Enforcing Normalcy: Disability, Deafness, and the Body.* London: Verso, 1995.

Garland-Thomson, Rosemarie. *Extraordinary Bodies: Figuring Physical Disability in American Culture and Literature.* New York: Columbia UP, 1997.

Linton, Simi. *Claiming Disability: Knowledge and Identity.* New York: New York UP, 1998. Cultural Front Ser.

"Meet Author J.K. Rowling." *Scholastic.* Scholastic, n.d. Web. 5 April 2014.

New Prater, Mary Anne & Tina Taylor Dyches. *Teaching about Disabilities Through Children's Literature.* Westport: Libraries Unlimited, 2008.

Nodelman, Perry. *The Hidden Adult: Defining Children's Literature.* Baltimore: Johns Hopkins UP, 2008.

OED Online. Oxford University Press, March 2014. Web. 5 April 2014.

Rowling, J. K. *Harry Potter and the Chamber of Secrets.* 1998. New York: Scholastic, 2000.

_____. *Harry Potter and the Deathly Hallows.* New York: Scholastic, 2007.

_____. *Harry Potter and the Goblet of Fire.* New York: Scholastic, 2000.

_____. *Harry Potter and the Half-Blood Prince.* New York: Scholastic, 2005.

_____. *Harry Potter and the Order of the Phoenix.* New York: Scholastic, 2003.

_____. *Harry Potter and the Prisoner of Azkaban.* New York: Scholastic, 1999.

_____. *Harry Potter and the Sorcerer's Stone.* New York: Scholastic, 1998. Rpt. of *Harry Potter and the Philosopher's Stone*, 1997.

Rubin, Ellen & Emily Strauss Watson. "Disability Bias in Children's Literature." *The Lion and the Unicorn* 11.1 (1987): 60–67. Web. 22 Jul. 2012.

Harry Potter and the Chronotope: Suggestive Possibilities for Theoretical Engagement_____

Margaret Zeegers

Explorations by readers

Readers, all readers, bring their own knowledge and understanding to every text they encounter. That knowledge and understanding has been developed out of their own cultural, social, personal and critical identities. Young people who come to J. K. Rowling's *Harry Potter* books bring to them a complete set of cultural, social, personal and critical baggage that add their own dimensions to their engagement with them, dimensions that may be encapsulated in the concept of the chronotope. It is their own experience of their own world that informs so much of their engagement with that of Harry Potter's. They go to school, only it lacks the excitement and intrigue of Hogwarts. They have their favorite teachers, and these are the ones who are not so much seen to be cool, but who are knowledgeable and fair in their genuine concern for students' well-being, such as Minerva McGonagall. There are the teachers that they particularly dislike, like Severus Snape, who does not appear to be on their side at all, and the reader tends to take up their attitudes toward him. They make firm relationships that form a solid group of best friends, such as the one that Harry, Hermione, and Ron form, only they have those otherworldly conceits that make them irresistible. Dudley Dursley may be unpleasant enough, and easily recognizable in their own worlds, but the likes of Draco Malfoy and his cronies are clearly dangerous to life and limb. Such characters deliver a whole new level to the concept of school bullies, and Harry and friends offer models of heroic action, providing a number of possibilities for variant readings of the hero and heroic action. Such explorations rest largely on concepts of intertextuality, where readers bring to the text prior learning or existing knowledge of a variety of fiction or indeed real-life narratives, interacting with developing interpretations as a text is read.

Carolyn Burke's concept of a Linguistic Data Pool (cited in Brown & Mathie) is a useful concept in this regard when examining young readers' responses to their literature. Burke represents young people's reading, writing, speaking, and listening skills as sitting over a vast reservoir of knowledge they have about language, a linguistic data pool. On the one hand, this pool of knowledge is drawn upon each time they have an encounter with texts. On the other, it is filled further every time they have another such encounter. The concept also gives rise to the concept of *Linguistic Spillover*, when ideas, words, phrases, plots, and particular textual features find their way from one language experience to another, an intertextuality that we ourselves are perhaps more aware of than young people when we engage texts (Brown & Cambourne 10). Intertextuality involves readers drawing upon a number of previous literary experiences that enhance whatever it is we are reading or writing (or saying, or listening to) at the time. As Brown and Cambourne put it, "All language learners have an ever-increasing pool of knowledge about language somewhere in their heads. This data pool is constantly being added to from a variety of sources [speaking, reading, writing, listening]. Once in the data pool this knowledge can be drawn upon when engaged in some other kind of language encounter . . . " (10).

The connections that are artistically made between readers' own real worlds and those of the books provide a rich vein for literary explorations. Kieran Egan has given some attention to the role of the emotions in the acts of imagination that readers perform, especially as they "try on" the heroic qualities that they admire in tales of heroes and heroic deeds in exalted language (81). It is more than the aesthetic responses that are normally associated with engagement with literature, and the chronotope allows for a full exploration of this.

The Chronotope

Literally "time space," the chronotope is described by Mikhail Mikhailovich Bakhtin as "the intrinsic connectedness of temporal and spatial relationships that are artistically expressed in literature" (84). In giving us the concept of the chronotope, Bakhtin gives us the site where spatial and temporal indicators are fused into one carefully thought-out, concrete whole; where "time thickens, takes on flesh, becomes artistically visible" and space "becomes charged and responsive to movements of time, plot, and history" (84). Space, depending on the chronotope, may be distant and fantasy-filled in foreign lands or extraterrestrial spheres. It may be filled with concrete, real people, speaking the language of the everyday and with events negotiating lived experience of day-to-day household goods and matters. It may be filled with people making pronouncements of higher-order beings with special powers. The fantasy chronotope, such as we see in the *Harry Potter* books, fills its space with the normal concerns of children at boarding school, with extra dimensions of what is distinctly not the everyday. The immediately recognizable unpleasantness of the Dursleys in an unremarkable suburbia sits alongside the overwhelming possibilities for good or evil of an extraordinary wizard world. That world certainly thickens and takes on flesh in its artistic visibility, and that space indeed becomes a charged one.

Maria Nikolajeva suggests that the chronotope allows discernment of text types, or genres. The time-space connection is evident in epic novels, romance novels, historic novels, parodies, and so on. The epic tale has a chronotope of its own. It has its beginning and end time points, but no matter what goes on between these points, none of it has any real bearing on the character or characters involved, for they do not even age throughout the trials of their epics. Epic tales have long served as models for children's books and stories, explains Rosemary Ross Johnston. The appeal of the epic tale in relation to young people's reading is that it provides ample scope for didactic approaches by adults: themes such as those of goodness, heroism, generosity of spirit, courage, skill and so on in the face of adversity are praised and valued as they are set against less desirable qualities of evil, cowardice, meanness of spirit and incompetence. The chronotope applied to children's and young adult literature shows that it is becoming more and more complicated as works in this field develop from relatively simple structures, based on epic story models, to complex personal and social interrelationships that provide enormous scope for young people to explore their world and thereby gain some meaning in relation to their experience of it. Given this, we may consider the chronotope as the organizing center for the fundamental narrative events of the novel (Ross Johnston), providing a tool to use in opening up for ourselves and young readers opportunities for enriched engagement in explorations of text types and characterisations they contain. What is more, it suggests ways in which we may expand horizons of literature and what it means for the reader in relation to enjoyment, appreciation, and pure reading pleasure (Zeegers). Developments in children's and young adult literature since the late twentieth century suggest that particular types of time and space connections show the emergence of a particular chronotope, the children's literature chronotope, one that is strongly in evidence in *Harry Potter.*

This is especially so when we consider that the very notion of childhood is a relatively recent development. Philippe Ariès, in his consideration of mediaeval attitudes to the child and childhood, has raised considerations of different eras and ways in which things change in this regard. His work has not been beyond critique,[1] but it has formed the basis of valuable discussion and debate on what we mean when we talk about the child and childhood. Karin Lesnik-Oberstein has gone so far as to pronounce that the child does not exist. She argues that what we see as that younger-than-we-are creature in our midst, while it is no doubt a living, breathing human being, is only a child insofar as our society has determined it to be so. Our society represents its characteristics, its properties, and its configurations as being non-adult. Maria Lassén-Senger proposes the myth of childhood as one that has evolved out of Victorian era romanticism that exaggerated the differences between adult and child to such an extent that unrealistic images of childhood emerged. Those images, she suggests, present themselves not only in everyday relations between adults and children, but also in the fictional young of the fiction texts in which they were depicted. Such discussions suggest that there are no naturally occurring universal descriptions for the child or to childhood in the field of children's and young adult literature.[2] What we have are multiple concepts and socially-determined literal and figurative experiences of childhood, created by adults, as suggested by Goldson (53).

Conditions for Becoming Readers

Yet the role of adults in children's and young adult literature is not to be discounted. The engagement with literature by children and young adults is based on the development of their literacy skills, on their knowledge and understanding of language and how it works. The work of Brian Cambourne has given us a useful set of conditions under which this may occur. Briefly, these eight conditions are immersion, demonstration, expectation, responsibility, use, approximation, and response. They are based on Lev Semyonovich Vygotsky's concept of the Zone of Proximal Development and Jerome Bruner's idea of scaffolding. Scaffolding is the social contexts in which children's language skills are supported by more knowledgeable others. Immersion has children surrounded by language in supportive environments, when more knowledgeable others demonstrate the range of language possibilities as they model their own linguistic engagements. That engagement is then extended to children, with the unquestioning expectation that the children will learn what is expected of them as fluent readers and capable writers. As this happens, children take on responsibility for their own learning, supported by their more knowledgeable others, to use the developing skills. An important aspect of this is the idea of approximation. Children approximate or mimic adult literacy behaviors and get supportive response from the adults or more knowledgeable others whose behaviors they are imitating. They will rejoice in such names as *Hagrid*, as appealing to them as to adults, even if for different reasons. The adults in their lives may have read the original description of *hag-rid* (or *haggard*, that is, having indigestion) given by Thomas Hardy's character Elizabeth in his 1886 *Mayor of Casterbridge* (the same character also refers to *dumble-dores* when she means *bumble bees*) and enjoy the word play. The younger readers may just enjoy the idea of the hag, or witch, in the name.

As the young become fluent readers themselves, the adults who have scaffolded their development to this point become increasingly marginalized in individual young people's engagements with books. John S. Mayher identifies this point of initial contact with one's own reading as an experience of rapture, brought about by experiencing, and not just hearing, a story that has the power to transport one into lives quite beyond one's own. He goes further, describing those who are thus transported as following up on that sort of delight. These young readers persist in the often frustrating task of developing reading skills so that they end up in effect living on a different planet, *The Planet of the Readers*. That planet is a psychological space of the chronotope. The reader's removal to a literary realm, joined with the habit of approximating adult behaviors and gradually acceptance of responsibility for one's own reading, creates the conditions of the children's literature chronotope.

Children's Literature Chronotope

The children's and young adult literature chronotope exhibits features of the works that are not new to adult readers, but they are to the young readers. Reducing the literature to its most basic level of setting, we can give it as a formula. We are able to identify a place that belongs to the child or the children on their own, or with limited adult presence. The authors construct such a place as a result of accident, design, or unfortunate circumstances. The very title of Nan Chauncy's book *They Found a Cave* suggests such a place. So many of the *Famous Five*, *Secret Seven* and *Adventure* books[3] employ this device often through the ubiquitous *hols* periods, where the children go off somewhere without their parents. We see a similar literary device in John Marsden's Tomorrow series,[4] where the stakes are considerably higher than they are for Blyton's young people. Harry Potter's boarding school, in a parallel time and space that is accessed by crashing through an invisible-to-ordinary-mortals portal in a barrier in a normal London train station to take the Hogwarts Express, takes this a step further to consider features of a parallel space and time. The parallel time and space principle is integral to the chronotope. Moreover, the time of this chronotope is the crucial period of young people's change and maturation from some stage of childhood to some stage closer to adulthood. As we follow Harry's story through the various books, we see him develop from a boy to a young adult, including his experience with hormone-fuelled moodiness in his adolescence, until in the end of the final book, when we see him as a young husband and father seeing his own and his friends' children off at King's Cross Station Platform 9¾ on their run to Hogsmeade Station. Throughout the series of the books, the space of this chronotope is that space remaining once adults are removed from center stage to places on the story's periphery. Hogwarts School of Witchcraft and Wizardry performs this function with a good measure of success.

Dialogics

The books are connected by the chronotope space. A further dimension of this is dialogics. Dialogics acknowledges that no text exists of and by itself. If we think of intertextuality here, we come close to what is meant by dialogics. Intertextuality means that all texts are tied to particular social actions and social institutions, and readers draw on their knowledge and understanding of these actions and institutions and of other texts as they are engaged in any particular text. The text is dialogic, and to participate in it, the reader draws upon other texts to gain as complete an experience as possible of the Harry Potter books. We see this in the words used by the young wizards-in-waiting in their learning of spells. The words they use call up wonderful evocations of the everyday language, layered with those of the magic arts. *Disapparate* has the tone of authority about it, to be sure, but it also appeals and makes sense as a clever combination of *disappear* and *dissipate.* A single word in one of many such presented in the books, it has a linguistic sophistication that has its own attractions for a young readership and takes up its own engagement with such word use. This is the same sort of thing that adults do when they engage in enjoyable word play.

In such ways, dialogics anticipates the rhythms of other works, of other readers and readings, other epochs, providing places to add them in. Chronotopes, Bakhtin suggests, are mutually inclusive in that they may be interwoven with each other, replace each other, oppose each other, even contradict each other. The real people (not just the characters) in an artistic work—the author, the listener, the reader—"may be (and often are) located in different time-spaces, sometimes separated from each other by centuries or great spatial distances . . . all located in a real, unitary, and as yet incomplete historical world," one which is not at all the same as the represented world in the text (Bakhtin 253). This real world cannot be chronotopically the same as that represented world.

Yet that real world induces readers to respond to the text as more than passive receivers; they engage in more than one-way processes, allowing the emergence of at least two (the author's and the reader's or listener's) meanings. Such meanings are only created against a background of previous texts. Each engagement by each reader is part of a dynamic process of interactivity between the author's reality, the text's fictitious reality, and the reader's reality (Nikolajeva). What develops is multiple, probably contested meanings, where interpretive strategies are not natural and universal, but learned, explains Stanley Fish (qtd. in Newton). That learning is not limited to classrooms, of course, but given our schooling system, much of it takes place there. Readers of the Harry Potter books live in their own real world, the one from which they are transported in the rapture of the reading.

They also relate to the representation of the real world of the Dursleys at 4 Privet Drive in Little Whinging, Surrey, picking up on the tone of *whingeing* in the address and the banality of *Privet Drive*. And then they have that extra piece of information on the original letter from Hogwarts: *The Cupboard under the Stairs*. The possibilities of deliberate oppression of a boy with the very plain name of Potter within the suburban ordinariness of another plainly-named family bring into play a multiplicity of suggestions in the address alone. Readers engage dialogics as they respond to the various suggestions of these features in the text. As the readers respond, they are themselves the ones that give this a depth of meaning. Readers will later add to what they have surmised about this represented world as the role of the owl, Hedwig, contrasts with the unremarkable postal system of the readers (and the Muggles of the book), and the interplay of magical and mundane increases in complexity to enchant the readers. Given multilayered realities of the readers' own world, the Muggles' world, and the wizards' world, with a further sub-category of the Mudbloods' world—in addition to the tangential, but involved adults in each of those worlds—those artistic transactions increase exponentially, and, as we know from the success of the books, readers really do relish them.

Parody

Such multiplicity has an edge to it. It opens up fields of literary parody, which Gary Saul Morson sees as a "special form of a more general communicative possibility" (Morson & Emerson 64) and evident in the carnivalesque works offered to us by Bakhtin for consideration (253). In children's and young adult literature in particular, it opens possibilities for parody of adult worlds. The chronotope contains close connections with adult worlds, with only temporary removal from them. Morson suggests that the question of parody gives rise to other questions (64). For our purposes, one of these is most pertinent: what function does parody serve for the parodist? Parody is not being used here as ridicule, mockery, or laughter, writes Linda Hutcheon (qtd. in Morson and Emerson). Parody here is being used in the sense that it allows a focus, even a "childist" one (to take up the term given us by Peter Hollindale on the subliminal, unspoken, taken-for-granted aspects of, in this case, the adult world). The purpose is to allow a temporary inversion of that world. In that moment of inversion, it is possible to hold up the world of the young as mainstreamed, not marginalized. It is a moment when the young occupy the time and space of the void created by adult absence. In such circumstances, they become decision makers, actors, and responsible agents. Pitting or matching their own skills and resources against the odds they encounter, they win, lose, or reach compromises that adults in the inverted target world might envy, from successes in quidditch to the successful defense of Hogwarts itself from such frightful and powerful attacks of the Death Eaters, unleashed by the evil forces of Voldemort and his supporters.

Individual young people may be quite plausibly represented as negotiating their world with all the fine qualities that even quite ordinary young people have and some more. Indeed, Rowling's characterizations of Harry, his friends and their families, and some of the more unpleasant students at the school are couched in terms that emphasize their ordinariness in the face of the extraordinariness of the conditions in which they find themselves. They are the ones with ordinary names, such as Ron and Neville; the adults are called things such as Severus and Sirius. In the parodic world, just as it is in the real world, some children are orphans and have to negotiate this world of theirs. It, too, is a world in which people die and grief is to be dealt with. Wizard and Muggle families alike love, laugh, quarrel, engage in romance, produce and raise children (wizards often with the aid of house-elves who take up some of the everyday drudgery of domesticity and housekeeping and such like) while they fight, or even produce, evil. People are made up of good and bad characteristics, and a number of adults are as apt as anybody to make stunningly stupid mistakes, all held up for young readers to scrutinize. Dumbledore and McGonagall are pillars of strength in a fragile world, but they do not have the final responsibility for saving it. The young people do. Snape is constantly questionable, but properly understood and respected at the end. The endearing Hagrid serves as a foil to these, and the stable father figure provided by Mr. Weasley is most welcome in the face of a number of ineffectual other adults that people the pages with a charming Dickensian sort of whimsy. And young readers respond.

The books explore aspects of children's and young adult worlds that contain within them fear, and loss, and grief, and despair. These are every bit as serious as those to be negotiated in adult worlds. Indeed, they are even more so, given their nature and intensity. Rowling presents such things for her young readers with great insight and sensitivity. The modern world realities of young people having to live with painful loss is a subject approached not only with authorial skill, but also some courage. The impulse to blame and condemn could have lurked at the edge of Rowling's writing, but the personal tensions that she presents are part of the parody of the adult world for children to understand, and this keeps didacticism and preaching firmly at bay.

Forgery

The books are good examples of Morson's point about parody: if parody is to be successful, it must draw upon a certain verisimilitude. If it does not, it is forgery (64). In works that we may consider forgeries, we see that authors invest them with adult values that have not yet been developed by young people, or worse still, with adult hypocrisies that are abhorrent to young people. They fall short of the intent of parody. Just as parody does, forgery foregrounds certain assumed features of a target world and exaggerates them as characteristic of that which is selected, but it does this with an intention to dupe and deceive. To depict the young people and their place in the time and space represented as more or less than they are, or perceived to be, smacks of adult dishonesty. Rowling has clearly established and maintained an honesty in her work that steers clear of any suggestions of forgery.

Books that do not manage this fail to live up to expectations of engagement with the world and the range of concerns that young readers may rightly look for in their reading. This is not the case with the Harry Potter books, as they treat the implied young readership to parody rather than forgery. They are based on close approximations of adult reader behaviors. They work through painful childhood and young adult issues with a focus on veracity that shows young readers authorial respect in the form of parody rather than forgery. There is the final battle for Hogwarts, in which good does triumph over evil, but the number on the death list of the good is to be squarely faced. Even Shakespeare's character Henry V allowed only four of his lords and twenty-five of the lower ranks to die, so as not to ruin the sense of the magnitude of the English victory in such a battle. Rowling pulls no such punches about good people dying in such a battle as the one she depicts. That would be forgery.

Conclusion

In an essay called "Living in New Worlds: Beyond the Boundaries of Literacy," I have discussed educators' tradition of engaging in pedagogical dialogue, that sort of teacher-instigated question-and-answer routine where children try to guess the answer that is sitting inside the teacher's head as the right one. Given this question-and-answer tradition, I would argue that taking up concepts of dialogics, parody, and forgery—when engaging reading with children and young adults—increases the scope of meaningful experience, indeed can spark rapture, in reading. It is possible to exploit the potential of the chronotope to enable young people to appreciate that they really have something to read and to say. Through the chronotope and related concepts applied in evaluations of literature for children and young adults, we may engage young people in the dialogic world that is open to us, writes Caryl Emerson. As adults, we ourselves reject forgeries when we engage in our own reading. Engagement in reading is not the place for universals, for each personality and point of view has its own valid part in dialogics. It is a place in which children may learn to approximate adult reading behaviors; it is in stark contrast with a monologic world, where truth is impersonal and distributed in much the same way as opinion in social network apps. The Harry Potter books draw readers by means of their representation of a tantalizingly possible reality, conceived as readers engage a clearly unreal, parallel world in parallel time. In that world, they may explore hero paths to be trodden in this world, right here and right now.

Notes

1. See Barry Goldson and Wendy Stainton-Rogers.
2. See, for example, Peter Bennett.
3. See, for example, Enid Blyton's *Famous Five Go Adventuring Again*, 1942; *The Sea of Adventure*, 1948; and *Good Old Secret Seven*, 1960.
4. See, for example, John Marsden. *Tomorrow, When the War Began: The Beginning*. Tomorrow Series. 2001.

Works Cited

Bakhtin, Mikhail Mikhailovich. "Forms of Time and of the Chronotope in the Novel." Trans. Caryl Emerson & Michael Holquist. *The Dialogic Imagination: Four Essays*. 1937–38. Ed. Michael Holquist. Austin, TX: U of Texas P, 1981. 84–258. Print.

Bennett, Peter. *The Illustrated Child*. New York: Putnam 1979. Print.

Bleich, David. "The Subjective Character of Critical Interpretation." *Twentieth Century Literary Theory: A Reader*. Ed. Ken Newton. London: MacMillan Basingstoke, 1989. 231–35. Print.

Blyton, Enid. *Famous Five Go Adventuring Again*. London: Hodder & Stoughton, 1942. Print.

_____. *Good Old Secret Seven*. Leicester: Brockhampton, 1960. Print.

_____. *The Sea of Adventure* London: Armada, 1948. Print.

Brown, Hazel & Brian Cambourne. *Read and Retell: A Strategy for the Whole Language/Natural Learning Classroom*. South Melbourne: Nelson, 1991. Print.

Brown, Hazel & Vonne Mathie. *Inside Whole Language: A Classroom View*. Sydney: Primary English Teachers Association, 1990. Print.

Bruner, Jerome. *Actual Minds: Possible Worlds*. Cambridge, Mass: Harvard UP, 1986. Print.

Cambourne, Brian. *The Whole Story: Natural Learning and the Acquisition of Literacy in the Classroom*. Auckland: Scholastic, 1993. Print.

Chandler, Daniel. *Semiotics: The Basics*. 2nd ed. London: Routledge, 2007. Print.

Chauncy, Nan. *They Found a Cave*. London: Oxford UP, 1948. Print.

Dentith, Simon. *Bakhtinian Thought: An Introductory Reader*. London: Routledge, 1995. Print.

Emerson, Caryl. "The Tolstoy Connection in Bakhtin." *Rethinking Bakhtin: Extensions and Challenges*. Eds. Gary Saul Morson & Caryl Emerson. Evanston, IL: Northwestern UP, 1989. 148–70. Print.

Fish, Stanley. "Interpreting the Variorum." *Twentieth Century Literary Theory: A Reader*. Ed. Ken Newton. London: MacMillan Basingstoke, 1989. 235–40. Print.

Goldson, Barry. "The Demonisation of Children: From the Symbolic to the Institutional." *Children in Society: Contemporary Theory, Policy and Practice*. Eds. Pam Foley, Jeremy Roche & Stan Tucker. London: Palgrave Macmillan, in association with the Open University, 2001. 34–41. Print.

Hardy, Thomas. *The Mayor of Casterbridge: The Life and Death of a Man of Character*. London: Macmillan, 1975. Print.

Hollindale, Peter. *Signs of Childness in Children's Books*. Woodchester Stroud, UK: Thimble, 1997. Print.

Hutcheon, Linda. "Modern Parody and Bakhtin." *Rethinking Bakhtin: Extensions and Challenges*. Eds. Gary Saul Morson & Caryl Emerson. Evanston, IL: Northwestern UP, 1989. 87–103. Print.

Lassén-Senger, Maria. "Child Power? Adventures into the Animal Kingdom: The Animorphs Series." *Children's Literature as Communication: The Chilpa Project*. Ed. Roger D. Sell, Amsterdam: John Benjamin, 2002. 159–76. Print.

Lesnik-Oberstein, Karin. *Children's Literature: Criticism and the Fictional Child*. Oxford: Clarendon, 1994. Print.

Marsden, John. *Burning for Revenge*. Tomorrow Series. Sydney: Macmillan, 2001. Print.

_____. *Darkness Be My Friend*. Tomorrow Series. Sydney: Macmillan, 2000. Print.

_____. *The Dead of Night*. Tomorrow Series. Sydney: Macmillan, 2000. Print.

_____. *The Night Is for Hunting*. Tomorrow Series. Sydney: Macmillan, 2001. Print.

_____. *The Third Day: The Frost*. Tomorrow Series. Sydney: Macmillan, 2001. Print.

_____. *Tomorrow, When the War Began: The Beginning*. Tomorrow Series. Sydney: Macmillan, 2001. Print.

Mayher, John. S. "Foreword: Welcome to the Planet of the Readers." *Teaching Reading in High School English Classes*. Ed. Bonny O. Ericson. Urbana, IL: National Council of English Teachers, 2001. ix–xii. Print.

Morson, Gary Saul. "Parody, History, Metaparody." *Rethinking Bakhtin: Extensions and Challenges*. Eds. Gary Saul Morson & Caryl Emerson. Evanston, IL: Northwestern UP, 1989. 63–86. Print.

Nikolajeva, Maria. *Children's Literature Comes of Age: Towards a New Aesthetic*. New York: Garland, 1996. Print.

Ross Johnston, Rosemary. "Childhood: A Narrative Chronotope." *Children's Literature as Communication: The Chilpa Project*. Ed. Roger D. Sell. Amsterdam: John Benjamin, 2002. 136–57. Print.

Rowling, J. K. *Harry Potter and the Half Blood Prince*. London: Bloomsbury, 1997. Print.

_____. *Harry Potter and the Philosopher's Stone*. London: Bloomsbury, 1997. Print.

_____. *Harry Potter and the Chamber of Secrets*. London: Bloomsbury, 1998. Print.

_____. *Harry Potter and the Prisoner of Azkaban*. London: Bloomsbury, 1999. Print.

_____. *Harry Potter and the Goblet of Fire*. London: Bloomsbury, 2000. Print.

_____. *Harry Potter and the Order of the Phoenix*. London: Bloomsbury, 2003. Print.

_____. *Harry Potter and the Deathly Hallows*. London: Bloomsbury, 2007. Print.

Shakespeare, William. *The Life of King Henry the Fifth*. London: Abbey Library. Print.

Stainton-Rogers, Wendy. "Constucting Childhood, Constructing Child Concerns." *Children in Society: Contemporary Theory, Policy and Practice*. Eds. Pam Foley, Jeremy Roche, & Stan Tucker. London: Palgrave, in association with The Open University, 2001. 26–33. Print.

Vygotsky, Lev Semyonovich. *Mind in Society: The Development of Higher Psychological Processes*. Cambridge, MA: Harvard UP, 1978. Print.

Webster, Roger. *Studying Literary Theory: An Introduction*. London: Edward Arnold, 1991. Print.

Zeegers, Margaret. "Living in New Worlds: Beyond the Boundaries of Literacy." *Idiom* 42.2 (2006): 57–65. Print.

From Sorcerer's Stone to Deathly Hallows: The Failed Quest for Immortality in the Harry Potter Series_____

Lana A. Whited

> *Therefore never send to know for whom the bell tolls, it tolls for thee.*
> (John Donne, Meditation XVII, *Meditations*
> *upon Divergent Occasions*, 1624)

"Hallows, not Horcruxes. Precisely," says Albus Dumbledore to Harry Potter while the two are conversing in King's Cross Station in the next-to-last chapter of J. K. Rowling's *Harry Potter and the Deathly Hallows* (713). Of all the conversations between The Boy Who Lived and his headmaster over Harry's seven years of wizarding education, this is probably the most significant. In addition to providing a structural frame for the entire series, the conflict of the Deathly Hallows—the Resurrection Stone, the Cloak of Invisibility, and the Elder Wand—against the seven Horcruxes is the dominant theme of the Harry Potter series. This begins with the introduction of the Resurrection, Sorcerer's, or Philosopher's Stone in book one and culminates in Harry's full understanding of Voldemort's Horcruxes and why they are inferior to the Hallows in the scene in King's Cross Station. The conflict embodied in the Hallows v. Horcruxes quest emblemizes the primary theme of the entire series: the futility of the quest for eternal life and the necessity of accepting the concept of human mortality.

Nicolas Flamel

The notion of immortality is introduced into the Harry Potter series on Harry's initial trip to Hogwarts, when Ron's Chocolate Frog card features a photo of Albus Dumbledore. Dumbledore is noted for three accomplishments, including "his work on alchemy with his partner, Nicolas Flamel" (Rowling, *Sorcerer's* 103). Although the titular stone has not yet been mentioned, it is implied in the reference to Flamel, the medieval alchemist who was, according to European legend, the only known maker of the Philosopher's Stone.[1] According to lore, Flamel used the stone to make "the elixir of life," a substance that greatly extended his lifespan and that of his wife, Perenelle. Flamel's name is used thirteen times in *Sorcerer's Stone*, including as the title of chapter thirteen. Most sources about Flamel date his birth to 1330. In Rowling's account, Flamel and his wife are expected to die at the end of *Harry Potter and the Sorcerer's Stone* because he and Dumbledore have agreed that it would be prudent to destroy the stone, after all the harm caused by Voldemort in pursuit of it. Just after the Christmas break in Harry's first year at Hogwarts (1991–92),[2] Hermione locates "an enormous old book" which indicates that Nicolas and Perenelle Flamel recently (to the book's publication) achieved the ages of six-hundred-sixty-five and six-hundred-fifty-eight, respectively.[3]

For a figure of the middle ages, Nicolas Flamel's life is surprisingly well documented. The Bibliothéque National in Paris contains works he both copied as a scribe and composed, and important legal documents concerning his marriage and death have been found (Merton). Clearly, Flamel did not anticipate immortality, as historical records indicate that he designed his own tombstone in the early fifteenth century[4] and executed his will just a few years before his death in 1418. There is no historical evidence of Flamel's having experimented with alchemy, although the walls of his home attest to his interest in mysterious figures and symbols; a book of designs called *Exposition of the Hieroglyphical Figures* and attributed to Flamel was originally published in France in 1612 and in England in 1624. A French author, Etienne François Villain, published *Histoire Critique du Nicolas Flamel et de Perenelle sa Femme* (*A Historical Critique of Nicolas Flamel and Perenelle His Wife*) in 1761; Villain contends that the English publisher of *Hieroglyphical Figures* amplified the legend of Flamel having come into possession of a mystical book and subsequently spending over twenty years attempting to translate and decipher it, with eventual success. Flamel's most recent editor, Laurinda Dixon, endorses this explanation: "Flamel was a real person, and he may have dabbled in alchemy, but his reputation as an author and immortal adept must be accepted as an invention of the seventeenth century" (xvii). Dixon's edition of *Exposition of the Hieroglyphical Figures* was published in 1994, and Rowling's incorporation of Flamel into her first Harry Potter novel appeared three years later.

Flamel's reputation as an alchemist seems to have come to full flower two centuries after his death, during the reign of Louis XIII, as European intellectuals became increasingly interested in science. At that time, a Flamel relative named Dubois, who had inherited Flamel's library but apparently not his intelligence, was interviewed repeatedly by Cardinal Richelieu; however, to the cardinal's frustration, Dubois was unable to discuss alchemy knowledgeably. Dubois performed tricks for the court using a powder he claimed to have been Flamel's, and the legend of Nicolas Flamel, alchemist, began to grow. When Dubois turned out to have a criminal record, Richelieu opportunistically threw him in jail, had him executed, and took the notebooks and papers said to have belonged to Flamel. Dixon writes that rumors of Flamel's knowledge of alchemy were "the creation of seventeenth-century editors and publishers desperate to produce modern printed editions of supposedly ancient alchemical treatises then circulating in manuscript for an avid reading public." Public awareness of Dubois' interaction with the French court also led vandals to ransack Flamel's tomb, where—purportedly—they did not find a body (Merton).[5]

Moving into the nineteenth century, rumors of Flamel's immortality were fed by a story recorded by Paul Lucas, a French physician and would-be archaeologist cut from the same cloth as Indiana Jones. Between 1699 and 1717, Lucas made three voyages for Louis XIV to Greece, Egypt, and Turkey. According to Merton, he was dispatched "to study antiquities and bring back any inscriptions or documents that could help forward the modest scientific efforts then being made in France." In *Voyage dans la Turquie* (*Voyages in Turkey*), published in 1719, Lucas relates the story of his having met a group of seven philosophers at Broussa who seemed "ageless" and who told them they met every twenty years at different locations on different continents to discuss ideas. During a discussion of human longevity, the group talked about the work of Nicolas Flamel and the power of the Philosopher's Stone and the Elixir of Life. They claimed to possess the stone and to know how the *Book of Abraham the Mage* had come into Flamel's hands in the first place—a detail about which little had previously been known. At a time when ideas often traveled at a snail's pace, Lucas was stunned by their familiarity with Flamel's life and work. To Lucas' even greater surprise, the group also claimed that Flamel and his wife were still alive and well and living in India, having staged their own funerals. Merton describes the response to Lucas' work: "The publication of Paul Lucas' book created a great sensation. In the seventeenth century, like today, there lived discerning men who believed that all truth came out of the East and that there were in India adepts who possessed powers infinitely greater than those that science so parsimoniously metes out to us."

Whatever the actual details of Nicolas Flamel's interest in alchemy—if any—it is apparent that his life had been eclipsed by his legend, scarcely a century after his death. So established is the legendary Flamel that he is described on a medical history website of the (US) National Institutes of Health as "A scholar and scribe [who] devoted his life to understanding the text of a mysterious book filled with encoded alchemical symbols that some believed held the secrets of the Philosopher's Stone" ("Who is Nicolas Flamel?"). Rowling resurrected Flamel for a new generation of readers, and Flamel's modern fans didn't have to wait long for a fictional series devoted exclusively to him: Michael Scott's *The Secrets of the Immortal Nicolas Flamel*, a six-volume set, which commenced in May 2007 with the publication of *The Alchemyst* and finished in 2012 with *The Enchantress*. In the tradition of Flamel's interest in symbols, each book cover is emblazoned with an icon of relevance to the story.

The emphasis on Nicolas Flamel in book one of the Harry Potter series makes clear that Rowling intends a discourse on issues of human mortality. Albus Dumbledore's intended destruction of the Philosopher's Stone at the end of that volume prefigures the conversation with Harry in King's Cross Station, Dumbledore's manifesto emphasizing the struggle for longevity over the quest for immortality. These scenes all form part of an extended argument for de-stigmatizing death. Dumbledore tells Harry at the end of the boy's first school year that death for the Flamels will be "like going to bed after a very, *very* long day. After all, to the well-organized mind, death is but the next great adventure" (Rowling, *Sorcerer's Stone* 297). In King's Cross Station at the end of Harry's seventh year, Dumbledore tells Harry that the boy approached the encounter with Voldemort far less frightened than his adversary because Harry had "accepted, even embraced, the possibility of death" (Rowling, *Deathly Hallows* 711). Rowling has spoken in interviews about writing the Harry Potter series—book one in particular—as consolation in the aftermath of her mother's death from multiple schlerosis in 1990. She maintains that her mother's death helped her relate to Harry and told Elizabeth Vargas in an interview that after her mother's death, "Death became the central theme" (Rowling, "A Year in the Life").

Immortality in the Harry Potter Series

Perhaps the second-most-important thing Albus Dumbledore says to Harry Potter comes at the end of *Harry Potter and the Chamber of Secrets*, when the great wizard affirms the importance of choice (another theme dominating these works): "It is our choices, Harry, that show what we truly are, far more than our abilities" (333). Dumbledore's own character is ultimately tainted by his having made the choice to seek the Hallows, and what he impresses upon Harry in King's Cross Station is Harry's understanding that Dumbledore is actually similar to Voldemort in having chosen to try to avoid death, in Dumbledore's case, through possession of the Elder Wand. Harry feels that he has the "odd" task of "defend[ing] Dumbledore from himself," reminding his professor that he (Dumbledore) sought immortality through less nefarious means than Tom Riddle did.

Rowling articulates the theme of embracing mortality through the folktale "The Tale of the Three Brothers." In his commentary following that story in *The Tales of Beedle the* Bard, Dumbledore says this tale "made a profound impression upon [him] as a boy" and that he "requested [it] more often than any other at bedtime" (94). Dumbledore articulates as the moral of this tale that "human efforts to evade or overcome death are always doomed to disappointment" (94). But rather than subscribing to this moral, Dumbledore has instead chosen to pursue the "curious legend" about the Deathly Hallows—that any person who legitimately acquired all three of the Hallows "will become 'master of death,' which has usually been understood to mean that they will be invulnerable, even immortal" (96). The central irony of Dumbledore's characterization is that although he realizes that "humans have a knack for choosing precisely those things that are worst for them," he nevertheless chooses what is worst for him (and certainly for his family, especially his sister, Ariana). Despite his understanding that the legend associated with the Hallows "contradicts the meaning of the original [tale]," Dumbledore seeks the magical objects and, in his quest, comes closer to uniting them than any other person (95). He found the Resurrection Stone in the home of Marvolo Gaunt, Voldemort's father; defeating Grindelwald, he became rightful owner of the Elder Wand; shortly before James Potter's death, Harry's father shows the Invisibility Cloak to Dumbledore, who asks to keep it for examination. At this point, Dumbledore might be said to possess all three of the Hallows, although not legitimately, as he recognizes the cloak as rightfully Harry's by virtue of Harry's descent in the Peverell line. Dumbledore's close proximity to actually becoming "Master of Death" seems to him a despicable thing. In King's Cross Station, he begs Harry's forgiveness, declaring, "I have known, for some time now, that you are the better man" (Rowling, *Deathly Hallows* 713). But a reader may perceive Dumbledore's closeness to the Hallows as ennobling rather than diminishing him. Like Jesus in the wilderness with Satan, Dumbledore has confronted his temptation and ultimately refused it; despite his curiosity concerning the Invisibility Cloak, he decides to destroy the Resurrection Stone in the culmination of *Harry Potter and the Sorcerer's Stone* in order to prevent Voldemort from possessing it. Surely it is more admirable to refuse temptation while staring it in the eye than to decline it in its absence. Regardless of Dumbledore's ambitious or self-serving choices as a young man, a reader most likely sides with Harry when Harry assures his headmaster that Dumbledore is too hard on himself. Dumbledore is, in the end, a great wizard and an effective mentor for Harry because of, not in spite of, his own human frailty.

Dumbledore's final act of mentorship toward Harry is redefining what it means to conquer death and informing his protégé that he—Harry—is death's true master: "the true master does not seek to run away from Death. He accepts that he must die, and understands that there are far, far worse things in the living world than dying" (Rowling, *Deathly Hallows* 720). The purpose of the entire scene is Dumbledore's explaining to Harry (and, by extension, to the reader), how the boy could have just had the Avada Kedavra curse fired at him but survived. When Harry expresses surprise that he might still be alive, Dumbledore explains that Harry's willingness to let Voldemort kill him "will . . . have made all the difference" (Rowling, *Deathly Hallows* 708).

The Phoenix

Rowling underscores her use of the immortality theme by her placement, at Hogwarts, of the mythological creature that represents longevity: the phoenix. The phoenix is an eagle-sized bird whose scarlet and gold plumage in direct sunlight might cause the bird to appear aflame (significantly, scarlet and gold are the house colors of Gryffindor). It experiences a cycle akin to a fiery molt: after a period of aging, when its plumage declines in splendor, it catches fire (on "Burning Day") and burns to ashes, from which it is then regenerated as a chick. This ability to begin its life cycle over again is the source of its reputation for longevity. Although the phoenix of myth and legend usually undergoes immolation every 500 years, Fawkes experiences shorter cycles, and Harry witnesses Fawkes' immolation in the first and fifth books.[6] The cycle of the phoenix gives it "the ability to take the full force of a Killing Curse and still be reborn" ("Phoenix," *Harry Potter Wiki*). For the same reason, it is immune to the stare of the basilisk, although eye contact between the basilisk and other creatures is normally petrifying at best and fatal at worst. Its near-imperviousness to death makes it a particularly apt symbol for Rowling's primary theme.

Most of the characteristics assigned to Albus Dumbledore's phoenix are not the invention of J. K. Rowling but borrowed from traditional bestiaries, or collections of beasts.[7] The creature is one of the oldest referred to in recorded mythology, appearing as early as the fifth century BCE, in the writings of Herodotus and later in the works of such major figures as Ovid and Pliny the Elder (first century CE). Accounts of the phoenix in European literature are derived mainly from Arabic, Indian, and Egyptian sources ("Phoenix," *Medieval Bestiary*). Details borrowed by Rowling from previous accounts of the phoenix include the primary myth of how the phoenix regenerates itself (the immolation cycle) and the phoenix's remarkable strength (Fawkes fetches Harry the sword of Godric Gryffindor and conveys him and his friends out of the dungeon where the basilisk confrontation occurs).

But Rowling adds three significant characteristics to the phoenix of myth and legend: she endows Fawkes with a beautiful song; she assigns healing properties to the phoenix's tears, and she attributes to Fawkes a loyalty that makes him a particularly appropriate symbol for Gryffindor house and a dedicated ally of Harry Potter. Because of this loyalty, Harry Potter benefits, at important junctures in his story, from all of the phoenix properties invented by his creator. Fawkes' ability to disappear and reappear at will, in a manner similar to apparition, also helps him to be exactly where Harry needs him.

The song of the phoenix is described in *Fantastic Beasts and Where to Find Them*: "Phoenix song is magical; it is reputed to increase the courage of the pure of heart and to strike fear into the hearts of the impure." Although *Fantastic Beasts* may be regarded by some readers as extracanonical,[8] the properties of the phoenix's song are amply demonstrated in the seven novels of the series, most notably in two scenes. In the climax of *Harry Potter and the Goblet of Fire*, Harry encounters the reconstituted Voldemort in the cemetery at Little Hangleton. Surrounded by Death Eaters and confronted with Voldemort's intention to kill him, Harry appears to be protected only by the tombstone of Voldemort's father, behind which he hides to deflect curses. Harry's back is against the proverbial wall; his adversary points out that he has "no Dumbledore to help him and no mother to die for him" (Rowling, *Goblet of Fire* 658). The Boy Who Lived appears on the verge of death. The strength that enables Harry to escape this dire predicament is essentially auditory and comes from two sources—Fawkes' song and the encouragement of Voldemort's victims (including, of course, Harry's parents), who emerge as apparitions from Voldemort's wand as a result of *priori incantatum*—the magical interaction of Harry's and Voldemort's wands, owing to their having phoenix feather cores derived from the same source and from the same source as the song that sustains Harry:

> And then an unearthly and beautiful sound filled the air . . . It was coming from every thread of light-spun web vibrating around Harry and Voldemort. It was a sound Harry recognized, though he had heard it only once before in his life: phoenix song.
> It was the sound of hope to Harry . . . the most beautiful and welcome thing he had ever heard in his life. . . . He felt as though the song were inside him instead of just around him. . . . It was the sound he associated with Dumbledore, and it was almost as though a friend were speaking in his ear. . . ." (Rowling, *Goblet of Fire* 664)

Sustained by the song and the encouragement of his loved ones, Harry experiences emotional resurrection and is able to get to the portkey that will return him immediately to Hogwarts, even retrieving the body of Cedric Diggory on his way. Similarly, in the denouement of *Harry Potter and the Half-Blood Prince*, Fawkes' lament at the conclusion of Albus Dumbledore's funeral helps Harry find the emotional strength to continue in his quest to destroy the Horcruxes.

The healing power of the phoenix's tears is also a Rowling invention—healing, of course, being a regenerative process. These tears are the only known antidote to basilisk venom; just as the phoenix's song can prompt emotional revival, the tears can revive a person physically, even from the brink of death. Thus, in the dungeon of the Hogwarts Castle, Fawkes helps Harry fight off the basilisk and protects him from the effects of the venom in another of the bird's key scenes in the series. During the third task of the Triwizard Tournament, when Harry sustains an acromantula bite in the maze, his wound is healed again by phoenix tears.[9]

The third quality Rowling creates for the phoenix—or perhaps for Fawkes specifically—is his loyalty. This is underscored by its XXXX Ministry of Magic classification, given "not because it is aggressive, but because very few wizards have ever succeeded in domesticating it" (Rowling, *Fantastic Beasts*). Dumbledore's phoenix, Fawkes, is said to be one of only two known domesticated phoenixes ("Phoenix," *Harry Potter Wiki*), a testament to the bird's loyalty and also perhaps to Dumbledore's character.[10] Albus Dumbledore and Fawkes' devotion to each other is underscored in the fact that the headmaster's Patronus is a phoenix and in the name he gives to his anti-Voldemort organization, the Order of the Phoenix. Harry's suitability as Dumbledore's protégé is marked by his phoenix feather wand core, which is described by wandmaker Olivander as the twin of the feather in Voldemort's wand. It is their shared loyalty to Dumbledore that brings Fawkes to Harry in two of his episodes of greatest need: in the Chamber of Secrets and the graveyard at Little Hangleton. Fawkes' service to both Albus Dumbledore and Harry Potter affirms their stance with regard to the quest for immortal life—rejection of immortality in favor of the longevity represented by their talisman bird. (By contrast, the creature loyal to Voldemort is a snake, representing temptation in traditional literary and Christian symbolism.) The phoenix's Ministry of Magic categorization is "rebirthing mortal." Its special ability to recreate itself significantly extends its lifespan, but does not convey immortality. This seems consistent with the fact that among the three brothers in Beedle the Bard's final tale, the author clearly recommends the tactics of the third brother—the one who is Harry's direct ancestor—in using the Invisibility Cloak to evade death for as long as possible.

It may be tempting to the reader to align Voldemort, rather than Harry, with the phoenix, as the quest for immortality is his, not Harry's. But in his essay "The Sacrifice of Love: Phoenixes and

Resurrection in Harry Potter," Ben Lavon explains the fundamental difference between the phoenix's cycle of rebirth and Voldemort's attempts to live forever: in achieving its rebirth, Lavon writes, the phoenix "does not defy nature . . . . [as] the phoenix is reborn in the wake of his own death" (5). In other words, the phoenix does not achieve longevity by avoiding death. Voldemort, on the other hand, attempts to extend his life artificially by creating Horcruxes, in which portions of his soul may be vested, so that he decreases his odds of experiencing death. Voldemort's process is also unnatural in that he seeks to preserve his soul, but not his body, whereas the phoenix revives in his physical form.

Harry, by contrast, not only accepts, but embraces his mortality. Just before the climax of *Deathly Hallows*, after he has experienced Severus Snape's memories through the Pensieve and learned that Dumbledore's plan for him will require his willing death, he becomes suddenly appreciative of his physical body. Having lain on the carpet of Dumbledore's office for several minutes adjusting himself to the knowledge that the only thing he has left to do is die, Harry finally sits up, "and as he did so he felt more alive and more aware of his own living body than ever before. Why had he never appreciated what a miracle he was, brain and nerve and bounding heart?" (Rowling, *Deathly Hallows* 692). His appreciation of his physical body is reminiscent of Hamlet's "What a piece of work is a man" speech, particularly in tone: "What a piece of work is a man! How noble in reason! how infinite in faculty! in form, in moving how express and admirable! in action how like an angel! in apprehension how like a god! the beauty of the world! the paragon of animals!" (Shakespeare, *Hamlet* Act II, Scene 2).

Voldemort, on the other hand, views his body as purely utilitarian and has no particular appreciation of it. He appears in *Harry Potter and the Sorcerer's Stone* as a parasite to Professor Quirinius Quirrel, who carries his master in a turban. He appears in *Harry Potter and the Chamber of Secrets* as a memory and an apparition. During Harry's third year and most of his fourth, because he lacks the physical competence to hold a wand, Voldemort is physically dependent on Pettigrew, a mediocre wizard. Not until the climax of *Harry Potter and the Goblet of Fire* does he return to functional physical form, through magic requiring Pettigrew's flesh and Harry Potter's blood.

Universality

In exploring the impossibility of immortality, J. K. Rowling taps into a thematic river that runs through much of the great literature of the Western world, beginning with the first known Western literary work, *The Epic of Gilgamesh*. Recorded in tablets now in the collection of the British Museum, *Gilgamesh* dates at least to the seventh century BCE and tablets that were preserved in the library of the Assyrian King Ashurbanipal (reigned 669–631) and originated in the biblical region of Ninevah in modern-day Iraq. The titular hero lived in the period between 2800 and 2500 BCE, and the *Epic* is a long poem narrating the story of his quest for immortality. Gilgamesh at first does not seem heroic. He is a king who feels entitled to have sex with the brides of men in his kingdom and who fights with other men for fun. The gods see his arrogance and send Enkidu, a man who has lived in the wild with animals, to challenge him. The two become great friends, but Enkidu dies, and the death of his friend reminds Gilgamesh that he, too, is mortal. He mourns, "How can I be at peace? Despair is in my heart. What my brother is now, that shall I be when I am dead. Because I am afraid of death I will go as best I can to find Utnapishtim whom they call the Faraway, for he has entered the assembly of the gods" (*Epic* 97). Gilgamesh does find Utnapishtim, a man who has survived a great flood, like Noah, and has become immortal. Utnapishtim gives him a challenge to pass in order to gain immortality, that of remaining awake for six days and seven nights. But Gilgamesh's fatigue prevents his meeting the challenge, and when he awakes disappointed after a week, Utnapishtim urges Gilgamesh to wash himself clean and then tells him "a secret thing, a mystery of the gods" (*Epic* 116). Informed that there is a plant at the bottom of the water that "restores his lost youth to a man," Gilgamesh retrieves the plant and sets it next to a pool of water, vowing to take it home to the elderly men of his village, saving a portion for himself (*Epic* 116). But while he is bathing in the pool, a serpent consumes the plant, and Gilgamesh recognizes that it would be imprudent to search for the plant or try to find more and decides instead to return to Uruk; in other words, he abandons his quest for immortality. Doing so humbles him and makes him a better man, as well as a better monarch. He returns home to admire the design of his city and to record his story on a stone tablet. It could be argued that the epic itself is Gilgamesh's immortality.

Because the books in the Harry Potter series are written in prose instead of verse, they are not true epics. They do, however, tell the story of a hero, a characteristic that they share with the earliest literature of Western civilization. Gilgamesh is quite a different type of hero from the boy wizard, however. While Harry Potter is humble and willing to face death, Gilgamesh, tries to avoid it. Ironically, Rowling's hero has faced a mortal blow and defeated it. It is his adversary, Voldemort, who strives for immortality. As early as the first book in the series, Lord Voldemort is trying to find the alchemist's stone that will make him immortal. Like Utnapishtim, Albus Dumbledore's friend Nicolas Flamel has found the stone that is the passport to immortality. Like Gilgamesh, Voldemort fails to acquire the means to live forever. But unlike the Mesopotamian king, Voldemort does not accept his death graciously; instead, as we learn in the last book of the series, *Harry Potter and the Deathly Hallows*, the evil wizard has killed others in order to split his soul in an unsuccessful effort to make himself immortal.

The ancient theme of the search for immortality as explored in *Gilgamesh* is best preserved by J. K. Rowling in "The Tale of the Three Brothers." Like the brother who wants the all-powerful sword, Gilgamesh sees himself as invincible, a fighter who cannot be beaten. Like the brother who wants the stone that brings loved ones back from the dead, Gilgamesh wishes he could resurrect his friend Enkidu. But after much exploration and consideration, Gilgamesh makes the same choice as the brother who takes the cloak that makes him invisible to Death; both men accept their mortality in the end and go peacefully to their deaths.

The centrality of the quest-for-immortality theme may help to account for the popularity of the Harry Potter series for adult readers. In his famous 1947 essay "On Fairy-Stories," J. R. R. Tolkien describes four gifts that fairy tales provide to readers: Fantasy, Recovery, Escape, and Consolation. These are experienced by the reader in the process of accompanying a character in a "Secondary World" through a "Perilous Realm," in which the reader can exercise his or her "fugitive spirit," thereby arriving at what Tolkien calls "the regaining of a clear view" (Tolkien 9). Discussing Escape, Tolkien writes,

> And lastly there is the oldest and deepest desire, the Great Escape: the Escape from Death. Fairy-stories provide many examples and modes of this—which might be called the genuine escapist, or (I would say) fugitive spirit. . . . Fairy-stories are made by men not by fairies. The Human-stories of the elves are doubtless full of the Escape from Deathlessness. . . . Few lessons are taught more clearly in them than the burden of that kind of immortality, or rather endless serial living, to which the "fugitive" would fly. For the fairy-story is specially apt to teach such things, of old and still today. (13)

It seems likely to the reader of Harry Potter that "Deathlessness" or "endless serial living" might be the best Voldemort could hope to achieve, were he to achieve his quest for immortality. And it is hard for that reader not to think of J. K. Rowling mourning her mother when Tolkien calls such fantasy stories "a prophylactic against loss" (10).

In his discussion of fairy (or faerie) stories, Tolkien is quick to recognize that they are customarily regarded as the literary province of young readers, a perception with which he takes issue: "it will be plain that in my opinion fairy-stories should not be specially associated with children" (5). To view these stories as exclusively for children is to limit them, Tolkien argues, in the same way that:

> a beautiful table, a good picture, or a useful machine (such as a microscope) [would] be defaced or broken, if it were left long unregarded in a schoolroom. Fairy-stories banished in this way, cut off from a full adult art, would in the end be ruined; indeed in so far as they have been so banished, they have been ruined. (5)

If any theme in such a work would be more meaningful to an adult readership than to children, surely it would be the theme of the desire for immortal life. Developmental psychologists tell us that until at least middle adolescence, young people cannot conceive that death is final. How, therefore, can a child reader possibly experience the resonance of the lines "Harry understood at last that he was not supposed to survive. His job was to walk calmly into Death's welcoming arms"? (Rowling, *Deathly Hallows* 691). Tolkien's discussion can bring readers to a fuller understanding of why Rowling has always steadfastly maintained that she did not write the Harry Potter series with an audience of children specifically in mind. It is the great blessing of childhood not to pay heed to one's mortality.

Of course, it is still worthwhile to introduce children to the idea that human beings do not live forever, which most will learn soon enough. Tolkien wrote in the same essay of the importance of children reading books that, like their clothing, allow room for growth ("Fairy Stories"). Of the four "gifts" contained in the fairy story, Tolkien believed that the most important was Consolation, an important part of which was what he called the "Eucatastrophe." Amy Sturges, a scholar of fantasy in general and Tolkien in particular, identifies the Eucatastrophe as a "joyous turn" when the reader suddenly glimpses:

> denial that there's universal final defeat. It's a glimpse of joy, a fleeting glimpse of joy, that is as poignant as grief when something turns, and after you've been through this dark night, after you've seen the danger, after the dragon has breathed in your face, then you have this joyous turn where things actually work out. And [Tolkien] says that this is a glimpse of truth. (qtd. in "Fairy Stories")

In the Harry Potter series, J. K. Rowling ultimately rejects the idea that a human life could last forever, replacing it with the notion that mortality is preferable, even beautiful. But perhaps the greatest magic of the books is the amount of consolation the story of Harry Potter offers to those facing the agony of human mortality. Stories of young readers finding solace in Harry Potter are legion. By pretending to be dead, fifteen-year-old Cassidy Stay of Texas survived an assault on her family that left her parents and four siblings dead. At her family's funeral, she quoted Albus Dumbledore: "Happiness can be found even in the darkest of times, if one only remembers to turn on the light" ("Happiness"). And Dumbledore asks Harry, "You think the dead we loved ever truly leave us? You think that we don't recall them more clearly than ever in times of great trouble? Your father is alive in you, Harry" (Rowling, *Prisoner of Azkaban* 427). Finally, Dumbledore assures Harry that he will continue to benefit from his mother's sacrifice:

> "Your mother died to save you. If there is one thing Voldemort cannot understand, it is love. He didn't realize that love as powerful as your mother's for you leaves its own mark. Not a scar, no visible sign . . . to have been loved so deeply, even though the person who loved us is gone, will give us some protection forever." (Rowling, *Sorcerer's Stone* 299)

The tombstone on James and Lily Potter's graves bears the words, "The last enemy that shall be destroyed is death" (Rowling, *Deathly Hallows* 328). Kendra Dumbledore's tombstone in the same churchyard features the quotation "Where your treasure is, there will your heart be also" (325). The quotation on the Potters' tombstone is 1 Corinthians 15:26 and that on Kendra Dumbledore's is Matthew 6:19. At a press conference kicking off her *Deathly Hallows* book tour in 2007, Rowling said that she considers these two quotations to "almost epitomize the whole series" (Garcia). The *Christian Post* article presents Rowling's comments as an affirmation that the Harry Potter series is a Christian allegory, after many years of shielding that fact from readers who might not have wanted to know so much of the author's intentions. The reporter, Elena Garcia, declares *Deathly Hallows* to be "about resurrection and life after death" and uses the phrase "Christian allegory." In the scene in Godric's Hollow, when Harry reads the inscription on his parents' stone and objects that he associates the sentiment with Death Eaters, Hermione steers him in the allegorical direction: "It doesn't mean defeating death in the way the Death Eaters mean it, Harry. . . . It means . . . you know . . . living beyond death. Living after death" (Rowling, *Deathly Hallows* 328).

But a close reading of Rowling's comments in the press conference and an examination of the Albus Dumbledore exegesis in King's Cross Station suggest something different. Of her stance on immortality, Rowling says, "On any given moment if you asked me [if] I believe in life after death . . . I think I would come down on the side of yes—that I do believe in life after death. [But] it's something that I wrestle with a lot" (Garcia). It is important to note that it is not the author, but the reporter insisting here on the Harry Potter series as a Christian allegory; Rowling's own position might be described as hopefully agnostic. The question of whether Harry has achieved or will achieve immortality is certainly not the focus of his conversation with Dumbledore following his final near-death experience with Voldemort.[11] Instead, when Harry expresses surprise that he might still be alive, Dumbledore tells him that the determining factor in his current state is his willingness to die, his surrender to the inevitability of his own death. Dumbledore redefines for his protégé what it means to be master of death: "the true master does not seek to run away from Death. He accepts that he must die, and understands that there are far, far worse things in the living world than dying" (Rowling, *Deathly Hallows* 720).

Just prior to his confrontation with Voldemort, Harry has been accompanied into the forest by the apparitions or shades of his loved ones: James and Lily Potter, Sirius Black, and Remus Lupin. While they assure Harry that death will not be painful, not a one of them provides him with any glimpses of immortality. Instead of the glory or joy of eternal life, they focus on the comfort of accepting death and of their continued presence with him. There is far more emphasis in the Harry Potter series that "the dead we loved [n]ever truly leave us" in the mortal realm than that we might enjoy their company in an afterlife (Rowling, *Prisoner of Azkaban* 427). Harry Potter shares distinct similarities with Jesus, and his creator adorns the graves of his parents and his mentor's parents' with Bible verses. The saga does not preclude Harry's enjoying an afterlife reunited with his loved ones—but it also neither endorses nor requires it.

Notes

1. As most readers are aware, *Harry Potter and the Philosopher's Stone* is the title of the original (British) first novel. The title was changed to *Harry Potter and the Sorcerer's Stone* by Rowling's American publisher, Arthur A. Levine of Scholastic Books (with Rowling's cooperation), due to concern that the word "philosopher" in the title would not entice and might confuse young American young readers. As Philip Nel has pointed out, the title change diminishes the connection with the alchemy suggested in the British title (262).

2. As Karin Westman has explained, the timeframe for the Harry Potter series is established in *Harry Potter and the Chamber of Secrets*, with the mention, in the fall of Harry's second year, of the 500th anniversary of the near-beheading of Sir Nicholas de Mimsy-Porpington, the Gryffindor House ghost. Thus, Nearly Headless Nick's party takes place on Oct. 31, 1992, and Harry, who entered Hogwarts the previous fall and turned 11 on July 31 of his entrance year, was born in 1980 (308).

3. This mention of Nicolas and Perenelle Flamel's ages raises a question of temporal consistency in the series. If Nicolas was born in 1330 (a date often cited), he would turn 665 in 1988, yet the book Hermione finds, which is described as "very old," says that Flamel "celebrated his six hundred and sixty-fifth birthday *last year*" and that Perenelle Flamel is 658 (220, emphasis mine). Obviously, if the Flamels had achieved those ages the year before the book's composition, it should be a fairly new book.

4. Images of the carvings and decorations on Flamel's house are available on many French tourism websites. Flamel's tombstone is preserved in the Musée National du Moyen Âge, or National Museum of the Middle Age, (formerly the Musée de Cluny) in Paris, and pictures of it are widely available online.

5. Most accounts of Flamel's life, including Merton's, indicate that his house was vandalized repeatedly in the years following his death due to his reputation as a successful businessman and philanthropist and his home's reputation for eccentric decoration (the symbols on the walls).

6. Ben Lavon has noted that the frequency of Fawkes' immolation marks a departure with the phoenix of medieval bestiaries.

---

7. At least two bestiaries are referenced in the Harry Potter series: Newt Scamandar's *Fantastic Beasts and Where to Find Them* (a book Rowling subsequently wrote for a charitable cause) and *The Monster Book of Monsters*, a textbook selected by Hagrid for Care of Magical Creatures Class.

8. For a discussion of what material is included in the Harry Potter "canon" and what is excluded, see M. Katherine Grimes' introduction to this volume.

9. Interestingly, in recent years, an alternative treatment for certain cancers and other pain-inducing ailments focuses on the use of a hemp-derived oil called "phoenix tears." For more information, see the website of the Phoenix Tears Foundation.

10. The other domesticated phoenix, "Sparky," is the mascot of a New Zealand quidditch team and is mentioned in *Quidditch Through the Ages*, not in the seven Harry Potter novels. According to Arabian legends, there can be only one living phoenix at any point in history ("Phoenix," *Medieval Bestiary*).

11. At least three times, Voldemort appears on the verge of killing Harry and actually pronounces the Avada Kedavra curse: in Godric's Hollow when Harry is 15 months old, in the Little Hangleton cemetery in the climax of *Goblet of Fire*, and in the confrontation in the Forbidden Forest in *Deathly Hallows*.

Works Cited

Dixon, Laurinda, ed. *Nicolas Flamel. His Exposition of the Hieroglyphical Figures (1624)*. London: Garland, 1994.

The Epic of Gilgamesh. Ed. N. K. Sandars. New York: Penguin, 1987.

"The Flood Tablet, Relating Part of the Epic of Gilgamesh." *The British Museum*. Web. 31 Dec. 2014.

"Happiness in the Darkest Times: J. K. Rowling Contacts Shooting Survivor." *The Guardian*. 7 Aug. 2014. Web. 1 Jan. 2015.

Lavon, Ben. "The Sacrifice of Love: Phoenixes and Resurrection in Harry Potter." Unpublished paper. Chapel Hill: University of North Carolina. 2009.

Merton, Reginald. "Nicolas Flamel." *Magicians, Seers, and Mystics. Alchemy Lab*. Ed. Dennis William Hauck, n.d. Web. 30 Dec. 2014.

Nel, Philip. "You Say 'Jelly,' I Say Jell-O': Harry Potter and the Transfiguration of Language." *The Ivory Tower and Harry Potter: Perspectives on a Literary Phenomenon*. Ed. Lana A. Whited. Columbia: U of Missouri P, 2002. 261–84.

"Phoenix." *Harry Potter Wiki*, n.d. Web. 31 Dec. 2014.

"Phoenix." *The Medieval Bestiary*. 15 Jan. 2011. Web. 1 Jan. 2015.

Rowling, J. K. *Fantastic Beasts and Where to Find Them*. 2001. eBook. Pottermore. Web. 2012.

_____. *Harry Potter and the Deathly Hallows*. New York: Scholastic–Arthur Levin Books, 2007.

_____. *Harry Potter and the Sorcerer's Stone*. New York: Scholastic–Arthur Levine Books, 1997.

_____. *The Tales of Beedle the Bard*. New York: Scholastic–Arthur Levine Books, 2007.

_____. "A Year in the Life." Interview with Elizabeth Vargus. *ABC News*. YouTube. Web. 2009.

Shakespeare, William. *The Tragedy of Hamlet, Prince of Denmark*. *The Complete Works of William Shakespeare*. Massachusetts Institute of Technology, n.d. Web. 1 Jan. 2015.

"Fairy Stories: Comparing Tolkien and Rowling Literature." Lesson 9. *MuggleNet Academia*. Podcast. Hosts Keith Hawk and John Granger. 10 Sept. 2012. Web. 29 Dec. 2014.

Tolkien, J.R.R. "On Fairy-Stories." *Essays Presented to Charles Williams*. 1947. PDF. *The Rivendell Community: Formation Materials*. The Rivendell Community, n.d. Web. 1 Jan. 2015.

Westman, Karin. "Spectres of Thatcherism: Contemporary British Culture in J. K. Rowling's Harry Potter Series." *The Ivory Tower and Harry Potter: Perspectives on a Literary Phenomenon*. Ed. Lana A. Whited. Columbia: U of Missouri P, 2002. 305–28.

Whited, Lana A., ed. *The Ivory Tower and Harry Potter: Perspectives on a Literary Phenomenon*. Columbia: U of Missouri P, 2002.

"Who Is Nicolas Flamel? and Other Historical Figures." *Harry Potter's World: Magic, Medicine, and Science*. Exhibit. National Institutes of Health US National Library of Medicine, 24 Aug. 2007. Web. 31 Dec. 2014.

RESOURCES

Chronology of J. K. Rowling's Life

Laurie Adams

July 1965	Joanne Rowling is the first of two daughters to be born to Peter Rowling and Anne Rowling (née Volant) in Chipping Sodbury, England.
June 1967	Dianne Rowling is born.
1970	Rowling family relocates to Winterbourne, near Bristol, whereupon young Joanne makes the acquaintance of a family named "Potter," whose children become her friends.
1970-1971	Rowling becomes "aware that people wrote books, they didn't just arrive" and begins to write her own stories, including a series, "Rabbit," featuring a rabbit.
1974	Another move takes the Rowling family to Tutshill, near Wales. At Tutshill Primary School, Rowling makes the acquaintance of a teacher named Mrs. Morgan, who will one day provide some of the inspiration for the character of Severus Snape.
1976-1987	Rowling attends Wyedean Comprehensive Secondary School and later, Exeter University. She describes herself during this time as an awkward, bookish, rural teen and very Hermione-like, underscored by her eventual promotion to Head Girl. Rowling, upon entering university, abandons plans to pursue modern languages (German) for a career as a bilingual secretary, as her parents had encouraged her to do. She instead opts for Greek and Roman studies and French.
1980	Anne Rowling is diagnosed with multiple sclerosis.

1987	Rowling is hired as a researcher by the African Research Department of Amnesty International's London office.
1990	The idea of Harry Potter germinates in Rowling's mind during a train ride from Manchester to London. Rowling's mother Anne dies at age 45. Rowling is deeply affected by this loss, which becomes incorporated into what she describes as her writer's "DNA," the twinned elements of death and morality.
1991	Within six months of her mother's death, Rowling begins the earliest drafts of Harry Potter while teaching English in Oporto, Portugal.
1992	Rowling and Portuguese journalist Jorge Arantes marry.
1993	Rowling's daughter Jessica Isabel Rowling Arantes is born. Rowling leaves Jorge Arantes later that year.
1994	Rowling relocates to Edinburgh, Scotland, and, unable to find full-time work, takes on a part-time position as a clerical assistant in a church. She applies for public assistance benefits. Rowling also begins treatment for depression, while continually working on her manuscript for the first Harry Potter installment.
1995-1996	Rowling begins teaching French at Edinburgh's Leith Academy. In 1995, she completes *Harry Potter and the Philosopher's Stone* and begins her search for an agent. Christopher Little, of the Christopher Little Literary Agency, accepts the manuscript and begins submitting it to major publishing houses.
1996	On the heels of twelve rejections from other publishers, *Harry Potter and the Philosopher's Stone* is accepted by Bloomsbury.

1997	Within a month of *Harry Potter and the Philosopher's Stone*'s June publication in the UK, publishing houses in the US enter a bidding war that results in a $105,000 advance for Rowling. This allows her to realize her dream of supporting herself solely by her writing.
	At her publisher's suggestion, Rowling adopts her grandmother's name, Kathleen, so that her book can be sold under the name J.K. Rowling. This ruse to obscure the fact Harry Potter was written by a woman was suggested because Bloomsbury believed doing so would make the book more appealing to boys.
	Harry Potter and the Philosopher's Stone wins the Nestlé Smarties Gold award for fiction.
1998	US publisher Scholastic launches *Harry Potter and the Sorcerer's Stone*, the title slightly altered from the UK edition for clarity with US readers.
	Harry Potter and the Philosopher's Stone wins Rowling the British Book Award for Children's Book of the Year.
July 1998	The second book in the series, *Harry Potter and the Chamber of Secrets*, is published in the UK.
June 1999	First US publication of *Harry Potter and the Chamber of Secrets*. Later in 1999, *Harry Potter and the Prisoner of Azkaban* is released in the UK and the US with a two-month gap between the UK and US release dates. The remaining books in the series would have the same release date in both countries.
July 2000	*Harry Potter and the Goblet of Fire* is first published.

March 2001	Rowling publishes two peripheral world-of-Harry-Potter-themed books for charity: *Fantastic Beasts and Where to Find Them*, published under the pen name Newt Scamander, and *Quidditch through the Ages*, published under the pen name Kennilworthy Whisp.
April 2001	Rowling's article "I Miss My Mother So Much," detailing Anne Rowling's battle with and death from MS, is published in *The Observer*.
2001	Warner Bros. releases the film version of *Harry Potter and the Sorcerer's Stone*. Rowling is inducted into the Office of the Order of the British Empire (OBE) for her contribution to literature for children.
December 2001	Rowling marries Dr. Neil Murray.
2002	Warner Bros. releases the film version of *Harry Potter and the Chamber of Secrets*.
2002-2003	The first three collections of scholarly essays on the Harry Potter series are published: *The Ivory Tower and Harry Potter,* ed. Lana A. Whited; *Reading Harry Potter: Critical Essays*, ed. Giselle Anatol; and *Harry Potter's World: Multidisciplinary Critical Perspectives*, ed. Elizabeth E. Heilman.
March 2003	Rowling's son, David Gordon Rowling Murray, is born.
June 2003	*Harry Potter and the Order of the Phoenix* is published.
2004	Warner Bros. releases the film version of *Harry Potter and the Prisoner of Azkaban*.

January 2005	Rowling's second daughter, Mackenzie Jean Rowling Murray, is born.
July 2005	*Harry Potter and the Half-Blood Prince* is published.
2005	Warner Bros. releases the film version of *Harry Potter and the Goblet of Fire*.
February 2006	Rowling's article "My Fight," detailing her efforts to help institutionalized children in Europe, is published in *The Sunday Times*.
July 2007	The publication of *Harry Potter and the Deathly Hallows* completes the epic series.
2007	Warner Bros. releases the film version of *Harry Potter and the Order of the Phoenix*.
2008	*The Tales of Beedle the Bard*, a collection of wizarding folktales noted in *Harry Potter and the Deathly Hallows*, is published.
June 2008	Rowling delivers Harvard's 2008 commencement speech, admonishing graduates not to fear failure and to be open to the empathy-building influence of imagination.
April 2010	Rowling's "Single Mom's Manifesto" appears in *The Times*, decrying Tory vilification of single mothers.
June 2010	The Wizarding World of Harry Potter theme park opens as one of the Islands of Adventure of Universal Studios, Orlando.
June 2011	*Pottermore* interactive website is announced by partners J. K. Rowling and Sony.

April 2012	*Pottermore* website is launched.
September 2012	Rowling publishes her first work of fiction specifically intended for an adult audience, *The Casual Vacancy*.
April 2013	Rowling publishes her first detective novel, *The Cuckoo's Calling*, under the pen name Robert Galbraith.
June 2014	Rowling's appeal to Scottish voters to maintain ties to the United Kingdom is published in *The Telegraph*.
June 2014	Rowling's second Galbraith novel, *The Silkworm*, is published.
July 2014	Rowling posts to *Pottermore* a 1,500-word short story detailing Harry Potter and his friends as adults, *Dumbledore's Army Reunites at Quidditch World Cup Final*.
August 2014	A biographical sketch of Celestina Warbeck, a fictional singer from the Harry Potter series, is posted on *Pottermore*.
October 2014	Six new writing shorts are posted on Pottermore, including biographical information about Dolores Umbridge and details about the thestrals, wizarding world leadership, Professor Trelawney's dismissal from Hogwarts, Azkaban Prison, and wizarding naming practices.
December 2014	J. K. Rowling publishes twelve new pieces on *Pottermore*, including information on Draco Malfoy, the inferi, and Severus Snape—especially about whether the Potions Master was a vampire.

Works by J. K. Rowling

Books

Harry Potter and the Philosopher's Stone (1997)

Harry Potter and the Sorcerer's Stone (1998)

Harry Potter and the Chamber of Secrets (1999)

Harry Potter and the Prisoner of Azkaban (1999)

Harry Potter and the Goblet of Fire (2000)

Fantastic Beasts and Where To Find Them, as Newt Scamander (2001)*Quidditch Through the Ages*, as Kennilworthy Whisp (2001)

Harry Potter and the Order of the Phoenix (2003)

Harry Potter and the Half-Blood Prince (2005)

Harry Potter and the Deathly Hallows (2007)

The Tales of Beedle the Bard (2008)

Wonderbook: Book of Spells (2012)

The Casual Vacancy (2012)

Writing as Robert Galbraith

The Cuckoo's Calling   (2013)

The Silkworm   (2014)

Material on the *Pottermore* website

Dumbledore's Army Reunites at Quidditch World Cup Final (2014)

Celestina Warbeck (2014)

Dolores Umbridge, The Atrium, The Carriages, Trelawney Is Sacked, Row Ninety-Seven, The Tattered Veil (2014)

Bibliography

Abanes, Richard. *Harry Potter and the Bible*. Camp Hill, PA: Horizon, 2001.

Anatol, Giselle, ed. *Reading Harry Potter: Critical Essays*. Westport, CT: Praeger, 2003.

_____. *Reading Harry Potter Again: More Critical Essays*. Westport, CT: Praeger, 2009.

Anelli, Melissa. *Harry, a History: The True Story of a Boy Wizard, His Fans, and Life Inside the Harry Potter Phenomenon*. New York: Pocket Books, 2008.

_____. *The-Leaky-Cauldron.org*. Leaky, Inc, n.d. Web. 9 Nov. 2014.

Bassett, David & Shawn Klein, eds. *Harry Potter and Philosophy: If Aristotle Ran Hogwarts*. Peru, IL: Open Court, 2004.

Beahm, George. *Fact, Fiction, and Folklore in Harry Potter's World: An Unofficial Guide*. Charlottesville, VA: Hampton Roads, 2005.

Blake, Andrew. *The Impossible Rise of Harry Potter*. New York: Verso, 2002.

Bridger, Francis. *A Charmed Life: The Spirituality of Potterworld*. New York: Doubleday, 2001.

Bryfonski, Dedria, ed. *Political Issues in J. K. Rowling's Harry Potter Series*. Farmington Hills, MI: Greenhaven, 2009.

Colbert, David. *The Magical Worlds of Harry Potter: A Treasury of Myths, Legends, and Fascinating Facts*. New York: Berkeley, 2001.

Errington, Phillip W. *J. K. Rowling: A Bibliography, 2007-2013*. London, Bloomsbury, 2015. Print.

Frankel, Valerie, ed. *Teaching with Harry Potter: Essays on Classroom Wizardry from Elementary School to College*. Jefferson, NC: McFarland, 2013.

Gierzynski, Anthony. *Harry Potter and the Millennials: Research Methods and the Politics of the Muggle Generation*. Baltimore: John Hopkins U P, 2013. Print.

Gish, Kimbra Wilder. "Hunting Down Harry Potter: An Exploration of Religious Concerns about Children's Literature." *Horn Book* May/June 2000: 262-71. Print.

Granger, John. *The Hidden Key to Harry Potter: Understanding the Meaning, Genius, and Popularity of Joanne Rowling's Harry Potter Novels*. Hadlock, WA: Zossima, 2002.

_____. *Looking for God in Harry Potter*. Carol Stream, IL: Tyndale House, 2004.

_____, James Thomas, & Travis Prinzi. *Harry Potter Smart Talk: Brilliant PotterCast Conversations About J. K. Rowling's Hogwarts Saga*. Unlocking Press, 2010.

Gupta, Suman. *Re-Reading Harry Potter*. New York: Palgrave MacMillan, 2003.

Hallett, Cynthia J. & Peggy J. Huey, eds. "J. K. Rowling: Harry Potter." New Casebooks. New York: Palgrave Macmillan, 2012. Print.

Hallett, Cynthia Whitney, ed. *Scholary Studies in Harry Potter: Applying Academic Methods to a Popular Text*. New York: Edmin Mellen, 2005. Print.

Heilman, Elizabeth, ed. *Harry Potter's World: Multidisciplinary Critical Perspectives*. New York: Routledge Falmer, 2003.

Highfield, Roger. *The Science of Harry Potter: How Magic Really Works*. New York: Penguin, 2002.

Kern, Edmund. *The Wisdom of Harry Potter*. Amherst, NY: Prometheus Books, 2003.

Kronzek, Allan & Elizabeth Kronzek. *The Sorcerer's Companion*. New York: Broadway Books, 2001.

Killinger, John. *God, the Devil, and Harry Potter*. New York: Thomas Dunne Books, 2002.

Lackey, Mercedes, ed. *Mapping the World of Harry Potter*. Dallas: BenBella Books, 2005.

Mulholland, Neil, ed. *The Psychology of Harry Potter: An Unauthorized Examination of the Boy Who Lived*. Dallas: BenBella Books, 2006.

Neal, Connie. *The Gospel According to Harry Potter*. Louisville, KY: Westminster John Knox, 2002.

_____. *Wizards, Wardrobes and Wookies: Navigating Good and Evil in Harry Potter, Narnia and Star Wars*. Downers Grove, IL: Intervarsity, 2007.

Nel, Philip. *J.K. Rowling's Harry Potter Novels*. New York: Continuum, 2001.

Nexon, Daniel & Iver Newmann, eds. *Harry Potter and International Relations*. Lanham, NY: Rowman & Littlefield, 2006.

Prinzi, Travis, ed. *Hog's Head Conversations: Essays on Harry Potter.* Vol. 1. Allentown, PA: Zossima, 2009.

Schafer, Elizabeth. *Beacham's Sourcebooks for Teaching Young Adult Fiction: Exploring Harry Potter*. Osprey, FL: Beacham, 2000.

Spartz, Emerson. *MuggleNet.com*, 1999. Web. 13 Nov. 2014.

Vander Ark, Steve. *The Harry Potter Lexicon*. 11 Sept. 2002. Web. Nov. 2014.

Vezzali, Loris, et al. "The Greatest Magic of Harry Potter: Reducing Prejudice." *Journal of Applied Social Psychology*. 44 (2014). *Wiley Online Library*. 23 July. Web. 15 Jan. 2015.

Weiner, Gary, ed. *Readings on J. K. Rowling*. Farmington Hills, MI: Greenhaven, 2003.

Whisp, Kennilworthy [J. K. Rowling]. *Quidditch Through the Ages*. New York: Scholastic, 2001.

Whited, Lana A., ed. *The Ivory Tower and Harry Potter*. Columbia: U of Missouri P, 2002.

_____. "McGonagall's Prophecy Fulfilled: The Harry Potter Critical Library." *The Lion and the Unicorn*. 27.3 (September 2003): 416–425. *Project MUSE*. 6 Aug. 2014.

About the Editors

Lana A. Whited is editor of the *The Ivory Tower and Harry Potter*: *Perspectives on a Literary Phenomenon* (U of Missouri P, 2002). An internationally-recognized expert on the Harry Potter series, Dr. Whited has contributed essays on Harry Potter to publications such as *The Lion and Unicorn* and *Through the Looking-Glass*. She regularly teaches a college course called "Harry Potter and the Hero Myth" and a Hogwart's Academy course in a middle school enrichment program. In October 2014, she served as keynote speaker for the Ravenclaw Conference of Edinboro University's annual Potterfest. A Salzburg Seminar Fellow, Dr. Whited also was a featured panelist in 2004 at a special symposium in Trebon, Czech Republic, sponsored by the Committee on Media and Culture of the Czech Parliament. Dr. Whited is professor of English and director of the Boone Honors Program at Ferrum College in the Blue Ridge Mountains of Virginia. In spring 2014, she was recognized with an Exemplary Teaching Award from the Board of Higher Education and Ministries of the United Methodist Church. She earned degrees from Emory & Henry College, The College of William and Mary, Hollins University, and the University of North Carolina at Greensboro.

M. Katherine Grimes is author of "Harry Potter as Fairy-Tale Prince, Real Boy, and Archetypal Hero" and co-author of "What Would Harry Do?" both in *The Ivory Tower and Harry Potter*: *Perspectives on a Literary Phenomenon* (U of Missouri, 2002). The former essay was used as the basis for a chapter in the book *Introduction to Mythology: Contemporary Approaches to Classical and World Myths*, edited by Eva M. Thury and Margaret K. Devinney (Oxford UP). Associate professor of English and English program coordinator at Ferrum College (Virginia), Dr. Grimes earned degrees from Catawba College, the University of North Carolina at Chapel Hill, and the University of North Carolina at Greensboro. Her primary areas of scholarly expertise are twentieth-century British and American literature. Her dissertation was entitled *The Motherless Child: Absent Mothers in Twentieth Century Southern Literature*.

Contributors_____

Danny Adams is the author of the historical novel *Lest Camelot Fall* (Musa) and co-author, with the late Philip José Farmer, of the short science fiction adventure novel *The City Beyond Play* (PS Publishing). His shorter work has appeared in *Appalachian Heritage, Asimov's Science Fiction, Ideomancer,* the *Journal of the American Chestnut Foundation, Mythic*, *Paradox*, *Space & Time*, *Strange Horizons*, and elsewhere. He is a librarian assistant at Ferrum College (VA) and a speculative fiction reviewer for *Publishers Weekly*. Danny and his wife Laurie live in the Blue Ridge Mountains of Virginia with numerous clever animals and a (but not *the*) hundred-acre wood. He can be found on Facebook as Madwriter and on Twitter as Madwriter1970.

Laurie Adams followed up a stint in broadcast media with a degree in Criminal Justice, both fueled by an intense curiosity about what exactly makes people tick. In addition to her journalism background, Adams has three publications to her credit in the *LAE Journal* (2010), the *International Journal of Business and Social Science* (2012), and the *Council for Undergraduate Research Quarterly* (2013). She currently works as a freelance writer.

Saradindu Bhattacharya earned his doctorate from the Department of English, University of Hyderabad (India) in 2014. His primary areas of research and scholarship are trauma and memory studies, young adult literature, celebrity culture, visual culture and new media studies. He has published essays on online representations of 9/11, digital avatars of new age spiritual gurus, and heroic and villainous celebrities in the Harry Potter series.

Danielle Bienvenue Bray earned her doctorate in English with a concentration in children's literature from the University of Louisiana at Lafayette in May 2012. Her dissertation, *Those Who Nurture: Food, Gender, and the Performance of Family in Fantasy for Young Readers* explores the performative act of food-sharing as a means of establishing a mother-child or nurturer-child relationship in a wide sample of fantasy novels for middle grades and young adult audiences. Dr. Bray is a lecturer in the University of Georgia's Department of English, where she teaches composition, multicultural literature, and dramatic literature. She is currently pursuing her MFA in children's literature at Hollins University.

Jenn Coletta teaches American sign language (ASL) at Clear Springs High School in Houston, Texas. She earned a BS *summa cum laude* in deaf education with a focus in English from Stephen F. Austin State University. She entered Hollins University's MA program in children's literature in summer 2013. Her thesis involves cults in dystopian literature, particularly in the Divergent series. She plans to pursue a PhD in children's literature.

Colette Drouillard is an assistant professor of library and information studies at Valdosta State University in Valdosta, GA. She earned her PhD in library and information studies from the Florida State University, College of Information. She teaches courses focused on library services for children and young adults as well as literature for children and young adults. Her areas of research focus primarily on reading motivation and reading interests of young readers.

Todd Ide is ABD in Michigan State University's doctoral program in curriculum, instruction, and teacher education. He earned three degrees from Western Michigan University: an MA in literature/genre studies, with a thesis on *Robinson Crusoe*; an MFA in fiction and creative nonfiction, with a thesis called *Loss: A Father's Story of Miscarriage*; and a BS in English, history, and political science/public policy. He has taught for twenty years, both in high school and higher education. He currently teaches at Grand Valley State University and Aquinas College, both in Grand Rapids, Michigan.

Jeanne Hoeker LaHaie earned her doctorate in English literature in 2012. Her dissertation, *Girls, Mothers, and Others: Female Representation in the Adolescent Fantasy of J. K. Rowling, Philip Pullman, and Terry Pratchett*, examines the roles of adult females in contemporary fantasy for children and young adults. Her most recent published work, "Theorizing Steampunk in Scott Westerfeld's YA Series Leviathan," considers the components of the genre as it is commonly written for adolescents. Dr.

LaHaie is a faculty specialist at Western Michigan University, where she teaches children's literature and rhetoric and composition.

Leigh A. Neithardt is a doctoral candidate in literature for children and young adults at The Ohio State University. She is the author of "The Problem of Identity in *Harry Potter and the Sorcerer's Stone*," included in *Scholarly Studies in Harry Potter: Applying Academic Methods to a Popular Text*, edited by Cynthia Whitney Hallett. She also has forthcoming a personal essay that incorporates disability theory, which will appear in an introductory disability studies textbook. Her dissertation research examines picture books that feature characters with disabilities using concepts of rhetorical narrative theory, and in particular, James Phelan's concept of Narrative Progression.

Christina Vourcos is a graduate student in English at Texas A&M University–Corpus Christi, where she also earned her bachelor's degree in liberal arts with a focus on English and journalism. She has worked for the university's student newspaper, *Island Waves*. Her graduate study focuses on British and American literature.

Crystal Wilkins graduated from The University of North Carolina–Greensboro with a master's degree in rhetoric and composition after earning her bachelor's degree in English from Ferrum College, where she has also taught composition and research. Her reading interests lean toward dystopian fiction, zombie survivalist fiction, and novels with potentially untrustworthy narrators. She lives in Virginia with her equally potentially untrustworthy Jack Russell Terrier. Ms. Wilkins is a benefit analyst for an insurance company. This is her first publication.

Margaret Zeegers is associate professor in the School of Education and Arts at Federation University of Australia. She is the author of the book *Grammar Matters* (2013, OUP); co-author of *Gatekeepers of Knowledge* (2010, Chandos, Oxford); and author of numerous scholarly articles in national and international refereed publications. Dr. Zeegers is immediate past president of the International Board on Books for Young People (IBBY) (Australia), editor of a national journal for primary school English and literacy teachers (*Practically Primary*), associate editor of the *Australian Journal of Language and Literacy* and an editorial board member for IBBY's journal, *Bookbird*. As IBBY (Australia) president, she was convener and judge of the Ena Noël Award for children's and young adult literature and Australian nominator for both the Astrid Lindgren Award and Hans Christian Andersen Award. In 2010, Dr. Zeegers was the Australian representative to the International Committee for the Peace Project, launched at the Nami Island Children's Book Festival (Korea), which brings together children's stories of peace.

Thorsrud, Harald 215
Tolkien, J. R. R. viii, 86, 143, 166, 167, 178, 319
Tolstoy, Nikolai 167
Tonks, Nymphadora 140, 284
Torah 28
Torregrossa, Michael A. 164
Trelawney, Sybil 134, 135
Triwizard Tournament 11, 61, 95, 112, 134, 284, 315
Troyes, Chrétien de 84, 92, 95
Twain, Mark 6, 14, 40, 50, 239

Umbridge, Dolores 39, 74, 90, 113, 114, 134, 136, 152, 186, 190, 277, 281, 334, 335
Universal Studios 7, 20, 333

Vargas, Elizabeth 310
Vezzali, Loris 73
Villain, Etienne François 307
Virgil 29
Voldemort, Lord 29, 112, 114, 134, 181, 188, 219, 281, 284, 318
Vonnegut, Kurt 44
Vygotsky, Lev Semyonovich 295

Wace 84
Walker, Alice 14
Wallace, David 124, 145
Warner Bros 240, 255, 332, 333
Watson, Emily Strauss 288, 290
Weasley, Arthur 170

Weasley, Bill 274
Weasley, Charlie 160
Weasley, Fred 30
Weasley, George 9, 42, 65, 274, 287
Weasley, Ginny 30, 39, 43, 70, 91, 123, 215
Weasley, Molly 131, 132, 133, 134, 140, 170
Weasley, Percy 31, 43, 214
Weasley, Ron 5, 18, 28, 31, 39, 42
Westman, Karin 323
Whitbread 51, 57
Whited, Lana A. vii, 9, 42, 46, 49, 77, 79, 144, 145, 211, 223, 240, 306, 325, 332, 341
White, T. H. 86, 92
Whitman, Walt 14, 38
Widdershins, Willy 184
Wigfield, Allan 244
Will, George 61
Wilson, Joe 199
Winerip, Michael 54
Winters, Sarah Fiona 132
Wolosky, Shira 201, 213
Wordsworth, William 38
World War I 42
Wright, Richard 5
Wynne-Jones, Tim 61

Young, Andre 184
Young, Rebecca De 213, 218

Zipes, Jazk 201